Business Ethics from the 19th Century to Today

David George Surdam

Business Ethics from the 19th Century to Today

An Economist's View

palgrave
macmillan

David George Surdam
Department of Economics
University of Northern Iowa
Cedar Falls, IA, USA

ISBN 978-3-030-37168-5 ISBN 978-3-030-37169-2 (eBook)
https://doi.org/10.1007/978-3-030-37169-2

This Palgrave Macmillan imprint is published by the registered company Springer Nature Switzerland AG.
The registered company address is: Gewerbestrasse 11, 6330 Cham, Switzerland

Acknowledgments

This book had its origins in conversations with my late dissertation advisor, Nobel Prize winner in Economics Robert W. Fogel. For years after I graduated from the University of Chicago, Bob (as he insisted his graduated students call him) would graciously take time from a busy schedule to discuss my latest work. He encouraged me to investigate topics in business ethics, and I attended his class on the subject at the Graduate School of Business at Chicago. He emphasized the historical phenomenon of changing views of what was ethical in business.

I later taught courses in business ethics at Loyola University of Chicago and the Graduate School of Business, University of Chicago. Many of the ideas for this book emanated from these courses.

As with most authors, many people helped me along the way. The following paragraphs are among the most pleasurable ones for me to write.

I thank graduate assistants Caroline Mutonyi, Madiha Ahsan, and Shanaya Alvares at the University of Northern Iowa, for processing thousands of the note cards and looking up articles and books. Undergraduate Kobe Diers provided help with a particularly tedious task (deleting 2102 superscripts representing endnotes). Matt Goodwin helped compile the citations and the bibliography.

There are plenty of friends in academia to thank. David Galenson, sole surviving member of my dissertation committee, has continued to support and encourage my endeavors; Louis Cain encouraged me to teach a course on the ethics of economic activities at Loyola University of Chicago. Professor Cain critiqued the chapters on late nineteenth-century American industrialists. Years ago, the late Max Hartwell sparked an interest in Great

Britain's industrial transformation. He also gave a struggling graduate student much-needed and appreciated encouragement.

Stanley Engerman provided comments on the sections covering business failures and the American Civil War; he has long been gracious in taking time to read my work and to offer encouragement. Professor Mark Wilson of UNCC carefully read the chapter on the Civil War and pointed me to several valuable sources, including Scott Marler. Marler, in turn, alerted me to some further interesting materials on the Civil War era; he also reviewed the Civil War chapter. Michael Haupert of the University of Wisconsin, LaCrosse, read the chapters on distributions of income and wealth, children, and twenty-first-century situations.

I thank the two anonymous reviewers for their useful comments, especially the reviewer who urged me to include descriptions of basic approaches to business ethics.

Librarians at the University of Chicago, Northwestern University, Notre Dame University, Chicago Public Library, University of Oregon, and University of Northern Iowa helped me locate manuscripts. The staff at the UNI inter-library loan department were unstinting in obtaining books from around the country.

My indexer on previous books, Sarah Statz Cords, found some articles in the Madison *Daily State Journal* for me.

I also thank Farzad Moussavi and Leslie Wilson, former and current Dean of the College of Business Administration of the University of Northern Iowa, who offered encouragement and support—both moral and financial (for research trips). Fred Abraham, Head of the Economics Department at the University of Northern Iowa, has long been a supporter of my work.

I appreciate Elizabeth Graber, Commissioning Editor for Palgrave Macmillan, for her interest in my work. Her encouragement and quick responses made my experiences with Palgrave Macmillan pleasant and enjoyable. Editorial Assistant Sophia Siegler and Project Coordinator Tikoji Rao were enthusiastic and gracious throughout preparing the manuscript for publication. Anish Divya thoroughly copy edited the manuscript and corrected several errors.

Contents

Introduction

By 1800, people across the world gained familiarity with impersonal trade with people in far-away places. Consumers found themselves interacting with strangers on a scale not experienced since, perhaps, the peak of the Roman Empire. Europeans, in particular, enjoyed goods found in East Asia and the so-called New World. Europeans would find the nineteenth and twentieth centuries filled with upheaval. A long-standing form of employer-worker institution—slavery—suffered a stunning collapse. Free labor became more assertive. A group of pioneering retailers transformed shopping for common people living in western Europe and North America. The industrialization of England and Holland spread across western Europe and the former British colonies in North America. A greater proportion of people, especially in America, began using consumer credit and investing in financial instruments. These financial tools required a learning process, and consumers often made mistakes. Neophyte consumers also proved prey for unscrupulous lenders and financial market manipulators.

New technologies and innovations created greater flows of information and greater impersonality between transactors. Better communication and transportation technologies opened vast vistas for fraudsters and also empowered consumers by creating more options in the marketplace and by helping identify unethical culprits. Despite continued fraudulent behavior, some business practitioners, religious thinkers, and philosophers formulated the idea that "business ethics paid," whereby ethical business practices would trump fraudulent actions. Other proposed ethical approaches included corporate social responsibility, stewardship, and stakeholder theory. Whether such theories, in themselves, raised the level of ethical practices remained unclear.

CHAPTER 1

Labor Resists

Labor and employer relations evolved considerably in America and Europe during the nineteenth century. Free labor struggled to get better working conditions and higher wages, leading to labor-management strife. Many workers decided that unionization was the best way to resist employers and to fight for better working conditions. Unions' endeavors to raise wages and to improve working conditions were perhaps inevitable in the face of increased productivity. All too many employers resorted to unethical actions to suppress worker interests, although unions, too, chose violent and unethical methods. Unions represented workers with sometimes diverse preferences. Craft unions and industrial unions had different goals and histories.

The coal mining industry may have experienced some of the most contentious labor and owner relationships in American labor history. West Virginia's coal mines provide an illustrative example that will be covered later in the chapter.

Business executives decided to promote welfare programs for their workers, in part to ward off unionization and government regulation. Workers chafed under even the paternalistic corporate welfare and other employer actions designed to foster greater productivity and harmony.

Economists derived new theories regarding the fairness of wages in the nineteenth and twentieth centuries. They hoped these new theories would rationalize the setting of wages and possibly stem discontent among workers.

D. G. Surdam, *Business Ethics from the 19th Century to Today*,
https://doi.org/10.1007/978-3-030-37169-2_1

Labor unions and large firms, though, occasionally united in supporting legislation that they knew would injure the interests of owners and workers at smaller plants or in other industries. Although workers were sometimes victimized, such victimization did not make them virtuous.

Worker Productivity and Malfeasance

Small business owners may be able to adequately monitor their employers' efforts and productivity. As businesses get larger, though, no one person can monitor all of the employees. Employees can employ deception to appear productive, including claiming credit for other workers' efforts. Employers resort to increasingly complicated performance measures; such efforts leave a "tremendous wiggle room for deceptive activities (Shulman 2007, 141)." Because such efforts may inundate decision makers with a torrent of information, people "start to pay less attention to the particulars of the information swamping them." The overload creates "obfuscation parading as clarity." The valuable signs can easily be missed (Vaughan 1996, 250).

Employers also worry about employees embezzling money, supplies, or goods. Employees and even managers have varying motives for embezzling. Modern American employers conduct investigations into prospective and current employees' credit-worthiness. Besides employees embezzling money to pay debts, some employees are getting revenge against their company for perceived grievances, while other employees are simply greedy. The conundrum for embezzling employees, though, is how to successfully deceive superiors, since embezzling employees are "subvert[ing] some set of social controls … and [need] to feign trustworthiness." Anthropologist David Shulman concludes that "organizations inevitably have structural and cultural blind spots in their social control, in part because casual deceptions are so important in an organization's dramaturgical infrastructure."[1] Shulman asks whether business organizations (and this applies to any organization, including non-profit and governmental) created cultures that "subtly encourage the rationalization of misconduct …. Individual excuses and justifications are a symptom of an underlying set of organizational mechanisms that allow both individuals and organizations to detach themselves from adverse moral assessments of deception." An organization that tolerates "slightly questionable behavior" may be unwittingly promoting an escalation of misbehavior, a domino theory of unethical behavior (Shulman 2007, 145–146, 164).

Workers and Compensation

There was a fairly close connection between productivity and wages. One of the results of the "marginalist revolution" in economic thinking during the 1860s and 1870s was the idea that wages would and should be set equal to the marginal revenue product of labor (the incremental increase in revenue from hiring an additional identical worker or unit of labor). The early proponents of the marginalist revolution thought that this economic finding would establish some sort of ethical rationale for a market-determined wage. Economic exploitation was defined as paying workers less than their marginal revenue product. However, complete unanimity regarding this belief was and is still lacking for the validity of this economic theory.

The problem with associating marginal revenue product of labor with an ethical distribution of incomes is that "The product or contribution is always measured in terms of price, which does not correspond closely with ethical value or human significance. The money value of a product is a matter of the 'demand,' which in turn reflects the tastes and purchasing power of the buying public and the availability of substitute commodities. All these factors are largely created and controlled by the workings of the economic system itself. Hence their results can have in themselves no ethical significance as standards for judging the system (Knight 1935, 55–56)."

Many people believe that such a process might create a disproportionate number of jobs with very low wages. For instance, some charities employ disabled people to put together crafts-type items; the pay is often very low, because the productivity level is so low (Schecter 2013, no page numbers; *WBEZ915* 2013, no page numbers). Is this ethical? Is it exploitive?

The demand for labor depends upon workers' marginal productivity (the incremental increase in output) and the market price of the output they produce. If workers' marginal revenue productivity (the incremental increase in revenue) increases, perhaps because the employer provides more capital per worker; workers become more proficient through gaining experience; workers attain more knowledge; or the price of the output increases—then the demand for workers increases and both employers and workers share the gains. Employers earn more profits, and workers receive higher wages.

The supply of labor depends on several factors, many outside of an individual worker's control (such as population changes, diseases such as the Black Death in medieval times, or other factors), including workers' willingness to work, which is the subjective trade-off workers make between more leisure and more income (which is converted into consumption). A worker's willingness to work at a particular job also depends upon workplace safety, amenities, and other factors. If a job is particularly nasty, fewer workers will be willing to take such a job at any given wage, reducing the supply of labor for that job and forcing the employer to pay higher wages.

All of this is tidily explained in any principles of microeconomics textbook. Students and the general public are entitled to wonder, "Does this stuff really work in the real world?" Economists studying historical data are often able to test whether such factors as danger, unpleasantness, and isolation affect the supply of labor for such jobs and therefore the wage.

Discontented Workers

Workers frequently accused masters of conspiring to suppress wages. Even Adam Smith recognized the tendency: "Masters are always and every where in a sort of tacit, but constant and uniform combination, not to raise the wages of labour above their actual rate. To violate this combination is every where a most unpopular action, and a sort of reproach to a master among his neighbours and equals." According to physician and author Andrew Ure, some owners, though, were practicing an early example of "efficiency wages" (later practiced by Henry Ford and his $5 day wage), whereby workers were paid more than the market wage in the hopes of motivating workers to work harder in order to keep getting the high wage (Smith 1981, 84; Ure 1835, 366).

Whether the workers' plight would have been better under socialism or communism was doubtful. Thomas Aquinas recognized the ills of the communist system, whereby workers were transformed into slaves regulated by central direction; he also predicted that the workers would rebel against the functionaries, as they "would have to drudge in return for meager rations, whilst the functionaries take it easy and enjoy the lion's share of the profits (Hoeffner 1985, 29)."

Pope Leo XIII highlighted the growing issue of labor and management strife. He issued an encyclical, *Rerum Novarum*, in 1891 and described the problem thusly: "some opportune remedy must be found quickly for the misery and wretchedness pressing so unjustly on the majority of the working class: for the ancient workingmen's guilds were abolished in the last century, and no other protective organization took their place." He disdained the socialist movement, arguing that "the working man himself would be among the first to suffer" from socialist programs. He based his belief upon an interesting argument: "Socialists, therefore, by endeavoring to transfer the possessions of individuals to the community at large, strike at the interests of every wage-earner, since they would deprive him of the liberty of disposing of his wages, and thereby of all hope and possibility of increasing his resources and of bettering his condition in life."

Pope Leo XIII, though, emphasized that the wealthy owner or employer should not "look upon their work people as their bondsmen, but to respect in every man his dignity as a person ennobled by Christian character." He countenanced the free bargaining over wages, except where one party held a disproportionate bargaining position. Otherwise, the state would be needed only to adjudicate non-compliance with the contract. Therefore, employers should not exploit their stronger bargaining position vis-à-vis workers: "to exercise pressure upon the indigent and the destitute for the sake of gain" was condemned. He then cast the employer's duties in a somewhat paternalistic light, requiring that employers grant their workers time to attend church services and to encourage their workers to shun dissipation and corruption. His concerns were quite similar to many of the leading industrialists, including those who used armed force to quell labor disturbances, despite their own attempts to improve workers' lives (George Pullman and Henry Ford, for example). The Pope worried about leisure time's potential for worker dissipation through alcohol, gambling, and other mean endeavors. He hoped workers would "turn [their] thoughts to things heavenly."

The Pope suggested that "wages ought not to be insufficient to support a frugal and well behaved wage-earner." In fact, the Pope thought that thrifty workers were capable of eventually amassing savings and becoming small capitalists. Such an eventuality was beneficial not only for creating a more even division of income and wealth but would make workers work harder with their own capital.

The Pope took the then controversial position that workers had a right to unionize and to strike but within bounds. He listed legitimate reasons for striking as impairment of health, lack of time for family and leisure, dangerous inter-mixing of genders, and other aspects. Some of labor's demands should be implemented, by the government if need be, in order to forestall strikes that injured trade and the general public, as well as the involved labor and management (Pecci 1891, paragraphs 3–5, 20, 41–47, 57).

An Unholy Alliance

Pope Leo XIII's fears about labor's vulnerability to owners' bargaining strength were borne out in America. American capitalists often developed friendly relations with local, state, and federal politicians and judges. In times of labor strife, these capitalists were often quick to call in judges (to issue injunctions), city police, National Guard, or employer-paid but legally deputized, private guards. Sometimes business owners subsidized police and National Guard units. Because of the various levels of government, management could "shop" for compliant officials. In the end, management's (and labor's) penchant for resorting to violence gave American labor history a bloody legacy. Of course, such heavy-handed, even murderous, tactics aroused the public's ire. Andrew Carnegie never shook off the legacy of the Homestead strike. How industrialists treated their workers often was the primary influence on the public's opinions regarding individual corporations.

On the other hand, many of the workers were immigrants. The Anglo-Saxon public feared the immigrants, whom they considered, literally, the unwashed. With the dissemination of the germ theory, educated Americans worried that crowding immigrants into unsanitary factories and slums was creating conditions ripe for infectious diseases. Such concerns eventually tainted the public's perception of the cleanliness of the products they bought (imaginative Americans could have wondered about the hands that sewed their garments or butchered their meat).

The Gilded Age and Progressive Age were marked by outbreaks of labor/management strife. Employers requested and received the assistance of state troops to suppress labor unrest almost 500 times between 1875 and 1910; by the 1890s, federal troops assisted employers in putting down striking workers (Marens 2013, 460, 462–463; Laurie 1989, 136–137; Hilkey 1997, 123).[2]

Some American consumers sided with workers, such as members of the National Consumers' League. These consumers decided to exercise their doubts regarding certain producers by boycotting those companies' products and favoring the products of employers who reputedly treated their workers well (Marens 2013, 464).

Industrialist Alfred Krupp was a pioneer in establishing worker welfare programs in Germany and offered an alternative to American employers' struggles with workers. From a modern vantage point, his efforts appear modest and perhaps ridiculously inadequate, but, "[Krupp] began doing something at a time few did; that his were among the first steps toward industrial social responsibility; that his welfare programs were effective within the larger context of German social history; and that they set the internationally renowned Krupp firm upon a path which it never abandoned."

Krupp exercised almost complete control over his firm, until a Founder's Crisis of the mid-1870s, when he began preparing for his son to assume his position. Krupp's motives for initiating and expanding his welfare program were comprised of humanitarianism and self-interest that reflected his astute and visionary understanding of the workers' desires and needs and the benefits for the firm. He was intent on rewarding loyal workers. He was also paternalistic and tried to control his workers' lives. He avoided the violent labor strife found in America.

Workers, of course, chafed at such heavy-handed scrutiny, but as a later Krupp chairman of the board, Heinrich Heider, observed, acknowledging that growing class consciousness on the part of the worker would have inevitably eventually created tension between Alfred Krupp and his workers, "The fatherly image embodied by Alfred Krupp was as a rule accepted with an almost childishly naïve gratitude. We still today should respect this feeling. It would be false to judge the social activity of the past by the standards of the present (McCreary 1968, 24–25, 38, 49)."

The Perils and Discontents of Coal Mining

In the public's mind, coal mining perhaps exemplified exploitation of workers. Coal mining in America varied across regions. Labor investigator Howard Lee described the West Virginia mines of the early 1900s. Pioneering West Virginia mine owners exploited the miners and the original landowners. He relates how eastern capitalists sent engineers to survey likely veins of coal; these agents then induced the inhabitants to sell their land for "mere pittances" of less than a dollar an acre. Somewhat confusingly, though, Lee described the early operators of coal mines in Appalachia as being short of capital but willing to work extensive hours. Some of these owners eventually became wealthy men with political influence. "They treated their workers and operated their mines just as they had been treated and had seen mines operated in their native lands and in Pennsylvania. They knew no other way."

The West Virginia mine owners wanted to control their labor force and resisted unions. The mine owners used a variety of means to keep the unions out; the tactics included getting injunctions from friendly local magistrates; imposing martial law; gaining influence over local government officials; maintaining excessive scrutiny of workers; employing thuggish mine guards; and blacklisting pro-union miners (Lee 1969, 7–8, 12). Although some of these tactics may have had legitimate uses, the owners used political and legal influence to gain disproportionate negotiating strength against the workers; such tactics raised ethical questions.

In retrospect, the miners' demands seem pretty reasonable. The Paint Creek, West Virginia miners wanted piece rates a half-cent per ton below those paid at union mines; rights of free speech and peaceable assembly; no more blacklists; no more compulsory purchasing at company stores; an end to "cribbing"; installation of scales; check-weighmen; and joint owner/worker scrutiny of "docking" for impurities (Wheeler 1976, 70). That miners included rights of free speech and peaceable assembly in their demands demonstrates how skewed bargaining power had been in the past. These demands appear consistent with most people's conception of simple fairness. The mine owners might have better forestalled union organization by not hiring expensive mine guards and avoided the recurring work stoppages had they acceded to most of these rather modest demands.

West Virginia mine owners held interesting attitudes toward a "ton." Most people regard a ton as consisting of 2000 pounds. Mine owners used "cribbing," a framework at the top of mine cars that increased the cars' coal-carrying capacity and required miners to load well over 2000 pounds to earn pay for a "ton." Workers naturally scorned such petty cheats. Mine owners also imposed edicts against adulterating coal with inferior coal or non-coal material (Lee 1969, 18; Wheeler 1976, 70).

Workers also despised the "Yellow-Dog" contract that mine owners often imposed upon workers. The contract required workers to sign away their right to join a union, and Lee, among other historians, considered it a pivotal tactic in repelling unionism. Lee observed that the contract "was supplied to the operators by the union itself. If the union had not violated its union contract with the Hitchman Coal & Coke Company [legal case], and had it not tried to induce that company's workers to break their individual contracts of employment, there would have not been any Yellow-Dog Contract in West Virginia .... The union did not provide these strikers with sufficient relief funds [so the miners began drifting back to work]." The mine owners allowed workers to return, if they signed individual contracts. "The union, however, began to pressure these workers to breach their contracts, return to the union, and continue the strike." The Hitchman Company filed for and won an injunction; the Supreme Court eventually upheld the Hitchman Company's actions (Lee 1969, 79–80; Wheeler 1976, 86).

Mine owners, too, had grievances. The West Virginia mine owners did not operate in a vacuum. They competed, often at a disadvantage due to their higher costs of transporting coal to users, with mine owners in Pennsylvania, Ohio, Indiana, and Illinois. These Great Lakes mines already faced unions and paid higher wages. The West Virginian owners remained viable competitors only by keeping wages and other expenses lower than their rivals. The operators in the other states negotiated with the unions facing them that such unions would try to organize (or infiltrate, depending upon one's perspective) the non-union mines in West Virginia. The West Virginia operators "were justified to some extent in their view of the union as an agent of their competitors, bent on damage to their competitive position." The existing unions, of course, understood and desired to bring more of their working brothers into organized labor, thereby strengthening the existing unions' leverage (Wheeler 1976, 75).[3]

There was also an element of lawlessness in the region. The mine operators often finagled deputy sheriff positions for trusted employees. The attractions of having one's own employees serve as law enforcement officers eventually became an element of abuse and hatred. One sheriff, Don Chafin, gained notoriety. Chafin became the county Democratic county assessor, county clerk, and sheriff after the war. He replaced the Baldwin-Felts mine guards with his own men. Eventually he had hundreds of men on the deputy-mine-guard payroll. Chafin was adept at skimming money off the expenses of his "feudal army." By 1921, he testified before the U.S. Senate Committee that he was worth $350,000, even though his salary was $3500 per year. The Senate committee stated, "The system of paying deputy sheriffs out of funds contributed by the operators, as the testimony shows has been done in Logan County … is a vicious and un-American policy." The committee then made the ironic statement, "It would be just as logical to have members of Congress paid by certain interests." The owners paid for such a large crew of deputies through charges upon coal tonnage; one wonders whether it would have been cheaper to simply accede to some of the workers' demands.

Because the owners held sway over the West Virginia legislature and local governments, the abusive law enforcement system persisted. Workers were as willing to resort to violence as were the mine owners. Both sides armed themselves, and the owners built fortifications. During the violence immediately after 1918, there were plenty of workers who were war veterans with familiarity with firearms and explosives (Lee 1969, 11, 22–24, 87, 91).[4] All too often, violence begat violence, with the old playground charge, "He started it!" becoming the justification for retaliation.

Unionization in Coal Mining

When workers organized and formed unions, they, in essence, created a monopoly of labor. In remote areas, a mine owner might be the sole employer for miles around, giving that owner some wage-setting power (what economists designate as monopsony power). Economic theory suggests that when a union faced mine owners, the outcome with regard to setting a wage was indeterminate. The outcome depended upon the relative bargaining powers of the unions and the owners. Both sides had incentives to increase their bargaining power. The owners could import replacement workers, hire mine guards and "detectives," or call upon their friends in the state house for local militia. The workers could arm themselves and deter the importation of replacement workers. They could also resort to the courts, with sporadic success.

One Colorado governor did not even wait to see whether a miners' convention would result in a walk-out before he declared martial law. The miners were incensed by this "unwarranted and uncalled for action" and instead of calling off their strike, decided to strike; the miners decided that returning to work in the face of the military would have been perceived as "cowardly surrender (Suffern 1915, 60)."

During a strike in 1912, the West Virginia governor Henry Hatfield—himself no stranger to violence, as a descendant of the Hatfield-McCoy feud—imposed martial law and allowed military tribunals to mete out justice. The tribunals, a violation of civil liberties, hastily arrested, convicted, and sent men to the state penitentiary. Howard Lee comments, "In civil life the judges of the military courts were laymen, many of whom did not know the difference between a felony and a misdemeanor, and their judgments reflected their lack of knowledge." In many cases, militia members did double duty as mine guards, so miners understandably viewed such "law enforcement" efforts as illegitimate. In fairness to Hatfield, he eventually forced the mine owners and miners to accept a brokered peace in 1912; the miners won some of their demands (Lee 1969, 33–35, 46; Wheeler 1976, 72).

Despite or perhaps because of mine violence, working conditions in West Virginia improved up to the mine war of 1920–1921. Workdays shortened and the company store system became less exploitative. Mine owners paid twice monthly, and mine safety improved. More importantly, mine wages, both in nominal terms and in purchasing power, rose between 1897 and 1918. The mine wars in West Virginia did not result from "progressive immiserization" of the workers. "Prior to both mine wars [1912 and 1920–1921], conditions, which had been improving, took a downward turn. This is quite pronounced in the case of the 1920–1921 mine war. A more concrete basis for the violent nature of the confrontation between labor and capital in West Virginia is that both sides considered that they were locked in a struggle to the death (Wheeler 1976, 82–83, 90)." The 1920–1921 general economic downturn in America may have contributed to worker discontent after the war.

Aspects of the Coal Mining Industry

Economists Price Fishback and Dieter Lauszus noted that coal companies were often not as powerful as reputed. Unions and miner mobility forced owners to offer competitive wages and conditions. By the 1920s, at least, much of any exploitation that had existed was probably waning. They added that the negative reputation of company towns emanated from the sole employer aspect: "In the company town, the employer was landlord, merchant, and politician rolled into one, and so became the focal point of discontent over all and all aspects of life. Further, since the company town was private property, employers could prevent trespassers and maintain political control over the town. Workers feared the abuse of this power and the violation of their personal freedom (Fishback and Lauszus 1989, 140–141)."

Because the nature of coal mines made supervision difficult, workers were often paid piece-rate wages. Miners were usually responsible for their own safety, aside from some basic safety-related "public-goods" that had economies of scale (being cheaper to provide for all, than if each individual had to provide such goods on his own): ventilation, mine gas inspections, watering, and providing pre-cut timbers. Mine supervisors or foremen assigned particular spaces for each miner (or pair of miners). The miner and his co-worker "made nearly all of the accident prevention decisions within his own workplace. He decided how often to timber the roof to prevent roof falls, and how large a blast to use in dislodging the coal."[5]

Contemporaries originally placed much blame upon mine workers themselves for accidents. Miners took short cuts with regard to safety; perhaps revealing inspectors' nativist prejudices, inspectors also accused recent immigrants as being especially lax. The recent immigrants' inability to speak English and possible lack of mining experience were often cited. Other inspectors, though, held mine owners accountable for not fulfilling their responsibilities with regard to safety. Fishback suggests that later historians, who vilified the mine owners, portrayed the miners as "helpless economic pawns in the coal operator's hands. They emphasized the geographical isolation of the mining towns and describe the operator as routinely meeting competition from other operators by reducing the wages of the working man directly or indirectly by increasing prices at the company store." Fishback pointed out that real wages for miners had, in fact, increased until the mid-1920s. Strangely enough, the United Mine Workers of America (UMWA) considered mine safety a secondary goal; the UMWA focused on increasing unionization of non-union mines, in order to strengthen its monopoly power in the industry. Therefore union and non-union mines would not necessarily have different safety records based solely on a union/non-union distinction (Fishback 2006, 271–275).

Mine owners often resisted miners' attempts to organize, claiming such attempts were a monopolization of labor, a restraint of trade. The owners, though, were more than happy to organize among themselves. Some mine owners wanted to combine to keep the price of coke sufficiently high, so they could pay their men a living wage. Of course, such a collusive agreement foundered upon individual mine owners' self-interest. In any event, the influx of foreign labor proved a convenient scapegoat for the low wages. Presaging the "Buy America" and anti-immigrant sentiments persisting in modern-day America, native-born miners wanted a ban on hiring foreign miners. Mine owners disagreed. Henry Clay Frick, for instance, refused to stop hiring Slavs and Italians (Sheppard [1947] 1991, 47–50).

Andrew Carnegie and Frick differed on their approaches to handling labor disputes. Frick wanted to take a militant and antagonistic stand against the workers, although in the past he had been in the forefront of making an agreement that gave his miners sufficient to live upon and with planned increases in wages; he also paid his workers in a timely fashion. Carnegie told Frick, "My idea of beating in a dispute with men is always to shut down and suffer; let them decide when they desire to go to work—say kindly, 'All right, gentlemen, let's hear from you … when a majority vote to start, start it is.'" Carnegie understood that workers resented replacement workers (scabs) and noted, "Who can blame them (Sheppard [1947] 1991, 42, 46–48; see also Standiford 2005, 223)?"

A year later, Carnegie wrote for public consumption in the periodical *Forum*: "To expect that one dependent on his daily wage for the necessities of life will stand by peaceably and see a new man employed in his stead, is to expect too much." He also preached to his fellow industrialists: "There is an unwritten law among the best workmen. Thou shalt not take thy neighbor's jobs." Of course, commentators then and now harped on the contradictions between Carnegie's remarks and his actions.

Carnegie had tempered Frick's attempt to quash a coal strike in 1887, but he was nonplussed to experience a significant increase in costs that his rivals, adhering to more hardline tactics, avoided. Carnegie had earlier surrendered in a fight with his workers. In 1885, Carnegie realized that his workers were restless upon hearing that his firm earned $3 million in profits; he decided to give a 10 percent raise. The skilled and experienced workers wanted a return to the eight-hour shifts that had been taken away earlier. To forestall a strike, Carnegie authorized the dismissal of hundreds of skilled operators and to bring in strikebreakers, but the rest of the workforce rebelled and forced Carnegie to retreat (Standiford 2005, 71).

In 1892, Carnegie headed to Scotland and left Frick in charge of the Carnegie Steel Company in Homestead, Pennsylvania. Frick's tactics led to violence, although some of his fellow executives applauded his adamant refusal to accede to the workers' union. Carnegie pleaded that he had nothing to do with the ill-fated decisions, saying he was incommunicado in Scotland. The incident tarnished Carnegie's standing in the public's eye; decades of charitable efforts never succeeded in erasing the smudge (Sheppard [1947] 1991, 50–51, 63).

The workers realized that Carnegie and Frick held the whip hand, with one telling Hamlin Garland, a writer for *McClure Magazine*, "We can't hurt Carnegie by six months' starving. It's our ribs that'll show through our shirts. A man working for fourteen cents an hour hasn't got any surplus for a strike." Another worker conceded, "There are lots of other jobs as bad." The workers were most aggrieved by the length of the work shift, not the work itself (Standiford 2005, 230–231).[6] As grim as these working conditions were, and by twenty-first-century standards, they were atrocious conditions, immigrants still clamored to come to America. These immigrants likely had some notion of what they were going to encounter, as their friends and family who had immigrated earlier corresponded with them.

Exploitation or Not

Although Tennessee Ernie Ford sang the deathless line, "Owe my soul to the company store," in "Sixteen Tons," the company store may have been more benign than legend has it. Some British factory owners paid wages in tickets or "tommy-books" redeemable only at the company store. As with many American coal miners, the factory owner required workers to use their tickets at the company store; any worker with the temerity to ask for cash was threatened with, "If you don't want tommy you don't want work." Not all company shops were exploitative, and some were respectable and were intended for the convenience of the workers. Although stores may have originally been exploitative, using scrip and charging high prices, economic historians have shown that by the 1920s or so, the stores served to monitor and reduce the cost of credit for both company and the worker. The company store also could charge lower prices for items it purchased in bulk. Stores located in isolated regions might naturally have charged more, as the costs of shipping merchandise to such locations might have been higher (Davis 1966, 273).

Coal mine owners in western Pennsylvania reportedly used company stores to exploit their workers in the late nineteenth century. Observers claimed that the stores, referred to as "pluck-me stores," not only charged exorbitant prices but induced owners to limit the hours that miners worked. The purpose of limiting the hours was to ensure that every dollar the miner earned went through the company store, "Otherwise, when pay day came, there would be a cash balance due him and a consequent loss of profit on a corresponding amount of store goods." The logic of this explanation seems dubious. Owners, therefore, overcrowded their mines with workers. Mine owners with company stores were better able to survive competition that drove profits from mining coal to zero; these owners survived based on their profits from the company store. Because of these supposed abuses, mine workers strove to eliminate the company stores in this region or at least to create a differential wage structure, whereby companies with stores paid more per ton of coal mined (*Annals of the American Academy of Political and Social Science* 1896, 162–164; Suffern 1915, 27).

Price Fishback disputed the standard depiction of company stores as exploitative. He acknowledged that the historiography tends to see the company stores in a negative light; journalists and a Senate investigation found higher prices at company stores than local trade stores. Fishback's thesis was "the company store's prices were part of an employment package offered to geographically mobile miners in a labor market with hundreds of mines." His argument revolved around the mobility of the miners (and, implicitly, the flow of information regarding wages and working conditions among mines). Mines may have been located in rural areas, but there were often several mines in relatively close proximity. Because the stores were somewhat isolated, the cost of transporting merchandise was undoubtedly higher for such stores, accounting, in part, for the higher prices than miners might have faced in more established towns. Mines also differed by regions; miners in West Virginia faced different conditions than miners in Illinois. Fishback argued that even a company operating a store monopoly in a non-union area faced constraints on its prices. He noted that a researcher who declared the company stores exploitative, also described the miners' mobility in response to better working conditions or wages.

To be sure, an Immigration Commission of 1907 discovered some cases of coerced buying and other anti-competitive tactics. But a Coal Commission in 1925 concluded that "the system of openly forcing employees to buy at commissaries is said to be no longer in practice." The two commissions' different dates are highly suggestive of a gradual evolution of company stores.

Congressional committees rarely collected prices from a large number of stores, so Fishback claims that the evidence from the scattered prices could be misleading. Even with this drawback, a table showing prices for December 1922 "show that in six of the ten comparisons the stores in mining districts—including independent and company stores—charged less than stores in manufacturing districts." Miners also frequently found better quality articles at the company store than at independent stores, according to 1908 and 1909 Immigration Commission investigations.

Assuming miners were both mobile and knowledgeable about working conditions between mines (both within and between regions), then a mine owner exploiting miners through high store prices would have to compensate by offering higher wages or other inducements above that of companies not exploiting miners in a similar fashion. In fact, some miners might have benefited from the differing wage/benefit packages. Single males would gravitate to mines paying higher wages and charging higher prices at the company stores, since such miners' propensity to purchase consumer goods would have been lower than miners with families. The mine owners' ability to exploit workers was inversely related to the workers' literacy and their understanding of English. Across the early decades of the twentieth century, workers were becoming more literate and the immigrants were gaining facility with English.

As company stores began to buy in bulk, they began receiving better wholesale prices. The stores, similar to most local retailers, often extended credit to the miners. The company stores had an advantage with regard to information of miners' ability and willingness to repay loans, as store operators usually had access to company payroll information. One other aspect of the mines' relative isolation was the lack of banks. The issuing of scrip—which sometimes was in response to miners' request for advances on wages due the following payday—may have been in response to a scarcity of currency; in addition, not having to handle cash reduced the mine owners' cost of security with regard to large sums of cash. Companies also acted as lenders to their "better workers," in order for those workers to purchase consumer durables and even houses. The intent was not to create debt peonage, but to help motivate workers to remain with the company; such policies incurred the risk of a worker repudiating the loan by moving away.[7]

Fishback found evidence that companies charging higher prices at their stores also paid higher wages. The workers appeared well-enough informed to force mine owners to offer competitive compensation packages. He concluded scrip was a more benign aspect than traditionally thought (Fishback 1986, 1011–1018, 1021–1023, 1029).

Fishback's work often dealt with conditions after 1900. The pioneering coal mine operators in the previous decades may have possessed greater monopsony power until new owners entered the local market. Fishback acknowledged such a process in his discussion regarding operators attempting to raise prices at the company store to offset the higher wages; he doubted that such a policy would work, as "the mines [had become] increasingly less isolated with increased mobility of miners and increased competition from independent stores." Certainly miner ownership of automobiles and access to railroad/bus transportation services reduced isolation; in fact, the likelihood of unionization appeared to be associated with greater isolation (Fishback 2006, 273–274).

In any event, allegations of coal mine owners acting unethically with respect to their workers may have been inaccurate. Economic analysis reveals, at the least, ambiguity with respect to some of these allegations.

Employer Welfare Capitalism

Several of the late nineteenth-century Quaker factory owners used social welfare programs to improve their workers' standard of living. Henry Ford gained acclaim for his five-dollar-day wage; there was a sinister ramification of his seemingly generous wage in that conveyor belts began running faster. Ford and similar employers made a show of building housing or creating social welfare programs for their workers, but many of these employers privately worried that putting more dollars into the pockets of their workers would lead to worker dissipation through spending on alcohol. On the other hand, the public seemed to think, at least initially, that such largesse implied that Ford and his compatriots were behaving ethically in other phases of their corporations. National Cash Registers had the ability to ward off punishment for violating the Sherman Act, as many people defended the company based upon its renowned social welfare programs. Publicist Ivy Lee rehabilitated International Harvester after the firm faced allegations of antitrust violations and an unfavorable magazine expose entitled "Making Cripples and Dodging Taxes." Lee emphasized the firm's social welfare programs and reversed the flow of public opinion (Marens 2013, 469).[8]

Welfare capitalism was an attempt to create worker loyalty and to forestall the formation of unions through positive motivations, including providing benefits and "harmonizing" worker, supervisory, and capitalist interests. Although providing carrots to motivate workers was calculated to undercut worker militancy and to present a good public persona, workers and owners recognized the latent coercion involved. Employers could still evict workers from company housing or eliminate coverage under the health care plan. Welfare capital had mixed effects (Edwards 1979, 91, 95; Surdam 2015, 68).

Some companies established company unions. The seeming contradiction in terms did point to such entities' weakness. Company unions developed in the first two decades of the twentieth century. The standard interpretation of company unions is that they were a devise to forestall the creation of an independent union and to implant "welfare capitalism." Such interpretations may have missed the key question of whether company unions resolved, if only partially, some of the issues that drove workers to demand unions. One feature stood out during the first two decades of the twentieth century: Employers began realizing that a high level of labor turnover was costly and that the employers needed to address low worker morale. Management could improve worker morale by creating procedures whereby workers could express concerns about shop floor conditions. Such concerns often revolved around the arbitrary behavior of immediate supervisors, such as foremen. During the 1920s, many large manufacturing companies, indeed, formed company unions, and these organizations reduced turnover rates and improved productivity growth. In addition, injury rates fell. The evidence suggested that "company unions ultimately benefitted both labor and management on the shop floor, while at the same time serving to prevent the distributional losses employers would have suffered had independent unions been successfully organized." A contemporary economist, Paul Douglas made the distinction clear: Company unions increased production and morale, but "independent unions insured that labor received its fair share of the gains."[9]

One researcher analyzed the available data and found that "those industries reporting the greatest success in reducing turnover through welfare measures were also those with the largest concentration of recorded welfare benefits." In 1919, firms that pioneered welfare capitalism, however, found themselves facing striking workers. The researcher found that the industries with the greatest success at cutting labor turnover using welfare benefits experienced the largest growth in strike activity during the late 1910s (Fairris 1995, 493–494, 502–506).

Independent trade unions, too, had flaws. There were disturbing aspects of trade unions, especially in comparison with "Friendly societies:" "the one [trade unions] intent on using the collective power of the work force to make a change in real wages and the other [friendly societies] developing a system of welfare services among members through cooperative effort." Economist Brian Griffiths cited the 1906 Trade Disputes Act that gave British trade unions "total immunity for torts 'alleged to have been committed by or on behalf of the trade union.'" A contemporary observer, jurist A.V. Dicey, claimed, "It makes a trade union a privileged body exempted from the ordinary law of the land." Sidney and Beatrice Webb, who were avowed socialists, admitted that the act was "nothing less than monstrous (Griffiths 1980, 114–115; Dicey 1914, xlvi)."

Such criticism of trade unions may surprise many readers used to thinking of such organizations as benign, even heroic. Union wage gains were associated with losses by non-unionized workers. Some union leaders, when confronted by this association, saw nothing wrong with extracting "from the society the highest possible reward for the labour power that we sell," a statement that echoed many so-called robber barons. Unions are monopolies of workers; that is how they bargain for higher wages (although wage gains are ultimately limited by productivity considerations). Unsavory practices of unions included opposing industrial change that jeopardized union jobs; contributing to higher unemployment; using intimidation and physical violence; and exercising coercive power over individuals (Griffiths 1980, 117).

By 1900, most of the "Gilded Age" industry titans were gone. Carnegie had sold his holdings to J.P. Morgan and U.S. Steel; Rockefeller had retired from Standard Oil, Vanderbilt was dead, and so on. The next generation of corporate executives was managerial and not entrepreneurial. The prevalence of oligopoly stabilized prices and profits in many industries; stabilized profits allowed managers to consider long-term employee betterment programs. These programs might raise costs, but such increased costs could be passed on, in part, to consumers. "Between 1900 and 1920, however, such long-established welfare folkways began to change, part of an evolution in overall bureaucratic procedure .... With increasing frequency, American big businessmen attempted to set up private 'welfare states' within their individual firms. These efforts to reduce worker dissatisfaction and socialist activity were frequently phrased in the late-nineteenth-century, Social-Gospel rhetoric of trusteeship."

With the tight labor market of the 1920s, especially after Congress enacted restrictive immigration laws, corporate leaders began to see employees not as expendable, but as valuable assets. Concerns over the cost of labor turnover spurred corporations to devise means of retaining good workers. Management began to see workers as "an individual with the potential, if his human capital were properly invested, to expand company profits. The New Era had created an image of the new economic man." In the face of government passiveness, business leaders seized the responsibility for providing social welfare. Corporate leaders feared that government involvement would mismanage things up by "over-supplying" welfare services, especially to the undeserving. They feared demoralization of the working (and unemployed) people. Business leaders also believed that corporation managers would better assess the costs and benefits of social welfare programs. One leader testified, "If you vote the money by Government assistance our general public will pay for it through taxation, which is very general and very indefinite." In contrast, social welfare provided by corporations would affect their costs and "the people who use the product will ultimately pay for that service." Historians Edward Berkowitz and Kim McQuaid concluded, "[W]elfare capitalism served a double function. It aided industrial efficiency and minimized governmental inefficiency (Berkowitz and McQuaid 1978, 121–122, 127–129)."

Workers Unite

Despite employer corporate welfare programs, employees still chafed at wages. Negotiating wages and working conditions remained contentious.

Many critics of free enterprise claim workers are at a disadvantage in negotiating wages and working conditions with employers. Economist Frank Knight suggests that "the popular notions regarding the intrinsic superiority in bargaining power of the employer are very largely false. This is true even apart from situations where there is effective monopoly in one form or another; and the monopoly factor itself may operate on either side (Knight 1939, 2)."

In any event, disgruntled workers followed time-honored forms of protest. "Consequently, workers were sometimes less than diligent in their duties and less than devoted to their employers. Absenteeism was high, 'soldiering' [shirking] was significant and sabotage was not uncommon." Prior to 1910, "many employers appear to have been preoccupied with other matters and were thus simply unaware of the costs associated with high labor turnover and low worker morale (Fairris 1995, 499)."

Knight's claim aside, workers resorted to unions, because individual workers were unable to exert enough bargaining strength to sway employers. Workers were vulnerable to work stoppages, as they often did not have any savings. Workers faced a long struggle to win recognition for unions and to gain federal legislation protecting the right to unionize and to strike. Some employers, though, recognized that "managing a disorganized mass of workers presented organizational difficulties that would not have existed to the same degree had a union been in place to enforce agreements and assuage employee concerns, although a union would certainly have set a price for its cooperation." Employers may have worried that if they allowed a union, and their competitors did not, they would be at a disadvantage. As jobs began requiring more skills and training, workers gained bargaining leverage, and employers could not cavalierly fire recalcitrant workers and hire replacements. Economists and Progressives began pressing for employers to recognize worker rights and to ameliorate the worst aspects of working conditions. John Bates Clark, an economist whose research led him to espouse setting wages solely based on market forces and workers' individual productivity, understood that collective bargaining "tend[ed] to equalize the strategic position of men and employers." German labor unions were more successful in unionizing large firms than were American unions. German legislators created stronger rights for union workers. The diverse working class, where ethnic and religious differences trumped animus toward employers, made organizing American workers difficult (Marens 2013, 458, 465).

British labor unions struggled to align the interests of all of their workers. Workers primarily sought higher wages; they did not necessarily agree on other union aims, such as unemployment or health insurance, working hours, and death benefits. Younger workers often had different priorities than did older workers.

Unions could use various forms of insurance to recruit members, to maintain discipline, and to enforce union decisions. Members who had paid in for years found themselves trapped; they could not incur the wrath of the union and be kicked out, lest they lose their old-age and funeral benefits (the benefits were not vested). These tactics resembled employers' desire to bind workers! Unemployment insurance helped maintain solidarity; unemployed members would not be tempted to accept really low wages out of desperation. Such solidarity, of course, was an important lever in bargaining with management. Unions often used the contributions as reserve funds in case of strikes, but such tactics did not always operate in the anticipated manner; union members worried about depleting the reserves through strike activities instead of using the reserves for benefits. The effectiveness of these benefits to maintain discipline varied between workers. Younger workers, with little paid in, were less easily disciplined, as expulsion meant losing little; younger workers might be more militant than older workers in agitating for pay increases, since they had more years to benefit from such increases. Older workers might be more cautious in incurring the displeasure of union officials, especially if they had old-age benefits at stake.

Union leaders understood that the unions' unemployment insurance policies came with moral hazard potential, whereby ineligible workers might try to obtain benefits or workers receiving unemployment insurance legitimately might prefer to remain unemployed instead of looking for and resuming work. Unions had to determine whether applicants for unemployment insurance were eligible for benefits. Craft unions required applicants to make claims at branch meetings, where they were well known to other workers. Workers who tried to fraudulently obtain benefits were punished by his fellow members. Once a worker received benefits, he had to sign a "vacant-book" daily at his branch; union officials could send the unemployed worker to job sites. If the worker refused a job offer, he lost his benefits, unless he could provide a good excuse for not taking the job. Friendly societies, on the other hand, had difficulty combatting moral hazard, since their members were dispersed among various occupations (Boyer 1988, 323, 328–331).

Conflicts Within Unions Over Hours

Unions faced difficulties in deciding their goals. Although many British and American progressives in the late nineteenth century bemoaned the lengthy workdays and weeks of workers, not all workers favored shorter hours, British and American iron and steel workers between 1890–1923, for instance. Foundries were unpleasant places to work by their nature; a blast furnace was, of course, hot, and dangers were omnipresent. The National Association of Blastfurnacemen in 1888 supported shorter hours, but many of its members were opposed to shorter working days if it entailed a reduction in pay. Only decades later, did a British Steel Smelters union "accept wages for an eight-hour day that would keep labor costs constant."

American iron and steel workers also opposed the eight-hour-day campaigns of the 1890s. American iron and steel companies began hiring immigrants from Eastern Europe. The industry recruited immigrants through labor agents and steamship companies. The immigrants were aware of working conditions, whether through the agents or, more likely, from letters from relatives already working in the industry. These immigrant workers, probably inured to working extremely long hours, wanted all the work they could get. "Russian steel laborers in Pittsburgh told an investigator they were glad to work extra days. A majority voluntarily reported on Sunday to clear yards and repair equipment. An immigrant characterized his twelve hour position: 'A good job, save money, work all the time, go home, sleep, no spend.'" The companies' tactic of hiring immigrants ended, when World War I turned off the spigot of immigrants; a few years later, the country enacted stricter immigration law.

After World War I, the American steel industry, as with many other industries, faced a general strike. Between the 1919 strike and 1923, the industry's labor policy on work hours changed quickly. Public opinion and government coercion pushed an unwilling industry toward granting shorter workdays. The industry leaders dithered, but threats by the government forced their hands. Judge Elbert Gary chairman of the board of U.S. Steel, informed President Warren G. Harding that the industry would stop the 12-hour day, because of "a strong sentiment throughout the country … and especially because it is in accordance with your own expressed views (Shiells 1990, 386, 389–390)." Employers across industries gradually acceded to shorter workweeks, giving Saturday afternoons off; then giving the entire day off; and finally shortening the workday. The last barrier became the eight-hour day. Possible factors explaining the decline in the workweek between 1909 and 1919 included higher wages; constrained immigration; increased unionization; federal government wartime labor policies; electrification of manufacturing; and various federal and state legislations. These factors created what labor economist Robert Whaples calls this "Great Decline" in the length of the workweek.

Another factor affecting working conditions and hours was the dawning realization that retaining employees for the long term was better than having constant turnover. The personnel boom of the World War I era was part of a trend toward a "high-wage-high-quality-low-turnover" employment relation. In order to sustain long-term productivity, employers began shortening work hours and offering paid vacation time. Whaples pointed out that industries where there were a few employers "had the greatest incentive to invest in future productivity through reduced hours, since they were the most likely to maintain long-term relations with their employees (Whaples 1990, 394, 404)."

In the process of getting shorter work hours, the W.K. [Will Keith] Kellogg Company's experience remains unique. Unlike most employers of the 1880–1920 years, Kellogg thought leisure was important for all people; he personally regretted not learning to play. He was also fascinated by mass leisure. "He believed that family, community, and personal and public health should be the first beneficiaries of the new wealth in time." He set up various daycares, playgrounds, parks, and amenities in Battle Creek.

During the slide into the Great Depression, Kellogg's decided to switch from three eight-hour shifts to four six-hour shifts. Company officials explained that spreading the work meant paychecks for hundreds more families. The company tried to maintain the purchasing power of the eight-hour day by raising the minimum daily wage or by increasing the hourly wage by 12.5 percent. The company official explicitly noted that the decline in the general price level contributed to sustaining the purchasing power of the pre-Depression wages. In other words, unlike other companies' work-sharing plans, Kellogg's did not put the burden of the plan upon the workers; Kellogg's split the costs of the short hours. The company's overall wage expense increased under the plan, but the company hoped that increased worker productivity would offset the higher wage bill. They alluded to Henry Ford's argument, if not proof, that shorter hours proved beneficial. By 1931, the idea of the six-hour day was attracting political and business attention, with President Herbert Hoover asking Kellogg to visit Washington, D.C. to discuss the plan. The following year, a large proportion of firms had reduced hours in order to save jobs; most reduced wages (although whether with respect to real wages was unclear).[10]

The Kellogg Company examined the six-hour policy after five years. The findings indicated overhead and labor unit costs fell, as did the number and severity of accidents. They considered the experiment an "unqualified success." The company's attitude began swinging back toward preferring longer hours during the 1940s (Hunnicutt 1992, 479–483, 492–495, 497). The company eventually succeeded in increasing the workday but only after decades of struggle.

Safety Legislation

In the Disneyfied version of *Mary Poppins*, the chimney sweep, Bert, played by Dick Van Dyke seemed a romantic, if scruffy, character. In reality, chimney sweeps led harsh lives. The boys tended to be small (malnourished); the work was arduous, dirty, and essentially health-destroying. The fine dust damaged many of the sweeps' lungs. Of course, mid-nineteenth-century London could not afford all of its workers pleasant working conditions.

Who should be responsible for workplace safety? From an economics perspective, the "who" issue may be of minor importance. Assuming workers and employers recognize the risk, assigning legal responsibility may be moot. Suppose the employer bears the responsibility. Implementing safety rules or equipment may cost money. The employer may be less willing to hire workers in the face of stringent safety requirements; the employer's demand for workers would fall, leading to a reduction in the market-clearing wage. If the employer does not implement these safety procedures and equipment, then fewer workers will want to work for the employer. The workers' reticence reduces their supply of labor, forcing the employer to pay more. In a sense, increased safety is similar to a tax. A (per-unit) tax drives a wedge between the wage offered and the net wage. If employees have to pay for the safety devices, then their willingness to work will fall and the market-clearing wage will rise. Workers will receive more in gross wages but will then pay out some of their wages to cover the safety costs.

Nineteenth-century employers and workers appeared to tolerate more dangerous working conditions than their descendants. During the construction of the Central Pacific Railroad over the Sierra Nevada Mountains in California, Chinese workers were lowered over cliffs in baskets to place and detonate dynamite. The trick was to raise them before the dynamite exploded. "On the Central Pacific the death rate was artificially increased by the unamiable Irish habit of exploding their blasts while the Chinese were still working in the cuttings beneath." Irish workers, too, faced similar dangers.

Another engineering marvel, the Panama Railway, was a literal death march: "The record for fatalities was probably set by the Panama Railway—at one point one worker in five was dying every month." The railway's doctor faced an overwhelming number of corpses; he hit upon the idea of selling unclaimed bodies to medical schools, thereby making the railway hospital self-sustaining (Faith [1990] 1994, 200–201; see also Holbrook 1947, 170).

Railroad workers faced hazards, too. Before the introduction of automatic couplers, trainmen had to stand between cars in order to insert a pin to link the cars. Trainman frequently lost fingers or were crushed between the cars. Early train cars lacked airbrakes, so brakemen ran atop the cars and manually applied the brakes. Exploding boilers on steamboats and locomotives were omnipresent dangers.

Over the years, state and federal regulations of the coal mining industry appeared. Price Fishback found that "the coal mining labor market in the early 1900s was more competitive than monopsonistic. Risk premia are found in wages, accident rates are unaffected by wage cuts, and … unions enhanced the welfare of their members." These results occurred even though many states had enacted mine safety regulations and the federal government launched a Bureau of Mines, but such regulations were often ineffective due to the legislatures' failure to adequately finance inspectors. Fishback concluded, "The quantitative analysis here supports [the] … view of the ineffectiveness of the Bureau of Mines and most state mining legislation. Conversely, the analysis shows that workmen's compensation legislation had no impact on coal mine safety (Fishback 2006, 270)."

Coal mining during World War II had injury and death rates comparable with combat troops: "Coal miners had the dirtiest, toughest, and most dangerous jobs in America, and the war made them worse [in the face of accelerated production schedules] … . Because little could be done to improve safety at a time of maximum effort, the mines became even more hazardous. Each week some 500 miners were killed or injured, a rate approaching that of combat. As of May 1943, the armed forces had sustained a total of 27,000 casualties, while in the same period 35,000 miners were injured—2000 fatally (O'Neill 1993, 208–209)."

Clearly, people were willing to accept greater risks in years past. Why did workers accept such risks? Was this because management and labor valued human life any less? An economist would ask, "What were their alternatives?" Was it because the opportunity sets facing pre-1900 people were much more limited than late twentieth-century Americans? Is safety a luxury good, in the sense that as incomes increase, workers demand an even greater proportional improvement in workplace safety?

More Leisure at Work

As worker productivity increased, workers negotiated for shorter work hours, vacation time, and better working conditions. By the 1920s, white-collar workers began getting coffee breaks. One can imagine Ebenezer Scrooge's conniptions if Bob Cratchit had the temerity to take a coffee break—bah, humbug, indeed. By mid-century, observers noticed that leisure was creeping into the workplace. *Business Week* cited the growing prevalence of coffee breaks and the now-ubiquitous snack machines. As late as the 1950s, though, some employees were only just beginning to be granted coffee breaks (*Business Week* 1953, I:146; Stewart 2013, no page numbers).

Movies from the 1950s showed business executives indulging in three-martini lunches while conducting business and even relaxing. A social observer noted, "These meetings represent, of course, the twentieth-century dream of the longish, relaxed lunch period … a rationalized break from the sales charts and a chance to down a few drinks that will keep the rest of the afternoon from becoming too strenuous (Kerr 1962, 32)." Workers began reading newspapers, conversing with friends, and engaging in other forms of leisure. Some supervisors found these behaviors abhorrent, but a younger breed of managers considered the behavior acceptable. An observer worried that "we will avoid exacerbating our consciences by pretending to work 35, although such subterfuges as time off for shopping and hairdos will actually cut the week to 30 hours or fewer (Havemann 1964, 89)."

The internet allows workers to surreptitiously (and sometimes not so surreptitiously) engage in non-business activities while at work. On occasion, workers have the gall to look for other jobs, while at their current jobs. Workers also gained paid vacation time, increased holidays and personal days, and sick leave across the twentieth century (Tooley 2010, no page numbers; Conner 2012, no page numbers; U.S. Bureau of Labor Statistics 1996, Table 5; Bowers 1927, 163–164).

By the twenty-first century, moreover, some workers were finding that play and work mixed. Silicon Valley companies often offered leisure and recreational facilities. Their workers who engaged in creative and technical work could use these amenities even during working hours. The companies hoped to attract and to retain scarce technologically savvy workers (Garber 2012, 30).

Various consulting groups advise employers on how to reduce such shirking behavior. Workers employ a variety of rationales for such behavior, but, the behavior appears almost universal among white-collar workers. Many modern American and European workers undoubtedly consider surfing the internet and doing personal business as a "perk" of the job. Certainly salaried workers may believe that how they allocate their time is their business, as long as the work gets completed. Workers engage in "time theft" by taking overly lengthy breaks or lunches, time card or clock theft (co-workers might punch in and out for them), internet time theft, "goofing off," and excessive personal time. Consultants suggest using devices to monitor internet usage and biometric devices to monitor check-in and check-out times to reduce time theft (*Time Well Scheduled* n.d., no page numbers; Donskey 2014, no page numbers).

Minimum Wage

Neoclassical economics suggests that in a competitive market for a particular type of worker, supply and demand considerations will determine the wage. If workers are disabled or otherwise impaired, the theory predicts a low wage, quite possibly a wage incapable of sustaining life. Many people find such an outcome deplorable and intolerable. In modern-day America, however, non-profit companies often have exemptions from existing minimum wage jobs and can pay wages far below the minimum wage (Schecter

2013, no page numbers). Presumably voters and legislators assume that such workers receive sufficient support from family or government programs so that the workers will not starve.

Setting wages by legislation is a long-standing practice. Medieval authorities in London during Edward I's reign fixed the wages of "masters" in crafts. One edict stated that "If any man of the city give more to any workman than is here written and commanded, let him be amerced [fined] to the city in forty shillings, without any pardon (Ashley 1913, 193)." It seems odd to penalize employers paying above the fixed wage rate.

Minimum wage jobs in America are actually pretty good jobs, both in comparison with jobs historically and with contemporary jobs in many countries throughout the world.

Workers in fast-food restaurants, for instance, labor under climate-controlled, hygienic conditions. Although some fast-food managers may be petty tyrants, it is unlikely that the management regime is as harsh as those found in the 1900s America. The national minimum wage of $7.25 per hour in 2020 provides an annual income well in excess of average incomes throughout today's world, much less incomes of the past.

There are drawbacks to the minimum wage. Raising the minimum wage causes business' costs to increase. Firm's and industry's supply curves shift to the left, raising prices and reducing quantity of output. Some of the former gains from voluntary trade disappear. A higher minimum wage may create unemployment. The amount of unemployment depends on how "binding" the minimum wage is and the sensitivities of supply and demand for labor with regard to changes in wages. If I establish a minimum wage of $9.00 per hour in 2021, the effect upon unemployment will be modest. If I establish a minimum wage of $15.00 per hour in 2021, the effect upon unemployment may be significant.

The federal government enacted a series of minimum wage laws beginning in 1938 ($0.25 per hour). Organized labor held mixed opinions regarding such laws, with Samuel Gompers, president of the American Federation of Labor arguing in 1914: "The American Federation of Labor is not in favor of fixing, by legal enactment, certain minimum wages. The attempts of the government to establish wages at which workmen may work, according to the teachings of history, will result in a long era of industrial slavery." Other people argued that a national minimum wage would have different effects on regional labor markets, especially in the

South where wages were lower. African-Americans sought legislation to redress differences in white-black wages. Economist Thomas Leonard documents another motive for minimum wage laws; Progressives viewed minimum wage laws as useful in culling the labor force of "unemployable" people, primarily immigrants and the less competent (Leonard 2005, 212–215; see also Nordlund 1997, 34–35, 40–41).

A study of the early effects of the minimum wage law, conducted by economist Yale Brozen, found that "An employment effect does stand out as an apparent consequence of the bunching of national minimum wage increases in the 1960s and the widened coverage of the Act, in this period, leaving fewer alternative occupations for those unable to obtain jobs in covered employment. The relative incidence of non-white teen-age unemployment rose to an unprecedented level in 1966." Part of the different experiences of white and non-white teenagers may be due to employer discrimination on the basis of race or ethnic background; Brozen, however, shows some evidence that employer discrimination of this form, if it existed, was quirky—"While the ratio of non-white to white teen-age unemployment rose from 1.8 to 2.4, the ratio of non-white to white employment in other age groups little affected by minimum wage rates declined from 2.4 to 2.1 for men and 2.2 to 1.8 for women."

Another factor driving the large unemployment difference between white and non-white teenagers might have been that the higher labor costs to small businesses drove out a greater proportion of small businesses in economically poorer neighborhoods. In other words, businesses that were just able to make a market rate of return in a poor neighborhood because of the low wage levels may have been driven out by the minimum wage induced hike in labor costs (Brozen 1969, 109–122).

Regardless of the cause of the greater non-white teenage unemployment, the long-run impact is significant. The main benefit of entry-level jobs is to inculcate job skills—the burger-flipping job is a stepping stone to better jobs. If the teenagers cannot reach the lowest rung of the job ladder, their chances for moving up later in life may be adversely affected.

More recently, economists David Card and Alan Krueger claimed that raising the minimum wage in New Jersey's fast-food industry *increased* the number of jobs, but theirs was a controversial if oft-cited finding. Subsequent research unearthed such unintended consequences as an increase in the number of high school dropouts in the wake of raising the minimum wage. More recent research has found, at most, modest deleterious efforts from raising the minimum wage by small amounts in the *short run* (Card and Krueger 1994, 772–793; Crofton et al. 2009, 445–464; Cooper 2015, no page numbers).[11]

Meanwhile, unions are quite aware of the beneficial aspect of preventing entry of potential substitutes for union labor. In an ironic twist on Marx, the unions are raising their lifestyles on the backs of the unskilled workers. Thus, it is easy to see why politicians may favor the minimum wage. From a political viewpoint, people who can't get jobs because of minimum wage may be unaware of deleterious effects of the law. Union workers who retain their jobs and gain higher wages are the beneficiaries. They can see tangible gains from the increased minimum wage. The lost jobs may be visible, as when the employer calls in some of his workers and tells them he must lay them off. Jobs that are not created because of the higher minimum wage are invisible job losses. The news media doesn't cover Ms. Doe's non-announcement that she was going to hire two new workers, but won't because of the higher minimum wage.

On a second level, even if all the unemployed workers recognized why they are unemployed, they may have a difficult time organizing against the minimum wage. If most of the adversely affected workers are teenagers who are spread geographically and occupationally, they may have difficulty combining efforts to lobby against the minimum wage; many of them may not even be able to vote.

Small businesses will be against the minimum wage, but, again, they are not particularly concentrated. Meanwhile, unions are concentrated blocs of votes; the unemployed workers are not concentrated and probably have difficulty in lobbying. Companies, such as larger corporations employing semi-skilled and skilled labor that pay well above the minimum wage may benefit, too, as smaller competitors, such as "Mom and Pop" companies may be priced out of the market. The Employment Policies Institute found that "roughly half the minimum-wage workforce is employed at businesses with fewer than 100 employees, and 40% are at very small businesses with fewer than 50 employees (Saltsman 2013, A13)." The canard that large corporations such as McDonald's and Walmart are ruthlessly exploiting workers by paying only the minimum wage is dubious.

Not all workers are covered by minimum wage laws. Some of America's most vulnerable workers were not covered. Initially southern growers lobbied to ensure their labor force was not covered. More recently, Speaker of the House, Nancy Pelosi, made sure that American

Samoan workers were not covered by the federal minimum wage statute; American Samoan workers toiled under a separate law that froze their minimum wages at $4.18–$5.59 depending on the industry. Apparently some of her most important constituents, including Star Kist Tuna ("tell 'em Nancy sent you"), ran canneries in American Samoa (*Washington Times*, January 12, 2007, no page numbers; Wang 2012, no page numbers).

Similar to 1930s movies showing harsh conditions on prison chain gangs, some businesses gain from having access to cheap labor. Prisoners can earn small amounts of money, but producers of similar goods who use non-prison labor cry foul. Federal prisons have a ***maximum*** wage: $1.15 per hour. Another study suggests that Americans would be better off, if prisoners were paid a minimum wage or higher: "virtually every stakeholder in the U.S. economy would be better off if people who were incarcerated were fully integrated into the U.S. labor force, and were responsible in meeting their obligations to their communities, families, and victims." Author Tom Petersik believes inmate workers should have the same basic worker rights as non-inmate labor (Kovensky 2014, no page numbers; Petersik 2000, no page numbers).[12]

People with disabilities are another group of workers not covered by the minimum wage. Various non-profit agencies provide training, sometimes housing assistance, and other social services to workers. In return, they pay these workers wages that, in some cases, barely rival what prison inmates earn. "Goodwill Industries … is among the nonprofit groups permitted to pay thousands of disabled workers far less than minimum wage because of a federal law known as Section 14(c). Labor Department records show that some Goodwill workers in Pennsylvania earned wages as low as 22, 38 and 41 cents per hour in 2009." Although some observers criticized the law, believing it exploitative, the defenders, such as Terry Farmer, CEO of ACCSES, a trade group, says that rescinding the law might, "force [disabled workers] to stay at home … or otherwise engage in unproductive and unsatisfactory activities." A disabled worker, who worked for Goodwill Industries, lamented, "We are trapped. Everybody who works at Goodwill is trapped." This worker, at least, made between $4.37 and $5.46 per hour (Schecter 2013, no page numbers).[13]

Women in the Labor Force

Women have worked as long as men, particularly in subsistence activities. Eve had to toil alongside Adam, according to the Biblical account. Women often ran the retail side of the family's production within the house. Women worked in the labor market as domestic servants, teachers, agricultural harvesters, and mill workers. The rise of big businesses with the attendant need for clerical staff was amenable to an infusion of women workers.

Women working in factories elicited varying degrees of disapproval. The American and British experiences with women in the labor market were somewhat similar. In many cases, people assumed that "female workers were young, transient, marginal, and exploited laborers (Goldin 1990, 6; see also Gersuny 1976, 137–138; Evans 1970, 114)." Some critics, including Friedrich Engels viewed poor women engaged in factory work as being inherently unchaste. Critics cited (or concocted) statistics claiming a vast majority of factory women lost their chastity, but such male musings may have contained more than a hint of prurience. Accusations of female promiscuity often used the number of children born out of wedlock, but such rates proved to be similar to those of women in agricultural districts; women in domestic service had higher rates of children born out of wedlock—the cliché of the exploitative son of the employing family may have had an element of truth. On the other hand, serious inquiry into working conditions revealed unhealthy aspects of factory work (although work in other venues was probably deleterious, too). For Victorian Age reformers and traditionalists, "Classing women and children together as helpless creatures needing the protection of strong men, they were indignant at the knowledge that women had to support themselves, that they suffered degrading wrongs as working women (McKendrick 1974, 166–167; see also Neff 1929, 14, 53–56)."

More salient, perhaps, were the arguments that women and children displaced men. A man losing a job might have meant *his* wife and children had to seek work in the market. Factory work certainly differed from domestic industry, where the family worked under their own roof. If the family worked in the factory, they might be together only for meals and sleep. British commentators worried that a large number of unemployed factory fathers wandering aimlessly during the day, while their wives and children worked, could prove demoralizing for all involved. The father's authority might deteriorate, and wife and older children might demand more discretion over their earnings. Such a specter was troubling, indeed (McKendrick 1974, 201; Neff 1929, 51).[14]

These issues aside, Neil McKendrick suggested historians were missing a salient point: Families where mothers and older children worked had higher aggregate incomes and likely enjoyed higher standards of living. He advocated recognizing that eighteenth- and nineteenth-century British families surmounted obstacles to carve out a life with some bright spots among the turmoil and to avoid, "the enormous condescension of posterity." He was disdainful of commentators, who dwelled on the negative aspects of working-class life and perpetuate "little more than propaganda, and propaganda is no less propaganda when it is on the side of the angels. Indeed, the kind of social history which lovingly picks over the scars and injustices of the past … has its descriptive uses but it does little to explain the past, and it does less than justice to the motives and aspirations and endeavours of those who actually suffered and achieved as a result of them (McKendrick 1974, 170, 209)."[15]

Women were crowded into occupations during the first half of the twentieth century that had relatively brief on-the-job learning processes. One could master the techniques of filing fairly rapidly. If the wage scale was based on seniority, a file clerk might earn a wage above the clerk's marginal revenue product. Firms having such jobs preferred to have a force of young, inexperienced workers, rather than experienced workers with relatively high wages. One way to cull the workforce was the "marriage bar." Once women got married, the expectation was that she would leave the labor force. For employers of jobs with relatively flat productivity increases after the initial training period, the marriage bar proved an effective way to replace expensive, experienced workers with rookies. Some firms offered inducements for their female workers to get married (and then to subsequently leave the job). The marriage bar disappeared during the 1950s, although flight attendants were still susceptible to such an institution for decades to come. The demographic changes during the 1920s and 1930s led to a dearth of young workers, and since young women were relatively scarce in later decades, employers began to re-think their attitudes toward married women workers (Goldin 1990, 171–175).

Did girls and women require protection? Mimi Abramovitz, among other historians, distinguishes the differing motives underlying Protective Labor Laws and Mothers' Pensions: seeking better working conditions versus legislation allowing single women to raise their children without entering the labor force. Abramovitz, though, points out that the "protections granted to women worked against them. Protective labor legislation based on motherhood, female frailty, and special privileges for the home became a justification for barring women from certain occupations and segregating women into low paid 'women's jobs (Abramovitz 1996, 188).'"

The Supreme Court had earlier decided that general hours legislation were unconstitutional, since the laws would violate the right of labor (and employers) to contract freely. Louis Brandeis and Josephine Goldmark wrote a brief defending the ten-hour law for women; they emphasized the alleged detrimental effects work had on women and their future offspring. During the first decade of the twentieth century, rising concerns about America's racial and ethnic composition fueled the eugenics movement. The 1908 Supreme Court, consisting mainly of Anglo-Saxon males, found Brandeis and Goldmark's argument compelling. Women got their ten-hour law, but the victory proved a mixed blessing, as the idea that women needed extra protection proved pernicious. Among advocates of women's rights the dichotomy between protective legislation and equal rights proved long-lasting. Economist Claudia Goldin reflects that "from the 1920s to the 1960s, many liberals opposed the ERA (Equal Rights Amendments), while conservatives supported it." Professional and the growing numbers of business women supported the ERA, while "social feminists" worried that "women would suffer by forfeiting protective legislation (Goldin 1990, 192–198; Blau and Kahn 2000, 75; Degler 1980, 415)."

One important reason for the persisting differences in wages between women and men was that women had a higher probability of exiting the labor market, whether temporarily or permanently. Regardless of gender, gaps in an employee's job history were usually deleterious to that worker's wage profile across his or her lifetime. During the nineteenth century, men and women frequently changed jobs. As jobs became more complex and required greater amounts of on-the-job training, employers were keen on ascertaining before hiring a worker whether that worker would stay on. Goldin explained how "firms often used sex as a signal of shorter expected job tenure." In addition, women with household responsibilities were at a disadvantage in landing and retaining jobs (Goldin 1990, 116).

Conclusion

The Great Depression reversed the prosperity of the 1920s and forced many firms to pare back social programs. Companies' reductions of social programs, however, coincided with the growing need for such programs. The Great Depression swept aside the efforts of private provision, whether through charities or corporate welfare. The 1930s also featured renewed strife between labor and management that persisted for the next two decades. By the 1950s, the rate of participation in labor unions peaked in the United States.

Employers differed greatly in their attitudes toward and their treatment of employees. A key factor was whether employers viewed their workers as a means to an end. Employers who worked directly with workers often developed a fellow-feeling that led to better treatment. Then again, many employers were barely making profits and felt pressed to wring as much out of their workers as possible to keep their businesses afloat.[16]

Even when employers sought to ameliorate conditions for their workers and viewed their workers as people and not as chattel or units of labor, they all too often assumed a condescending attitude toward their employees. Perhaps being successful made the industrialists haughty or imbued them with a sense that their expertise in one endeavor made them adept at another.

Notes

1. Carl Gersuny chronicles employee pilfering in New England textile mills (1976, 144–146).
2. Alan Trachtenberg reported "close to 37,000 strikes, involving 7 million workers on record between 1881 and 1905—provide dramatic indices of turmoil (Trachtenberg 1982, 80)."
3. Coal mine operators in other states had conspired to get railroads to charge higher rates to West Virginia operators (Wheeler 1976, 88).
4. Mother Mary Jones came to West Virginia during one of the strikes. She allegedly exhorted miners to, "Arm yourselves, return home and kill every goddamned mine guard on the creeks, blow up the mines, and drive the damned scabs out of the valley (Lee 1969, 27)." Howard Lee got this quote from a transcribed copy of Jones' speech retained by the secretary of the West Virginia Coal Operators Association. Given that Ms. Jones' name is now the title of an esteemed liberal periodical, one wonders how *Mother Jones* readership would react to knowing that she advocated armed violence with—guns.

5. The safety measures were, in effect, apportioned according to the party, who could better or more conveniently make the decision. Presumably, if transactions costs were low, using a Coasian argument regarding an initial assignment of property rights (or responsibility), an efficient level of safety would be chosen, regardless of whether miners or operators made safety decisions.
6. At one point, Carnegie was proud that he paid his men an average of $1.40 a day compared with the local average of $1.35. In 1898 he paid $13.5 million in wages and reputedly gained $11.5 million in profits (Standiford 2005, 240).
7. Companies issuing scrip often did so at full value; some miners sold their scrip to independent individuals, saloons, and storekeepers. Independent individuals often paid 65 to 85 percent of the face value and then turned around and bought provisions from the company store. Coal mine owners quickly prohibited such transactions (Fishback 1986, 1022).
8. Ford defended his assembly line system, denying that it took skill out of work (Hall 1998, 414; Seabright 2004, 158–59). Ford was blunt in his autobiography: "Without the most rigid discipline we would have the utmost confusion … . There is not much personal contact—the men do their work and go home—a factory is not a drawing room (Ford and Crowther 1923, 111–112)."
9. See Fairris (1995, 498) for arbitrary foremen; Nelson (1982, 335–357); second quote Douglas (1921, 89–107).
10. David Roediger and Philip Foner thought the shorter workday was simply camouflage for the real goal: cutting wages (1989, 245–248; Hunnicutt 1992, 478).
11. Government officials' and social activists' belief that they know better than do employers and business owners recurs. Proponents of the minimum wage often assert that employers will benefit from raising the minimum wage; such an argument leaves unanswered the obvious question, "If it is so beneficial, why don't employers do so voluntarily?"
12. Because convict labor was not voluntary, employers exploiting such labor could be seen as acting unethically, even though their actions were legal. Rebecca McLennan documented how the American judicial system gave "official recognition and implicit approval" to involuntary servitude (McLennan 2008, 109–111, see also 8). The businessmen involved showed scant regard for the humanity under their control, and their ethical behavior surely ranked among the worst examples in modern business ethics (Blackmon 2009, 96, 327, 362–364; McLennan 2008, 122). De Beers Mining Company exploited native people in the gold and diamond fields (Newbury 1987, 17–18, 23).

13. In a sense, the argument is that such employers are exploiting their workers for the workers' own good.
14. The rising earnings of American women suggest that the father's earnings may prove to be less important to families in the future; whether fathers will spend their days wandering aimlessly remains to be seen.
15. McKendrick later took to task commentators unwilling to examine the available data, admittedly a difficult endeavor. He revealed his scorn in the memorable statement: "There is a kind of social history which will always dwell lovingly on cancer of the scrotum in climbing boy chimney sweeps, or exploit the quick reaction to stories of the rampant immorality of the mill-hands, of female workers stumbling home 'blear eyed with drink and beastliness (McKendrick 1974, 170–171).'"
16. This point was made by Kathryn Edin and H. Luke Shaefer: "The decision makers rarely meet the rank and file.…Only employers who know their employees personally can exercise the discretion to discern whether someone like Rae [fired for missing a shift, when her transportation proved unavailable], the two-time 'cashier of the month,' has missed her shift because she's shirker or is a valued employee who has hit a rough patch (Edin and Shaefer, *$2.00 a Day*, 165)."

Bibliography

Abramovitz, Mimi. *Regulating the Lives of Women: Social Welfare Policy from Colonial Times to the Present* (Boston, MA: South End Press, 1996).

Annals of the American Academy of Political and Social Science. "'Company Stores' in the Pennsylvania Mining Districts," 7(1), January 1896, 162–164, no author.

Ashley, William J. *An Introduction to English Economic History and Theory. Part 1: The Middle Ages* (New York, NY: Longmans, Green, 1913). 9th Edition.

Berkowitz, Edward and Kim McQuaid, "Businessman and Bureaucrat: The Evolution of the American Social Welfare System, 1900–1940." *Journal of Economic History* 38(1), March 1978, 120–142.

Blackmon, Douglas. *Slavery by Another Name: The Re-Enslavement of Black Americans from the Civil War to World War II* (New York, NY: Anchor Books, 2009).

Blau, Francine and Lawrence Kahn. "Gender Differences in Pay." *Journal of Economic Perspectives* 14(4), Autumn 2000, 75–99.

Bowers, Glenn A. "Nesday Chemical Company." *Harvard Business Reports* 4, 1927, 162–170.

Boyer, George. "What Did Unions Do in Nineteenth-Century Britain?" *Journal of Economic History* 48(2), June 1988, 319–332.

Brozen, Yale. "The Effect of Statutory Minimum Wage Increases on Teen-Age Employment." *Journal of Law & Economics* 12(1), April 1969, 109–122.

Business Week. "A Big Fast-Growing Market: The Leisured Masses, Part I." September 12, 1953, 142–143, 145–46, 148, 150, 152.

Card, David and Alan Krueger. "Minimum Wages and Employment: a Case Study of the Fast-Food Industry in New Jersey and Pennsylvania." *American Economic Review* 84(4), September 1994, 772–793.

Conner, Cheryl. "Employees Really Do Waste Time at Work." *Forbes*. July 17, 2012. www.forbes.com/sites/cherylsnappconner/2012/07/17/employees-really-do-waste-time-at-work/, viewed January 9, 2016, 9:00am.

Cooper, Preston. "What the Card-Krueger Study Tells Us about the Minimum Wage." *Foundation for Economic Education*. December 18, 2015. https://fee.org/articles/what-the-card-krueger-study-tells-us-about-the-minimum-wage/, viewed March 5, 2018, 10:25am.

Crofton, Stephanie, William Anderson, and Emily Rawe. "Do Higher Real Minimum Wages Lead to More High School Dropouts? Evidence from Maryland Across Races, 1993–2004." *American Journal of Economics and Sociology* 68(2), April 2009, 445–464.

Davis, Dorothy. *A History of Shopping* (London, UK: Routledge & Kegan, 1966).

Degler, Carl. *At Odds: Women and the Family in America from the Revolution to the Present* (Oxford: Oxford University Press, 1980).

Dicey, Albert. *Lectures on the Relation between Law & Public Opinion in England during the Nineteenth Century* (London: Macmillan, 1914).

Donskey, Jordann. "Time Theft: Top 7 Ways Employees Steal Time." *EPAY Systems*. September 22, 2014. www.epaysystems.com/time-theft-top-7-ways-employees-steal-time.

Douglas, Paul. "Shop Committees: Substitute for, or Supplement to, Trades-Unions? *Journal of Political Economy* 29(2), February 1921, 89–107.

Edin, Kathryn and J.H. Luke Shaefer. *$2.00 a day: living on almost nothing in America* (Boston: Houghton Mifflin Harcourt, 2015).

Edwards, Richard. *Contested Terrain: The Transformation of the Workplace in the Twentieth Century* (New York, NY: Basic Books, Inc., Publishers, 1979).

Evans, Robert, Jr. "Evolution of the Japanese System of Employer-Employee Relations, 1868–1945." *Business History Review*, XLIV(1), Spring 1970, 110–125.

Fairris, David. "From Exit to Voice in Shopfloor Governance: The Case of Company Unions." *Business History Review* 69, Winter 1995, 493–529.

Faith, Nicholas. *The World the Railways Made* (London: Pimlico, [1990] 1994]).

Fishback, Price. "Did Coal Miners 'Owe Their Souls to the Company Store'? Theory and Evidence from the Early 1900s." *Journal of Economic History* 46(4), December 1986, 1011–1029.

Fishback, Price. "The Irony of Reform: Did Large Employers Subvert Workplace Safety Reform, 1869 to 1930?" *Corruption and Reform: Lessons from America's Economic History*, edited by Edward Glaeser and Claudia Goldin (Chicago, IL: University of Chicago Press, 2006), 285–318.

Fishback, Price and Dieter Lauszus, "The Quality of Services in Company Towns: Sanitation in Coal Towns during the 1920s." *Journal of Economic History* 49(1), March 1989, 125–144.

Ford, Henry and Samuel Crowther. *My Life and Work* (Garden City, NY: Doubleday, Page & Company, 1923).

Garber, Megan. "Perks and Recreation: In Silicon Valley, a New Breed of Tech Company Tries to Enforce Fun." *The Atlantic*, December 2012, 28–32.

Gersuny, Carl. "'A Devil in Petticoats' and Just Cause: Patterns of Punishment in Two New England Textile Factories.' *Business History Review* L(2), Summer 1976, 131–152.

Goldin, Claudia. *Understanding the Gender Gap: An Economic History of American Women* (New York, NY: Oxford University Press, 1990).

Griffiths, Brian. *Morality and the Market Place* (London, UK: Hodder and Stoughton, 1980).

Hall, Peter. *Cities in Civilization* (New York, NY: Pantheon Books, 1998).

Havemann, Ernest. "The Emptiness of Too Much Leisure: Automation and a Shrinking Work Week Bring a Real Threat to All of Us." *Life*, February 7, 1964, 76–90.

Hilkey, Judy. *Character Is Capital: Success Manuals and Manhood in Gilded Age America* (Chapel Hill, NC: University of North Carolina Press, 1997).

Hoeffner, Joseph Cardinal. *Economic Systems and Economic Ethics: Guidelines in Catholic Social Teachings* (Cologne, Germany: Ordo Socialis, 1985).

Holbrook, Stewart. *The Story of American Railroads* (New York, NY: Crown Publishers, 1947).

Hunnicutt, Benjamin. "Kellogg's Six-Hour Day: A Capitalist Vision of Liberation through Managed Work Reduction." *Business History Review* 66(2), Summer 1992, 475–522.

Kerr, Walter. *The Decline of Pleasure* (New York: Simon and Schuster, 1962).

Knight, Frank. "The Ethics of Competition." *The Ethics of Competition and Other Essays* (New York, NY: Harper & Brothers, 1935). 41–75.

Knight, Frank. "Ethics and Economic Reform. I. The Ethics of Liberalism." *Economica* 6(21), Feb. 1939, 1–29.

Kovensky, Josh. "It's Time to Pay Prisoners the Minimum Wage." *New Republic*. August 14, 2014. http://www.newrepublic.com/article/119083/prison-labor-equal-rights-wages-incarcerated-help-economy, viewed February 12, 2015.

Laurie, Bruce. *Artisans into Workers: Labor in Nineteenth-Century America* (New York, NY: Hill and Wang, 1989).

Lee, Howard. *Bloodletting in Appalachia: The Story of West Virginia's Four Major Mine Wars and Other Thrilling Incidents of Its Coal Fields* (Morgantown, WV: West Virginia University 1969).

Leonard, Thomas. "Eugenics and Economics in the Progressive Era." *Journal of Economic Perspectives* 19(4), Fall 2005, 207–224.

Marens, Richard. "What comes around: the early 20th century American roots of legitimating corporate social responsibility." *Organization* 20(3), 2013, 454–476.

McCreary, Eugene. "Social Welfare and Business: The Krupp Welfare Program, 1860–1914." *Business History Review* XLII(1), Spring 1968, 24–49.

McKendrick, Neil. "Home Demand and Economic Growth: A New View of the Role of Women and Children in the Industrial Revolution." *Historical Perspectives: Studies in English Thought and Society in Honour of J.H. Plumb*, edited by Neil McKendrick (London, UK: Europa Publications, 1974), 152–210.

McLennan, Rebecca. *The Crisis of Imprisonment: Protest, Politics, and the Making of the American Penal State, 1776–1941* (Cambridge, UK: Cambridge University Press, 2008).

Neff, Wanda. *Victorian Working Women: an Historical and Literary Study of Women in British Industries and Professions, 1832–1850* (New York, NY: Columbia University Press, 1929).

Nelson, Daniel. "Company Union Movement, 1900–1937: A Reexamination." *Business History Review* 61(3), Autumn 1982, 335–357.

Newbury, Colin. "Technology, Capital, and Consolidation: The Performance of DeBeers Mining Company Limited, 1880–1889." *Business History Review* 61, Spring 1987, 1–42.

Nordlund, Willis. *The Quest for a Living Wage: The History of the Federal Minimum Wage Program* (Westport, CT: Greenwood Press, 1997).

O'Neill, William. *A Democracy at War* (Boston, MA: Harvard University Press, 1993).

Pecci, Pope Leo XIII, *Rerum Novarum*. 1891. vatican.va/content/leo-xiii/en/encyclicals/documents/hf_l-xiii_enc_15051891_rerum-novarum.html.

Petersik, Tom. "The Economics of Inmate Labor Force Participation." *Executive Summary*. The Center on Crime, Communities & Culture. September 2000. http://www.correction.org/Secondary%20Pages/InmateLabor.html.

Roediger, David and Philip Foner. *Our Own Time: A History of American Labor and the Working Day* (London, UK: Greenwood Press, 1989).

Saltsman, Michael. "Who Really Employs Minimum-Wage Workers?" *Wall Street Journal*, October 29, 2013, A13.

Schecter, Anna. "Disabled workers paid just pennies an hour—and it's legal." *NBC News*. June 25, 2013, no page number. http://investigations.nbcnews.com/_news/2013/06/25/19062348-disabled-workers-paid-just-pennies-an-hour-and-its-legal, viewed September 22, 2013.

Seabright, Paul. *The Company of Strangers: A Natural History of Economic Life* (Princeton, NJ: Princeton University Press, 2004).

Sheppard, Muriel. *Cloud by Day: The Story of Coal and Coke and People* (Pittsburgh, PA: University of Pittsburgh Press, [1947] 1991).

Shiells, Martha. "Collective Choice of Working Conditions: Hours in British and U.S. Iron and Steel, 1890–1923." *Journal of Economic History* 50(2), June 1990, 379–392.

Shulman, David. *From Hire to Liar: The Role of Deception in the Workplace* (Ithaca, NY: Cornell University Press, 2007).

Smith, Adam. *An Inquiry into the Nature and Causes of the Wealth of Nations*, edited by R.H. Campbell and A.S. Skinner (Indianapolis, IN: Liberty*Classics*, 1981).

Standiford, Les. *Meet You in Hell: Andrew Carnegie, Henry Clay Frick, and the Bitter Partnership that Transformed America* (New York, NY: Crown Publishers, 2005).

Stewart, Art. "Time Theft Is a Bumpy Road for Employees." *Internal Auditor*, February 5, 2013.

Suffern, Arthur. *Conciliation and Arbitration in the Coal Industry of America* (Boston: Houghton Mifflin, 1915).

Surdam, David. *The Big Leagues Go to Washington: Congress and Sports Antitrust, 1951–1989* (Urbana, IL: University of Illinois Press, 2015).

Time Well Scheduled. Time Theft in the Workplace. n.d. https://timewellscheduled.com/time-theft/.

Tooley, Heather. "Personal Internet Usage in the Workplace—A Serious Epidemic." January 17, 2010, http://voices.yahoo.com/personal-internet-usage-workplace-serious-5284153html?cat=15, viewed June 12, 2013, 3:01pm.

Trachtenberg, Alan. *The Incorporation of America: Culture and Society in the Gilded Age* (New York, NY: Hill and Wang, 1982).

Ure, Andrew. *The Philosophy of Manufacturers: Or, An Exposition of the Scientific, Moral, and Commercial Economy of the Factory System of Great Britain* (London, UK: Charles Knight, 1835).

U.S. Bureau of Labor Statistics. "Economic News Release." 1996. http://www.bls.gov/news.release/ebs.t0.5html.

Vaughan, Diane. *The Challenger Launch Decision* (Chicago, IL: University of Chicago Press, 1996).

Wang, Nick. "American Samoa Minimum Wage Freeze Approved by Congress." *Huffington Post*, July 19, 2012, www.huffingtonpost.com/2012/07/19/american-samoa-minimum-wage_n_1687975, viewed September 22, 2012.

Washington Times. "GOP hits Pelosi's 'hypocrisy' on wage bill." January 12, 2007, www.washingtontimes.com/news/2007/jan/12/20070112-120720-2734r.

WBEZ91.5 "Labor laws allow workers with disabilities to earn less than minimum wage." May 28, 2013. http://www.wbez.org/print/107389.

Whaples, Robert. "Winning the Eight-Hour Day, 1909–1919." *Journal of Economic History* 50(2), June 1990, 393–406.

Wheeler, Hoyt. "Mountaineer Mine Wars: An Analysis of the West Virginia Mine Wars of 1912–13 and 1920–21." *Business History Review* L(1), Spring 1976, 69–91.

CHAPTER 2

Early Nineteenth-Century Changes

Many historians associate the decades after the Civil War with rampant unethical behavior in business, what Mark Twain memorably labeled, "The Gilded Age." But such antics were also plentiful during the antebellum era. "Mammon had become the national saint," prior to the Civil War (Rhodes 1912, III;80). A historian remarked that after the war, "To so many persons the accumulation of wealth had become the one absorbing and all important object in life that the methods by which the end was gained, no matter how abominable, shocked nobody. Falling into the general way gradually, and long familiar with it, better men were condoning such perverted moral standards. Many of sound consciences were intimidated, or were brought to believe in the hopelessness of protest. Public opinion seemed oppressed and silenced by prolonged experience with wrong (Oberholtzer 1922, II:539)." A business ethicist espousing deontological or teleological theories in 1850 or 1870 might have, at best, been greeted with blank stares, or, at worst, hoots of derision. On the other hand, observers and historians may be guilty of exaggerating the persuasiveness of unethical behavior, given America's economic growth across the nineteenth century.

Such colorful figures as Commodore Vanderbilt, Jay Gould, Jim Fiske, and Daniel Drew became legendary for larger-than-life exploits rivaling Davy Crockett or Mike Fink. Vanderbilt and the three financiers fought for control of rail traffic in New York; their fight was a financial equivalent of bare-knuckle, no-holds-barred brawling (albeit in top hats and frocks).

D. G. Surdam, *Business Ethics from the 19th Century to Today*,
https://doi.org/10.1007/978-3-030-37169-2_2

Part of the public's fascination with these tycoons' actions was that few understood what was actually going on. The tycoons' financial machinations were beyond the experience of most Americans; this veil of ignorance allowed the tycoons' friends and enemies and newspaper reporters to embellish, misinterpret, or outright fabricate events.

The nineteenth century witnessed a quickening of technological change in Europe and the United States. Better communication and transportation services enabled American and European business owners to expand their trading network but also triggered more impersonal business relationships. A buyer and seller might never meet personally, and opportunities for confidence men expanded. Banking and finance underwent significant transformations to meet the needs of a more sophisticated economy (Sandage 2005, 100–101).

The introduction of new technology raised novel ethical issues. The larger endeavors required a new form of organization, but limited liability corporations raised ethical issues. The state governments' ability to grant incorporations gave rise to corruption.

Is Technology Good?

Is technological change a good thing? The popular reaction to new technology is often hostile, as new technology displaces older technologies. Is there such a thing as an ethically neutral innovation? Usually someone loses (producers of existing products) when innovation occurs, even though society overall is better off. Given that there are winners and losers, it may be possible to employ a bribery criterion: If winners (the providers using new technology) can compensate the losers and still have a positive gain, is this a good technology? Of course, such a bribery program is difficult to implement, as identifying who loses and how much losers should be compensated are difficult questions. This form of "compensation" only rarely occurs. There is also the question whether such losers deserve to be compensated, as no one's livelihood is guaranteed in perpetuity.

Technology rarely arrives in a perfected form. There are inevitable defects, but such defects often lead to death and injury. Driver-less cars promise to be a boon, but there will be accidental deaths along the way. Such accidents, of course, provide rival competitors with opportunities to criticize and slander the new technology. Steamboat boilers tended to explode, killing people by hideously scalding them. Steamboat captains and many passengers wanted to go faster, sometimes to beat a rival steamboat to a port. Because the engineers had not completely discerned how much pressure their boilers could handle, to use a responsibility-shirking passive voice: mistakes happened. It took a few decades before Congress established an effective regulatory agency—the Steamboat Inspection Service. One scholar observes that legislators were dilatory in creating a safety agency until a really big disaster, then there was a scramble to legislate. "Cynics refer to this process as 'tombstone technology (Fielder 1994, 287).'"

Importance of Information

For millennia, business owners relied upon trusted agents to conduct business on their behalf in far-flung ports. Business historian Alfred Chandler Jr. observes that loyalty and honesty outweighed business acumen in the choice of associates, so sons, sons-in-law, and long-standing friends continued to be partners or agents. Business acumen might have been less important in the past due to the inadequate information available upon which to make decisions. Given the slowness of transportation, reports of prices determined by fluctuating market forces of supply and demand were almost inevitably obsolete. The scope of markets remained circumscribed, and trusted friends and family assumed an importance rivaling business acumen.

During the nineteenth century, however, changes in communication, transportation, and printing technologies created new flows of business information. The growth of cities and expanded markets made it feasible for businessmen to establish exchanges that compiled and disseminated relevant information, thereby raising the benefits of business acumen. "[M]erchants were served by a growing number of specialized ancillary enterprises—banks, insurance companies, shipping lines, and freight forwarders. Specialization lowered information and transactions costs as well as the costs of financing and transporting the flow of goods through the American economy (Chandler 1977, 38–39, 48)." What transpired for the American economy generally did so in western Europe, too.

Businessmen valued information about technology. In today's world, Americans and Europeans charge developing countries with stealing intellectual property. Few Americans are aware that early American textile manufacturers engaged in intellectual thievery and espionage. Samuel Slater immigrated from England to the United States; although he did not steal blueprints of Richard Arkwright's machinery designs as some alleged, his memory was keen and durable. He could recreate such machinery. The fledgling U.S. government, intent on developing its own manufacturing capabilities, sometimes offered bounties for textile machinery. The British, of course, resisted such intellectual theft, and passed laws prohibiting export of ideas. Whether the British Parliament's latter actions were ethical seemed to go unstated. The British, centuries before, had enticed Flemish textile producers to immigrate to Britain, bringing their know-how with regard to woolen textiles (Tucker 1981, 297–313; Josephson [1934] 2011, 11).[1]

American manufacturers also enticed British skilled workers to migrate. British employers responded by giving some workers pay raises and bonuses for remaining in their employ. Once the English workers arrived in America, they were the object of spirited bidding by other American manufacturers; the skilled workers could demand and receive good pay and some autonomy. On the other hand, skilled workers currently in America disliked the importation of skilled labor (Marburg 1941, 2–3, 5).

Early Nineteenth-Century Views of Business Morality

Many Americans appeared bewildered by the rapid pace of change and the accumulation of wealth. There was a lively debate about the rising prominence of big business owners and business ethics. Commentators described businessmen and their practices in the early nineteenth century. Reverend Henry Ward Beecher condemned much business behavior that induced men to compartmentalize their behavior (Beecher 1851, 154).

A Massachusetts doctor sent some advice to his brother in 1807. In his letter, he asked, "Is your knowledge of this business greater than Macombers? [No reference to Macombers was provided, aside from that he appeared to have had some success in business.] Are you more skilfull in the arts and duplicity necessary in trade than he is? Are you more likely to collect a bad Debt than he is? Can you expect to be more successful in detecting Theives than he [spelling in original] (*Bulletin of the Business History Society* 1941, 94)?" Although an ethical businessperson might disagree with the advice to be duplicitous, the other advice rings true, even today.

Dishonest or fraudulent speculation worried Joshua Bates. He disputed the maxim that participants in a business transaction had every right to "buy as cheap as he can, and sell as dear as he can." Carried to an extreme, the maxim implied that "every degree of deception, every kind of speculation, every species of fraud, and almost every act of pecuniary oppression" was justified. He urged his readers to refrain from deception and take no advantage of ignorance or necessity of the other party. If the other party made a mistake in pricing an item, Bates urged readers not to take advantage. He decried deceptions produced by "a direct falsehood, a crafty insinuation, an evasive answer, or any other artifice, the motive is the same; the injury is the same; and in the view of Him, who looketh on the heart, the guilt is the same." Bates resorted to the tactic of warning that God monitors all. By taking advantage of people facing some desperation, Bates claimed such a person would have perpetrated one of the "worst kinds" of fraud that demonstrates "great cruelty and peculiar hardness of heart. It is extortion. It is oppression. It is robbery (Bates 1818, 5–10, 13)."

An anonymous author writing in *Hunt's Merchants' Magazine* in 1841 contended that there was a "general morality of trade," explaining that "since all men may be called traders ... [and] it is so hard to say who is a merchant and who a huckster." He called trade "a divine institution." The author gave an interesting rationale for compensating the merchant for "his opinion and time." He then provided an excellent description of a middleman's functions: "Your grocer, at the corner, keeps on hand, at the risk of fire, waste, and damage, goods which, were you to seek them in the places where they were produced, would employ all your time and strength. Is he not to be paid for doing you this service (*Hunt's Merchants' Magazine* 1841, 526–528)?" He might have added that the grocer, in the case of goods with variable quality, provided a service of (presumably) selecting goods of high quality relative to price.

Unitarian minister and abolitionist Thomas Higginson took a more benign view of wealth seeking. He later became one of the group that helped finance radical abolitionist John Brown. He saw wealth as "admirable or base" depending upon how it was attained (a precursor, perhaps, of Robert Nozick's process theory of distributive justice). He cited the need for wealth that subsidized science, literature, and art.

Higginson understood that unethical behavior occurred in business, and that some acquired property through chicanery. Such chicanery, however, was not solely a province of commerce. He noted that some merchants claimed, in a monumental misjudgment, "that the day for making great fortunes is gone by." Higginson observed that an unscrupulous person would want everyone else to be scrupulous. Higginson recognized the allure for young men entering business in the antebellum years to get ahead early by cutting ethical corners. He differed by attributing some of this temptation to "foolish parents" who "impressed on him [a son] … [making a living] as his first duty."

The ministerial side of Higginson emerged, when he described "two kinds of worldliness." Some men believed that this life was the only existence, so they tried to seize all they could. Other men, believing in an afterlife, attempted to use their financial gains to buy their way to salvation. Higginson advocated a stewardship approach to business. "God hath placed you (says the *Qur'an*) to be his vice-regents on earth; he offered his trust to the mountains and the stars and they humbly declined it; he hath appoint man, and now man hath become selfish and unjust (Higginson 1853, 21–23, 26, 29–30)!"[2]

Higginson saw commerce as necessary to "facilitate the production and distribution of wealth. These functions are both legitimate and important." He disagreed with Cicero's beliefs that trade was a situation whereby the merchant "can only gain by some trick," or that "the gain of one merchant is necessarily another's loss." He instead recognized that "any new branch of Commerce is a gain to one or many, and no loss to any—a net gain, consequently to the community." This occurred because, merchants created value by shifting goods and services, "from a place where it is superfluous or useless to a place where it is precious." Higginson demonstrated a profound grasp of commerce and trade. His article, published in Freeman Hunt's *Merchants' Magazine*, was widely read, and many readers undoubtedly agreed with him.

Having described the nature of business, Higginson discussed the potential for the "Business Man" to do God's work. He quoted an anonymous business friend of his as stating, "I feel, when I stand at my desk, that I am worshipping God with every stroke of my pen." He argued that because businessmen were involved with "the most dangerous edge-tools in the community, viz., dollars and cents," that such participants needed to exercise strict moral behavior motivated by intrinsic honor and honesty. For the Business Man an opportunity and temptation were given through his role as an, "an important element in the community." The opportunity arose from the businessman's ability to serve mankind (or at least his townspeople) and to demonstrate by example the differences between virtue and debased behavior. The businessman had been given much responsibility: "as stewards of God we have our commission on our office in the privilege of discharging it .... Nothing shall convince me that the opportunity of a good action is not its own exceeding great reward."

He concluded by exhorting businessmen to resist temptation and to be good stewards. If others chose to gain wealth through unscrupulous means, the true Christian should, "Wrap yourself in your own virtue, and seek a friend and your daily bread. If you have, in such a course, grown gray with unstained honor, bless God, and die!" For some readers, such an outcome might not have seemed too appealing (Higginson 1853, 22, 33–36, 38–40).

Low Status of Businessmen

"Were businessmen professionals?" became a contested question. Formal education remained the surest marker of social status and gentility in eighteenth- and nineteenth-century America. Businessmen were not considered professionals during the early 1800s. As late as 1856, many people believed commerce and trade required little but "industry and attention," so most of its practitioners were "dull, ignorant" people, but one writer demurred and argued that "as much preparation is necessary in assuming the occupation of the merchant as in embracing any of the learned professions .... There is scarcely any branch of knowledge which may not be advantageously used in the counting-house, and a liberal education tells as well on the merchant's cash-book as in the lawyer's briefs (Casseday 1856, 55)."

Edwin Freedley, author of *A Practical Treatise on Business*, noted the condescension shown to businessmen, in this case by a clergyman: "A mere merchant! A mere man of business! Who would be content with such a designation? What respect can one feel for such a character?" Freedley took the novel approach of criticizing the ministry; he mentioned that the clergyman who voiced the derogatory remark made $3500 per annum "out of his moral and religious sentiments." If true, this clergyman was doing handsomely indeed, as $3500 was probably several times the annual earnings of most working-class Americans in the 1850s. Freedley attributed motives of avarice to clergy; he argued that ministers failed to be "profitable" teachers of mankind, "opting to sell moral advice for private profit instead of speaking from their disinterested concern for the civic good (Freedley 1853, 23–24, 27)."

A twentieth-century historian remarked that antebellum professionals often exploited their arcane knowledge by establishing monopolistic practices to limit the supply while simultaneously striving to increase the demand for their services. Such behavior naturally incurred ill-will (Brown 1992, 13, 22; Augst 1997, 52).

Merchants and traders, among business practitioners, dealt in abstractions; they did not make tangible goods. They provided a service. Thomas Higginson remarked how business required "mental engagement in details that lack intrinsic interest (Higginson 1853, 22; Augst 1997, 55, 72)." Higginson and Ralph Waldo Emerson understood that elevating the businessman's cultural reputation required a transformation from "the anxious devotion to gain, so antithetical to liberal learning, into a moral discipline of the senses." David Hume and Francis Hutcheson had argued during the eighteenth century that "the manners of men are made gentle and civilized by the *doux commerce* of public exchange (Augst 1997, 56)."

As American businesses became larger, a class of managers developed. Managers' work included esoteric aspects; people did not understand businesspeople, "[who] performed functions which the folk could not understand and of which they were suspicious; banking and stock-brokering were outside the limits of their experience, and the retail merchant they felt they could understand only too well—he was a man who bought cheap and sold dear, who could not be trusted, and who made money with little or no exertion." The process of alienation between businesspeople and the general population occurred: "Often the point of contact has been one where friction might develop. This friction has tended to change into actual hostility, the suspicion which came from lack of understanding (Porter 1944, 115)."

Another author claimed that other professionals would benefit from "the practical experience and intelligent observation required in the counting-house. And the counting-house should be conscious of its nobility … to compel all the world to acknowledge the virtue and value of its lessons (Casseday 1856, 56)." Freedley, too, argued that business developed character and a "mastery of the informal social knowledge." He chided critics of businessmen, stating that the canards that "any fool can get money" and that business required no intellectual ability were erroneous (Freedley 1853, 31; see also *Hunt's Merchants' Magazine* 1851, 782; Augst 1997, 63, 73).

Americans began to honor businessmen [not businesswomen, of whom there were few at this point in time]. Whether or not businessmen supplanted farmers as the ideal American citizen, the elevation of businessmen was noticeable enough that Edgar Allen Poe could satirize them in his story, "The Business Man." Poe transformed a heretofore respectable merchant into a mugger, who employed the latest business methods and jargon (Sandage 2005, 73).

Success Manuals

Americans' desire to get ahead spawned a new route to financial success. Those who did not make money through business could write "success manuals" and possibly gain a measure of financial prosperity. Although many of these authors mouthed what became platitudes—"diligence, honesty, frugality, industry, reliability"—and so forth, these platitudes were no less true for becoming clichés. Historian Judy Hilkey examined nineteenth-century success manuals. "In the world depicted in the success manual, 'character was capital' and 'manhood was everything.' Success writers defined character and manhood not only as the means to success, but as success itself, a nonpecuniary notion of success in which the 'worthy' ... might be joined together in a common set of beliefs about what it meant to be a man and what it meant to be a success (Hilkey 1997, 5)."

Americans read self-help books from the colonial days; they avidly consumed books on attaining wealth. Benjamin Franklin penned successful and lucrative advice books: "The way to wealth, if you desire it, is as plain as the way to market. It depends chiefly on two words, industry and frugality; that is, waste neither time nor money, but make the best use of both. Without industry and frugality nothing will do, and with them everything. He that gets all he can honestly and saves all he gets will certainly become rich." To modern ears, this is all cant. What proved interesting was that Franklin added a caveat, perhaps a sop to the religious sensibilities of his time: "[I]f that Being who governs the world, to whom all should look for a blessing on their honest endeavors, doth not, in His wise providence, otherwise determine." In other words, Franklin acknowledged the role of Chance masquerading as providence; hard work and honesty did not guarantee wealth, as there were stochastic events in every person's life that might derail their wealth-seeking endeavors (Franklin 1902, 155; McConnell [1930] 1973, 45).

Hilkey argued that these success manuals "helped legitimize and establish the hegemony of the new industrial order that emerged in the Gilded Age." The authors sometimes expressed ambivalence about the changing society, since many of them grew up in preindustrial Jeffersonian America, so they sometimes offered “a critique as well as a defense of the new order.” They struggled to “reconcile themselves to the uncertain, sometimes unpromising possibilities [the new industrial order] represented.” Hilkey did not find the authors to be shills or “self-conscious ideologues in the service of the plutocrats of the new industrial order. In general, success writers were small-time but ambitious ministers, educators, and publicists who were in a good position to take the pulse of those in the American heartland.” The authors hoped that their books might “win for themselves success of the pecuniary sort while offering much-needed encouragement and reassurance to their public.”

To persuade doubters, inculcated with years of hearing religious leaders bemoan wealth and the pursuit of it, success manual writers made distinctions between the proper and improper ways to amass riches. They lauded the old-fashioned, slow accretion of wealth through diligent industry and thrift; the new-fangled path to wealth involving speculation—which many deemed as gambling—was scorned. For those cases where men (and occasionally women, such as famous investor Hetty Green) gained quick wealth through speculation and financial manipulation, religious leaders and success manual writers shrugged their shoulders and rationalized the aberration thusly, if inaccurately: “only honestly acquired wealth could give true enjoyment and that the corrupt wealthy usually lost their fortunes.” Other supporters of wealth accumulation, such as Reverend Thain Davidson, stressed that “It is no sin to be rich … wish to be rich or to try to be rich.” A person erred only in “being too eager after riches.” In the right hands, money was a force for good; presumably these wise wealth holders might view their responsibility as a trustee instead of an owner. Gilded Age readers, though, might have wondered about Davidson’s subtle distinction.

Success writers interpreted the Parable of the Talents (Minas) in Matthew 25:21, 26–30 to be a celebration of “the importance of improving one’s lot and to make the point that heaven helps in proportion to how much one helps oneself.” Hilkey argued that the parable was, at best, ambiguous, especially in the context of the success writers. These writers stressed self-reliance and self-help, whereby an individual helped himself or herself by seizing opportunities. The paradox arose as the same writers “preached loyalty, duty, discipline, and sometimes even blind faith in the ultimate beneficence of the established order.”[3]

The mantra "character is capital" served a dual purpose. For young men of modest means, the mantra afforded hope, even if illusory, that they could overcome their financial disadvantage by exhibiting sterling character. The mantra also suggested that not only the few but the many might use their character to improve their lives by becoming "rich without money (Hilkey 1997, 7, 96–98, 129)."

One success manual writer, George Hewitt, listed some unethical activities that young men should avoid: "misrepresentation on the part of the seller"; "grinding the faces of necessitous workmen" by paying "starvation wages"; "speculating with borrowed capital"; "trading in futures which is nothing but gambling"; and "taking advantage of bankruptcy laws … to evade the payment of … just debts (Hewitt 1895, 413)."

Success manuals evolved throughout American history. During the early 1800s, a modest yeoman ideal dominated, with its emphasis on self-reliance and honesty. After the Civil War, a new school of behavior arose. Horatio Alger's Ragged Dick character proved popular. Ragged Dick was, in his way, a conman, a trickster. He exemplified the idea that "fortune favored the impudent." In the more cynical postbellum world, "success demanded boldness, energy, 'push,' decision, earnestness, 'true grit,' and above the Algerian quality of pluck." Americans, though, were not the sole worshippers of "pluck," as the British also admired pluck. What was pluck? Was it simply to "go forth and seize the main chance? Ragged Dick seized his chance and parlayed it into, if not riches, middle-class respectability; Ragged Dick demonstrated the idea that young men should proclaim themselves, or as one writer put it: self-trumpeting (Halttunen 1982, 203)."

Hilkey observed that the Horatio Alger "rags-to-riches" fables would have seemed perverse to earlier generations. By the later years of the nineteenth century and well into the twentieth century, salesmen and men looking for the main chance "would have either offended or baffled the authors of most Gilded Age success manuals, who believed that *character*, *willpower*, and *manhood* rather than personality was the key to success." Twentieth-century success manuals took a more self-serving and predatory approach to success, including manipulating people and self-aggrandizement (Hilkey 1997, 3–4).

In addition to his being alert and assertive enough to seize his chance, Ragged Dick was not just some street urchin. Contemporaries labeled Dick's asset as "charm." Young men were exhorted to "cultivate the friendly spirit." Personal magnetism became recognized as a useful skill, one that, at least, could be cultivated to some extent by even the sourest soul. Ragged Dick's charm induced people "to follow and obey him whether they will or not" or what was sometimes referred to as "executive ability." In today's world, he would be feted for his social intelligence, an ability to insinuate himself into the good graces of helpful adults. At about the time Ragged Dick made his literary appearance, John D. Rockefeller, who was not known for his charm, and other similar real-life characters were climbing the economic ladder without Ragged Dicksian charms. Over the years, the advice books depicted new routes to success. Initially young men were to concentrate on maintaining their inner virtues, but by the postbellum years, young men were encouraged to "manipulate appearances to their own advantage … putting on the appearance of business." One way to project success was to spend lavishly, to acquire the trappings of success. Such deception raised obvious ethical questions about the propriety of presenting a false appearance of prosperity. Ragged Dick lied about living in a swanky apartment; floundering businessmen were instructed to act as though nothing was amiss (Halttunen 1982, 203–205).

American Get-Ahead Attitude

Americans had long been imbued with a spirit of getting ahead. The lack of a rigid social hierarchy allowed citizens of modest means to dream of financial and social success. Americans in the 1800s spent much time and effort trying to get rich and, often, the quicker the better. Given nineteenth-century individuals' uncertain lifespans, an emphasis on "quick" may have been more prudent than for twenty-first-century Americans facing more stable and longer lifespans.

American males could transform themselves overnight; a simple change in scenery afforded opportunities to forge or assume new personalities and histories. Such "shape-changers" were reportedly common during the late antebellum years. One such method was the "suicide dodge," where men faked suicides to gain sympathy and cash (*New York Times*, April 28, 1859, 8).

Nineteenth-century Americans struggled with reconciling getting ahead with the sleazy aspects that often accompanied such go-getting, as examined by historian Karen Halttunen. Early on, success manuals warned young people against becoming confidence men or painted women; in the latter case, painted women were not necessarily prostitutes but more frequently women of fashion, "who poisoned polite society with deception and betrayal by dressing extravagantly and practicing the empty forms of false etiquette." Americans worried about these characters, since "the hypocrisy of the confidence man and the painted woman did not lie simply in a discrepancy between what they practiced and what they preached." They were adept at luring, "the guileless into granting them confidence." Although these characteristics are not laudable, they appear to be relatively innocuous to modern readers, but to Americans of the mid-nineteenth century, such deceptions were not taken lightly, as fears of hypocrisy undermined social confidence and might "reduce the American republic to social chaos."

Nineteenth-century Americans were proud of their republic, but they were keenly aware of both the novelty of their form of government and its fragility. Many Americans based their defense of liberty upon their republican virtues. The growing taste for luxury, a far cry from the Puritans' and Quakers' insistence on modest lifestyles, threatened liberty by inducing people to forsake: "the republican virtues of industry, sobriety, frugality, and simplicity." Such a transformation would endanger their liberty and turn (free, white) Americans into slaves.

Louis Godey's *Lady's Book* was an example of an antebellum American paean to consumerism that was de rigueur reading for middle-class American women. Not only did the periodical keep middle- and upper-middle-class American women informed about fashion, its editor Sarah Josepha Hale ran articles and editorials pertaining to issues affecting women. Even *Godey's Lady's Book* commented on the dangers of fashion (Halttunen 1982, xiv–xv, 9, 67). Successful business owners, therefore, faced a conundrum: success in money making could easily trigger spending money on luxuries and a surrender of liberty.

Godey's periodical proved successful, but he ran into unscrupulous characters willing to trade on his name and reputation. Of course, as his periodical grew in popularity and subscriber lists lengthened, so did the temptations for scammers. Godey had initially sent traveling agents to solicit and collect subscriptions; a year's subscription to his magazine cost $3, which was quite high for the times. He identified his agents with letters of introduction and also by listing their names on the cover of his magazine. These precautions were not sufficient. In 1837, con artists posing as subscription agents collected money and then absconded. Godey responded by placing advertisements in local newspapers where such scams occurred. In the era before photographic identification, ferreting out such con artists proved difficult.[4]

One historian Elizabeth Nelson pointed out why fraudulent subscription collectors proved successful. The usual story of fraud had naifs from the countryside venturing into a town or city and being scammed. The fake Godey's agents instead went forth and collected money in towns and in rural areas. Because the fake agents did not have any publishing expenses, they were willing to take almost any amount in return for an annual subscription. Subscribers were not taken aback by the fake agents' willingness to discount the subscription, since haggling was common. In fact, the subscribers who paid in advance proved to be easy marks. Once these "subscribers" discovered they had been defrauded, they naturally wanted their money back or to receive the annual subscription. Godey, on the other hand, blamed the defrauded subscribers for not asking to see written confirmation that the agent was a true Godey's agent or for a receipt. He did not honor the fraudulent subscriptions, which antagonized people. Godey then used one scammer's success to demonstrate the popularity and geographical spread of *Godey's Lady's Book*, demonstrating that Godey was, at least, willing to turn a sour situation to his advantage (Nelson 2004, 69, 71–72).

Eventually a caricature arose. Americans often created bigger-than-life characters, or in some cases, individuals created their own bigger-than-life persona, such as David Crockett. The master trickster often originated from New England, saying little or answering questions with questions. He peddled stuff and often bested the local yokels. By mid-century, the Yankee was a national myth: "I am Sam Slick the Yankee peddler .... I can ride on a flash of lightning and catch a thunder-bolt in my fist (Rourke 1931, 73)." Other characterizations of the Yankees depicted a "mercenary, hypocritical, philistine, an evil genius of duplicity whose sharp practices exploited the confidence placed in him by his fellow men. But on the other hand, he was thrifty, industrious, ascetic, 'a cracker barrel mentor, a Romantic rustic given to apothegms on trust in oneself, in one's fellow man, and in the benevolence of 'Natur [sic].'" Such a self-reliant and self-confident character "was not simply a confidence man, but a 'man of confidence,' uniquely suited to represent the American nation in an age of democratic patriotism (Halttunen 1982, 30–31)."

Americans and Europeans alike noted the "Yankee Trader." Presumably, Southern gentlemen would not resort to such sharp trading as the Yankee trader. The Yankee peddler was a stock character, but only one of several associated with "the Yankee." He was often described as "long-backed, thin" and "angular." English men and women were bemused by the

Yankees (typically of New England). Tall tales surrounded the character: "in each [tale] the Yankee was a looming figure .... But he was always the symbolic American .... Half bravado, half cockalorum, this Yankee revealed the traits considered deplorable by the British travelers; he was indefatigably rural, sharp, uncouth, witty. Here were the manners of the Americans! Peddling, swapping, practical joking, might have been national preoccupations." The Yankee was contrasted with the Briton, who was—in the eyes of the Americans—"still wicked, still mannered and over-polished, either rich or nefariously seeking riches, and always defeated by simple rural folk to the accompaniment of loud laughter." Yankees and Britons, however, were kin, "there was no contrast ... a gawky Yankee lad proved to be the son of an English nobleman." Another writer observed that the character was supernaturally shrewd: "If you met him in a tavern and he drew you into a trade, he soon quietly stripped you of everything you had (Rourke 1931, 4, 7, 16–17; see also Josephson [1934] 2011, 20)."

Ben Jonson and Daniel Defoe had noted similar characteristics among early eighteenth-century British traders. Jonson described a *projector* as one who found ways to enrich themselves, by suits, marriages, or by undertakings. It was the art of relying upon one's wits. Defoe was less flattering, defining *projectors* as "being masters of more cunning than their neighbors, turn their thoughts to private methods of trick and cheat, a modern way of thieving ... by which honest men are gulled with fair pretenses to part from their money." He concluded, "A mere projector is then a contemptible thing, driven by his own desperate fortune to such a strait that he must be delivered by a miracle or starve; And when he has beat his brain for some such miracle in vain, he finds no remedy but to paint up some bauble or other ... and then cry it up for a new invention, gets a patent for it, divides it into shares and they must be sold." The projector then wheedles some "honest coxcomb" into parting with his money for a share "and then (*nascitur ridiculus mus*) the adventurer is left to carry on the project, and the projector laughs at him." Defoe admitted the unfair tarring of all speculators: "the just contempt we have of the former sort [masters of cunning] bespatters the other [honest men], who, like cuckolds, bear the reproach of other people's crimes." He lauded the honest projector, who, "having by fair and plain principles of sense, honesty, and ingenuity brought any contrivance to a suitable perfection, makes out what he pretends to, picks nobody's pocket, puts his project in execution, and contents himself with the real produce of the profit of his invention (Defoe [1697] 2003, 1285–1286)."

Another way to measure the public's attitudes toward businesspeople is to consider folk tales and songs. Folklorists document some songs and sayings that reveal the businessman in an unflattering light. A rhyme summarizes the attitude, although just how general the attitude was held is uncertain: "The miller he stole corn. The weaver he stole yarn. The little tailor he stole broadcloth. For to keep these three rogues warm." The miller possibly incurred the most ire among the peasants, since peasants had to have their grain milled; millers became renowned for their acquisitiveness.

One of the few examples of a businessman portrayed favorably in folklore was Paul Bunyan, "the Brobdingnagian lumberman." Portrayals of Bunyan have him working alongside the other lumberjacks; his activities were easily understood by people, even those who never saw a lumber camp. Bunyan was portrayed as being generous with food, but he also was capable of chicanery. In one tale, he tried to reduce his payroll: "Discovering in the spring that he had no money on hand, Bunyan suddenly rushed into camp shouting that they had been cutting government pine and were all to be arrested …. [after the men scattered] Bunyan cleared his camp without paying his men a cent for their labor (Stewart and Watt 1916, 647–648; Porter 1944, 116–117)."

There were some real-life businessmen who resembled the caricatures from folklore. Phineas T. Barnum exploited his shrewd understanding of human nature. He asserted that people liked being flimflammed by good-natured tricks that he labeled "humbugs." He was a master showman. He revealed in one of his early books, that his wealth was based on illusion and deceit, of "obtaining money under false pretences from the public." In later years, Barnum presented a rehabilitated view of his activities. He admitted to relying upon humbug early in his impresario efforts but realized that to persist in the entertainment industry, he had to provide quality amusement at reasonable prices. An editorial in the *New York (Daily) Times* compared him to small-time cheats, who adulterated sugar or coffee or counterfeited bills of exchange. These men seldom got rich and often ended up in prison. Their failure was that, unlike Barnum, "they do not act upon a shrewd knowledge of human nature. They do not enlist the weaknesses of their victims on their side. They neither pique their curiosity, nor tempt their credulity, nor give them any chance to laugh at the cheat as a good joke. They are mere prosaic, common-place, and therefore unsuccessful, swindlers." According to this editorial writer, Barnum reveled in the public acknowledgment and admiration that he is "just the shrewdest and the sharpest Yankee that this hemisphere has yet produced (*New York Times*, December 16, 1854, 4)."[5]

Barnum's antics were not unique. An author published, *How to Get Money: Or, Eleven Ways of Making a Fortune*, which "taught readers to run up vast debts, hide assets, duck and default on payments, and abscond into the night. … 'Smile at honest men for lack of brains.'" This author had also published a book on how to detect and catch fraudsters (Sandage 2005, 76). One wonders whether the publisher offered the two books as a boxed set.

Forms of Business Organizations

In addition to new personalities, businessmen faced new challenges in raising sufficient capital. They had to be careful in forming partnerships. A partnership, similar to a sole proprietor, faced unlimited liability. The unlimited liability constricted the formation of socially useful businesses and made raising capital difficult. From an ethical standpoint, however, limited liability rankled many observers, who believed that people seeking limited liability were violating a sacred business trust to meet their liabilities. There arose a tension between perceived equity and efficiency.

Partnerships suffered from potential opportunistic behavior by one of the members. Lurking over partnerships was the threat of unlimited liability; if your partner made a mistake, you could be liable to pay back the entire amount lost. Partners had full ownership rights and could dissolve the partnership whenever they wanted. Even if the other partner or partners were willing to buy out the departing partner, an untimely dissolution was fraught with potential for major losses. Assets might have to be sold at below-market prices or business relationships with customers and suppliers might be disrupted. A partner, therefore, could hold up the other partners, or, "a partner could attempt to extract a greater share of the firm's revenue just by threatening dissolution." Nineteenth-century courts were hesitant to block any proposed dissolution, even if one partner was clearly damaged (Lamoreaux and Rosenthal 2006, 130–131, 135).

Economists Eric Hilt and Katharine O'Banion traced the development of limited partnerships in New York during the antebellum years. French law permitted a *societe en commandite*, whereby some partners were outside investors and granted limited liability. This legal form of partnership worked well, but English and American resistance was based on tradition: "opponents of this innovation argued the form was 'contrary to the whole genius and spirit of the English law,' and successfully resisted its introduction [in England] until the twentieth century (Hilt and O'Banion 2009, 615–616)."

Corporation law evolved during the nineteenth century. The big advantage of incorporation was the limited liability for the shareholders. Such limited liability encouraged investors to pool their capital with other investors, some or many of whom were not personally acquainted. Because of this advantage, investors seeking to incorporate had to secure a charter from their state legislature. Banks and transportation companies were often already regulated by legislators, so it was natural that they were early supplicants for charters. The process involved persuading legislators by various means. Because of the time and expense involved, companies seeking charters tended to be banks, insurance, manufacturing, and utility companies. New banks faced especially contentious hearings, as the incumbent banks sought to prevent the chartering of potential rivals. Corruption ran both ways; aspiring corporations could bribe legislators, or legislators could hold up legitimate projects by threatening to deny a charter. Although suspicious of special charters in general, many Americans were willing to put aside their skepticism, when they believed a charter would benefit them directly. Citizens also hoped that a successful project would begin to pay taxes and alleviate a state's need for taxation (Hilt 2008, 651; Wallis 2005, 214–215).

Economist John Wallis describes how "Corruption was generally defined as the few benefiting at the expense of the many." He quotes Andrew Jackson, who admitted the futility of running a completely honest and impartial government, but hoped that "we can at least take a stand against all new grants of monopolies and exclusive privileges, against any prostitution of our Government to the advancement of the few at the expense of the many …. I have now done my duty to my country (Wallis 2005, 239–240)."

The new form of organization was not perfect upon birth. Incorporation and limited liability created possibilities for deception and fraud. Compared with twenty-first-century regulations, the incorporation laws of, say, 1825 were simple and primitive. A savvy twenty-first-century investor might look in askance at these nascent corporations. First of all, there were no prospectuses to peruse. Although double-entry accounting had existed for centuries, the profession had yet to standardize financial reporting. Because of financial institutions' greater vulnerability to fraudulent behavior, their charters more frequently—but not universally—required annual financial statements (Hilt 2008, 648, 652, 659).

In contrast to Great Britain and the United States, Germany was a relative latecomer to industrialization, roughly a century later. The Germans followed the French laws regarding business organizations. The French law was more hospitable to joint-stock companies, but even anonymous companies with limited liability needed authorization of the state. There was no rush toward incorporation in Germany during the first half of the nineteenth century; some of the 74 German corporations founded during this time were railroads. Manufacturing firms found it difficult to get government permission for incorporation. The government's early reluctance to support corporations might have resulted from a bias toward landed wealth and "the more familiar class of 'honest and dependable' small producers and merchants." The bankers and projectors seeking incorporation often included Jews, which may have stiffened government resistance: "The corporation became inextricably linked for many with stock jobbing—the word 'agiotage' recurs repeatedly in the literature of the period; and with the triumph of Mammon—usually depicted with pseudo-Semitic features—over sobriety, industry, and all the other 'German virtues.'" Against the entrenched interests, though, was the growing clamor for government support of corporations to offset Germany's relative poverty and backwardness. The lure of creating very large heavy industries to compete with British and French firms also proved a strong argument (Landes 1966, 106–107).

Brazil was also a latecomer to creating corporations. The country enacted new regulations that had made it easier to form corporations and limit investors' personal liability. One provision of the new regulation allowed companies to start operating with just 10 percent of their capital raised; the companies could start trading stock at the 20 percent threshold. The rules led to a stampede of investors, small and large, and incorporations of businesses. The Brazilian experience was similar to the infamous internet boom of the 1990s. The mania eventually imploded, creating prolonged economic doldrums. The real problem was that Brazilian investors lacked reliable ways for ascertaining which businesspeople to trust. Brazilian investors learned a harsh lesson; you had to be careful in whom you trusted enough to invest your money. The elimination of unlimited liability did not eliminate the possibility of loss of money invested. In many local economies, business actors interacted repeatedly, and individuals gained reputations for honesty and reliability. The "Who

You Know" aspect was important. As economies became more complex, impersonal relationships became prominent. "Because institutional mechanisms of trust eliminate the need to know the right people, increasing reliance on institutional trust marks an important moment in market formation." Initially financier and entrepreneur maintained "highly personal relationships," but in the twentieth century, "the consolidation and maturation of financial institutions rendered these personal connections inadequate and hence less important to business finance (Hanley 2014, 187–189)."

Types of Corruption

The combination of government and business, especially big business, has often proved toxic for citizens. Progressives and other critics of business could not decide whether "business corrupted government" or the other way around. Over a century before the Progressive Era, eighteenth-century British and American political thinkers characterized the situation as "the king and his ministers … manipulating grants of economic privileges to secure political support for a corrupt and unconstitutional usurpation of government powers." During the eighteenth and nineteenth centuries, executive patronage increased in England. By using national debt and corporate charters as means of tying the financial community to the government's policies, the Crown began to threaten the independence of Parliament. The Jeffersonians among the Americans feared that Alexander Hamilton's proposed national financial system, replete with national debt, would lead the fledgling nation down the same, corrupt path. These abuses threatened the treasured British balanced government and conferred greater power onto the crown.

Systematic corruption and venal corruption were two forms of corruption, according to John Wallis. Systematic corruption results when politicians "deliberately create rents by limiting entry into valuable economic activities, through grants of monopoly, restrictive corporate charters, tariffs, quotas, regulations, and the like. These rents bind the interests of the recipients to the politicians who create them." The politicians hoped to create a coalition that will allow them to control the government. "Systematic corruption occurred when politics corrupted economics." Venal corruption was the reverse: "the pursuit of private economic interests through the political process. Venal corruption occurs when economics corrupts politics." Classical thinkers viewed venal corruption as endemic within people. Philosophers and concerned lawmakers tried to develop a government that "could resist systematic corruption. By eliminating systematic corruption, they hoped to mitigate the problems of venal corruption as well." Wallis identifies systematic corruption as the greater of the two evils. "Venal corruption, by comparison, is small potatoes in terms of social welfare and economic growth." Systematically corrupt governments, on the other hand, "are rent creating, not rent seeking, governments. The survival of a systematically corrupt government depends on limiting access to markets and resources in order to create rents that bind the interests of the ruling coalition together. Systematic corruption prevents development because it cripples markets." How Americans escaped systematic corruption is a crucial question.

The federal government remained shackled with respect to internal improvements, forcing states to devise ways of financing economic development and simultaneously avoiding systematic corruption. Individual states' dual goals required some experience and revisions before getting the rules straight. In New York, Martin Van Buren exhibited systematic corruption by issuing bank charters to political allies in return for political and financial support. Other states used systematic corruption to generate tax revenues. In the contested election of 1824, Andrew Jackson charged Washington, D.C. as being rife with corruption. Jackson had a plurality of both the electoral and popular vote but lost the election, when Henry Clay threw his support to John Quincy Adams; Jackson felt vindicated in his charges of corruption.

With New York State as an example of what not to do, other states developed a solution to getting economic development without systematic corruption. Rather than use charters and other laws to limit entrance into industries, several states started granting corporate charters to all applicants. The idea was that "some problems of government were not caused by bad men, but by bad governments." The state legislatures had to create a system whereby the incentives were aligned with the desired outcome. The states often re-wrote their constitutions to embody the new approach; these constitutions usually contained provisions "requiring legislatures to pass general incorporation laws (Wallis 2006, 24–25, 39–40, 43, 45, 49)."

There were other forms of corruption. Economists Edward Glaeser and Claudia Goldin characterized "corruption" as having three elements: "(a) payments to public officials beyond their salaries; (b) an action associated with these payments that violates either explicit laws or implicit social norms; and (c) losses to the public either from that action or from a system that renders it necessary for actions to arise only from such payments." Their description encompassed a variety of corruption, legal and illegal. "Honest graft ... is the gain of wealth by public officials through private information .... The expropriation of this information involved a loss of wealth to the public, but it was not necessarily illegal." An example would be if a legislator knew the route of a proposed railroad (a staple of some western television and movie plots from *Once Upon a Time in the Old West* to *Blazing Saddles*) and bought up land before the information became public. The legislator gained wealth from the original landowners, who might have held out for a higher price had they possessed the same information. Such action might not land "honest grafters" in jail, but the activity certainly violated public norms. George Washington Plunkitt's description of honest graft was summarized by his boast that he wanted his epitaph to read: "George W. Plunkitt. He Seen His Opportunities, and He Took 'Em (Glaeser and Goldin 2006, 7–8; Riordon 1963, 1)."

Glaeser and Goldin argue that the late nineteenth century in America was characterized by a massively larger government, due in part to the Civil War, "more valuable public assets, more aggressive regulation, and bigger-stakes litigation." These factors hiked the potential gains from corruption. Countering these impetuses toward greater corruption were "legal penalties, career or social costs, and internal psychic pain. Thus, the overall costs of corruption come from the size of the potential penalties and the probability that these costs are imposed that are in turn a function of information flows, social opprobrium, and the legal system." Some people might scoff at the very idea that New York City's Tammany Hall politicians could have incurred, "internal psychic pain."

Despite the attention paid to corruption in America during the nineteenth century, Glaeser and Goldin suggest that corruption increased for the first three quarters of the century but declined from the mid-1870s to the 1920s. They used newspaper reports of corruption as a measure of corruption (Glaeser and Goldin 2006, 3–22). As in many spheres, increased competition among newspapers forced them to improve quality, or as Matthew Gentzkow, Glaeser, and Goldin put it, "to provide more information relative to spin." In cities with multiple newspapers, readers could choose among sources; usually one of the newspapers would have an informative report (Gentzkow et al. 2006, 215).

Improved Business Ethics

Herbert Spencer discussed ethical lapses in English businesses in the late nineteenth century. He claimed that fraudulent dealings infected all classes of the commercial world. He went on to describe how buyers in the clothing trade bribed and accepted bribes as a matter of course. But he also noted that retailers selling cheap clothes were poor judges of good-quality goods and therefore susceptible to being defrauded. The wholesaler or manufacturer plied the naif with food and drink and sold him a bill of shoddy clothes masquerading as superior goods (Spencer 1878, 107–108, 110–111).

Despite many dubious examples of business behavior, there were offsetting signs of improved business ethics. Economist Alfred Marshall believed that the growth of the joint-stock company reflected improved business ethics. He wrote that most shareholders were "almost powerless," as they had difficulty finding out what was going on, so they were unable "to exercise an effective and wise control over the general management of the business." Mitigating this potential drawback, though, was "the marvelous growth in recent times of a spirit of honesty and uprightness in commercial matters, that the leading officers of great public companies yield as little as they do to the vast temptations to fraud which lie in their way. If they showed an eagerness to avail themselves of opportunities for wrongdoing at all approaching that of which we read in the commercial history of earlier civilization, their wrong uses of the trusts imposed in them would have been on so great a scale as to prevent the development of this democratic form of business." He concluded, perhaps over-optimistically, "There is every reason to hope that the progress of trade morality will continue, aided in the future as it has been in the past, by a diminution of trade secrecy and by increased publicity in every form (Marshall [1920] 1979, 253)."

Conclusion

Americans and their British counterparts found an increasingly impersonal market during the nineteenth century. The growing extent of the market and changing technologies offered opportunities for most people to elevate their material standard of living but at a potential cost of being defrauded or exploited. Consumers, investors, and businessmen had to learn quickly in order to benefit from the economic and technological upheavals and not to become one of the defrauded.

Businesspeople were seen as uncouth, ill-educated, and unsavory. Yet they led the transformation of America during the nineteenth century by developing and exploiting new technologies. They were quick to exploit the advantages of a limited liability incorporation, both for the legal protection from creditors and for the ability to stymie potential rivals. Such shenanigans created potential for corruption on the part of legislators and businesspeople.

Notes

1. Regarding British textile producers stealing ideas and personnel from Flemish producers (Lipson 1921, 10–14, 21).
2. It is interesting that Higginson would quote from the *Qur'an* to Americans.
3. In verse 15: "he gave five talents, to another two, to another one, to each according to his ability." This is a nifty counterpoint to Marx's "To each according to his need." In any event, the passage seems to approve of the master, whether justly or not, making returns on his talents. Donald Hay remarked that "the reward for good servants is increased responsibility (Hay [1989] 2004, 50–51)."
4. Godey's subscriber list was potentially quite valuable, but there's no indication that he sold the list to other vendors.
5. There was a rarely mentioned aspect of Barnum's character. Barnum sought a seat in the Connecticut legislature, wishing only to vote for the Thirteenth Amendment and for an amendment to the state constitution allowing black suffrage. He argued that whites needed to cast off their prejudice toward blacks, who had shown their nobility by not seeking revenge upon their masters during and after the Civil War (Renda 2002, 243–244).

Bibliography

Augst, Thomas. "The Commerce of Thought; Professional Authority and Business Ethics in 19th-Century America." *Prospects: An Annual of American Cultural Studies* 27, 1997, 49–76.

Bates, Joshua. *A Discourse on Honesty in Dealing* (Middlebury, VT: J.W. Copeland, 1818).

Beecher, Reverend Henry. "The Benefits and Evils of Commerce," *Hunt's Merchants' Magazine* 24(2), February 1851, 147–156.

Brown, JoAnne. *Definition of a Profession* (Princeton, NJ: Princeton, University Press, 1992).

Bulletin of the Business Historical Society. "To Enter Business or Not to Enter? A Letter of 1807 Considers the Question." Vol. XV(6) December 1941, 93–95. No author.

Casseday, Ben. "Dignity of the Mercantile Class." *Hunt's Merchants' Magazine* 35(1), July 1856, 54–56.

Chandler, Alfred Jr. *The Visible Hand: The Managerial Revolution in American Business* (Cambridge, MA: Harvard University Press, 1977).

Defoe, Daniel. *An Essay Upon Projects* (Project Gutenberg Etext, [1697] 2003), https://ia600503.us.archive.org/2/items/anessayupon proje04087gut/esprj10.txt, viewed December 12, 2015).

Fielder, John. "The Ethics and Politics of Automobile Regulation." in *The Ford Pinto Case: A Study in Applied Ethics, Business, and Technology*, edited by Douglas Birsch and John Fielder (Albany, NY: State University of New York, 1994), 285–301.

Franklin, Benjamin. "Advice to a Young Tradesman." *Little Masterpieces*, edited by Bliss Perry (New York, NY: Doubleday & McClure, 1902), 153–155.

Freedley, Edwin, *Practical Treatise on Business: or How to Get, Save, Spend, Give, Lend, and Bequeath Money: with an Inquiry into the Chances of Success and Causes of Failure in Business* (Philadelphia, PA: Lippincott, Grambo, 1853).

Glaeser, Edward and Claudia Goldin. "Corruption and Reform: Introduction." *Corruption and Reform: Lessons from America's Economic History*, edited by Edward Glaeser and Claudia Goldin (Chicago, IL: University of Chicago Press, 2006), 3–22.

Gentzkow, Matthew, Edward Glaeser, and Claudia Goldin. "The Rise of the Fourth Estate: How Newspapers Became Informative and Why It Mattered." *Corruption and Reform: Lessons from America's Economic History*, edited by Edward Glaeser and Claudia Goldin (Chicago, IL: University of Chicago Press, 2006), 187–230.

Halttunen, Karen. *Confidence Men and Painted Women: A Study of Middle-class Culture in America, 1830–1870* (New Haven, CT: Yale University Press, 1982).

Hanley, Anne. "Is It Who You Know? Entrepreneurs and Bankers in Sao Paulo, Brazil, at the Turn of the Twentieth Century." *Enterprise and Society* 5(2) 2014, 187–225.

Hay, Donald. *Economics Today: A Christian Critique* (Vancouver, BC: Regent College Publishing, [1989] 2004).

Hewitt, George. "Motive and Method." *Portrait and Principles of the World's Great Men and Women, with Practical Lessons on Successful Life by Over Fifty Leading Thinkers*, edited by William King (Springfield, MA, King-Richardson, 1895), 411–414.

Higginson, Thomas. "Conscience in the Counting Room: Or the True Interests of the Merchant." *Hunt's Merchants' Magazine and Commercial Review*, Vol. 28, No. 1, January 1853, 19–40.

Hilkey, Judy. *Character Is Capital: Success Manuals and Manhood in Gilded Age America* (Chapel Hill, NC: University of North Carolina Press, 1997).
Hilt, Eric. "When Did Ownership Separate from Control? Corporate Governance in the Early Nineteenth Century." *Journal of Economic History* 68(3), September 2008, 645–685.
Hilt, Eric and Katharine O'Banion. "The Limited Partnership in New York 1822–1858: Partnerships without Kinship." *Journal of Economic History* 69(3), Sept. 2009, 614–645.
Hunt's Merchants' Magazine. "The Morals of Trade." Vol. 5, No. 6, December 1841, 526–530. No author.
Hunt's Merchants' Magazine. "Mercantile Miscellanies." Vol. 24, No. 5, May 1851, 782.
Josephson, Matthew. *The Robber Barons: The Great American Capitalists, 1861–1901* (New Brunswick, NJ: Transaction Publisher, [1934] 2011), September 8, 1883, 281–285.
Lamoreaux, Naomi and Jean-Laurent Rosenthal. "Corporate Governance and the Plight of Minority Shareholders in the United States before the Great Depression." *Corruption and Reform: Lessons from America's Economic History*, edited by Edward Glaeser and Claudia Goldin (Chicago, IL: University of Chicago Press, 2006), 125–152.
Landes, David. "Structure of Enterprises." *The Rise of Capitalism* (New York, NY: Macmillan, 1966). 99–111.
Lipson, Ephraim. *The History of the Woollen and Worsted Industries* (London, UK: a. & C. Black, 1921).
Marburg, Theodore. "Aspects of Labor Administration in the Early Nineteenth Century." *Bulletin of the Business Historical Society* 15(1), February 1941, 1–10.
Marshall, Alfred. *Principles of Economics* (London, UK: Macmillan Press, [1920], 1979). Eighth Edition.
McConnell, Donald. *Economic Virtues in the United States: A History and an Interpretation* (New York, NY: Arno Press, [1930] 1973).
Nelson, Elizabeth. *Market Sentiments: Middle-Class Market Culture in Nineteenth-Century America* (Washington, DC: Smithsonian Books, 2004).
New York Times. "The Lesson of Barnum's Life." December 16, 1854, 4, no author.
New York Times. "The Last Confidence Game-The Suicide Dodge." April 28, 1859, 8. Reprinted from the *Cincinnati Gazette*.
Oberholtzer, Ellis. *A History of the United States since the Civil War* (New York, NY: Macmillan, 1922). 5 vols.
Porter, Kenneth. "The Business Man in American Folklore." *Bulletin of the Business Historical Society* 18(5), November 1944, 113–130.
Renda, Lex. "'White Man's State in New England': Race, Party, and Suffrage in Civil War Connecticut." *An Uncommon Time: The Civil War and the Northern*

Home Front, edited by Paul Cimbala and Randall Miller (New York: Fordham University Press, 2002).

Rhodes, James. *History of the United States from the Compromise of 1850 to the Final Restoration of Home Rule at the South in 1877* (New York, NY: Macmillan, 1912). 8 vols.

Riordon, William. *Plunkitt of Tammany Hall: A Series of Very Plain Talks on Very Practical Politics, Delivered by Ex-Senator George Washington Plunkitt, the Tammany Philosopher, From His Rostrum—The New York County Court House Bootblack Stand* (New York, NY: E.P. Dutton, 1963).

Rourke, Constance. *American Humor: A Study of the National Character* (New York, NY: Harcourt, Brace, 1931).

Sandage, Scott. *Born Losers: A History of Failure in America* (Cambridge, MA, Harvard University Press, 2005).

Spencer, Herbert. *The Morals of Trade* (New York, NY: D. Appleton, 1878).

Stewart, K. Bernice and Homer Watt. "Legends of Paul Bunyan." *Wisconsin Academy of Sciences, Arts, and Letters* 1916.

Tucker, Barbara. "The Merchant, the Manufacturer, and the Factory Manager: The Case of Samuel Slate." *Business History Review* 55(3), Autumn 1981, 297–313.

Wallis, John. "The Concept of Systematic Corruption in American History." *Corruption and Reform: Lessons from America's Economic History*, edited by Edward Glaeser and Claudia Goldin (Chicago, IL: University of Chicago Press, 2006), 23–62.

Wallis, John. "Constitutions, Corporations, and Corruption: American States and Constitutional Change, 1842 to 1852." *Journal of Economic History* 65(1), March 2005, 211–256.

CHAPTER 3

Examples of Mid-Nineteenth-Century Business Ethics in America

The growing American economy, both in terms of output and in landmass, created opportunities for entrepreneurs. The primitive but improving communication and transportation facilities meant that businessmen made more transactions, especially with respect to granting and obtaining credit and merchandise with strangers. The transactors rarely saw each other, and the precarious nature of frontier purchasing power meant a great number of bankruptcies. New scientific knowledge gave rise to new medical nostrums and an increasing dependence upon strangers for foodstuffs.

Americans also experienced increasing tensions between regions. Although the fault line between slave-owning and non-slave-owning regions would eventually ignite into civil war, business developments differed, too. Bumptious northerners sought the main chance, while southerners maintained a gentlemanly veneer. Southerners had to watch their bottom lines but opted to pretend that they were paternalistic and patrician. Certainly, business ethics during the Civil War failed to disabuse the notion of the rapacious Yankee businessman, who was willing to make profits from the national crisis. Some of these Yankee businessmen, such as Philip Armour, reputedly started their fortunes by wartime profiteering.

Bankruptcy, impure and dubious food and drugs, and wartime business activities were examples of the changes facing Americans in the nineteenth century. Some Americans remained devoutly religious and based their ethical behavior upon Biblical precepts, but other contemporaries were

D. G. Surdam, *Business Ethics from the 19th Century to Today*,
https://doi.org/10.1007/978-3-030-37169-2_3

more free-wheeling. The attitude was that as long as actions were within the law or, at least, not explicitly against the law, such actions, if profitable, were desirable.

Bankruptcy

Paying Your Debts

A basic ethical expectation in commerce is for businesspeople to pay their bills and to repay their loans on time. As the use of credit expanded, this standard behavior became crucial for the smooth operation of commerce. If one merchant failed to pay his bills on time, his creditors might become financially vulnerable in turn. Bankruptcy could easily prove contagious, spreading insolvency from business to business.

Bankruptcy release held the promise to restore honest businesspeople's ability to operate a business and to remove the stigma of bankruptcy. The economy needed honest risk-takers, who were willing to open new businesses. Under a draconian bankruptcy regime, such honest entrepreneurs could be knocked out of the arena completely due to one unfortunate venture. On the other hand, the potential for dishonest borrowers to defraud creditors was real enough. The ethical premises, though, were troubling. As historian Scott Sandage points out, "Legal release from debts seemed to violate two rules of capitalism: keeping your promises and taking responsibility when your actions harm others." The conundrum was that "Failure was at once anathema and endemic to maturing capitalism (Sandage 2005, 64)."

The term "bankrupt" originated from a "medieval Continental custom of breaking the bench (hence, *banca rupta*) of a banker or tradesman who had absconded with the money or goods of his creditors."[1] The Anglo-American tradition of bankruptcy initially focused on the action and not necessarily the insolvency of the bankrupt (Treiman 1938, 189–193, see also Weisberg 1986, 35).

Perpetual Hope, Frequent Failure on the American Frontier

Opening a store in newly settled territories during the early years of the United States was a risky venture. The majority of the customers depended upon a lumpy income, as money flowed in at harvest time and flowed out the rest of the year; when farmers harvested their crops, they simultaneously placed the crops on the market and drove down prices. Exacerbating this aspect was a shortage of currency and dubious banks; farmers, retailers, and artisans operated in a rudimentary economy. A retailer or wholesaler had to become adept at ascertaining good versus bad bank notes. The uncertainty of the soundness and appropriate discounts for bank notes could easily lead to ill-will if a consumer presented a bill and held a different opinion than the retailer as to its value. The merchant hewed to a fine line; if he erred on the side of caution, a rival merchant might usurp his business, but if he paid too much for the notes, his own solvency could be jeopardized. Some farmers simply refused to accept that a bank note was worth less than its face value (Atherton 1971, 137; Foulke 1941, 275–276; Atherton [1949] 1968, 177–179).

Despite the ferocious mortality rate of fledgling mercantile efforts—estimated anywhere from 33.3 to 97 percent—Americans with small capital accumulations continued to start businesses. Henry David Thoreau claimed, "a very large majority [of merchants], even ninety-seven in a hundred, are sure to fail, is equally true of the farmers." The 97 percent figure, as with many bogus statistics through the ages, became a fact in the minds of many Americans, until debunked decades later by Bradstreet's credit agency (Thoreau [1947] 1977, 287–288; Jones 1849, 49).

American wholesalers wanting to sell their goods to a wider customer base often had to extend credit to merchants on the frontier. American borrowers were often people of scant means and modest social standing. Wholesalers usually did not have social connections with their borrowers. Merchant newcomers faced a daunting challenge in ascertaining which farmers they could safely extend credit. Not until the 1840s would there be any credit-rating services. John Beauchamp Jones and his brother solved the problem by boarding with a farmer; they discovered that the farmer was an honest, prudent man with good judgment. This farmer supplied them with the necessary information regarding the credit-worthiness of his neighbors (Sandage 2005, 7).

Given the isolation of the frontier, a bankrupt could easily move elsewhere and escape past failures; the likelihood of a new neighbor recognizing the escapee's prior financial woes was low. Nor would such a borrower suffer loss of social status and disgrace by reneging on a loan. Flight, though, often meant sacrificing family ties and friendships; the refugee also gave up knowledge of conditions in their original locale and had to learn such information anew.

On the other hand, overtrading occurred when a retailer "relied on credit to extend a business's normal operations beyond the prudent limits of its capital." In modern parlance, such activity might be compared with leveraging, buying the biggest house the bank will approve. Retailers overborrowed in hopes—perhaps based on the anticipation of new settlers moving into a frontier community—of enlarging their profits; wholesalers, too, participated by extending credit to even dubious retailers in hopes of increasing their sales and interest payments (Balleisen 2001, 57, 171–173). Such speculation and overtrading could be societally useful, if the speculators and overtraders proved sagacious, but sagacity was hardly ubiquitous.

Profiting from Bankruptcy

It was an ill bankruptcy that benefited no one. Similar to a poker player with the smallest amount of cash at a table, many shoestring entrepreneurs could not outlast even short runs of misfortune before the game was over. Potential beneficiaries from someone's bankruptcy included private assignees and receivers, sheriffs and auctioneers, newspapers publishing bankruptcy information, lawyers, and astute observers. These activities, although necessary, struck many antebellum people as disreputable because they benefited from the misfortune of others. Although these salvagers displayed the much-honored willingness to take the initiative, in this context, they were viewed as unscrupulous and sordid.

In the aftermath of the wave of bankruptcies, a cottage industry of bankruptcy services arose. Former bankrupts were often adept at salvaging assets. The bankruptcy act of 1841 created a significant increase in bankruptcies and a corresponding increase in salvaging services. Even the legal expenses quickly drained the available funds to compensate creditors, and frequently court officials reaped more than did creditors. Bankrupts benefited doubly from the act, as they were freed of past debts and were well-positioned to become salvagers. One debtor was fortunate enough to preside over his own bankruptcy proceedings, thanks to a judge who appointed him. Even attorneys who went bankrupt from land speculation found themselves busy handling bankruptcy cases (Balleisen 1996, 474, 477–478, 480–485, 488–489).

Lawyers and former bankrupts provided consulting services for bankrupts. Some former bankrupts engaged in speculation, bidding for the remains of other bankrupts. Although historian Edward Balleisen labels these scavengers as "vulture capitalists," the speculators may have performed a valuable service. Just as flies and carrion clean the environment of the decaying dead, these financial services cleansed the body economic. Speculators with cash could hope to find bargains. Former mercantile owners were often best placed to get the most out of the remaining assets; they might have been better able to wring more payment out of past-due accounts payables that had contributed to their business' demise. Many bankrupts could easily outbid any other interested parties for the legal title to the overdue accounts, as they usually had superior knowledge regarding their former accounts. In many cases, they might have been able to re-acquire such assets at auction for a fraction of the value. Especially important was knowledge of who actually had the best title to a plot of land; just because someone had a deed did not make them the owner. On occasion, bankrupts simply purchased items of sentimental value at auction, such as personal possessions (Balleisen 1996, 501–504, 2001, 19, 136–139, 143, 153).

Identifying Bankrupts

In America, the 1841 Bankruptcy Act provided information on insolvents, since court records were open to the public. One British publisher had been printing a list of bankrupts for years, so Americans pushed for similar publications. James Gordon Bennett of the New York *Herald* considered doing so, but his paper only printed the names of bankrupts in the southern New York district. A few other publishers compiled pamphlets listing bankrupts in their region (Balleisen 1996, 498, 2001, 148–149).

Enter Lewis Tappan, who was a struggling mercantilist and a staunch abolitionist. His brother, Arthur, and he applied their Christian principles to their business practices. Their mercantile endeavors foundered during the depression of 1837, along with a fire that damaged their business. Lewis decided to separate from his brother's partnership in hopes of prospering. He was well into middle age and worried about providing for his family. He considered opening a cotton-goods store, but a friend—also an abolitionist—persuaded him that selling goods based upon slave labor was wrong (Wyatt-Brown 1966, 433–435).

Tappan turned to rating borrowers. Although valuable in theory, credit information could be manipulated. Prior to credit-rating agencies, east coast wholesalers often required letters of reference from clergymen, bankers, and lawyers before extending credit. If such professionals who wrote the letters were unknown to the easterners, the letters were of doubtful value. A creditor could conspire with a debtor to defraud a potential creditor. The original creditor could supply overly laudatory information about the debtor in order for the debtor to get credit from which to pay the original creditor. The debtor, of course, hoped that by misleading Peter to pay Paul, the debtor could forestall the denouement, if only for a little longer (Balleisen 2001, 83).

Tappan believed that an entrepreneur could earn a good living while serving fellow merchants by providing better information on individual's credit-worthiness. Such information would help stymie reckless businesses that "overtraded" from getting credit, while enhancing the opportunities of credit-worthy merchants. Ultimately the credit information would "encourage honorable and prudent behavior by both debtors and creditors (Balleisen 1996, 496)."

Tappan devised the method of eliciting credit reports from local lawyers and merchants regarding local businessmen. The reporters initially earned money only from pursuing collection cases, not from filing reports. Critics of Tappan's efforts decried his reliance on "spies" reporting on friends and fellow business owners' activities; these critics asserted that no man of honor would stoop so low. Some of Tappan's reporters were reputedly too young and inexperienced to be providing opinions as to other business owners' credit-worthiness. Other observers, though, argued that men who resisted collection of credit information were likely worried that any such reports on their credit would be unfavorable; honest debtors, though, worried about the power wielded by credit-reporting agencies. A more serious issue was the conflicting interests inherent in being both a reporter and a debt collector. In any event, Tappan's staff of scribes transcribed the reports into large volumes. Tappan then charged interested wholesalers and other businessmen to examine the information held on a particular merchant or buyer. To control against theft of the information, Tappan required the inquirer to hear the reports *read* by one of his clerks at the Mercantile Agency's office. By 1845, Tappan possessed a reputation for providing reasonably accurate reports; as historian Lewis Atherton concluded, "Such hysterical charges [of inaccurate reports] of course exaggerated the faults of mercantile agencies. Their very survival depended on fair and accurate reports;" Tappan improved the weaker aspects of the system as the company matured (Atherton 1946, 541, 550–551; Sandage 2005, 109–111, 154; Madison *Daily State* 1858, 166).

Tappan found that protecting his intellectual property was difficult. He imposed strict limitations upon access to the credit information. The

Bradstreet Agency began business a few years after Tappan's Mercantile Agency; other less-permanent companies entered the industries. Stealing information became easier, when the Mercantile Agency began allowing subscribers to borrow the reference books. Some subscribers, as well as competitors, shared the books with non-subscribers. Copycat companies baldly (and badly) plagiarized Tappan's findings while undercutting his prices. Tappan faced the ironic twist that many of the subscribers to the Mercantile Agency failed to live up to their obligation to pay promptly for their subscriptions. He implored them to remit their payments, so that he could improve his services (Madison *Daily State* 1858, 166, 171–174, 182; Balleisen 1996, 497; Wyatt-Brown 1966, 441).

Conclusion

Bankruptcy no longer carries the same stigma as in the past. Americans joke about credit card debt. Indebted Americans seek credit counseling and, unless fraud is involved, have no fear of jail or prison.

As bankruptcy laws evolved, the laws lost much of the "express moral content." Americans' attitudes toward the bankrupt business operator shifted from viewing merchant debtors as "elusive social deviant" to "noble and vulnerable statesman of society whom the law should protect from the cruel contingencies of economic life."

With the expansion of credit for consumer purchases in the twentieth century, a new aspect of bankruptcy developed. Consumers with over-extended debt loads—sometimes through copious purchases of consumer goods or because of misfortune (illness, job layoff)—began seeking debt relief through bankruptcy. Public attitudes toward consumer bankruptcy mirrored previous attitudes, with some commentators linking bankrupt consumers with wasteful spending and moral irresponsibility. Consumer advocates, on the other hand, argued that businesses enticed consumers to borrow beyond prudence. A commentator concludes, "In this world, we cannot readily tell the virtuous from the villainous (Weisberg 1986, 4–5, 138)." Another legacy of the nineteenth century, credit-rating agencies, is thriving, but consumers are urged to periodically check on the accuracy of such reports. The reports, of course, rely upon the ubiquitous electronic network of machines compiling data. Gone are Lewis Tappan's clerks laboriously transcribing reporters' messages (Sandage 2005, 274).[2] An industry even prospers by claiming to be able to "clean" bad credit histories.

Bad Food, Bad Drugs

Although patent medicines might seem to be a straightforward case of unethical behavior, the situation was much more complicated. There were plenty of people involved. Newspapers in America and Great Britain found that stories about better dying through chemistry spurred readership. People seemed to revel in accounts of death by poisoning; such reporting was not merely prurient, though, as it served to raise awareness of dangerous products. Newspaper publishers also received large amounts of advertising revenue from purveyors of patent medicines. A greater number of consumers began buying food from businesses instead of producing food themselves; what goes into food became a vexing question.

Quack, Quack, Everywhere a Quack

Although some suggest that the pejorative, "quack," derives from quacksalve, an ingredient in many patent medicines, the term dates back centuries. Historian Roy Porter suggests the term carried "the same kind of emotional venom as … insults like heretic, revisionist, dunce, scab …. It pointed a finger against incompetence: quacks are all mouth and no skill. It also branded a man as a fraud, a cheat." Ben Jonson in his play *Volpone; or The Fox*, characterizes quacks as, "These turdy-facy-nasty-paty-lousy-fartical rogue, with one poor groat's-worth of unprepared antimony … are able, very well, to kill their twenty a week (Porter 1988, 16; Jonson 1811, IV:248)."

Physicians rarely possessed much ability to cure or palliate most medical conditions well into the twentieth century. Quacksters, therefore, faced less competition than in today's world.

Adulterating Food and Drugs

Better living through chemistry might have been a title of a 1950s-style education film, but throughout the nineteenth century, advances in chemical analysis created a race between unscrupulous producers and investigators ferreting out adulteration. Many producers adulterated their products by substituting cheaper (but often deleterious) for legitimate ingredients. If producers using adulterated ingredients gained a major cost advantage over scrupulous producers, the cheaters might have succeeded in driving out the scrupulous producers (Akerloff 1970, 488–500).

Radical socialists and communists viewed adulteration and other deceitful methods as "proof of the fundamental character, and underlying incentives of, of capitalist economy." For these observers, capitalism accentuated the "greed of gain, the lust to accumulate money." These radical commentators raised a crucial point: Were customers "apathetic or dangerously ignorant about the nature of the foods they ate?" In other words, using historians Michael French and Jim Phillips' phrase, were customers "sophisticates or dupes?"

At first blush, the argument that customers were and remain dupes has plenty of support. Not many consumers, even educated consumers, understand the nature of the ingredients in, say, a candy bar or the intricacies of their laptop computer. On the other hand, consumers who are aware of their ignorance regarding chemical ingredients may have recourse to expert opinion. Modern-day Americans can watch advertisements on television touting some drug; if the drug looks useful, a person can surf the internet to find out information (granted the information on the internet is of varying quality) *or* they can query their physician. The beauty of informed consumers is that they perform a social benefit. Not all of us have to devote the time and effort to become informed on a particular good or service; those that invest such resources provide third-party benefits for other consumers. Vendors often argue that their customers are well-informed, rational actors, thereby placing responsibility upon the customers (French and Phillips 2003, 448, 451, 453).

Consumers tolerated widespread adulteration for several reasons. One, of course, was sheer ignorance that substances were being added. The cheaper ingredients may have led to lower prices that would have attracted consumers. Some consumers, even knowing that the food was adulterated, preferred the taste, color, or texture; people sometimes forgot how the unadulterated product tasted (Whorton 2010, 150).

There were limits to adulteration, though. With the rise of chemical analysis, outside parties could publish information regarding the "purity" of food products, or if the product was purchased on a repeated basis, consumers might be able to ascertain whether the product was adulterated or not. If these possibilities existed, then consumers could punish the errant producer by buying a substitute product. Economists posit that "firms will not have an incentive to cheat on quality … if the present value of expected profits from repeat sales exceeds any temporary increase in profits due to shirking on product quality (Klein and Leffler 1981, 615–641; see also Law 2003, 1116)."

Producers of high-quality products faced a challenge: How could these producers educate consumers that their product was, indeed, high quality? Your parents' admonition regarding "your reputation matters" was accurate. High-quality producers wanted to earn a reputation for superior products; low-quality producers wanted to usurp a reputation for superior products. In order for reputation effects to work well, consumers had to be able to easily recognize differences in quality, either before purchasing or soon after using the product. This is not to say, however, that there were no legitimate reasons for offering a (recognizable) low-quality product; a market offering a continuum of readily ascertainable qualities could better match consumer needs. A carpenter presumably needs a better hammer than a renter putting up a few paintings.

Product branding is one way to establish a reputation. From ancient times, producers of food and other goods put their name or mark on the product. This tactic became more widespread during the nineteenth century. Producers invested in their reputation by incurring the extra expense to make higher-quality goods or to provide higher-quality services. Product brands, then, sent signals to consumers that the producer intended to produce a high-quality product now and into the future. The growing sophistication of adulterating products, though, tempted even reputable producers, especially when adulteration created significant cost savings. Although maintaining one's reputation was important, a producer might well prefer to do so in the cheapest manner possible. If a producer was successful in convincing consumers of his or her product's high quality, then consumers would be willing to pay a premium for such a product, reversing the process whereby bad products drove out good products (Law 2003, 1116–1117).

Brand names and standardization can be great benefits for consumers. Some social critics believe that the "McDonaldization" of the world is an unmitigated evil that creates a "pernicious homogeneity" in consumption. An economist argues that, "instead of creating homogeneity in consumption, the existence of brand names has provided consumers on a global scale with more choice than ever in history. Travelers driving across the United States can depend that a quick meal at McDonalds is a known quality, as is a night in a Best Western or Holiday Inn (Wilkins 1994, 21)."[3]

Was there a serious threat to health from adulterated foods and quack elixirs? Some contemporaries, although estimating that between a sixth and a fifth of America's food supply was adulterated, revealed little evidence that the adulterants had physically harmed anyone. A business ethicist observed, "Given the state of medical record-keeping at the time, it is impossible to determine accurately the damage actually done by patent medicine use or poisonous food additives." A writer in the *Independent* observed, "Probably very few reform laws would gain sufficient popular momentum to be passed unless the people had an exaggerated idea of the evils to be prevented and the efficiency of the proposed laws." The writer was in favor of the Pure Food and Drug laws but noted that Americans already had safer food than in the past: "no chemical ever added is so poisonous as the ptomaines which develop in food which is not properly preserved." The authorities skewed the results by testing primarily items suspected of being tainted. The terms "adulterated" and "artificial" could be confusing (Wood 1985, 407–409, 411–412, 414–415; *Independent* 1905, 49–51).[4]

Americans and Europeans of the twenty-first century now consume large amounts of food additives. Many of these additives are intended to make food more attractive or to preserve it for long periods of time. One ironic use is that of polyphosphates: "universally deployed to increase the bulk of meat and fish ... [by] absorb[ing] more water." The magic of science has allowed modern-day producers to resort to the old trick of watering (and salting) the cattle before selling. Scientist Walter Gratzer concludes, "the process is commended in advertisements to producers and butchers on the grounds that it allows them to sell water in the guise of meat (Gratzer 2005, 213–214)."

Ethical Quandary of Third-Party Sellers

Similar perhaps to modern-day owners of convenience stores wrestling with the ethics of selling lottery tickets and installing gambling, excuse me, gaming machines, druggists, chemists, grocers, and others selling patent medicines faced a moral quandary. The patent medicines, similar to the lottery tickets, were profitable; the nineteenth-century retailer refusing to sell such products stood to lose significant sales, so considering relinquishing the sale of such products was no mere armchair ethical exercise (Crellin 1967, 223; Atherton [1949] 1968, 78).

Newspaper publishers found that sensationalized stories about bad drugs and bad physicians sold newspapers. Publishers often took a contradictory stance toward patent medicines. Some editors inveighed against nostrums while accepting cash for advertisements placed with their papers. James Gordon Bennett of the New York *Herald* bragged, "Send us more advertisements than Dr. Brandreth does—give us higher prices—we'll cut Brandreth dead—or at least curtail his space. Business is business—money is money (Young 1961, 81; Okun 1986, 172)."[5]

The *New York Times* demonstrated such contradictions. The *Times* ran a story regarding a fatal drug oversight in Mobile, Alabama. Adjacent to the article was an advertisement for Mrs. Winslow's Soothing Syrup that cured or alleviated stomach and bowel irritations, giving "health and comfort to mother and child." What the *Times* decried in one article, it earned revenue for in an advertisement. Even the *Journal of the American Medical Association* (*JAMA*) accepted advertisements from dubious vendors. The advertising revenue was needed, but *JAMA* was certainly jeopardizing its reputation by doing so. As medical journals gained credence, imitators tried to usurp this prestige by publishing phony journals that touted nostrums. Some publishers of reputable journals decided to rationalize their actions by claiming that other publishers would accept such advertisements anyway (*New York Times*, April 24, 1867a, b, 5; Young 1961, 207–208).

Calls for Regulation

With regard to patent medicines, knowing the ingredients could be a matter of life or death. Alcohol was one of the more benign ingredients, compared with morphine, cocaine, and opium. The Women's Christian Temperance Union, appalled at the inclusion of addictive and dangerous ingredients, opposed the use of patent medicines (apparently, some of the members unwittingly or wittingly got their alcohol through daily tonics). Consumer advocates pushed for accurate labeling that preserved the right of consumers to purchase, "oleomargarine, glucose syrup, coffee mixed with chicory, whiskey 'aged' over night, and other worthless or addictive tonics and remedies." The accurate labeling, though, would protect reputable producers and make it difficult for disreputable producers to dupe consumers; in today's parlance, the advocates wanted "informed" consumers (Wood 1985, 410–412).

New York City was a focal point of the battle over adulterated food and drugs. By the mid-nineteenth century, the *New York Times* bemoaned the fact that most wine, but particularly inexpensive weak wines contained "sugar of lead." The newspaper listed a chain of adulteration: "Our coffee is chicory, our chicory Venetian red, and our Venetian red brick dust, in which, lost is the labor that attempts to discover either thein [sic] or caffeine." But most of the newspaper's ire was directed to the producers of swill milk. The editorialist claimed that 9847 (a suspiciously precise number) children under the age of two had died from consuming the foul liquid, but the writer did not provide any source for this astonishing claim (*New York Times*, March 9, 1854, 4; see also Olmstead and Rhode 2008, 353–358).[6]

Naturally, some business owners supported the food and drug laws, especially those who could easily satisfy the edicts. Those who were unable to do so, of course, opposed the laws. The American Proprietary Association was vehemently against such laws. A middle group supported the idea in the abstract but had reservations about the details. Economist George Stigler argued that businesses seek government regulation that provides direct subsidy, control over entry, powers affecting substitutes or complements, and price-fixing; several of these aspects arose during the debate over pure food and drugs (Stigler 1975a, 116–119).

Economists often hold a somewhat skeptical attitude toward regulation. George Stigler developed a theory that firms in an industry may co-opt ostensibly unfavorable regulation and transform it to minimize the industry's discomfiture or to even gain benefits. The idea of firms "capturing" regulators has proved influential, but other social scientists tout a "public interest" motivation for regulation. Michael French and Jim Phillips applied these theories to the regulation of food, beverages, and drugs in the United Kingdom between 1875 and 1938. They acknowledged the possibility of firms capturing regulators: "producers constitute a relatively small coherent group, possessing relevant expertise, information and financial resources, plus a keen interest in the outcome of regulations touching on their business affairs." They denoted two scenarios for capture. In one scenario, a group of firms within an industry, "decides on [their] regulatory objectives and lobbies successfully for suitable legislation." In the second scenario, the firms within an industry must thwart another interest group's attempt to regulate the industry. The firms within the regulated industry react "to ensure that the final character of any measures suits its purposes rather than those of the original advocates of intervention. While these two forms of 'capture' could result in identical outcomes, they involve rather different processes in terms of how regulation is initiated and the relationships between different lobbies." Industries, though, are vulnerable to exaggerated charges of doing harm. Regulatory entrepreneurs are sometimes adept at presenting dramatic if misleading evidence that motivates the public to clamor for regulation; on many occasions, the crises are not as dire as depicted. In other cases, firms in an industry are envied and subsequently threatened by producers of rival goods (or sometimes similar goods). Producers who are losing in the marketplace may disparage their rivals by claiming fraud and danger. By appealing to the public interest, such firms may be able to squelch their more-successful rivals or to prevent the entry of potentially formidable rivals (French and Phillips 2000, 6, 8, 11; Stigler 1975a, 116–119). The long-standing feuds between local butchers and meat packers or butter and margarine producers exemplify the process.

Regulations' Limitations

An economist found that pure food and dairy regulations had minimal effects upon prices, suggesting that the market-power thesis was not a big factor. There was one exception, though; the butter industry was battling oleomargarine and wanted restrictions against the new product. What legislation was passed only slowed down the rate of decrease in butter prices. Some producers tried to pass oleomargarine for butter; because butter sold at a premium, the incentive to deceive consumers was tempting (Law 2003, 1113–1115).

Large, well-established firms often backed legislation. British food producers, such as Colman's, Fry's, and Van Houten's, "declared their willingness to have the manufacturer's invoice accepted as warranty, especially for proprietary or packaged goods, so that action under the Safe Food and Drugs Act (SFDA) would be brought against the producer rather the retailer .... Indeed, several producers had attempted to gain a market advantage from the 1875 legislation by invoking its legal guarantee in packaging or marketing materials."

British Parliamentarians found industry leaders such as George Cadbury persuasive; Cadbury claimed that large, reputable producers did not need regulation, as the impetus to maintain their reputation through branded goods and the force of market competition were sufficient. Some producers, such as Jeremiah Colman bemoaned the 1872 Food Act that levied fines upon his mustard that contained turmeric, chilies, and other ingredients; Colman argued that such additives made his product more pleasing to customers' palates. Colman pointed out that he sold his mustard as a "manufactured condiment" rather than as pure mustard. In a similar vein, Joseph Storrs Fry testified that he added sugar and starches, including arrowroot and sago, in order to make his cocoa more soluble and better tasting. Colman and Fry said their products were accurately labeled and would now run afoul of proposed amendments to the food act (French and Phillips 2000, 35–36, 46, 156).

In the United States, the Food and Drug Administration found it difficult to write legislation to curtail fraudsters duping the public. If using the mails was blocked, fraudsters recruited door-to-door salespeople. Other fraudsters, such as Dudley LeBlanc and his Hadacol and Adolphus Hohensee, played the victim card, claiming to be persecuted visionaries. Many customers believed such bleatings and blamed government officials and the big pharmaceutical companies for hounding LeBlanc and Hohensee, who were folk heroes (Gratzer 2005, 207).

Conclusion

Although it is true that some dubious products, such as Lydia Pinkham's various elixirs persisted, Ms. Pinkham (she was long dead by the time her products reached their greatest popularity) and her purveyors never amassed the fortunes that retailers Marshall Field and Julius Rosenwald did (Stigler 1975b, 179; Sullivan 1927, 2:512–513).

Despite a plethora of regulations, grocery stores sell food containing additives, and consumers still seek out miracle cures from persuasive schemers. Market forces create an impetus for quality food and drugs, but competition does not completely eliminate fraudsters.

Customers must seek advice from trusted experts and rely upon their own efforts to ascertain product quality and purity.

Food poisoning remains common, and opioid overuse demonstrates that useful drugs can be abused. The desire to be cured or to be out of pain remains strong; there remains many suppliers willing to supply dubious cures. Eternal vigilance and competition in the marketplace remain consumers' strongest defense along with hiring trusted experts for consultation.

Wartime Ethics

The American Civil War was a watershed event in the history of business ethics in America. The federal government's spending soared and its oversight initially lagged. Northerners faced a buffet of temptations, and many businessmen and government officials subscribed to the idea that it was an ill war that brought no easy money. Antebellum businessmen gorged themselves at the government troughs during times of peace, so wartime corruption was not a new phenomenon or something peculiar to the subsequent Gilded Age.

Business Ethics Aspects

Business ethics considerations infused the struggle. The key issue trigging the war was slavery, although both sides cloaked their rationales for going to war; southerners argued they had a right to secede under a state's right doctrine, while northerners argued the Union was sacred. Had there been no controversy about the morality and the ultimate extent or expansion of slavery, however, the impetus toward secession would have been absent or muted. Although the abolition movement had scored successes in Great Britain and the United States—a prohibition on the trans-Atlantic slave trade, as well as the abolition of slavery in England and its former colonies and in the northern states—slavery retained its vitality in many places.

A more immediate question, though, was whether southern planters should honor their debts to northern businesses. Historian Scott Marler believed that, "For most Louisiana merchants, the ingrained habits of intra-mercantile honor died hard. A businessman's reputation for integrity demanded that obligations contracted in good faith be respected." Some southern businessmen attempted to repay their debts after the war. Northerners often chose to believe that the southern businessmen opted for secession in hopes of evading debts; notorious Union general and politician Benjamin Butler argued that the prospect of repudiating debts was a key "inducement to the commercial classes of the South to go into the Rebellion." Marler concluded, "although there is no evidence for insinuations that merchants backed secession to gain windfall profits from cancelling their outstanding debts, perceptions are often as important as reality (Marler 2013, 125–126)."

Some New York business executives sympathized with the southerners. Richard Lathers, a northern businessman from South Carolina, favorably contrasted southern planters with northern businessmen; he considered southern planters as "gentlemen of culture" who upheld "a remarkably high standard of public and private integrity." Northerners, instead, pursued wealth and frequently succumbed to the temptations of engaging in fraud and corruption. John A. Dix, Democrat but later a general in the Union Army, believed that merchants "were partly to blame for the frenetic speculation and ensuing economic collapse [due to the Panic of 1857] and were consequently obliged to aid innocent victims of rapid economic expansion." Many of his fellow Democrats had no stomach for war and urged a peaceful secession (Bernstein 1990, 134, 141).

Many New York merchants held common cause with southern planters to uphold free trade and white supremacy. They talked openly about New York City seceding from the Union and becoming a free city. These merchants, mostly Democrats, found the Republicans' hurried passage of the Morrill Tariff perturbing. These men would later find Lincoln's Emancipation Proclamation anathema. Despite these defections, a historian wrote, "it is fortunate that the business leaders did rally to the defense of the Union. Their money, leadership, and talent for organization enabled them to furnish the floundering Federal government badly-needed regiments quickly (Frost 1961, 278; see also Bernstein 1990, 143, 145)."

Antecedents of Corruption

Government spending for internal improvements such as canals and railroads was a well-established tradition before the Civil War. After the Erie Canal radically transformed New York's economy, governments eagerly sponsored and financed canals and railroads; such endeavors had mixed benefits. Although efforts to gain legislative approval of charted private endeavors often inspired corruption, in the case of canals the opportunity for corruption lay more in the bidding and building by private contractors. By examining ratios of actual expenditures to estimated costs, two economists reveal that subsequent canal building, as well as large public projects in the twentieth century, suffered greater relative cost over-runs than the original Erie Canal project (Engerman and Sokoloff 2006, 3–4, 12–16, 18–24).

Antebellum businesspeople were accustomed to offering payments as persuasive tools. The Erie Canal backers gave land to legislators. An example of the disreputable behavior of the railroad officials and legislators occurred in Wisconsin. Because legislators in that state voted on whether to approve charters of incorporation, investors with legitimate projects could face obstacles in proceeding. Therefore, even honest entrepreneurs faced the unsavory task of persuading legislators who opposed granting charters, whether out of heartfelt belief or to protect cronies, with financial inducements, including bribes (Gras 1945, 116).

Railroad managers of the LaCrosse and Milwaukee attempted to bribe Wisconsin legislators in 1858. Historian Mark Summers wrote, "It is hard to say which was more depressing, the lack of ethics or the lack of finesse on both sides ... the thieves had come to see stealing as one of the privilege of office .... A few officials accepted their bribes as though they were fees for services rendered and felt no remorse .... Buying lawmakers was a hallowed tradition." When the railroad officials attempted to recall the bonds, some legislators waxed indignant. S.W. Barnes [no first name given] whined, "But it is of recent occurrence that having obtained the benefits ... they should repudiate the very means by which they succeeded (Summers 1987, 110–111, Madison *Daily State Journal*, July 31, 1858, no page numbers)."[7] The legislators were brazen, with only two bothering to deny the charge of corruption.

Early Days of Chaos

To equip the troops required to suppress the rebellion, the Lincoln administration needed to rush purchases of supplies and armaments for the expanding army and navy. Some historians contended that early in the Civil War, "the contractors and officials ... reveled in a saturnalia of graft." Ludwell Johnson described Union war effort as exhibiting, "favoritism, greed, dishonesty and treachery." Historian Stuart Brandes argued that many commentators alleging widespread corruption "have based their assessment on the improvised, haphazard procedures of the early days of the war rather than on an examination of full record of the conflict." He concluded, "the real Civil War was a mixed record of waste and efficiency, of profit and loss, of fraud and sacrifice," but by 1865, "the troops recognized the growing efficiency and basic selflessness behind the war effort (Shannon 1928, I:71–73; Johnson 1966, 115; Brandes 1997, 68, 107)."

To augment the military's small peacetime cadre of administrators, the federal government benefited from having access to a pool of trained, experienced businessmen, who were adept at managing large organizations. The Lincoln administration elevated members from this pool of talent to high government positions to help the various cabinet members. Some northern businessmen volunteered their services. Brandes believed that increased congressional scrutiny and military quartermasters, "boldly streamlined the procurement process, most by shifting contracting from the states to the federal government. These measures reduced, but could not eliminate the incidence of profiteering." He conceded that such ethically dubious practices as "extortionate pricing and degraded quality" and "plunder, privateering, trading with the enemy and bounty jumping" continued on occasion (Brandes 1997, 68; Wilson 2006, 58–60).

The War Department's Commission on Ordnance and Ordnance Stores concluded in July 1862 that the early days of the war were marked "by the lack of system which prevailed .... The general government itself employed, directly or indirectly, numerous agents not acting in unison, and often becoming, therefore, competitors of each other .... Under a system so ill considered, extravagance was unavoidable." The Commission, though, criticized the use of middlemen, "who had never dealt in arms and knew nothing of their value." The end result of employing such naifs was that large numbers of useless weapons resided in government arsenals, many of which, "being entirely unfit to be placed in the hands of civilized troops." The Commission characterized some of the middlemen as "mere speculators and adventurers," and chided buyers who did not deal directly with the arms manufacturers. These speculators gained contracts that they then sub-contracted to legitimate producers. The Commission characterized such middlemen as "generally rapacious and unscrupulous." Presumably the Commission adjusted the contracts awarded to such nefarious characters. The Commission also cited some men, who claimed to be able to procure contracts by use of political influence; in return, they demanded commissions for their services. The Commission noted that reputable businessmen were hesitant to seek contracts, due to the odium attached to the contracting process. This hesitance was regrettable: "In no class of persons are the qualities which distinguish the best business men of our country—talent, integrity, enterprise, resource, perseverance—more needed than in them. But if wholesale slurs affecting their character, because of their relations to the government, finally render the very name of a contractor a reproach, what can be the result, except that the honest and the reputable will stand back, and that their places will be filled by men careless of their good name, if only money can be made by the sacrifice (U.S. Congress, Senate 1862, 14–18)."

As the Civil War progressed, allegations of price gouging became common. Increased demand for war supplies would have triggered increases in prices regardless of any corruption, so holders of inventories of war supplies in 1861 would have inevitably enjoyed initial windfall profits. The general price level doubled during the war, so much of the increased prices of munitions, armaments, and supplies may have reflected the general rise in prices. The government successfully prosecuted few alleged war profiteers. Newspaper editors and public anger might have exerted some effect upon businessmen, but others chose to be, "Vultures that prey upon the hearts of the dead on the battlefield, are human compared with monsters who furnish rotten blankets and rotten meat to the living in camp (*New York Daily Tribune*, May 25, 1861, 4; Brandes 1997, 102)."

Once President Lincoln decided to blockade southern ports, the need for a greatly expanded navy became urgent. Secretary of the Navy Gideon Welles enlisted businessman George Morgan to buy ships for the navy on commission. Morgan purchased 89 ships and received over $95,000 in commissions, which greatly exceeded President Lincoln's annual salary; Morgan apparently saved the navy hundreds of thousands of dollars through astute purchasing, but although he charged the usual 2.5 percent, some Congressional representatives resented his pocketing the tens of thousands of dollars in commission. Historian Stuart Brandes believed that Morgan's services could have been obtained at a lower cost, but given the exigency of the situation, Morgan performed a good service for the nation (Brandes 1997, 78).

The Union forces required considerable transport for troops and supplies within the interior of the country. Steamboat owners and railroads profited greatly from the war. The government opted to pay a flat rate per soldier per mile, so railroads scrambled to gain lucrative contracts for transporting large numbers of troops long distances. Sometimes the railroad officials "persuaded" military officers to choose their lines via side payments to the officers. One officer admitted accepting such persuasion from a railroad executive (U.S. Congress, House 1861, 2:631; Brandes 1997, 76).

Financing the War

The federal government used a combination of taxes, borrowing, and inflation to generate sufficient revenues to fight the war. An over-reliance upon taxes might have squelched production in the North. The North (and the Confederacy) knew the lesson of inflation; the deathless phrase, "Not worth a Continental!" from the Revolutionary War still echoed. Floating bonds to American citizens was a salute to the confidence in the growing economic power of the northern states and also avoided foreign indebtedness; the bonds also promised to moderate the inevitable rise in prices to a tolerable level. A key question was whether northerners would purchase enough of the war bonds. Few Americans were familiar with buying and selling bonds, and most Americans associated bonds with bankers (often with a tint of disrepute); certainly the Jacksonian distrust of big banks persisted (Lawson 2002, 43).

Financier Jay Cooke had petitioned Salmon Chase, Secretary of the Treasury, for the right to market war bonds on an exclusive basis. Cooke had been more successful than most bankers at selling bonds in the early years of the war, so Chase eventually relented. Matthew Josephson highlighted Cooke's alliances with various political leaders: "Cooke would have, by his own principles, not the slightest doubt or scruple in combining forces with the statesmen (Josephson [1934] 2011, 36, 54)."

As with many innovators of financial instruments, Cooke faced accusations of fraud. Other critics complained about the hundreds of thousands of dollars the government paid him for marketing the bonds. Cooke did not intend to be a "Dollar-a-year" man, as some executives were during World War II. He received a commission of 0.375 percent (later reduced to 0.25 percent of the price of the bonds), but given the immense value of the bonds he marketed, his commissions burgeoned. His commissions seemed outrageous to contemporaries, but having sold millions of dollars of bonds, his commissions do not appear to have been excessive, hovering around one-eighth of 1 percent. Cooke, himself, blandly justified his commissions: "We could not be expected to leave our comfortable homes and positions here without some great inducement and we state frankly that we would if we succeeded expect a fair commission from the treasury (Josephson [1934] 2011, 55–57; see also Lawson 2002, 46)."

Cooke understood how to market the bonds to a wide spectrum of the northern public, and he performed a valuable service for the government. Henrietta Larson, a biographer of Cooke, stated, "The Secretary's [of the Treasury] report on the cost of the loan showed that it had been remarkably low." Another historian lauded Cooke's wartime activities for: "his truly amazing success in selling government bonds to finance the Civil War after others had failed in the undertaking (Larson 1936, 148; Brandes 1997, 100; Hower 1936, 85)."

Trade Between the Belligerents

A particularly sordid aspect of the Civil War was trade between the belligerents. Trade between belligerents was nothing new for Americans. During the War of 1812, American citizens, especially in New England and New York, traded with their Canadian neighbors, who were supposedly enemies.

During the Civil War, Federal and Confederate officials recognized the importance of international and intra-regional trade for the Confederacy. Southern cotton growers collectively possessed price-setting power in the world market for raw cotton; the thousands of southern cotton growers supplied 70–80 percent of the raw cotton used by England, France, and New England during the antebellum years. Southern growers were unable to exploit their dominance in the market by collectively reducing the supply of raw cotton and reaping correspondingly higher prices, but the Confederate government might have levied an export duty upon cotton that would have exploited the region's price-setting power. Such a reduction in the crop would have freed up manpower to fight in the military while providing tax revenue from which to issue bonds to finance the war. Both Abraham Lincoln and Jefferson Davis recognized cotton's potential to affect European governments' actions regarding the Civil War. Lincoln sought to ensure that sufficient cotton reached European and New England producers to alleviate the economic dislocation (Surdam 2001, 111–117).[8]

After the Union defeat at Bull Run in July 1861, the Lincoln administration ordered a blockade of southern ports. The administration, however, did not institute privateering, as previous presidents had done during wartime. The blockade proved effective, especially as it drove a huge wedge between the prices of cotton at southern ports and ports in Europe and New York. As the price of raw cotton rose in New York City and Liverpool, its price stagnated at southern ports. Prices of flour and other foodstuffs skyrocketed at southern ports (and were even higher inland). If a northerner could ship packed meat and flour from New York City to a southern port in return for raw cotton, he stood to treble his investment; one observer estimated that such a trader might reap as much as a sixfold or greater gain (Surdam 1999, 301–302). As siren calls go, a potential sixfold gain on one's investment was well-nigh irresistible.

As Union military fortunes improved after the capture of Norfolk, Memphis, and New Orleans in 1862, Lincoln countenanced trade through these river ports. In some cases, he hoped to succor Unionists and to foster goodwill with former Confederates. Some of his generals disagreed with his policy. General William Tecumseh Sherman, although initially in favor of trading with the locals, eventually believed the trade benefited Confederate troops; a fellow general lamented, "Memphis has been of more value to the Southern Confederacy since it fell into Federal hands than Nassau [a key staging point for European and New York contraband destined for import into the Confederacy] (U.S. War Department 1902, Ser 1, 39:22)."

The interesting question is why Lincoln encouraged efforts to get raw cotton, when such federal programs were rife with potential for unethical behavior and scandal? He, himself, was quite scrupulous with regard to his personal finances. Massachusetts textile manufacturer Edward Atkinson persuaded Lincoln that because the price of cotton in New York City quadrupled, the southerners were collecting as much revenue as they had in 1860—a specious argument as the volume of raw cotton shipped was just one-ninth the antebellum volume (never mind the fact that southerners did not get all of the revenue from cotton sold in New York or Liverpool). Lincoln, though, found this argument useful; he re-phrased it, saying: "Better give [southerners] guns for it [cotton] than let [them], as now, get both guns and ammunition for it .... And if pecuniary greed can be made to aid us in such effort, let us be thankful that so much good can be got out of pecuniary greed." Lincoln had it reversed: The between-the-lines trade eliminated the greatly increased transportation costs, so southerners got "guns and ammunition" from the between-the-lines trade and only "guns" through the blockade (Lincoln 1953, VIII:163–164; Surdam 2001, 196).

Lincoln wanted a permit system that would keep any trader or group of traders from monopolizing the trade, so he insisted that all loyal citizens have an opportunity to apply for permits. Treasury officials were to verify the prospective trader's loyalty and claims that he possessed or controlled cotton within the south. The Treasury Department would pay three-fourths of the current market price for cotton; traders were allowed to send non-contraband items down south, but these items could only be no more than one-third the value of the cotton. To forestall a drain on the nation's supply of gold and to avoid succoring Confederate finances, prospective traders could only use Greenbacks to buy cotton. This policy failed to get sufficient cotton, so Congress passed the Purchasing Act of July 1864. This act did not create much of a flow of raw cotton—just 55,000 bales (out of the 1.5 to 2.0 million bales exported from the south during the war).

Although the system appeared well designed (if one ignores the dubious premise underlying the trade), Treasury Agent Hanson Risley was lax in checking whether prospective traders actually possessed cotton within the south. He approved permits for Lincoln's friends Leonard Swett, Provost-Marshal Ward Lamon (both from Illinois), and Samuel Noble, a Georgia planter, who claimed to own tens of thousands of bales of cotton scattered throughout the South. Risley did not ask how these men, some who had never dealt in cotton before, could possibly control such large amounts of cotton. Thurlow Weed, whom Lincoln relied upon as an ally in the key state of New York, also vouched for some prospective traders. It is not surprising that many men, enticed by the potential gains from the legalized trade, exploited their contacts with Honest Abe. Friends of Abe or friends of friends of Abe often received the coveted trade permits (Surdam 1999, 301–312).

Weed, Swett, Lamon, and most of the other permit holders were staunch Unionists. Perhaps they justified their actions in two ways. First, Lincoln stated that getting cotton was in the national interest. These traders were enriching themselves by getting cotton while simultaneously serving the national interest. Second, even if the traders recognized the specious rationales underlying the administration's policies toward cotton, each individual could persuade himself that his minuscule number of bales was not injuring the war effort. The traders' quest for permits was legal, but their actions in obtaining such permits induced them to engage in fraud and deceit.

Many northerners were skeptical of Lincoln's policies toward raw cotton. The congressional committee of 1864 rebuked the trade, as it "induced a spirit of speculation and plunder among the people, who have entered into a disgraceful scramble for wealth during a time of war, waged to save the life of the nation, and has fed that greed of gain which must wound the public morals .... It is believed to have led to the prolongation of the war, and to have cost the country thousands of lives and millions upon millions of treasure." The New York *Herald* editorialized that the war "was kept alive and the war prolonged by villainies carried on from our side [of] the lines by a league of the copperheads and of corrupt men in the confidence of the government (U.S. Congress, House 1865, 1–2; New York *Herald*, July 21, 1865, 2, 4)."

Conclusion

The Civil War introduced large-scale government expenditures and mobilization of troops, transportation and telegraphic services, and productive capacities. Most of the businesspeople fulfilled their contracts honorably and capably.

The Lincoln administration's policy of permitting inter-belligerent trade in order to get raw cotton was a dubious venture that could have jeopardized the war effort. The policy induced politicians and businesspeople to consider or to engage in dubious practices. Political partisanship, though, may have provided a counter to unethical activities, as numerous committees investigated allegations of wrongdoing; trying civilians in military courts, a questionable act in itself, deterred other potential miscreants. Secretary of War Edwin Stanton and Secretary of the Navy Gideon Welles were honest administrators, who strove to eliminate waste and corruption with the aid of civilian and military administrators; Lincoln, on occasion, impeded their efforts in order to mitigate political fallout from the blockade (Neely 1991, 94, 105–106). Whether business morals declined in comparison with antebellum practices was difficult to ascertain. Certainly, the activities of some businesspeople during the war presaged the consolidation of industries and development of new methods of finance and organization.

These examples revealed the opportunities for operators, scrupulous and unscrupulous and also the frequent ambiguity of ethical standards. America of the nineteenth century was a dynamic society. The national pastime of seeking the main chance drove many Americans to undertake new and novel, sometimes dubious endeavors. Although unethical behavior occurred, America became an economic powerhouse, and the benefits eventually percolated down to workers.

Notes

1. Thomas Safley referred to *banca rotta*, or "brokenbank," whereby the tables on which merchants transacted their business were broken (Safley 2009, 56).
2. The Equifax debacle occurred during the writing of this manuscript. Since consumers never gave Equifax and its two competitors expressed permission to collect information, one could argue that Equifax had an elevated duty to protect consumers' information.
3. Marion Crane, the woman on the lam in Alfred Hitchcock's *Psycho* would have been better served stopping at a national-brand motel instead of the Bates Motel.
4. The same author, in reviewing a previous article, "Death in the Pot!," excoriated chemists who, "are always defending adulteration of food, especially when it is done by large corporations which are able to pay fat fees for expert (?) testimony on the witness stand (*Independent* 1901, 1149)."
5. Benjamin Brandreth tried to cultivate a persona of public-spirited citizen through acts of charity, lack of ostentation, and willingness to keep his workers on the payroll during slack times (Young 1961, 88). Of course, paying for charity from funds acquired through selling dubious products raises troubling ethical questions.

6. Duffy used the 9847 figure without comment (1968, 430); for adulterated coffee, see (Okun 1986, 214). The 1850 Census listed New York City as having a population just over half a million. Losing almost 10,000 children should have raised an uproar.
7. Edward Glaeser and Claudia Goldin reported that "gifts of railway stock given to congressmen and others during the Credit Mobilier scandal were perfectly legal at the time (Glaeser and Goldin 2006, Introduction, 11)."
8. For detailed discussions of cotton's importance in the western world's economy during the 1860s, see Surdam (1998, 113–132); Surdam (1994, 122–145); Beckert (2014, 261–265).

Bibliography

Akerlof, George. "The Market for 'Lemons:' Quality Uncertainty and the Market Mechanism." *Quarterly Journal of Economics* 84(3), August 1970, 488–500.

Atherton, Lewis. "The Problem of Credit Rating in the Ante-Bellum South." *Journal of Southern History* 12(4), November 1946, 534–556.

Atherton, Lewis. *The Southern Country Store, 1800–1860* (New York, NY: Greenwood Press: [1949] 1968).

Atherton, Lewis. *The Frontier Merchant in Mid-America* (Columbia, MO: University of Missouri Press, 1971).

Balleisen, Edward. *Navigating Failure: Bankruptcy and Commercial Society in Antebellum America* (Chapel Hill, NC: University of North Carolina Press, 2001).

Balleisen, Edward. "Vulture Capitalism in Antebellum America: The 1841 Federal Bankruptcy Act and the Exploitation of Financial Distress." *Business History Review* 70(4), Winter 1996, 473–516.

Beckert, Sven. *Empire of Cotton: A Global History* (New York, NY: Knopf, 2014).

Bernstein, Iver. *The New York City Draft Riot: Their Significance for American Society and Politics in the Age of the Civil War* (New York, NY: Oxford University Press, 1990).

Brandes, Stuart. *Warhogs: A History of War Profits in America* (Lexington, KY: University Press of Kentucky, 1997).

Crellin, J.K. "Pharmaceutical History and Its Sources in the Wellcome Collections. 1. The Growth of Professionalism in Nineteenth-Century British Pharmacy." *Medical History* 11(03), July 1967, 215–227.

Duffy, John. *A History of Public Health in New York City, 1625–1866* (New York, NY: Russell Sage Foundation, 1968).

Engerman and Sokoloff. "Digging the Dirt at Public Expense." *Corruption and Reform: Lessons from America's Economic History*, edited by Edward Glaeser and Claudia Goldin (Chicago, IL: University of Chicago Press, 2006), 95–122.

Foulke, Roy. *The Sinews of American Commerce* (New York, NY: Dun & Bradstreet, 1941).

French, Michael and Jim Phillips. *Cheated not poisoned? Food regulation in the United Kingdom, 1875–1938* (Manchester, UK: Manchester University Press, 2000).

French, Michael and Jim Phillips. "Sophisticates or Dupes? Attitudes toward Food Consumers in Edwardian Britain." *Enterprise & Society* 4(3), September 2003, 442–70.

Frost, James. "The Home Front in New York during the Civil War." *New York History* 42(3), July 1961, 273–297.

Glaeser, Edward and Claudia Goldin. "Corruption and Reform: Introduction." *Corruption and Reform: Lessons from America's Economic History*, edited by Edward Glaeser and Claudia Goldin (Chicago, IL: University of Chicago Press, 2006), 3–22.

Gras, Norman. "Shifts in Public Relations." *Bulletin of the Business Historical Society* 19(4), October 1945, 97–148.

Gratzer, Walter. *Terrors of the Table: The Curious History of Nutrition* (Oxford, UK: Oxford University Press, 2005).

Hower, Ralph. "Some Remarks on Private Banking: Study of Jay Cooke given to Members." *Bulletin of the Business Historical Society* 10(6), December 1936, 85–88.

Independent. "Food Adulteration Scares." Vol. 53(2737), May 16, 1901, 1148–1150.

Independent. "The Exaggeration of Food Adulteration." January 5, 1905, 49–51.

Johnson, Ludwell. "Northern Profit and Profiteers: The Cotton Rings of 1864–1865." *Civil War History* 12(2), June 1966, 101–115.

Jones, John. *The Western Merchant: A Narrative. Containing Useful Instruction for the Western Man of Business Who Makes His Purchases in the East; also, Information for the Eastern Man Whose Customers Are in the West: Likewise, Hints for Those Who Design Emigrating to the West. Deduced from Actual Experience* (Philadelphia, PA: Grigg, Elliot, 1849). [Used Luke Shortfield as pseudonym.]

Jonson, Ben. *The Dramatic Works of Ben Jonson, and Beaumont and Fletcher* (London, UK: John Stockdale, 1811). 4 vols.

Josephson, Matthew. *The Robber Barons: The Great American Capitalists, 1861–1901* (New Brunswick, NJ: Transaction Publisher, [1934] 2011). September 8, 1883, 281–285.

Klein, Benjamin and Keith Leffler, "Role of Market Forces in Assuring Contractual Performance." *Journal of Political Economy* 9(4), August 1981, 615–641.

Larson, Harriet. *Jay Cooke, Private Banker* (Cambridge, MA: Harvard University Press, 1936).

Law, Marc. "Origins of State Pure Food Regulation." *Journal of Economic History* 63(4), December 2003, 1103–1130.
Lawson, Melinda. *Patriot Fires: Forging a New American Nationalism in the Civil War North* (Lawrence, KS: University Press of Kansas, 2002).
Lincoln, Abraham. *The Collected Works of Abraham Lincoln*, edited by Roy Basler (New Brunswick, NJ: Rutgers University Press 1953). X vols.
Madison *Daily State*. July 31, 1858.
Marler, Scott. *The Merchants' Capital: New Orleans and the Political Economy of the Nineteenth-Century South* (Cambridge, MA: Cambridge University Press, 2013).
Neely, Mark, Jr. *The Fate of Liberty: Abraham Lincoln and Civil Liberties* (New York, NY: Oxford University Press, 1991).
New York Daily Tribune. "Army Peculation." May 25, 1861, 4.
New York Herald. July 21, 1865, 2 and 4.
New York Times. "Adulterated Drugs, Drinks, and Diet." March 9, 1854, 4.
New York Times. "Fatal Poisoning by a Druggist's Mistake." April 24, 1867a, 5.
New York Times. "Sure to Regulate the Bowels." April 24, 1867b, 5.
Okun, Mitchell. *Fair Play in the Marketplace: The First Battle for Pure Food and Drugs* (Dekalb, IL: Northern Illinois University Press 1986).
Olmstead, Alan and Paul Rhode. *Creating Abundance: Biological Innovation and American Agricultural Development* (New York, NY: Cambridge University Press, 2008).
Porter, Roy. "Before the Fringe: 'Quackery' and the Eighteenth-Century Medical Market." *Studies in the History of Alternative Medicines*, edited by R. Cooter (London, UK: Palgrave Macmillan, 1988), 1–27.
Safley, Thomas. "Business Failure and Civil Scandal in Early Modern Europe." *Business History Review* 83(1), Spring 2009, 35–60.
Sandage, Scott. *Born Losers: A History of Failure in America* (Cambridge, MA, Harvard University Press, 2005).
Shannon, Fred. *The Organization and Administration of the Union Army, 1861–1865* (Cleveland, OH: Arthur H. Clark, 1928), 2 vols.
Stigler, George. "Can Regulatory Agencies Protect the Consumer?" *The Citizen and the State: Essays on Regulation* (Chicago, IL: University of Chicago Press, 1975a). 178–188.
Stigler, George. "Theory of Economic Regulation." *The Citizen and the State: Essays on Regulation* (Chicago, IL: University of Chicago Press, 1975b). 114–144.
Sullivan, Mark. *Our Times: The United States, 1900–1925. Vol. II. America Finding Herself* (New York, NY: Charles Scribner's Sons, 1927). 6 vols.
Summers, Mark. *The Plundering Generation: Corruption and the Crisis of the Union, 1849–1881* (New York, NY: Oxford University Press, 1987).

Surdam, David. "Cotton's Potential as Economic Weapon: The Antebellum and Wartime Markets for Cotton Textiles." *Agricultural History* 68(2), Spring 1994, 122–145.

Surdam, David G. 1998. King Cotton: Monarch or Pretender? The State of the Market for Raw Cotton on the Eve of the American Civil War. *Economic History Review*, 51, February, 113–132.

Surdam, David. "Traders or Traitors: Northern Cotton Trading During the Civil War." *Business and Economic History* 28(2), Winter 1999, 301–312.

Surdam, David. *Northern Naval Superiority and the Economics of the American Civil War* (Columbia, SC: University of South Carolina Press, 2001).

Thoreau, Henry. *The Portable Thoreau* (New York, NY: Penguin Books, [1947] 1977).

Treiman, Israel. "Acts of Bankruptcy: A Medieval Concept in Modern Bankruptcy Law." *Harvard Law Review* 52(2), December 1938, 189–215.

U.S. Congress. House. *Government Contracts.* 37th Cong., 2nd Sess. Report No. 2 (Washington, D.C.: GPO, 1861), 2 vols.

U.S. Congress. House. *Trade with Rebellious States.* House Report No. 24, 38th Cong., 2nd Sess. (Washington, D.C.: Government Printing Office, 1865).

U.S. Congress. Senate. *Letter of the Secretary of War, transmitting, In answer to a resolution of the Senate, a copy of the report of the commission on ordnance and ordnance stores made to the War Department.* 37th Cong., 2nd Sess. Ex. Doc. No. 72. (Washington, D.C.: GPO, 1862).

U.S. War Department. *The War of the Rebellion: A Compilation of the Official Records of the Union and Confederate Armies in the War of the Rebellion* (Washington, D.C.: Government Printing Office, 1880–1902).

Weisberg, Robert. "Commercial Morality, the Merchant Character, and the History of the Voidable Preference." *Stanford Law Review* 39(1), November 1986, 3–138.

Whorton, James. *The Arsenic Century: How Victorian Britain Was Poisoned at Home, Work, and Play* (Oxford, UK: Oxford University Press, 2010).

Wilkins, Mira. "When and why brand names in food and drink?" in *Adding Value: Brands and Marketing in Food and Drink*, edited by Geoffrey Jones and Nicholas Morgan (London: Routledge, 1994), 15–40.

Wilson, Mark R. *The Business of Civil War: Military Mobilization and the State, 1861–1865* (Baltimore, MD: Johns Hopkins University Press, 2006).

Wood, Donna. "Strategic Use of Public Policy: Business Support for the 1906 Food and Drug Act." *Business History Review* 59(3), Autumn 1985, 403–32.

Wyatt-Brown, Bertram. "God and Dun & Bradstreet, 1841–1851." *Business History Review*, XL(4), Winter 1966, 432–450.

Young, James. *The Toadstool Millionaires: A Social History of Patent Medicines in America before Federal Regulation* (Princeton, NJ: Princeton University Press, 1961).

CHAPTER 4

Rise of Industrialization

The rise of mass production in such industries as textiles, meat packing, chemicals, tobacco, iron, and oil changed American and European economies. Capturing the benefits of large-scale production often resulted in industry concentration (Chandler 1977, 282–283).

Rapid technological changes created incredibly lucrative opportunities for those willing to take the risks in harnessing the new technologies to a marketable form. Cornelius Vanderbilt, Andrew Carnegie, James Duke, and John D. Rockefeller were not always the innovators, but they recognized how the technologies could meet consumer and business needs. Two scholars characterized these upheavals: "A hallmark of the market system in times of rapid change is to bestow enormous wealth on a few lucky or greedy individuals, and to dispossess many good people …. Moral outrage is natural." These authors acknowledged that the market system and the attendant upheavals conferred material benefits that improved the living standards of the poor, such as better nutrition and the ability to finance public health infrastructure. The transformation created social upheaval and disrupted societal mores (Friedman and McNeill 2013, 63–64).

The era spawned the introduction of so-called robber barons, but these characters differed in their business practices. Ethical issues swirled about the century's prize technological advance: railroads. From financing to setting rates, the public took a keen interest in railroad executives' and owners' activities. Railroads, of course, were not the only new, large-scale

D. G. Surdam, *Business Ethics from the 19th Century to Today*,
https://doi.org/10.1007/978-3-030-37169-2_4

industries. The public gradually realized that under certain circumstances, large-scale and even monopolistic firms benefited consumers, reversing millennia of suspicions toward and disapproval of monopolies. The public expected responsible use of concentrated economic power, especially when such power was granted under state-granted incorporation privileges.

Origins of the "Robber Baron" Concept

Historian Hal Bridges traces the history of the "Robber Baron" depiction of the Gilded Age industrialists and financiers. He identifies an article in *The Nation*, circa 1869, in which the author referred to Cornelius Vanderbilt as "a lineal successor of the mediaeval baron." Henry Demarest Lloyd's *Wealth against Commonwealth* in 1894 developed the argument of the rapacious robber barons, although Bridges characterized Lloyd's work as propaganda. Lloyd's work, though, exerted great influence upon the public's perception of the industrialists (Bridges 1958, 1–3; see also Godkin 1869, 431–432).

Carl Schurz, a German immigrant to American and Civil War general, possibly coined the term "Robber Barons" in a speech at Harvard, comparing the big business leaders of 1882 to the feudal nobility of the Middle Ages; just prior to Schurz' speech, Lloyd may have inspired Schurz' choice of words. It didn't take long for the epithet to capture the imagination of Americans: "by 1900 'Robber Baron' not only had become a journalistic synonym for a certain disreputable type of big businessman but carried the further insinuation that pernicious conduct was typical of all big businessmen, amounting to nothing less than a wholesale indictment of the entire business elite (Tipple 1959, 511)."

The industrialists were motivated by a mixture of goals. Allan Nevins speculated (and speculation was pretty much all any commentator could do in this case) that John D. Rockefeller was motivated not solely by greed of gain, but by "competitive achievement, self-expression, and the imposition of their wills on a given environment (Nevins 1940, I:603–622, II: 707–714)."[1]

Matthew Josephson's entertaining *The Robber Barons* was typical of the portrayals of industrialists as relentlessly opportunistic and unscrupulous characters. He published his book in 1934. His lack of training in economics and the still raw emotional edge of the industrialization of the United States during the previous half-century colored his effort. In his preface he acknowledged that the industrialists transformed the American economy into an efficient "corps of producers," but accompanied by, "an uncontrolled appetite for private profit." He claimed that this was a "great inherent contradiction whence so much disaster, outrage and misery has flowed."

An example of Josephson's flair for the colorful and amusing anecdote was his depiction of Daniel Drew. Drew was known for his "handkerchief trick." On a hot day, when things were looking bleak for Drew's holdings, he would pull out his bandana handkerchief "to mop his brow before sitting down with some fellow speculators. A slip of paper bearing a 'point,' or tip, fell to the floor; a bystander put his foot on it." As Drew hoped, the greedy speculators read the missive and bought Erie Railroad stock; Drew's missive proved deceptive, and the speculators founded themselves "gulled.

William Vanderbilt, son of Commodore Cornelius Vanderbilt, gained infamy with his quote, "The public be damned." In today's world, Vanderbilt would have claimed to have been quoted out of context. For once, such a plaint would have been correct. Josephson, no admirer of business leaders, observed that Vanderbilt was explaining that he terminated some trains between Chicago and New York, because such trains were not profitable, even though the public wanted the trains. "'The public be damned. I am working for my stockholders,' he had answered his interlocutor. 'If the public want the train why don't they pay for it?'" Vanderbilt had never heard of corporate social responsibility or stakeholder theory. His famous outburst, however, had thrown a harsh light upon the inordinate power enjoyed by the railroad barons (Josephson [1934] 2011, viii, 19, 187).[2]

Many of the historians writing in the first half of the twentieth century were characterized by a historian, Richard Hofstadter, as a "discontented professoriat of the Progressive Era," including Charles and Mary Beard and Vernon Parrington. These professors disliked American business civilization, and they resented the businessman-dominated boards of trustees at their universities. Some of the businessmen violated academic freedom by pressuring presidents to terminate scholars with contrary views. More importantly, historians writing in the first decades of the twentieth century often lacked access to the business records; instead they relied upon the "sensational and sordid events." The Beards, at least, recognized that the business expansion had "never been subjected to scientific analysis."

Charles Francis Adams Jr. had been a railroad executive and in his private correspondence bemoaned that some of his contemporaries, such as Daniel Drew, Cornelius Vanderbilt, and Jay Gould resembled or exceeded "the old robber barons" in terms of thievery. Adams admitted that he wished he had been more successful financially, so that he could have bequeathed a larger sum to his alma mater Harvard (Hofstadter quoted in Bridges 1958, 5–6, 8–9; Beard and Beard [1927] 1933, II:198).

Many prominent historians admitted that John D. Rockefeller cut costs and improved efficiency within the oil industry, but they still viewed his achievements as ill-gotten. One damned Standard Oil and Rockefeller with faint praise: "Rockefeller exploited every possible technical advance and employed fair means and foul to persuade competitors either to sell out or to join forces .... Rockefeller competed ruthlessly not primarily to crush other refiners but to persuade them to join with him, to share the business peaceably and rationally so that all could profit .... Competition almost disappeared; prices steadied; profits skyrocketed (Folsom [1987] 1996, 122–123; see also Garraty 1991, 519–520)."

Allan Nevins took a more nuanced stance in his biography of John D. Rockefeller. He quoted economist Alfred Marshall, who attributed the Standard Oil trust to, "a combination of exceptional constructive ability and astute destructive strategy." Nevins concluded Rockefeller and his associates used methods that were sometimes "morally wrong as well as unlawful" but these were "a natural and even inevitable response to the cutthroat competition of the times." Few Americans knew that Germany, among other countries, was promoting industrial cartels. Nevins and another historian also highlighted the fact that business ethics were changing during the late nineteenth century (Bridges 1958, 10).

Business historian Norman (N.S.B.) Gras took a pragmatic view of business ethics. He pointed out that business owners are "not in business for the love of our fellow-man, but that [they] are content to serve him for a profit." He argued that business owners had to be selfish in order to survive, but their success depended upon providing service to society. "[S]ince the service provided to the public is vital to society, there is complete justification for the policy." The public usually does not understand this aspect and, instead, demands that businessmen provide services without profiting: "The New Deal championed profitless prosperity and got nowhere in a short time." Gras cautioned, "But human selfishness may be conciliatory, broad-gauged, and keyed to the long-time point of view; in other words, the selfishness may be intelligent." He suggested that businesspeople should employ public relations to inform and to educate (and not to obfuscate or mislead) the public (Gras 1945, 102).

The Industrialists and Their Critics

Historians and economists have tried to ascertain whether the leading industrialists represented the Horatio Alger rags-to-riches story. Andrew Carnegie certainly rose from poverty to sheer wealth, and John D. Rockefeller (and his brother William) grew up in modest circumstances. But John Pierpont (J.P.) Morgan was born into wealth, and many of the later executives, not the original entrepreneurs, hailed from families with enough wealth to give them excellent educations. Historian Ralph Andreano recounted how difficult answering this question was, because of difficulties in definition and conceptual aspects, such as including family wealth and occupation. Andreano pointed out that in the early twentieth century, Jewish immigrants of modest means and education assumed leading positions in the motion pictures, retail, and textile industries. He concluded that "there is not sufficient statistical evidence at present to reject the Horatio Alger legend (Andreano 1973, 228–230, 241–243)."

There were some rags-to-riches entrepreneurs in Japan, a country with a more rigid social structure than America. Zuiken Kawamura was a more colorful if somewhat less reputable entrepreneur, who started as a laborer and became extremely wealthy and was made a *hatamoto*, a member of the elite within the samurai. His story is truly an exemplar of a Horatio Alger story. Because of his abilities to cut costs and still do good work, he outbid his construction competitors and won many projects. Bakufu officials often enlisted his advice on projects, which undoubtedly helped his own business. When a fire in 1657 hit his large town, he immediately "ran by day and night, with all the cash that he could lay his hands on, to Kiso, the major lumber supply region for Edo." He immediately purchased all the lumber in Kiso, using his cash as a down payment. He apparently did not inform the Kiso lumbermen of the fire. With the lumber, he could command very high prices back in his devastated town; he made a tremendous killing (Yamamura 1973, 179–180).

Historian Carl Destler studied the careers of 43 leading industrialists of the antebellum era. He found that "considerable success in exploitation of business opportunities involving little or no risk" characterized many of their ventures. Several of these men contributed to the development of monopoly or speculative techniques; a few pioneered new ways of manipulating legislators. Only four of them created innovation in the principles of sound corporate finance: James J. Hill, Edward H. Harriman, J.P. Pierpont Morgan, and John D. Rockefeller. Although 36 of the 43 used some form of monopoly power in their ascent, only two-thirds of these charged exorbitant rates once they achieved monopoly power. He castigated the Erie ring, Rockefeller clique, and Huntington group: their "effect upon the general level of business and civic ethics was seriously degrading …. The huge private fortunes of the 'Big Four' [Collis Huntington, Leland Stanford, Charles Crocker, and Mark Hopkins] were the measure of their success in reaping at little or no risk rich profits in construction and monopolistic operation, to which they added the returns from canny speculation in California real estate." Several of these men either controlled or manipulated the press; Destler singled out the Standard Oil as unique: "not only in the propaganda that emanated from its members and in the press it subsidized in defense of monopoly and large-scale organization as such, but also in the subsidy it gave a supposedly learned journal, *The Social Economist*, and its editor, George Gunton, even after he became a professor at Columbia University," but these antics may have occurred fairly late in the Standard Oil's experience.[3]

Destler admitted that the first generation of Standard Oil men "rate somewhat higher as entrepreneurs," although they initially gained success by "muscling in" upon the nascent oil industry as allies of the Erie Railroad ring. "The daring, ruthlessness, and tactical skill with which this venture was carried out will long command admiration as a masterpiece of the piratical art." He chided the Standard Oil for contributing little to the "improvement of the basic technology of petroleum" prior to the twentieth century, but he acknowledged Rockefeller group's "consummate skill in lowering production costs, in merchandising, and in maintaining the efficiency and altering the legal form of an organization … and showed great tenacity of purpose in maintaining the monopoly that they had achieved by illicit methods (Destler 1946, 40–49)." In reaching his conclusion, Destler relied upon Ida Tarbell's *Standard Oil* and Allan Nevins *John D. Rockefeller*, so, at least, he had a mix of opinions.

Another study of the careers of prominent late nineteenth- and early twentieth-century business entrepreneurs by economic historian Jonathan R.T. Hughes, dubbed some of the industrialists as, "The Vital Few." He made the point similar to this book that "morals change." The early 1900s featured the muckrakers, who did much to shape modern-day understanding of the so-called robber barons. Hughes observed: "The muckrakers left a baffling morass of special pleading and bias which is great fun for the reader but which is largely incoherent except as entertainment." He was less interested in the Rockefeller's and Morgan's "moral eccentricities" than in examining the economic environment in which they operated. Hughes used economics to analyze the industrialists' actions: "We don't ask whether a man's acts were 'good' or 'bad' in a moral sense." These leaders of American industry, though, may have been, in part, creations of their era, who reaped extraordinary rewards for their unique skills.

For instance, according to Hughes, the London *Economist* described J.P. Morgan in an obituary: "Mr. Morgan ... was a typical American banker—quick, resolute, highly speculative, well versed in all the arts of the stock exchange, in company promotion, in the control of banks and other corporations, and, above all, in trusts, pools, syndicates and agreements. All his competitors regarded him as their superior. He was the Napoleon of Wall Street (Hughes [1965] 1986, 403–404)."

For Destler, J.P. Morgan was a mixture of good and bad. He applauded Morgan for ending the abuses associated with the financial management of many railroad companies, but he repeated the accusations that Morgan manipulated the stock market (Destler 1946, 46).

Morgan was a man of rectitude; he had his code of business behavior and adhered to it. He believed in the importance of "character." His religious background was a legacy of his ancestors—staunch Episcopalians. Similar to John D. Rockefeller, he espoused religious strictures regarding behavior, and both served their churches. Morgan was a long-time vestryman, and one imagines it took a brave soul to refuse to put money in the offering plate with J.P. Morgan watching. Hughes, while not subjecting Morgan to amateur psycho-analysis, observed that "Morgan would be an easier subject for his biographers if he had in fact been the stereotyped ogre of railroads and banks and steel that the muckrakers wrote about." During the Panic of 1907, just before Morgan took his famous walk across Wall Street, he exhorted the Protestant clergy of the city: "It is time for reaffirming faith. Beseech your congregations on Sunday to leave their money in the banks (Hughes [1965] 1986, 408–410; Silk 1983, D2)."

Morgan's critics chided him for speculating in the gold market during the American Civil War. In fact, Morgan's father opposed his son's involvement in speculation. Hughes derided the historians who described Morgan's speculations with opprobrium; these historians apparently thought Morgan should have ignored financial realities in his gold speculations and bought gold at the government prices, but he would have gone broke doing so. "Biographers should read books about banking." Hughes' snide but appropriate remark is useful; many actions considered disreputable if not unethical reflects a commentator's bias against or ignorance about business activities.

Certain of the London *Economist's* laudatory statements might attract a muckraker historian wielding "an opprobrious pen," but economists might interpret Morgan as simply an exceptionally adept practitioner of "organization and reorganization." Hughes suggested, though, that Morgan did not "create his own world" but exploited the "advantages that came his way." Morgan was, in essence, an exceptional man of his times (Hughes [1965] 1986, 404, 412). Morgan happened to live during interesting times, and he understood and was willing to take his opportunities with regard to America's industrial transformation.

Gilded Age "Robber Barons" need to be distinguished from beneficial businessmen, who built good railroads or provided quality products at often ever-cheaper prices. In Burton Folsom's view, the true robber barons are those who exploited government largesse: "Market entrepreneurs made decisive and unique contributions to American economic development. The political entrepreneurs stifled productivity (through monopolies and pools), corrupted business and politics, and dulled America's competitive edge." The market entrepreneurs, including John D. Rockefeller, James J. Hill, and Charles Schwab, "usually innovated, cut costs, and competed effectively in an open economy." The political entrepreneurs, including Leland Stanford, Charles Crocker, Henry Villard, and the Union Pacific builders, who "tried to succeed primarily through federal aid, pools, vote-buying, or stock speculation (Folsom [1987] 1996, 131–132)."

There was a dichotomy in American attitudes toward petty capitalists and industrial capitalists identified by business historian Norman Gras. Much sentiment lies with the former, while animus is directed toward the latter. Sensational muckraking journalists, such as Ida Tarbell and Lincoln Steffens, matched by the wondrous literary talents of Jack London and Upton Sinclair, highlighted alleged perfidy and malfeasance by the industrialists; their writings held sway among the reading public, possibly because many Americans, anxious about the rapidly changing economy, were predisposed to suspect the worst about the rich industrialists. Gras concluded that "the work of Rockefeller and the others, when appraised from the social point of view, appears to have been actually for the public welfare. If so, the shades of Ida Tarbell, Henry Demarest Lloyd, and John Moody may well pass on to their final resting place of quiet oblivion. For some time the evidence has been accumulating that they were journalists and not too white [referring to "yellow" journalism] (Gras 1941, 49–50)."

Morgan, Rockefeller, and their contemporaries operated in an economic free-for-all. To be sure, there were rules governing business behavior, but the evolution of business activities quickly rendered many time-honored regulations obsolete. Their actions were, strictly speaking, not illegal, even if reprehensible in the eyes of many. Competition became, to use the clichés, ruinous and cutthroat. The public needed some readily identifiable target upon which to vent their frustrations and fears regarding the economic whirlwind swirling about them. Morgan, Rockefeller, and Carnegie became handy scapegoats. Hughes summed up the situation thusly: "A nation which wanted more, not less, competition in industry had a right to change the rules of the game of American capitalism. But it is only justice to observe that, in the process, Morgan became the victim of ex post facto proceedings. But so did many others (Hughes [1965] 1986, 419)."

As the pioneers of America's postbellum wave of industrialization retired or died, their places were taken by heirs or by professional managers. A historian, Constance Green, noted, "The builders of a business, unscrupulously or fairly intent though they may be upon establishing their power, have at least the justification of creating." She thought that "the inheritance of power may be one factor in its abuse .... The second generation made it their first concern to entrench themselves in control, regardless of consequences to employees, community as a whole, or stockholders (Green 1943, 23, 25; Beard and Beard [1927] 1933, II:175)."

A study of the backgrounds of the critics of the so-called Robber Barons by business historian John Tipple found that "compared with big businessmen, they [a sample of 50 representative critics] were a decidedly more homogenous group by origin and outlook as well as in the uniformity of their aims. Virtually all of them were native born .... The majority grew up in small towns, mostly in the Midwest, and came from middle-class families having professional or small business standing." Not too surprisingly, these critics' educational attainments "were far above the average of their day." They were a mix of academics, including economists Richard Ely and Thorstein Veblen; novelists, including William Dean Howells and Upton Sinclair; a President or two, including Woodrow Wilson; and just two major executives: Charles Francis Adams Jr. and Thomas Lawson.

Tipple wondered whether these critics had a personal reason to oppose Robber Barons, but he found only two with any adverse experiences with businesses: Ida Tarbell and Thomas Lawson. Tarbell's father, Frank Tarbell, had been involved with the oil boom in Pennsylvania, when Ida was very young. Certainly, contemporaries wondered whether her criticisms of John D. Rockefeller and Standard Oil were related to her father's unhappy experiences with Standard Oil. Lawson stated that Standard Oil executives had "outmaneuvered" Tarbell in some speculative dealings. Tipple related how the rest of the critics were "so far removed from the actual conflict that their over concern seemed contrived and tempted the businessman to dismiss them as mere agitators or mischief makers." Other potential sources of animus included "literary faddism, loss of status, and simply to the frustrations of certain intellectuals."

Muckraking, for instance, proved a surprisingly popular, albeit brief, style of journalism. In fact, Ida Tarbell, Lincoln Steffens, Ray Stannard Baker, and others inadvertently became muckrakers, as a result of their editors and publishers assigning or encouraging their investigations. Once muckraking turned these writers into celebrities and possibly moderately wealthy, they plowed furrows in the muckraking world. These journalists, aside from possibly Tarbell, had no obvious pre-muckraking dislike of big business, so the business elite's dismissal of muckrakers as "embittered intellectuals suffering from personal frustration or obsessed by an impelling sense of social inferiority," was probably erroneous. The muckrakers' may have simply catered to underlying public sentiment, once they overcame their surprise at the initial public reaction to their exposes. Tipple wrote, "it became incontrovertibly clear that the critics had never been alone in the assault but were serving only as an eloquent vanguard for an ever-increasing number of anxious and indignant Americans." Lincoln Steffens found the contradictions between honesty and wealth, morality and success, and so on worth delving into; he wanted to find the sources of these contradictions, and, as with many other Americans of his time, wanted faces to go with the contradictions. Given that many of business elite eschewed publicity and acted in secrecy, it was easy for muckrakers to present them as shadowy figures, Rorschach tests so to speak, for Americans to project their fears.

There was another key source of animus toward the business elite. Farmers' incomes displayed some inverse relationships with big business, but whether there was a causality going on was obscure. The general trend of industry replacing agriculture as the basis of the American economy, of course, created social and economic tension. Farmers fared relatively badly with respect to income during the last decades of the nineteenth century, and their Granger movement and populism reflected anger and anguish at economic forces. The big business leaders were an obvious target. When agricultural prices tilted back toward farmers, their agitation against big business diminished somewhat (Tipple 1959, 512, 517–520).

Precursors to Mass Markets

Railroads and telegraphs contributed to the rise of large-scale enterprises. Alfred Chandler Jr. observed that railroads enabled many smaller companies to enter and to compete in national markets. Telegraphs allowed owners and managers to communicate with a widespread net of assistants, associates, and other parties, thereby facilitating centralized control. The legal environment in the years before the Sherman Antitrust Act of 1890 also allowed horizontal combination. Until the Sherman Act, common law provided limited, if any, guidance as to what legal restraints existed to stymie the formation of cartels; state legislatures were in the vanguard of creating antitrust statutes. Chandler observes that the early mass producers did not turn to mass production in order to capture the economies of scale in production. Instead, they recognized that the new transportation and communications systems opened up much larger markets. "The potential of that market had impelled them to adopt the mass production machinery." Because wholesalers were often unable to order and maintain sufficient inventories that ensured customers could always obtain their products, the manufacturers began to create their own marketing and merchandising enterprises.

Chandler noted that horizontal integration was not a "viable long-term strategy," as many mergers failed unless they also vertically integrated into distribution and marketing. More often, some firms within a cartel succumbed to the temptation to cheat by clandestinely cutting prices or by lying about their sales. The lack of a legally binding contract proved insurmountable in most cases. From an ethical perspective, though, was it unethical to cheat on a cartel agreement of dubious ethical and legal character? Merger was usually the only way to ensure stable prices; the creation of a holding company proved a good vehicle to consolidate the many companies under centralized control. Often, though, holding companies required the approval of increasingly suspicious legislators. The trust company involved firms turning stock over to a board of trustees and receiving trust certificates. New Jersey's legislature approved a general corporation law that allowed trusts a year or so ahead of the passage of the Sherman Antitrust Act (Chandler 1977, 287, 290, 315–319).[4]

To Mass Produce or Not to Mass Produce

Alfred Chandler Jr. wrote extensively on the rise of big corporations in American economic history. His main insight was, "that modern business enterprise took the place of market mechanisms in coordinating the activities of the economy and allocating its resources." He characterized the transformation: "the visible hand of management replaced what Adam Smith referred to as the invisible hand of market forces." Although the market undergirded the demand for products, business owners and managers controlled the production, distribution, and investment processes. Concurrent with economy of scale was the need for managerial skills that could keep the factories going at high capacity and marketing skills to ensure buyers for the output. The genius of Standard Oil, General Motors, DuPont, and U.S. Steel was that they possessed management, organizational, and marketing skills to both produce and to sell large amounts of output (Chandler 1977, 1; Seabright 2004, 165).

Was America more conducive to mass production than Europe? Economic historian David Landes argues that because the American Constitution prohibited state-legislated barriers to interstate trade, the United States presented a much larger market than most European countries with their borders and different languages. In addition, America may have been socially and culturally ready for a mass market. European producers tended to cater to the upper class, but American lower- and middle-class consumers were willing to buy cheap standardized goods. Landes' insight may explain why "a number of episodes of striking economic growth in the premodern world were not sustained" due to the lack of mass demand (Landes 1998, 306; Seabright 2004, 159–160).[5]

A hierarchy of managers and executives became permanent and empowered, creating a class of salaried managers. These salaried managers required education, training, and experience to develop specialized skills. The rise of business bureaucracies meant that "selection and promotion became increasingly based on training, experience, and performance rather than on family relationship or money." These trends created an increasing separation between ownership and management. These managers were focused on "long-term stability and growth of their enterprises to those that maximized current profits." Other countries' industrialists relied upon family ties with varying results (Chandler 1977, 6–11).[6]

Telegraphs

Telegraphs are a good example of an industry that eventually became consolidated in the hands of a few. Telegraphs displayed some similarities to railroads and not just because telegraph lines were often erected alongside railroads. As with railroads, telegraph lines incurred heavy start-up costs. Competing telegraph companies needed some level of cooperation at terminal stations and standardization of dispatch and delivery. Telegraph companies quickly realized that consolidation was needed for long-haul message services and elimination of duplication of services (Du Boff 1980, 463). The Western Union Telegraph Company became the first nationwide monopoly in 1866.

The telegraph proved an admirable tool for financiers. Getting information ahead of rival investors was paramount. Decades earlier, England awaited news from the fields of Belgium in June 1815. The Rothschilds banking family understood the importance of getting accurate and relevant information quickly. They had established a commercial intelligence collection system, adroitly using the available transportation and communications technologies. Holders and potential buyers of English consols [a form of bonds] were on tenterhooks; victory over Napoleon would boost the consols, but the reverse would sink the consols. A Rothschild agent obtained a Dutch gazette announcing the allies' triumph and sailed to England. Nathan Rothschild received the news and hurried to the London Stock Exchange, arriving ahead of Wellington's envoy. According to legend cited by Frederic Morton, Rothschild pulled a double bluff. Instead of buying consols, Rothschild sold consols. Similar to a modern-day Warren Buffet, other investors watched Rothschild's actions; these investors now concluded from Rothschild's actions, that Napoleon had defeated the allied armies, as presumably they knew of the family's well-developed communications system. Rothschild continued to sell consols, convincing any remaining skeptics that the battle was lost. "Nathan kept on selling, his round face motionless and stern, his pudgy fingers depressing the market by tens of thousands of pounds with each sell signal. Consols dived, consols plummeted—until, a split second before it was too late, Nathan suddenly bought a giant parcel [of consols] for a song. Moments afterwards the great news broke, to send consols soaring." Morton concluded with a melodramatic flourish: "We cannot guess the number of hopes and savings wiped out by this engineered panic. We cannot estimate how many liveried servants, how many Watteaus and Rembrandts, how many thoroughbreds in his descendants' stables, [Rothschild] won that single day (Morton 1962, 49–50)."

Now this was a memorable story, and it attributed an almost superhuman cunning on Nathan Rothschild's part. From an ethical viewpoint, did he have a duty to announce the news? Was he responsible for other investors making erroneous inferences from his, admittedly deceptive, tactics? After all, he ran the risk of losing a fortune, had the news broken earlier or something disrupted his plans. According to historian Niall Ferguson, however, the story of selling consols was simply a legend. Nazi Joseph Goebbels embellished the story to make it appear that an "oleaginous Nathan" bribed a French general to "ensure the Duke of Wellington's victory;" Rothschild then misreported the battle's outcome to trigger the sell-off of consols described above before buying them. Ferguson reports that "Far from making money from Wellington's victory, the Rothschilds were very nearly ruined by it. Their fortune was made not because of Waterloo, but despite it (Ferguson 2008, 80–81, 84–85)." Because of the Rothschilds being synonymous with staggering wealth, people easily believed the legend.

American investors, too, ached to receive news promptly. In Boston, Samuel Topliff established a news room in a coffee shop. "He was the first to hear of a ship as she came within sight of the 'telegraph' station in Boston harbor, and one of his rowboats collected the first news of foreign ports from the in-coming vessel. This marine 'telegraph' was an ingenious arrangement of semaphores, which had been used for signaling the approach of vessels from hill to hill, since the year eighteen hundred. A series of stations along the coast from Edgartown to Hull told Boston and Salem of the approach of vessels as soon as they entered Vineyard Haven (*Bulletin of the Business Historical Society* 1928, 11–12)."

Merchants exchanged information amongst themselves "regarding prices and the probable course of trade." One company informed its agent, "I can only say this that if we do not pay strict attention in writing & answering our Letters [sic] every post, we had better leaving writing, at all. [sic] and trust all to Chance (Bruchey 1958, 279–280)." Of course, such news was often stale.

Telegraphs, therefore, fulfilled a dream of investors hungry for fresh news. Speculators and investors may have, indeed, provided the needed patronage to make telegraphs profitable. Because the Philadelphia Exchange opened an hour ahead of the New York Exchange, jobbers sought messages from Philadelphia, in order to get a jump ahead of their rivals. The almost instantaneous communication between the two cities forced the two exchanges to synchronize their hours. Before long, a less legitimate use of telegraphs emerged. The idea of "fake news" is nothing new, the recent American Presidential election notwithstanding. Unscrupulous speculators sent false information on the price of flour, when a ship arrived in Boston. Newspaper editors wrung their hands and wrote that the new technology "is too vast and too important to the public to remain in private hands. Government should control it and extend its links over the Union." Despite the occasional misuse of telegraph information, an economic historian concludes that "Availability of instant communication dramatically improved the functioning of markets, above all else by increasing price information. Traders could now carry out arbitrage operations swiftly and, given the nature of such transactions, it must have been easy for many individuals to mistake them for 'fraud'—especially since fraud did indeed occur. Yet nothing indicates that dishonest messages outnumbered legitimate dispatches. Thanks to the telegraph, operations once unimaginable now became feasible, and, for the first time, publicly visible (Du Boff 1980, 475–477)."[7]

Railroads in America

Railroads and waterways were crucial to American economic development. Farmers and retailers keenly followed railroad rates and power.

George Stephenson, pioneer of steam locomotion, expressed railroad economics simply: "where combination was possible, competition was impossible." He told the House of Commons that government should veto the construction of competing lines, in order "to protect the public against the heavy rates of traffic which would be required to remunerate the capital involved in their construction .... He saw that a line once built must impose a tax on the community, if only to keep itself in existence." If builders constructed a rival line that divided the available revenue in the locale serviced, the lines would compete and drive rates to disastrous levels; the lines would therefore be compelled to combine instead of competing (Adams 1869, 150).

Railroad owners incurred large initial investments in tracks, roadbeds, rolling stock, and other equipment. The greater the shipments or number of passengers, the more the owners could spread their expenditures on railroad infrastructure and equipment (fixed costs); in other words, the busier the railroad, the more its average cost fell. This cost structure implied that costs would be lower if there was just one firm instead of multiple firms.

Railroad management required reams of statistics in order to keep the trains running safely and profitably. The old ways of collecting, collating, and analyzing data required improvement. The Italian double-entry book-keeping techniques proved inadequate, and railroads began innovating and developing new techniques that now underlie modern accounting. It did not take long before canny railroad executives devised ways to mislead with statistics. Alfred Chandler Jr. observed that clever and unscrupulous promoters could manipulate the accounts to gull potential investors into believing the company's future was rosy. When construction was under-way, promoters could shift operating expenses to construction accounts to benefit investors while hurting customers. Such chicanery presaged modern-day accounting shenanigans, including Enron. Henry Varnum Poor and Charles Francis Adams Jr. urged reform of railroad accounting standards and suggested having outsiders auditing railroads' books (Chandler 1977, 111, 134–135, 190).

The railroad building of the 1840s and 1850s was marked by exuberant projectors possessing insufficient capital. Adams excoriated the rickety financing behind many railroads. Funds ran out at inconvenient times, and investors, trying to salvage their capital, started incurring debt, preference stock, and finally first, second, and third mortgages. At first, the investors based their debt upon actual railroad property, but eventually some dis-covered they could fraudulently get loans on "something thereafter to be created." Financial instability left many railroads susceptible to the machi-nations of predatory financiers (Adams 1869, 143).

Railroads led to widespread and voluminous trading of securities. During the 1850s, stock trading became ever more sophisticated, and the New York banks and Wall Streets developed techniques to facilitate specu-lation. Well-known, if sometimes infamous, railroad stock manipulators appeared as early as the 1850s (Chandler 1977, 92).

British investors in American railroads found such investments to be turbulent. The Americans were engaged in recurring rate wars, whereas British railroads enjoyed pools and agreements that stabilized prices. The British railroad executives may have looked with condescension and moral outrage at their American peers. Beatrice Webb, whose father was the president of the Grand Trunk railroad in Canada, wrote, "the circum-stances of mid-Victorian Capitalist enterprise were hostile to any fixed standard of morality." She observed, "The presidents of American railways, international financiers, company promoters and contractors, were forceful men, frequently of magnetic personality and witty conversation; but the common ideal which bound them in a close fraternity was a stimulating mixture of personal power and personal luxury; their common recreation was high living. Uniquely typical was the life on board a president's car on an American railway; above all, the consciousness of personal prestige and power; obsequious attention of ubiquitous officials; contemptuous bargaining with political 'bosses' for land concessions and bills through legislatures—altogether a low moral temperature." One researcher suggested that smug British commentators attributed Americans' low level of business ethics to the fact that the United States was a young country facing rapid development, "and where there are temptations to haste to be rich (Webb 1926, 7; Currie 1960, 207)."[8]

In America, railroad securities were often the playthings of speculators, some scrupulous, others not so. Matthew Josephson described one speculator's strategy: "'To buy up two or more bad roads, put them together, give the united roads a new name, call it a good, prosperous line, with immense prospects … get a great number of people to believe all this, then make large issues of bonds, for further improving and enhancing the … property.'—then to sell it all at a profit to purchasers who came along. Should these be unable to run it profitably, and be obliged to go into liquidation, then Mr. Gould or his agents would very likely be found on hand at the sale and take back the road at a greatly reduced price (Josephson [1934] 2011, 64–65)." This scenario would seem to require a large number of naïve investors willing to be in a yo-yo-esque investment.

Gilded Age Americans were proud of their transcontinental railroad. The builders of the Central Pacific and Union Pacific railroads overcame financial, physical, and political obstacles. Although their triumphs were and remain impressive, there was a seamy underside to their efforts. The federal government supported the railroads with land grants. Many boosters of the railroads thought these land grants would repay themselves, as the railroads triggered prosperity and population growth. They feared that without the land grant inducement, private builders would not attempt the project for years to come. The land grants, therefore, were needed to raise the private rate of return. As the railroads would be socially useful by lowering transportation costs and providing more reliable transportation, the difference between the social rate of return and the private rate of return without a land grant was the key question. If the private rate of return without the land grant was too low, the railroad would not be built (Mercer 1970, 604–605).

Underlying the transcontinental railroad was corruption. Adams had harsh words for the Union Pacific and the Credit Mobilier: "what this Credit Mobilier is seems to be as much shrouded in mystery as is the fate of the missing $180,000,000 .... The members of it are in Congress; they are trustees for the bond-holders, they are directors, they are stockholders, they are contractors; in Washington they vote the subsidies, in New York they receive them .... the whole thing seems to be a species of thimble-rig [a gambling game featuring a pea and three thimbles; the nimble of fingers can consistently cheat naïve bettors] (Adams 1869, 147)."[9]

Railroad Rates

Railroad rates concerned the public. Progressives worried that if large companies got rate discounts, the discounts would reinforce their competitive advantage versus the smaller producers. The rate wars were a critical factor in American economic history: "this shift from a high- to a low-rate policy, however unseemly and inequitable the process by which it was achieved, transformed the American economy as no other single factor did (Martin 1976, 193)."

Western farmers began relying upon railroads to ship their crops to eastern ports and on to Europe. At first, only one railroad served many farm locales, prompting fears of monopoly rates and inspiring the Granger movement that peaked in the late 1860s and early 1870s. Midwestern farmers' complaints about railroads waxed and waned with fluctuating railroad freight rates. Railroad expansion, however, created competition among the railroads and in conjunction with the Panic of 1873, reduced rail freight rates below even what the Grangers had agitated for. By 1875, Charles Francis Adams Jr. proclaimed the Granger movement a "phenomenon of the past (Adams 1875, 395)."

Farmers also expressed dissatisfaction with the buyers of their farm products and sellers of consumer goods. Farmers, of course, sold homogeneous products, thereby being perfect substitutes with other farmers growing the same crop. Because of the large numbers of producers, colluding to boost prices was nearly impossible. The farmers believed easterners manipulated the terms of trade in ways that injured farmers' interests, but during grain market upswings, some of the farmers' animus dissipated.

By 1901, Midwestern farmers seemed more "placid" about trusts than groups such as professional engineers (Galambos 1975, 95–97).

The railroads suffered from volatile rates; their attempts to stabilize rates usually failed, as individual lines cheated on agreements. By the 1880s, railroad presidents and other observers avidly sought ways to stabilize rates. A general traffic manager for the Chicago, Milwaukee & St. Paul, A.C. Bird [no first name given] told a Congressional committee that fluctuating rates were disastrous for railroads and other businesses. Given the public animus toward industrial collusion, the railroad men realized that some sort of government intervention was necessary. They wanted the nascent Interstate Commerce Commission (I.C.C.) to focus only upon maintaining rates and dividing railroad traffic. Beyond that, they opposed additional regulation. As with most business executives, the railroad officials wanted the "Goldilocks" amount of government intervention—not too much, not too little, but just right. Other people disputed the railroads' plea for control of rates (Cochrane 1943, 15–16).

The usual interpretation of the creation of the I.C.C. rested upon western farmers' fears that discriminatory and high railroad rates jeopardized their prosperity, even survival. Instead of western farmers agitating for the I.C.C., historians have shown that affluent New York City merchants were prime movers behind the law. The New York City merchants were unhappy that railroads had diminished their locational advantage. The Erie Canal had boosted New York's trade with the interior of the country and made the city the premier economic power. Businessmen in river towns also found themselves losing their advantages with the spread of railroads. Among railroad men, many recognized that the industry could not spare itself from destructive price wars, so they, too, became advocates of regulation. These groups, of course, had different views on what sort of regulations were desirable, but the coalition was sufficiently strong to get a law passed. A historian mused that "in the short run everyone got something from the 1887 Act." He cautioned, though, that the long-run effects were not so benign (Zerbe 1980, 344; see also Martin 1974, 340–341).

Railroad expert Albert Fink asserted that pools were necessary to stabilize freight rates and maintain the flows of eastbound traffic. As Albro Martin pointed out, though, "the businessmen of New York City, influential beyond their numbers and seeking allies wherever they could find them, set out to smash pooling once and for all." These New York businessmen lobbied the New York Assembly to form a special investigation under Alonzo Hepburn. Martin characterizes the Hepburn Committee of

1880, as "the very model of what a public investigatory body should not be," but, really, no one should be too surprised by a staged, "independent," investigatory commission. The commission relied upon the New York Chamber of Commerce and the Board of Trade while shunting railroad experts to the sidelines: "the witnesses for the railroads [such as William Vanderbilt] saw themselves as passively answering [or being pilloried in the New York City press] what they considered fatuous and inane charges from a group of ignorant, envious men with the most palpable axes to grind." The railroad men, as would John D. Rockefeller and Standard Oil, failed to understand the importance of public relations in an era of cheap newspapers. Francis Thurber, an instigator who had pushed for the committee, stated with arrogance, "The Committee believe that New York has a prior claim to this trade [importing and interior jobbing], as it first settled and naturally belongs here. The railroads have no right to break up the jobbing trade of this city, and transfer it to the interior of our own or other states." Another New Yorker later boasted that "every charge made by my clients [the New York business community] … seriatim [was] overwhelmingly proved," but Martin calls this "legal puffery."

A Senatorial hearing in 1882 headed by Shelby Cullom proved less biased and more astute. Martin described the hearing's report as revealing "a remarkable grasp of the situation" that "should have made the members of the old Hepburn Committee blush with shame." In particular, evidence presented at the Cullom hearings demonstrated that rate differentials were justifiable, but the New York businessmen continued to consider such differentials iniquitous. The recommendations of a proposed Senate bill, based on the Cullom report, included allowing long-short-haul discrimination (which the Hepburn Committee vociferously opposed) and remained silent about pooling (Martin 1974, 354–357, 361).

By 1897, men such as Francis Beattie Thurber had changed their minds regarding pooling. They joined fellow foe of pool and rate differentials, John Reagan, in recanting. Thurber, speaking as president of the U.S. Export Association, told members of the annual dinner of the New York Chamber of Commerce, "Senator Platt was right, and I and those who were with me were wrong." Between the Hepburn Committee and 1897, Thurber recognized that railroads had unique aspects. Martin believed the railroads needed to form cartels; by 1906, the railroads had been transformed into six or seven systems (Martin 1974, 369–371; see also Nash 1955, 193–194; Gilchrist 1960, 47).

Conclusion

Railroads, telegraphs, and cheap printing lowered transportation and communication costs, thereby enlarging market size, and helped create national demand for products. These improvements were conducive to the creation of large-scale production and distribution. Had industrial leaders eschewed the advantages of large-scale production and distribution, the American economy would have been very different. Consumers would have been worse off. The process of getting from the old to the new economy was fraught with dubious business behavior. Whether it could have been achieved under more genteel and ethical behavior remains a question unanswered. As railroad freight rates fell, farmers ceased their agitation against the industry. Investors learned caution and gained sophistication in choosing stocks, although new waves of investors required absorbing the costs of learning how to invest.

Historian Louis Galambos summarized the 1890s as a time "when attitudes were in flux and middle-class America was uniquely unsettled by the tides of social change," but various groups differed on what the main issue was. For some farmers in the Midwest, prices were paramount, but southern farmers worried more about the concentrated economic power of the trusts (Galambos 1975, 255). By the time the Supreme Court made some trust-busting rulings, the decisions may have been moot. Much of American industry consisted of oligopolies, and the trusts' time had passed. The American public appeared to have accepted large-scale businesses as a permanent feature of the economy.

Notes

1. For alternative explanations, see Schumpeter ([1934] 1983, 93); Sombart (1930, III:200); Bridges (1958, 10).
2. Gras provided the full quote in its context (Gras 1945, 113).
3. Charles and Mary Beard also studied the business leaders of the early twentieth century (Beard and Beard [1927] 1933, II:175).
4. Chandler identified just eight nationwide trusts: cattle, cordage, petroleum, cottonseed oil, linseed oil, sugar, whiskey, and lead processing. The first two trusts proved ephemeral (Chandler 1977, 320).
5. Charles Sabel and Jonathan Zeitlin argued that there were alternatives to mass production. They observed that mass production did not eliminate all small firms (Sabel and Zeitlin 1985, 137, 155–165).

6. The Ford family continued to play a role in managing the auto company for a few generations; Radio Corporation of America's (RCA's) David Sarnoff tried to pass power to his son. In most cases, family-owned business might be fortunate enough to have a sufficiently competent son to carry on the firm, but the good fortune needed for a third or fourth generation of talented progeny proved too elusive for many companies.
7. Du Boff observed that newspaper editors had to compete with investors for scarce wire time (476).
8. Of course, Americans probably feel the same way about business ethics in developing countries, as witness American disdain for paying or receiving bribes in foreign countries, never mind the fact that bribery was prevalent throughout American history.
9. Interestingly enough, the Disney version of *Davy Crockett, King of the Frontier* had a character named Thimblerig accompany him to the Alamo. Whether Davy should have included such a character in his entourage never occurred to little boys of the 1950s and 1960s or, apparently, to their parents. At least it was the great character actor, Hans Conried, in the role as Thimblerig. Conried would later voice Snidely Whiplash, Dudley Do Right's nemesis.

Bibliography

Adams, Charles F., Jr. "Railroad Inflation." *North American Review*. No. CCXXIL, January 1869, 130–164.

Adams, Charles F., Jr. "The Granger Movement." *North American Review* Vol. 120, No. 247, April 1875, 394–424.

Andreano, Ralph. "A Note on the Horatio Alger Legend: Statistical Studies of Nineteenth Century American Business Elite." *Business Enterprise and Economic Change: Essays in Honor of Harold F. Williamson*, edited by Louis Cain and Paul Uselding (Kent, OH: Kent State University Press, 1973), 227–246.

Beard, Charles and Mary Beard. *The Rise of American Civilization* (New York, NY: Macmillan, [1927] 1933), 2 vols.

Bridges, Hal. "The Robber Baron Concept in American History." *Business History Review* XXXI(1), Spring 1958, 1–13.

Bruchey, Stuart. "Success and Failure Factors: American Merchants in Foreign Trade in the Eighteenth and Nineteenth Centuries." *Business History Review* XXXII(3), Autumn 1958, 272–292.

Bulletin of the Business Historical Society. "Business and the Coffee House." II(3), May 1928, 11–13. No author.

Chandler, Alfred Jr. *The Visible Hand: The Managerial Revolution in American Business* (Cambridge, MA: Harvard University Press, 1977).

Cochrane, Thomas. "Some Social Attitudes of Railroad Administrators at the End of the Nineteenth Century." *Bulletin of the Business History Society* 17(1), January 1943. 15–21.

Currie, Archibald. "British Attitudes Toward Investment in North American Railroads." *Business History Review* XXIV(2), Summer 1960, 194–215.

Destler, Chester. "Entrepreneurial Leadership Among the 'Robber Barons': A Trial Balance." *Journal of Economic History* (6), Supplement: *The Tasks of Economic History*, May 1946, 28–49.

Du Boff, Richard. "Business Demand and the Development of the Telegraph in the United States, 1844–1860." *Business History Review* 54(4), Winter 1980, 459–479).

Ferguson, Niall. *The Ascent of Money: A Financial History of the World* (New York, NY: Penguin Press, 2008).

Folsom, Burton Jr. *The Myth of the Robber Barons: A New Look at the Rise of Big Business in America* (Herndon, VA: [1987] 1996).

Friedman, Daniel and Daniel McNeill. *Morals and Markets: The Dangerous Balance* (New York, NY: Palgrave Macmillan, 2013). 2nd edition.

Galambos, Louis. *The Public Image of Big Business in America, 1880–1940: A Quantitative Study in Social Change* (Baltimore: Johns Hopkins University Press, 1975).

Garraty, John. *The American Nation* (New York, NY: HarperCollins, 1991). 7th ed.

Gilchrist, D.T. "Albert Fink and the Pooling System." *Business History Review* XXIV(1), Spring 1960, 24–49.

Godkin, Edwin. "The Vanderbilt Memorial." *The Nation* Vol. IX, November 18, 1869, 431–432.

Gras, Norman. "A New Study of Rockefeller." *Bulletin of the Business Historical Society* 15(4), October 1941, 49–58.

Gras, Norman. "Shifts in Public Relations." *Bulletin of the Business Historical Society* 19(4), October 1945, 97–148.

Green, Constance. "What Has the Business Administrator Contributed to Society?" *Bulletin of the Business History Society* 17(1), January 1943, 22–26.

Hughes, Jonathan. *The Vital Few: The Entrepreneur & American Economic Progress* (New York, NY: Oxford University Press, [1965] 1986), expanded edition.

Josephson, Matthew. *The Robber Barons: The Great American Capitalists, 1861–1901* (New Brunswick, NJ: Transaction Publisher, [1934] 2011), September 8, 1883, 281–285.

Landes, David. *The Wealth and Poverty of Nations: Why Some Are So Rich and Some So Poor* (New York, NY: W.W. Norton, 1998).

Martin, Albro. "The Troubled Subject of Railroad Regulation in the Gilded Age—A Reappraisal." *Journal of American History* 61(2), September 1974, 339–371.

Martin, Albro. "James J. Hill and the First Energy Revolution: A Study in Entrepreneurship, 1865–1878." *Business History Review* L(2), Summer 1976, 179–197.

Mercer, Lloyd. "Rates of Return for Land-Grant Railroads: The Central Pacific System." *Journal of Economic History* 30(3), September 1970, 602–626.

Morton, Frederic. *The Rothschilds: A Family Portrait* (New York, NY: Atheneum, 1962).

Nash, Gerald. "The Reformer Reformed: John H. Reagan and Railroad Regulation." *Business History Review* XXIX(2), June 1955, 189–196.

Nevins, Allan. *John D. Rockefeller: The Heroic Age of American Enterprise* (New York, NY: Charles Scribner's Sons, 1940). 2 vols.

Sabel, Charles and Jonathan Zeitlin. "Historical Alternatives to Mass Production." *Past & Present*. No. 108, August 1985, 133–176.

Schumpeter, Joseph. *Theory of Economic Development*. (New Brunswick, NJ: Transaction Books, [1934] 1983).

Seabright, Paul. *The Company of Strangers: A Natural History of Economic Life* (Princeton, NJ: Princeton University Press, 2004).

Silk, Leonard. "Economic Scene: I.M.F.'s Goal of Confidence." *New York Times*, September 30, 1983, D2.

Sombart, Werner. "Capitalism." *Encyclopedia of the Social Sciences*, edited by E.R.A. Seligman (New York, NY: Macmillan, 1930), III:195–208. 15 vols.

Tipple, John. "The Anatomy of Prejudice, Origins of the Robber Baron Legend." *Business History Review* XXXIII(4), Winter 1959, 510–522.

Webb, Beatrice. *My Apprenticeship* (New York, NY: Longmans, Green, 1926).

Yamamura, Kozo. "Economic Responsiveness in Japanese Industrialization." *Business Enterprise and Economic Change: Essays in Honor of Harold F. Williamson*, edited by Louis Cain and Paul Uselding (Kent, OH: Kent State University Press, 1973), 173–197.

Zerbe, Richard. "The costs and benefits of early regulation of the railroads." *Bell Journal of Economics* 11(1), Spring 1980, 343–350.

CHAPTER 5

Ethics of the Firm and Strategic Behavior

Businesses, large and small, used various tactics to combat rivals. Drawing a distinction over which tactics were ethical and which were not was contentious. Courts and legislatures often adjudicated disputes. How did the large industrialists come to dominate their industries? Did they use fair methods or foul? Did they gain dominance through sheer efficiency in production or by using nefarious means?

Businesspeople are not the only group using ruthless and unfair tactics to gain dominance. Monopoly is a game that not only businesspeople can play. American political parties have a nifty duopoly; there are two main parties—Republicans and Democrats. Legislators get to make up the rules of the game. They create franking, seniority, and other factors that favor incumbents. Incumbents win a disproportionate number of elections. Although sports fans and pundits bemoan competitive imbalance in sports, congressional leader Emanuel Celler, who chaired committees investigating professional team sports, won over 20 elections in a row. He could have taught monopolists a thing or two about winning.

What were some forms of strategic behavior that conferred benefits and dominance for aggressive business executives? Firms used corruption and bribery of government officials, so-called predatory pricing, and other unfair and unethical, if not illegal, tactics. In some cases, the public mistakenly criticized large firms for unfair pricing, because the public did not understand the difference between predatory pricing and reduced prices due to better efficiency. The United States, though, took a different attitude toward cartels than did Germany and Japan.

D. G. Surdam, *Business Ethics from the 19th Century to Today*,
https://doi.org/10.1007/978-3-030-37169-2_5

Unfair Competition

Political scientist William Stevens made a key insight that lawyers and economists define "unfair competition" differently. For lawyers, "a method which is legal is not unfair. To the economist, on the other hand, legality per se is no criterion of fairness." Stevens, writing in 1914, claimed that "Nearly every large combination or trust and frequently smaller ones also reveals at some point in its history one or more instances of the use of such unfair methods." His list of unfair methods was lengthy and worth quoting: "Local price-cutting; Operation of bogus 'independent' concerns,' Maintenance of 'fighting ships' and 'fighting brands'; Lease, sale, purchase or use of certain articles as a condition of the lease, sale, purchase or use of other required articles; Exclusive sales and purchase agreements; Rebates and preferential contracts; Acquisition of exclusive or dominant control of machinery or goods used in the manufacturing process; Manipulation; Blacklists, boycotts, white-lists etc.; Espionage and use of detectives; Coercion, threats and intimidation (Stevens 1914, 282–283)."[1] In the case of using detectives, the Pinkerton and Burns agencies were "particularly vilified for using deception and violence to help destroy unions and break strikes (Shulman 2007, 57–58)." On occasion, coercion, threats, and intimidation may have included violence, sabotage, and arson, and one might as well add them to the catalog of infamies.

Stevens described how a firm with many sales territories might cut prices in a single territory to stymie local competition. He noted how the customers might benefit initially from the price cut, but he denied that this justified local price-cutting. He made the odd statement, "any gain to the consumer under this method, in addition to causing a corresponding loss to some other consumer, is obviously of a temporary character," but his reasoning seems fallacious. His conclusion that successful price-cutting squelched local competition and might result in the large firm exercising its newly won price-setting power to raise prices above the original level, may have been incorrect. Modern-day economists pointed out that some national chains, such as Walmart, that prided themselves on national pricing might be vulnerable to local chains or individual firms who cut prices. Price-cutting, therefore, could work in either direction, strong against weak or weak against strong (Stevens 1914, 284–285; Carlton and Perloff 2005, 355–356, 359).

A variation of the localized price-cutting method was for an established firm to resurrect a dormant brand and to sell such a brand at low prices in a local market to achieve basically the same result as the price-cutting mentioned above. These resurrected brands were known as "fighting brands." "They are said to be sold at prices below the cost of production solely to the customers of the independent organization or organizations."

Some firms used another tactic that Stevens deemed exploitative. In order to buy or use a piece of equipment, the buyer or lessee had to use a product manufactured by the same producer of the equipment. The Crown Cork and Seal Company manufactured tin caps (think of the old-fashioned bottle caps that required the use of a "church key" to flip the cap). The company owned patents on the Jumbo capping machine. Firms desiring to lease (they could not buy the machine) the capping machine were required to use the Crown company's caps. A few decades later, the International Business Machine (IBM) company leased business machines to firms and required them to use only IBM punch cards; IBM was able to ascertain how much firms used the machines by the amount of punch cards purchased.[2]

One rather dubious, even disrespectful, National Cash Register Company stunt was to create a "historical room" at the company's factory. The so-called graveyard was a display of business machines manufactured by defunct companies; each exhibit showed "the name of the company, date at which they went out of business, amount of money lost, etc." Stevens bemoaned this piece of intimidation, but whether such practice was unethical seems debatable. He thought the room was designed to forestall competition, presumably because potential customers would be dissuaded from buying cash registers from other companies, lest they buy from a potentially doomed company.[3]

Stevens recognized that some companies gained market dominance by being more efficient or producing superior products. He admitted that these firms are beneficial, but he immediately advocated regulating such superior firms in order to "insure that they will give the public in the form of lower prices the benefit of their superior efficiency (Stevens 1914, 289–292, 484–486)." His economic analysis seems faulty, because even monopolists who find ways to cut costs pass on some of the savings to customers (although the proportion of the savings going to the customers depends upon the customers' sensitivity to price changes).

An economist identified one tactic that sometimes proved effective: "the *institution of spurious suits* at law [italics his]." A firm could harass another firm with baseless accusations, such as the ever-popular "infringement of patents." Even if the plaintiff lost and had to pay its legal costs, the expense might have been worthwhile, if the rival's legal expenses drove it to bankruptcy. The early years of the phonograph and motion picture industries in America exemplified the fights over patents. RCA's David Sarnoff allegedly tied up Philo Farnsworth's patent regarding television for years (Watkins 1927, 78–79; see also Stashower 2002, 162–169; Ritchie 1995, 13–14).

Commercial bribery was another common practice. Myron Watkins noticed that the Federal Trade Commission dealt with numerous cases where one firm diverted patronage away from competitors through bribing the competitors' employees. "It is hard to say just what are the exact limits of legitimate inducements to trade." Another way to divert customers was through advertising. Cheap newspapers and periodicals, radio, and then television inundated consumers with messages. Just where was the line separating acceptable and unacceptable was difficult to discern; European and American laws countenanced a degree of "puffery," relatively innocuous falsehoods or misleading statements. "Such deception may inflict a very considerable amount of damage upon more honest competitors .... The rewards go, not to those who best forecast demand and who produce at lowest cost, but to those who succeed in fooling the consuming public (Watkins 1927, 80–81)."

Sources of Monopoly Power

Adam Smith had identified the monopolies of his time as the guild corporations and the joint-stock trading companies, government-granted monopolies (such as the East India Company), and collusion-inspired cartels, while ignoring the penny-ante local monopolies (local blacksmith, retail merchant). "People of the same trade seldom meet together, even for merriment and diversion, but the conversation ends in a conspiracy against the publick, or in some contrivance to raise prices." You might think Smith would immediately advocate for antitrust laws; people rarely recalled his next sentence: "It is impossible indeed to prevent such meetings, by any law which either could be executed, or would be consistent with liberty and justice." He ended with the rather bland assertion, "But though the law cannot hinder people of the same trade from sometimes assembling together, it ought to do nothing to facilitate such assemblies; much less to render them necessary (Smith 1981, 145)."

Smith also recognized the fragility of most cartels. Collusion to fix prices had often been an ephemeral enterprise. After all, suppose we agree with our Marxist friends: Capitalists were rapacious, unscrupulous people, people who would sell their granny down the river (or for a few pieces of silver). In their greed, capitalists would collude against the public to increase their gains. However, here the Marxist depiction of grasping capitalists ran into a problem: If capitalists were greedy, unscrupulous bastards, why should they adhere to a collusive agreement, especially since the rewards of cheating (chiseling) were so high? There was an inconsistency here. Perhaps the early economists were correct in their neglect of antitrust laws. Note, too, that consumers gained, at least temporarily, as cheating members cut their prices. In a sense, the cartel members' self-interest afforded an element of protection for consumers.

Two examples of cartels' fragility suffice. A manufacturer stationed his confederates "outside the building [where the collusive agreement was being negotiated], and, as soon as a price settlement was reached, [he] stroll[ed] casually over to a window and, by fingering the shade in a prearranged way, indicate[d] to him the level agreed on, whereupon the salesman would proceed to undercut the price his employer was even then pledging himself to maintain." In another case, "following the organization of a pool, one of the participants, hurrying to the telegraph office to wire his own deviation from the agreed-upon price, was shown by mistake a message filed a few minutes before by a fellow member quoting customers a price even lower than the more virtuous one had contemplated offering. He immediately revised his own offer, downward (Sullivan 1927, 2:322)." The hands had not even cooled after the handshake, before each party cheated.

Preventing and detecting cheating by cartel members is difficult. Cheaters do not announce their malfeasance. Punishing cheaters may prove impossible. You cannot go to a judge (in the United States at least) and say, "She cheated on our collusive agreement to charge monopoly prices to the public." Collusion is illegal in the United States. Of course, if a cartel is successful and profits rise, envy rears its ugly head. Other industrialists will note the cartel's success; profits attract rivals. How to keep these latecomers from trespassing upon the cartel's preserve is an interesting question.

Some industries found it difficult to stabilize prices, even with the development of trade associations. Cotton textile manufacturers had trade associations in the early 1900s. Repeated calls to curb production usually failed, as there were always "manufacturers who were hesitant, uncertain, and, as yet, unwilling to turn their backs on the old style of rough and tumble competition." One member stated, "My personal preference would be to stay out of the Institute [Cotton-Textile Institute]. My choice always will be to have a free hand to run our own business as we see fit to run it, and regardless of what anybody else does." An opponent described attempts to chastise an unnamed rival, who was involved in the association [but apparently cheated]: "Bastard, First Class. He runs his mills twenty-four hours a day, six days in the week, fifty-two weeks in the year. When he goes to New York he lunches alone at the Automat .... He makes the finest cloth in the market, because if he did not, the customers would reject every yard of it. He has never curtailed for the good of the industry." The opponent sarcastically remarked, "Join me at the automat for lunch someday." It is difficult to tell whether he was angrier at his unnamed rival for being so proficient in producing high-quality cloth or for cheating on the agreement. A decade after the Cotton-Textile Institute's failure in 1927 to curb production, the Roosevelt administration's National Recovery Agency tried to stabilize production output, but the attempt failed, in part because there was so much excess capacity that the limits failed to actually cut output (Galambos 1964, 45, 47).

Such attitudes gave rise to the manufacturers' new credo that *virtue* entailed establishing and maintaining prices. "There are some manufacturers who have the courage to establish prices and maintain them. Their price is their price and they refuse to dicker. But there are some who lack the courage and the strength. And just so there are some purchasing agents who do not haggle. They ask for bids from suppliers whose product is acceptable and the low man gets the business. But there are others who seem to consider their function one of dollar squeezing .... After all, it gets down to a very simple consideration of plain honesty (Whitehorne 1928, 493)."

However, many of today's monopolies were based upon government fiat, as Smith predicted. Utility companies became monopolies with the blessings of the state (Smith 1981, 135).[4] In modern times, cable television companies were classic examples of government-mandated monopolies. The United States has long created monopoly power through the patent system, trademarks, and copyrights.

Predatory Pricing

The general public, weaned perhaps upon tawdry plot lines in novels, movies, and television, believes that predatory pricing was a commonly used way to drive competitors out of business. Economist Lester Telser analyzed conditions where a firm might use either the threat of or the actual imposition of predatory pricing to attain monopoly power. Predatory pricing was a situation where the predatory company slashed its price so low that a potential entrant could not make a profit and was therefore deterred from entering the market or a rival (typically smaller) was forced out of business. In economics parlance, predatory pricing occurred, when a firm priced its output below the marginal cost of producing the output. In the short run, the firm absorbed losses from predatory pricing; the hope was by absorbing such losses, the firm would drive out its rival(s). An alternative way to create monopoly power was to merge the competing companies, although such acts might run afoul of U.S. antitrust laws. Firms threatening or actually pursuing predatory pricing were, in essence, playing a game of "chicken." Who would blink first? In such a game, the monopolist's and the target victim's abilities to maintain or to withstand predatory price depended partly upon available capital funds.

Simply reducing price is not sufficient to indict a firm of practicing predatory pricing. Firms may slash prices to below cost for reasons other than forcing out rivals. They use below-cost pricing as a means of introducing a new product (think of the free samples—prices get no lower than free samples—handed out to passers-by). Retailers may use "loss leaders" as ways to induce customers into their stores, in the hopes that customers buy other items in addition to the loss leaders.

The drawback to predatory pricing is always the injurious aspect to the predator in terms of losses on sales. As I tell my students, predatory pricing is akin to telling a rival, "I'll keep punching myself in the face, until you leave." The threat often is not credible, as predatory pricing is rarely in the interest of the predator. At best, the predator might hope to recoup the initial losses by being able to charge monopoly prices later, but this hope depends upon how easily rival firms can re-enter the market. In a sense, driving out rivals with predatory pricing becomes a "Whack-a-Mole" game. Telser suggests that the threat of cutthroat price competition needs to be backed by a stockpile of funds, although he writes, "Although reasonable men would not engage in predatory pricing, the threat of such cutthroat competition sets limits to the price of merger, and the share of monopoly return going to the successful entrant (Telser 1966, 260)?" Some observers believe that modern-day predatory pricing in the retail arena is unlikely: "The idea of Walmart driving out all the competition is ludicrous. They should drive out people who are overcharging; that's American capitalism. But there are just so many players in the pharmaceuticals industry and so much competition in the retail end, that driving out all the competition would be virtually impossible (Kristof, June 14, 1994, 4:1–2)."

Legal scholar Richard Easterbrook's advice is worth noting: "the courts should not consider a predatory pricing suit until after a firm has been driven from business *and* the alleged predator has raised its price. Only then could one be sure that it was predation and not vigorous competition that drove the rival out of business (Carlton and Perloff 2005, 355–356, 359)."

Bribery and Government-Provided Services

A standard unfair tactic is bribery. Some businesspeople use bribes and other blandishments to gain contracts and business. What constitutes bribes can be ambiguous.

For many centuries throughout Europe and America, if citizens wanted services from their local government official, they paid officials directly upon provision of the services. By the beginning of the twentieth century in America and other countries, however, most government officials were paid fixed salaries. In today's America, a rare exception occurs when Americans pay a justice of the peace or a county clerk for providing a civil marriage ceremony.

Prior to paying fixed salaries, payments to government officials were, according to historian Nicholas Parrillo, of two basic types: facilitative payments and bounties. Modern-day people are probably more familiar with the latter. The government offered a bounty for "performing a task that the affected person did not want and might resist." Bounty hunters abounded in movie and television westerns; often they were despised by law breakers and law abiders alike. The bounty payment, of course, promoted adversarial relations; the officer gained when the affected party was adversely affected. A facilitative payment, in contrast, was "a sum that an officer received for performing a service that the affected person wanted or needed." The facilitative payment system was akin to private transactions in the market, as it "tended to promote reciprocal exchange between the officer and the recipient of the service, working to the benefit of both."

Facilitative payments, however, could easily lead to extortion, whereby officers unlawfully took payments that were not authorized by statute, custom, or usage. There were some subtleties within the definition. Three elements could make an undue payment unlawful. The officer had to coerce the affected party to make a payment; the officer lied about the amount due; or the affected party "intended the payment to induce the officer to breach his duty." To modern eyes, the latter action constituted bribery. If none of these elements was present, the payment, although undue, was lawful. Eighteenth-century mores allowed for an affected person to compensate or reward an officer with a tip or a gratuity for doing his duty. Such payments could also be used to induce an officer to perform the service quicker or better or even to get the officer to perform his duty at all. In addition to lawful gratuities and ingrained custom, the doctrine of *quantum meruit* dictated that "any person who performs a valuable service for somebody else is entitled to reasonable recompense for it." If a benefited party did not make such recompense, the officer could sue for such.

Defenders of facilitative payments asserted that such payments "induced prompt, attentive, and faithful service" by government officials. Modern-day bribery in developing countries might have created "a valuable and efficient degree of flexibility." Critics, though, rebutted such arguments by asserting that negotiations between officers and affected parties all too often meant monopoly pricing by the officers; allowed officers to support themselves without the legislature's approval; and repudiated the idea that the citizen had a *right* to the service from disinterested government officers.

The American federal government's role expanded during the nineteenth century. Officers attracted affected parties by offering good customer service. In the wake of increasing immigration applications; settlers' claims for western lands; and veterans' claims after the Civil War, officers had plenty of opportunity to earn fees. Parrillo noted that due to competition between officers, officers "became famous (or notorious) for indulging applicants."

Legislators were aware of the officers' willingness to indulge customers, but Congress acquiesced in the practices. Such indulgences in return for fees smacked of corruption in the eyes of some contemporaries, but Parrillo asserted that a definition of corruption revolving around "the exercise of public power for a private interest" was too broad; he amended this to include the necessary condition that the exercise violates the law. Under this definition, the officer's liberality might not have been corrupt, since it was lawful to accept payment for services and legislators knew and tacitly approved of the liberality in approving applications. An alternative definition of corruption highlighted the tailoring of a law to fit the "peculiar needs" of a particular individual or group; in the cases of immigrants, land applicants, and pension applicants, though, Congress approved of the catering to these groups' "peculiar needs." Parrillo concluded that the officers' actions were not corrupt, especially as Congress approved of such largesse. As the century drew to a close, however, Congress began to recognize the scarcity of tax revenues and available land, as well as the dilution of voting power by long-standing American citizens in the face of increasing numbers of immigrants-turned-citizens. Congress then pressed for tightening standards for approving affected parties' applications, and the "customer service" model was replaced by a more impersonal and indifferent approach (Parrillo 2014, 1–2, 11–14, 18–22). Clearly facilitative payments were rife with potential abuse; in all too many countries around the world today, citizens resort to cash payments to motivate officials to perform necessary duties.

Bounties, however, seemed more conducive to the will of the government. By creating incentives for officers to act on the behest of the government, bounties promised to help enforce government directives "in the face of the contrary preferences of those affected." Those very incentives, however, could boomerang. As mentioned, the depiction of bounty hunters in American westerns revealed a drawback of the system: Bounty hunters alienated much of the citizenry. Bounties created incentives for enforcement but at the cost of potentially undermining the acceptance of a law.

The United States relied upon customs duties for much of its revenues during the country's first century. Customs officials were initially selected from local notables; although using local officials helped keep the customs laws acceptable to the populace, the officials were not keen to rigorously pursue cheaters in order to earn bounties. In the event, most shippers willingly paid the duties. The task of enforcing customs duties eventually fell to alien imposition; the political parties began using customs collections as patronage. The Civil War spurred the search for revenue, and the customs officials, especially newly created customs detectives, became more diligent in ferreting out evasion in order to collect bounties. These later actions infuriated merchants and shippers and threatened to alienate them from the federal government. The government, of course, relied upon the general goodwill and compliance of merchants and shippers, so the alienation was a potent threat. After a few years, Congress abolished the customs detectives.

Bounties gradually lost their attraction, as the public and government clashed over the tactics employed by bounty seekers, who were often outside the local community. Officers, intent on collecting bounties, might not exercise the discretion "necessary to sand off the hard edges of modern state power so it can win acceptance by the population." Parrillo observed, "The effective implementation of legislative will depended on a large degree of mass voluntary cooperation by the affected individuals, and bounties turned out to undermine such cooperation. The officer's monetary incentive to impose sanctions on laypersons placed him in such an adversarial posture toward them as to vitiate their trust in government and elicit from them a mirror-image adversarial response."[5]

By creating a system of fixed salaries, the official became "distanced … from the wishes of the layperson (in contrast to the facilitative payment) without radically alienating the two from each other (in contrast to the bounty). Compared with the two old forms of compensation, the salary placed the official in a middle distance vis-à-vis the population (Parrillo 2014, 3–4, 21–25, 30, 36–37 40–42)."

Corruption During Industrialization

Bribery has been known since at least Old Testament times. Isaiah 33:15–16 reads, "He who walks righteously and speaks uprightly, who despise the gain of oppressions [reject gains from extortion], who shakes his hands, lest they hold a bribe … his bread will be given him, his water will be sure."

Economists Raymond Fisman and Edward Miguel describe some aspects of bribery. "If bribe givers and takers are doing a halfway decent job of it, there's no obvious paper trail paper trial of what took place. Bribes don't appear in companies' tax returns, nor are they reported to shareholders in annual reports or cash-flow statements [in the United States]." With respect to tax returns, some countries, however, encourage reporting bribes to officials in other countries. Germany, the Netherlands, and Switzerland disdain bribery within their borders, but their companies may pay bribes to officials of other countries: "Not only was it permitted, it was tax deductible as a business expense. As a result, multinational corporations based in these countries would regularly report large bribe payments in tax returns. This practice largely came to an end with the passage of national laws related to the 1997 OECD Anti-Bribery Convention (Fisman and Miguel 2008, 18)."[6]

Although most governments have laws prohibiting bribery, there are few laws (or any good way to enforce) pertaining to transnational bribery. The OECD agreement left a big loophole: "Advocates of tough anti-bribery measures cautioned that the new treaty could prove a disappointment. For one thing, it would not outlaw most payments to political party leaders, even though party politicians were often central decision makers about government policy or simply proxies for actual government officials (Andrews 1997, no page numbers; Nichols 1997, 306, 357)." Although donating to political parties and legislators was legal, the line between political contributions and bribes seemed vague.

Tommy Suharto (former Indonesian ruler) and his siblings made money by helping foreign companies gain valuable trade considerations, including tax holidays, winning concessions, and so on. Fisman and Miguel asked a pertinent question, "What is the value of companies' political connections?" They suggested charting Suharto's health with an involved company's stock price; if Suharto's health declined, presumably, so would the company's stock value. To a degree, such blandishments resembled those used by Greek city leaders to get grain thousands of years ago.

In China, a local official Lai Changxing was popular with his constituents of Xiamen, because he kept prices of commodities artificially low for the city's poor, although he did so at the expense of government tax revenue. From the residents of Xiamen's perspective, Changxing was a benign, if corrupt, official. Fisman and Miguel commented that "One problem with the view that corruption speeds commerce is that paying bribes to reduce red tape is only half the story. Suppose that companies are willing to pay bribes to do an end run around the rules. Then government officials on the receiving end of these bribes will realize that they can make even more money by raising tariffs further, or throwing ever more regulatory barriers in companies' paths." This would create a not-so-virtuous downward spiral. "In many countries, like China, the rule enforcers are the rule makers as well, so they may start creating onerous new laws for the sole purpose of extracting larger bribe payments. Companies' willingness to pay bribes helps cause the red tape in the first place (Fisman and Miguel 2008, 28, 34, 66–67, 220)."

Lest Americans feel smug about their country's anti-bribery stance, Fisman and Miguel demonstrated that the U.S. Congress did not see fit to make it illegal to bribe congress people until 1853. True, "voting on matters where a member of Congress had a conflict of interest was illegal," but so were many other activities. The authors mentioned that one legislator was expelled for spitting, but none of the august bodies of legislators was ever evicted for bribe-taking or conflict of interest. Perhaps a gentleman's agreement was in force. Such sleazy actions continued to modern times. Although U.S. Senators were probably better educated and more intelligent than the average American (they are certainly far wealthier), their ability to pick winning stocks was impressive. The cynical and uncharitable among American voters might attribute such success to inside information or a friendly broker (see Hillary Clinton for turning $1000 into $100,000 by astute investments in the cattle futures market). Fisman and Miguel charted Vice-President Dick Cheney's ties with Halliburton; Democrats and others charged Cheney with dubious dealings with Halliburton. The authors argued that Halliburton (and other companies associated with Cheney) stock prices should have moved inversely with Cheney's health ups and down (fortunately for their research efforts, Cheney's health fluctuated considerably, thus giving statistical substance to their regression analysis). They found no such relationship (Fisman and Miguel 2008, 51, 220).

Corruption marked Africa's modernization during the postwar era. Political scientist Samuel Huntington notes that corruption can create a link between those gaining or grabbing political power with people controlling wealth, thereby allowing the two groups to assimilate (Huntington 1969, 61).

American cities during the Gilded Age and through the Progressive Era were notoriously and shamelessly corrupt. There were a few defenders of city politicians and office holders, such as New York City's George Washington Plunkitt. Plunkitt unabashedly bragged about making a lot of money, but he claimed to practice only "honest graft." He described how cities used to be small and poor, lacking many temptations, "lyin' around for politicians. There was hardly anything to steal, and hardly any opportunities for even honest graft." It was easy to keep track of the paltry sums entrusted to the city government. He had his own moral compass, so to speak: "Understand, I ain't defendin' politicians of today who steal. The politician who steals is worse than a thief. He is a fool [which was probably the worst thing a person could be, in Plunkitt's estimation]. With the grand opportunities all around for the man with a political pull, there's no excuse for stealin' a cent." In a classic statement of ethics being a function of opportunities, "it don't mean that the politicians of 1905 are, as a class, worse than them of 1835. It just means that the old-timers had nothin' to steal, while the politicians now are surrounded by all kinds of temptations and some of them naturally—the fool ones—buck up against the penal code."

Plunkitt was an ardent foe of civil service testing. He argued that most Democratic and Republican politicians agreed that "when a man works in politics, he should get something out of it." Proposed civil service testing threatened to destroy political parties: "Civil service would gobble up everything, politicians would be on the bum, the republic would fall and soon there would be the cry of 'Vevey le roi!' The very thought of this civil service monster makes my blood boil (Riordon 1963, 31–32, 38)."[7]

The Progressives fought long-standing corruption within cities. Some cities, such as Chicago, were notoriously corrupt. New York City's Boss Tweed and Tammany Hall are legendary. Economist Rebecca Menes considers the question, "How did corruption *not* cripple [economic] growth?" She cites a number of factors creating incentives for corrupt officials to act within some bounds, including open borders of cities (it was relatively easy to move to a less-corrupt urban area) and the discipline of the municipal bond market and ballot box. "Rapid city growth rewarded the circumspect grafter with opportunities for ... 'honest graft (Menes 2006, 64; Riordon 1963, 3).'"

Plunkitt considered politicians using inside knowledge of planned government projects to buy the affected property and make quick profits as "honest graft"; he denied taking money from the city treasury. He called "blackmailin' gamblers, saloonkeepers, disorderly people, etc." practitioners of "dishonest graft"; he compared his use of knowledge with "lookin' ahead in Wall Street or in the coffee or cotton market." He claimed that none of his fellow politicians practiced dishonest graft; he admitted that "I seen my opportunity and I take it .... Ain't it perfectly honest to charge a good price and make a profit on my investment and foresight? Of course it is. Well, that's honest graft (Riordon 1963, 3–5)."[8]

Nineteenth-century America, though, may well have presaged today's modernizing economies. Huntington argued that corruption may have a way of "surmounting traditional laws or bureaucratic regulations which hamper economic expansion. In the United States during the 1870s and 1880s corruption of state legislatures and city councils by railroad, utility, and industrial corporations undoubtedly speeded the growth of the American economy." Another scholar suggested, "Many economic activities would be paralyzed, were it not for the flexibility which *bakshish* contributes to the complex, rigid, administrative system." A similar situation occurred in postwar Brazil, where high rates of legislative corruption occurred simultaneously with rapid industrialization; entrepreneurs received cooperation from rural legislators. Huntington suggested that, to some degree, "the only thing worse than a society with a rigid, overcentralized, dishonest bureaucracy is one with a rigid, overcentralized, honest bureaucracy. A society which is relatively uncorrupt—a traditional society for instance where traditional norms are still powerful—may find a certain amount of corruption a welcome lubricant easing the path to modernization. A developed traditional society may be improved—or at least modernized—by a little corruption: a society in which corruption is already pervasive, however, is unlikely to be improved by more corruption (Huntington 1969, 68–69; Weiner 1962, 235)."

Law professor Susan Rose-Ackerman analyzes corruption in her book, *Corruption and Government*. She identifies key aspects underlying corruption: What are the incentives for corruption and how does corruption lead to inefficiencies and inequities; the different meanings of corruption across societies and across time; and how the private and public sectors' basic structures affect the prevalence of corruption. One aspect is of especial interest. During the mid-1950s, my parents and other parents petitioned Oregon senator Richard Neuberger to get an exemption from the immigration laws to allow them to adopt children from South Korea. Suppose that upon successful conclusion of the senator's efforts, that my parents sent him some gifts commemorating the arrival of their children (small crafts or artwork from Korea). Would this constitute a bribe or simply a tangible expression of gratitude? As Rose-Ackerman points out, drawing the "legal line between praiseworthy gifts and illegal and unethical bribes" is difficult. She focuses on cultural and historical factors that explain why different societies maintain their attitudes toward corruption; she hopes to "point out when the legacy of the past no longer fits modern conditions."

A difficulty in analyzing the effects of bribes and corruption is accounting not just for the immediate, direct but also indirect effects and effects across time. Rose-Ackerman describes how some economists (and perhaps her examples demonstrate why many people hold economists in low repute) create economic models to show how bribery may make outcomes more efficient. A simple case where people wait in line for government-provided goods or services may be improved, if people who place high values upon their time can bribe officials to move them ahead in the queue, such as airlines allowing people to pay extra to jump the queue. Another example revolves around tax collectors; if the government has a mandated minimum tax revenue target and employs tax collectors, then it may be efficient for the tax collectors to accept bribes as long as the target revenue is met. Businesspeople operating in business environments where corruption is common may justify making such payments. They may argue that the bribery serves to make the economy more efficient, than if they complied with the often inapt regulations. "Bribers are better off than they would be in an honest system in which they had to comply with the law."

Rose-Ackerman rebuts these arguments by identifying long-term consequences. Tolerating bribe-taking in one endeavor may inspire such behavior in other endeavors. In the case of tax collectors, the bribe-taking can easily lead to arbitrary and unjust tax payments; in the case of allowing people who are willing to pay a bribe to move ahead in a queue means that honest people must wait in line for a longer period. Corruption may also hinder state reform, as firms willing to bribe resist reform; such resistance may erode the government's legitimacy in the eyes of the citizens.

Businesspeople engaging in bribery, though, face potential drawbacks. By using illegal advantages, the bribe-payers may face extortionate demands. Similar to a postwar film noir plot, once a businessperson enters the murky waters of corruption, their ability to control events fades. Bribing a police officer or official may result in further demands for payments; the bribe payer cannot depend upon delivery of the promised services. Bribery can increase the amount of uncertainty in a business environment; certainly the bribe payer hopes to gain a certain outcome, but because a bribe is usually not enforceable, uncertainty does not disappear: "Individualized attempts to reduce uncertainty can, at the level of society, increase uncertainty. As a consequence, potential entrants will view the economic environment as risky and unpredictable."[9] Since a businessperson willing to bribe is often not a particularly scrupulous operator to begin with, such persons are rarely innocent or victims.

Creating incentives to forestall bribery and corruption is challenging. "Incentive systems can be effective, but they must be designed with care to avoid giving bureaucrats monopoly power that they can use to extract increased levels of rents (Rose-Ackerman 1978, 5, 16–17, 21–23, 85–108)." Chester Norman notes, "Officials must be unable to create onerous new conditions that they can then waive in return for payments. Thus British reformers in the 1830s urged that salaries be substituted for fees as a means of remunerating public officials. A parliamentary committee worried that accepting fees exposed a high official 'the suspicion of occasioning impediments to the exercise of [official] functions (Chester 1981, 135; Rose-Ackerman 1999, 79).'"

Financing Large-Scale Industry

Access to capital is crucial for many entrepreneurs. Not all potential borrowers face equal opportunities to get sufficient capital to start their businesses.

In comparison with British industrialists, who often financed start-ups with funds from personal savings, friends, and family or expansion out of accumulated profits, French and, more importantly, German industrialists found themselves needing large sums of capital in order to build very large plants in concentrated industries. The "backward" German economy also faced a shortage of entrepreneurial talent compared to the advanced British economy (Gerschenkron 1968, 120).

German banks pioneered joint-stock industrial finance, beginning in the 1840s and maturing during the last decades of the nineteenth century. The banks and industry cooperated in heavy manufacturing, mining, chemicals, and electrical engineering. The banks did not simply float securities of new and existing companies, "the point is that they retained an interest in their offspring and exercised a continuing influence on, if not control over, their operations. Moreover, with increasing financial concentration, a few large banks—notably the four 'D' Banks (Deutsche Bank, Dresdner Bank, Darmstadter Bank, Discontogesellschaft)—came to dominate entire industrial and commercial sectors." This phenomenon was unique to Germany (and to a lesser extent, Austria): "small wonder that it was German scholars and polemicists who developed the concept of 'finance capitalism.'"

Although economists usually disdained monopolies and cartels due to their inefficiencies, if there were economies of scale associated with larger firms, then monopolies and cartels sometimes proved beneficial: "there is good reason to believe that the German system generally used of proportioning market shares to capacity pushed cartel members to invest more and faster than they would have done otherwise. In the long run, thanks in part to dumping in times of market contraction, these investments paid well." It was not only the technical economies of scale that came into play. The large-scale, impersonal firms accentuated the skills and talents of engineers and technicians. These factors combined with the investment banks, whose skills in research and promoting large, complex business organizations helped persuade the public of the benefits of a German approach to industrialization (Landes 1966, 109–110).

The German bankers, similar to American bankers of the 1890–1930 period, disdained untrammeled competition that rendered prices volatile and solvency tenuous. "The banks refused to tolerate fratricidal struggles among their children. From the vantage point of centralized control, they were at all times quick to perceive profitable opportunities of cartelization and amalgamation of industrial enterprises. In the process, the average size of plant kept growing, and at the same time the interests of the banks and their assistance were even more than before devoted to those branches of industry where cartelization opportunities were rife." In a sense, then, the Germans benefited from their tardiness to the industrialization process (Gerschenkron 1968, 121).

Prior to World War II, Japanese banks, too, were connected to nonbanking companies though interlocking directors and auditors. Bank presidents were often major shareholders in the bank, so management was tied to ownership. Bank presidents often directed or audited nonbanking companies in which they owned large blocs of shares. In essence, these banks were created to ensure funding for their industrial allies. These "organ banks" lent large amounts of money to a small group of industrial companies, thereby violating the necessity to diversify the banks' risks. In this way, these Japanese "organ banks" were similar to banks in today's Russia and many developing countries. Lest American readers feel smug about American banks, banks in the United States often exhibited similar behavior during the nineteenth century. During Japan's Showa Financial Crisis, there were many bank runs, as people worried about poor-performing banks (Okazaki et al. 2005, 1083, 1087, 1091).[10] Japanese bankers' cronyism clashed with J.P. Morgan's approach. Morgan testified that the principal of lending was not predicated primarily on whether a potential borrower had money or property, "No sir; the first thing is character … because a man I do not trust could not get any money from me on all the bonds in Christendom (Strouse, July 7, 2002, 4:9)."

Russian backwardness emanated from several sources, of which serfdom was a primary one. In addition to the backward labor force, Russian industrialists faced a crippling shortage of capital; low standards of honesty and ethical behavior among business participants; and public distrust that made it difficult for banks to collect capital. Therefore, Russian banks could not act as did German banks. The paucity of capital and low business ethics—"where fraudulent bankruptcy had been almost elevated to the rank of a general business practice"—pretty much forced industrialists to seek governmental assistance in accumulating sufficient capital to establish large industrial firms. "There is no doubt that the government as an *agens movens* of industrialization discharged its role in a far less than perfectly efficient manner," due to incompetence and corruption. Despite these drawbacks, Ivan Vyshnegradski and Serge Witte made significant progress in industrializing Russia prior to The Great War. The Russians, as would the Soviets decades later, disdained investment in light industry and focused on large-scale enterprises; similar to German banks, the Russians tried to favor concentration and coordination among industrialists (Gerschenkron 1968, 124–125).

Counterexamples

Another tactic was for former rivals to form a cartel, but not all attempts to form cartels succeeded. There was a Whiskey Trust that failed repeatedly, due, in part, to cheating by cartel members and also by retailers (Clay and Troeksen 2002, 999–1021; Troesken 1998, 755–773).

Some large firms purposely limited their dominance of their industry. The DuPont company decided not to attempt to monopolize their industry. The company opted to dominate the industry through more efficient production that would reduce their unit costs below that of their smaller rivals. Arthur Moxham, one of their executives, advised in 1903 that an absolute monopoly would not be advantageous. It was better to produce roughly 60 percent of the market; he did not argue this because of legal constraints: "The essence of manufacture is steady and full product. The demand for the country for powder is variable. If we owned all therefore when slack times came we would have to curtail product to the extent of diminished demands." Then he made the telling point that if DuPont normally produced 60 percent, when there was a downturn in the market, the company could keep producing at capacity by lowering its price. The rival firms would bear the shortfall in demand (Chandler 1977, 442). This strategy was clever, but did it injure DuPont's rivals in an unfair way?

If you were up against one of the late nineteenth-century industrial Colossuses, you would have been fortunate to have drawn U.S. Steel. The famous merger of Carnegie Steel with the other participants created a gigantic firm. Carnegie Steel was, of course, the linchpin of the merger; Carnegie's insistence on minimizing costs meant that his firm was more efficient than its rivals (Hughes [1965] 1986, 239; Standiford 2005, 49). The American public naturally feared and was in awe of the new company, which dwarfed the other trusts, including Standard Oil. The new firm was in the bulls-eye of the antitrust forces.

Some industrialists prevailed because of superior business acumen tied with a ruthlessness tainted by occasional unscrupulous behavior. Rockefeller's peer Andrew Carnegie was astute, but he was also capable of engaging in calumny. When he realized that Allegheny Bessemer's new process was a superior and cheaper method, he immediately told railroads that the new method did not produce quality rails. He basically used some pseudo-scientific explanation for his claim, but the railroads listened. Eventually the Allegheny backers began doubting their own process, and the company foundered; Carnegie and Henry Clay Frick eventually bought out Allegheny and continued to use the direct rolling method (Standiford 2005, 88).

Carnegie pushed his men and his blast furnaces hard; he also willingly scrapped furnaces that became technologically obsolete and replaced them with superior furnaces. "Carnegie Steel thoroughly deserved its international reputation as the most relentless, ruthless competitor in the steel industry (McCraw and Reinhardt 1989, 593–594)."[11] Carnegie scrutinized cost figures for his companies and had a keen understanding of his rivals' costs. He was a pioneer in demanding accurate and timely accounting figures, possibly a legacy from his days working with Edgar Thomson and the Pennsylvania Railroad. Carnegie knew when he could undercut a rival's price. Charles Schwab, a Carnegie executive, recollected that "Carnegie never wanted to know the profits. He always wanted to know the costs." Such diligence in keeping statistics meant that he could gauge the effectiveness of individual workers, supervisors, and shifts. He rewarded those who performed well while simultaneously exhorting them to greater productivity (Standiford 2005, 47–48). Economic historian Jonathan R.T. Hughes considered J.P. Morgan's creation of U.S. Steel to be his masterpiece. At the outset, the firm controlled the majority of steel output but such control was not sustainable in the long run. Critics thought it an act of hubris to think such a gigantic firm could be efficiently managed, but Morgan "fooled them all. U.S. Steel was not the road to monopoly control of the American economy; the securities were placed with ease, and Carnegie did not get to foreclose [as he had hoped, when he agreed to the deal] (Hughes [1965] 1986, 430)." Schwab performed as capably for U.S. Steel as he had for Carnegie, at least in the beginning.

Morgan's contributions to American economic growth were summarized by Jean Strouse: "Morgan essentially provided that guarantee, choosing solid properties and taking what he called 'moral responsibility' for companies whose securities he under-wrote. When a road he had backed went bankrupt, he and his partners stepped in, saying in effect, 'we control the company, or no bailout.'" Morgan and his associates then applied, "'Morganization' involved scrutinizing every aspect of a railroad's operations, restructuring its finances, raising capital, settling lawsuits, firing managers, hiring new ones, appointing directors, and keeping vigilant watch over the company's finances, sometimes for decades, until solvency was restored." To be sure, Morgan had plenty of critics, since he was focused, "with building giant trusts and maintaining the international value of the dollar [more] than with the struggles of American farmers and workers or the social costs of industrialization. Nonetheless, in a time of cowboy capitalism he was an honest broker representing thousands of widely dispersed stock- and bondholders who owned 'new economy' railroads but had no effective control over the managers who ran them. In the course of his career he helped make American markets credible to foreign investors, kept the flow of capital moving east to west and transformed railroad securities from high-risk speculations into stable, long-term investments (Strouse, July 7, 2002, 4:9)."

After Schwab eventually proved ineffective as the head of the company, Morgan selected Judge Elbert Gary to run the company. Gary was an altogether different leader than Carnegie. In some ways, one might be tempted to label Gary a failure. The company's share of the American market fell from two-thirds to one-third; on the other hand, the company earned strong profits. More important, from Gary's point of view, was that the company stabilized the industry (avoiding the disruptive price wars) and avoided running afoul of the Sherman Antitrust Act—both supreme achievements (McCraw and Reinhardt 1989, 595–596).

Morgan was willing to organize conglomerates in ways that skirted the existing laws. Gary became a trusted lieutenant by informing Morgan that if he [Morgan] would divulge what purposes he had in mind with regard to a particular strategy, Gary would ensure the strategy would be carried out in a lawful way, if only barely so. Gary was not an entrepreneur like a Rockefeller or Carnegie nor was he an organizing genius as was J.P. Morgan. Gary, though, represented a new generation of industry leaders. He understood that the public and legislators were going to insist on proper behavior, so firms should gain a good reputation in the eyes of these groups. Gary frequently publicized his beliefs, and, in truth, liberalized some corporate policies. In an address delivered on June 17, 1922, Gary stated that U.S. Steel respected the rights of customers, employees, and competitors. He pledged that the company would provide accurate financial information. Whether he actually believed this was not the point; the key was his belief that by gaining the perception of playing fair, U.S. Steel could avoid the same government interference and ultimately the breakup that befell Standard Oil (McConnell [1930] 1973, 106).

Gary was forthright about his strategy. He testified in *U.S. v. United States Steel Corporation* that the company tried to eliminate or moderate fluctuations in prices, even when it could have reaped short-term gains from allowing prices to soar. His testimony might have seemed self-serving, but U.S. Steel customers testified to the accuracy of Gary's claims; in contrast to the pre-merger pricing policies, witnesses left no doubt as to their preferences for Gary's tactics. These witnesses and Gary's testimony convinced the court: "[N]o testimony has been produced on this record that a return to the old trade war system of ruinous competition would … benefit the public interests. On the contrary, the proof is that present business methods and ethics are more to be desired." So even though U.S. Steel possessed price-setting power, the court apparently deemed its use of such power to have been in the public interest.

The Supreme Court also contrasted U.S. Steel's behavior toward its rivals with, implicitly, Standard Oil's. It cited U.S. Steel's cooperation with its rivals with regard to price (although this, surely, was prima facie evidence of price-fixing). "There is no evidence that it attempted to crush its competitors or drive them out of the market, and in its competition it seemed to make no distinction between large and small competitors. In fact, its conduct towards it competitors … has been conspicuously free from that business brutality, meanness, and unfairness which characterized the conduct of certain large corporations found guilty of violating the Anti-Trust Law."

Gary was known for giving dinners for industry leaders, where the assembled steel operators would discuss prices. These dinners were dubious under the antitrust laws regarding cooperation among firms in an industry, but Gary had stopped them well before 1911 and the antitrust case against U.S. Steel. U.S. Steel determined and publicized what the price would be for the upcoming year and then exerted effort to maintain that price. Some U.S. Steel executives complained that such a policy was injurious to the company, as—in a turnabout from the public's perception—small firms cheated on the fixed price and "poached" some of U.S. Steel's market share. Aside from Gary's testimony before Congress, there was other evidence demonstrating his sincerity in seeking price stability. U.S. Steel's policy was to be the last to cut prices during recessions and the last to raise prices during upturns. The strategy did, in fact, cost the company market share, but it also helped maintain profit percentages (McCraw and Reinhardt 1989, 599–604, 612).

Why did Gary and U.S. Steel pursue such a counterintuitive approach to exercising their market dominance? Gary's legal training and experiences as a corporate executive made him wary of triggering antitrust actions. Morgan may have been influenced by Gary's caution, when he selected Gary to replace Charles Schwab. Gary suggested to Morgan in 1901, before assuming the reins of U.S. Steel, that the Attorney General was likely to attack U.S. Steel as a monopoly if it maintained its market share: "I also think that if the Corporation with its business is properly managed and it is allowed to continue in business until it has proven that the intentions of the managers are good, that there is no disposition to exercise a monopoly or to restrain legitimate trade, then in that case, if there is a contest, the company will be held to be legal (Tarbell 1925, 123–124)."

U.S. Steel prevailed in the antitrust case, although two economic historians suggested that had justices Louis Brandeis and James McReynolds not recused themselves, the 4–3 verdict in favor of the company might have been reversed. The verdict likely hinged upon U.S. Steel's dramatic loss of market share from its initial 66 percent. Although Gary's tactics of stabilizing prices at the expense of market share was important, the actual operation of U.S. Steel also contributed. Carnegie was famous for squeezing out added productivity and cutting costs, as were other industrial behemoths; the railroads had pioneered the use of data upon which to base decisions. These firms discovered and exploited economies of scale and scope, but U.S. Steel, despite the Carnegie heritage, operated more as a "loose federation." Despite this seemingly lackadaisical approach, U.S. Steel's utilization rate remained above the industry's rate for a quarter century. The corporation focused on vertical integration and constructing new plants in what is now Gary, Indiana. Once Gary realized that further expansion of capacity was likely to invite antitrust action, he had the firm reduce its expansion plans.

Gary also eschewed the secretiveness of Rockefeller and other industrial leaders. Although such close-to-the-vest policies may have been astute, in the hands of muckrakers the silent approach triggered suspicions of nefarious activities and gave scope for overheated imaginations. Gary publicized the new company's intentions as early as the very first *Annual Report* and its "Policy as to Prices" piece that announced price stability as its goal. The fact that the company published an *Annual Report* was novel; the act gained much public approval. McCraw and Reinhardt concluded that "the U.S. Steel story becomes not just an epic of administrative failure, or an example of oligopolistic inevitability, or, necessarily a harbinger of American industrial decline. It may be all three; but fundamentally it is a story of political economy. It constitutes a vivid instance of the interrelated nature of public policy and business behavior." It revealed that success in early twentieth-century American business was not achieved solely in the marketplace but also in the eyes of the public (McCraw and Reinhardt 1989, 614–617, 619).[12]

Surprising Effects on Labor

The consolidation of firms had two main ramifications for employees. By consolidating several medium-sized firms into one very large firm, many managers became redundant as well as workers. Those workers who remained, however, often enjoyed higher wages. The Commercial Travelers' National League testified that mergers reduced the number of commercial travelers, but "practically all the other witnesses who gave evidence on this point that the Standard Oil Company pays good wages and gives steady employment to its men." A similar tale occurred with the American Sugar Refining Company and several of the steel manufacturers; several of the steel manufacturers reported proportionally larger pay raises for its workers than for its white-collar workers. Of course, the job losses among the executives and other white-collar workers in the wake of mergers played out differently than for unskilled or semi-skilled workers. The white-collar workers were more articulate and may have had better access to a sympathetic press than did the laborers. The large corporations also appeared more amenable to using organized labor. In the steel industry, several of the larger firms used union labor although not exclusively. The executives testified that they were, "on the whole inclined to favor labor organizations," but one is entitled to ask whether such testimony was self-serving.

There was one aspect of the consolidation that many historians did not comment upon. As the smaller companies and their management were subsumed, critics warned that the "opportunities for independent management of business enterprises [diminished], and that in consequence the mental and moral fiber of the community is weakened." Even supporters of consolidation lamented the reduced opportunities for individual initiative, although they asserted that the overall gains more than offset the sentimental loss of initiative. Certainly being on the corporate ladder afforded people with opportunities to demonstrate initiative, and there were still plenty of market niches for entrepreneurs to fill or to create (U.S. Industrial Commission 1900, 29–32).

Organized labor was ambivalent about trusts. The socialists, perhaps surprisingly, viewed the trusts with some equanimity, since they viewed the concentration of capital as fulfilling Marx' prophecy. In the *Workmen's Advocate*, an editorial stated, "trusts and pools are playing their part in the development of that state of society in which every citizen shall indeed have opportunities, now as at present unequal, but equal (Gordon 1963, 159)." Foes of socialism worried that the concentration of economic power in the hands of a few trusts "will lead to the popular belief that the concentration of all business enterprises under one general management is a good thing and that thus State socialism may creep in." Another commentator accused a speaker of assuming "the socialistic attitude of encouraging trusts as a step toward socialism (first quote Sears 1956, 390; second quote Hatfield 1899, 15)."

With respect to their treatment of labor, Rockefeller and Carnegie, though, could be rightly accused of not delving too deeply into working conditions of their subsidiaries. Their involvement in coal and other mining endeavors made them tangentially, at least, culpable for some of the violent incidents that occurred in these industries.

Other Nations React Differently

American animus toward big business was not inevitable. Germans were not as avidly anti-monopolistic and anti-collusion as the Americans. The Germans had a Trade Regulation Act (1869) with a clause reading "All trade is open to everyone, unless this statute provides exceptions from or limitations upon this rule." This act seems pretty straightforward. A German Supreme court ruling of 1897, though, sent Germany down a different path than that followed by the Americans in the wake of the Sherman Act. In the *Saxon Woodpulp Manufacturers Association* case, the court ruled that the cartel agreement was not a violation of the Trade

Regulation Act. The court explained that the cartel intended to benefit the society in general and did not impair liberty of any individual. The jurists argued that the cartel was fostered to prevent the "ruinously low prices" that occurred under vigorous competition; such low prices, as seen in America during the early years of the oil industry, created much consternation for firms, consumers, and the nation. Cartel agreements to preclude injurious low prices, therefore, benefited the public interest. With respect to individual liberty, the German court took the stance that it would restrain freedom of contract by ruling against the proposed cartel.

The German court ruling in 1897 apparently was distrustful of competitive pricing. Although the 1897 decision acknowledged that cartels created for the purpose of exploiting consumers would be held in conflict with the public interest, the court failed to establish any standard for ascertaining which cartels were acting in the public interest. The German government also intervened on occasion to compel participation in cartels, particularly during the Nazi era. The government promulgated an Ordinance Against Abuse of Economic Power in 1923 that required cartel agreements to be written. The Ordinance also created the possibility that a cartel could penalize non-participants, but only with permission of the President of the Cartel Court. The cartels fixed prices, and cartel members went to extraordinary length to compel membership within the cartel. One critic claimed to have seen a circular letter with the instructions pertaining to a recalcitrant independent: "He, and his customers, must be pursued as beasts of prey, for we know no mercy. In this matter one becomes a member, or he will be vanquished as an enemy."

If one was fixated by the sheer size of German industrial cartels, then the government's policy made sense. One might understand why the Nazis and their Soviet counterparts equated size with efficiency. In the Soviet case, their factories proved adept at times at producing large amounts of stuff that Russian consumers did not want to buy. In Germany, critics accused the cartels of charging Germans higher prices than foreign buyers. Another critic thought cartel pricing was akin to a levy on the poor (Marburg 1964, 80–86).

Japan, too, allowed its industrialists latitude. Japanese businesses engaged in what two writers described as "a vast back-scratching system." The end result was a "softened market competition within and across firms in the giant conglomerates called *keiretsu*." Japanese firms and the government worked to avoid anyone losing face. These tactics made Japanese firms strong competitors in foreign markets, or at least did until 1990 or so. When firms got in trouble, banks and the government stepped in to remedy the situation (Friedman and McNeill 2013, 71–72).

Why were Americans so insistent on antitrust policy in the late 1800s, when German and Japanese governments seemed willing to encourage industrial concentration? Historian Richard Hofstadter speculated that American antitrust sentiment "had little to compete with in the way of aristocratic, militaristic, or labor-socialist theories." Given the jarring rapidity of transformation of the economy and the society, Americans made "some frightening projections into the future .... A nation that had gone so fast from competitive small enterprise to corporate giantism might readily go with equal speed from corporate giantism to a system of monopolistic tyranny." The public also had ambivalent feelings about antitrust. "They were living in a society that wanted to reap the benefits of large-scale enterprise, as well as to prevent the evils of monopolization (Hofstadter 1965, 192, 195–197)."

Legislators recognized the cost-saving (and ultimately lower prices) afforded by large firms exploiting economies of scale. They wanted to protect such companies, as Senator Nelson Aldrich (R-RI) attempted with his proposed rider to a tariff upon sugar: "That this act shall not be construed to apply to ... combinations ... made with a view or which tend, by means other than by a reduction of the wages of labor, to lessen the cost of production or reduce the price of any of the necessaries of life, nor to the combinations ... made with a view ... to increase the earnings of persons engaged in any useful employment (Grandy 1993, 365, 367–368)." Senators were, therefore, more concerned about the means whereby a producer gained monopoly power and not with a strict definition of monopoly as a sole producer.

State governments took the lead in prosecuting trusts, although their efforts were often for naught. State prosecution simply induced trusts to incorporate in another state, thereby creating a whack-a-mole aspect. Trusts were so unpopular that both Republicans and Democrats declared their hostility. Presidential candidate James G. Blaine made the ill-advised statement that trusts were "private business affairs" and that trusts existed in countries without protective tariffs. His Democratic opponents pounced upon his statement, "If Mr. Blaine had tried his best to do or say something for the good for the Democratic candidates, he could not have done better than he has done in his Portland speech. Let him deliver that speech in the West and there will be a stampede to the party that opposes trusts and upholds the rights of the poor man to live (*Public Opinion* 1888, 425; Gordon 1963, 159–160)."

No one bothered to ask economists to testify regarding trusts, despite the fact that some prominent ones had addressed the trust issue in academic journals. One economist stated that "[the majority of men in all ranks] are gradually learning that in those lines of industry which involve large capital, under concentrated management, the old theory of free competition is as untenable as it was in the case of railroads. That a great deal of our productive industry is thus monopolized hardly admits of doubt (Hadley 1886, 41)." Some economists were undoubtedly left off the witness list, because they held favorable views of trusts. One wrote, "Strictly speaking, concentration of capital does not drive small capitalists out of business, but simply integrates them into a larger and more complex system of production, in which they are enabled to produce wealth more cheaply for the community and obtain a larger income for themselves." The author noted that "By the use of large capital, improved machinery and better facilities, the trust can and does undersell the corporation; but that is not destroying competition .... The competition between trusts naturally tends to reduce the profits to a closer margin than would the competition between corporations for the reason that the larger the business transacted, the smaller the percentage of profit necessary to its success. Thus, instead of concentration of capital tending to destroy competition, the reverse is true (Gunton 1888, 389–390)."

In the end, the Sherman Antitrust Act passed unanimously in both the House and the Senate, except for one contrary vote in the Senate. The trust movement collapsed, as executives discovered that most of the combinations failed to pay common dividends in the years immediately following their formation (Sears 1956, 391–392).

Conclusion

German and Japanese attitudes toward large-scale companies differed from the Americans. These countries' governments embraced big firms. The American animus toward large companies demonstrated different countries' attitudes toward the ethical aspects of industrialization and large-scale firms.

Large-scale American corporations and trusts incited fears of industrial hegemony. Executives sometimes resorted to bribery of and undue influence over legislators. The public sometimes misunderstood predatory pricing, often confusing reduced prices emanating from a vicious policy designed to drive out rivals from price reductions reflecting lowered costs of production from improved production processes.

Notes

1. Fans of Mel Brooks' *Blazing Saddles* might add stampeding cattle through the Vatican.
2. See pages 460–469 for discussion of American Tobacco Company restricting sellers of their cigarettes from selling other brands—the company offered an additional commission for sellers who complied with the edict.
3. A modern-day take on this might be to issue bubble-gum cards of your defunct or soon-to-be-defunct rivals, listing similar business statistics.
4. For intervention in trade, Smith described how colonial enterprises received exclusive rights (575).
5. Parrillo offered the American income tax system as an example whereby people generally obey the laws at rates far higher than a Benthamite calculation of marginal gains from cheating versus the marginal cost from being detected and fined would predict (Parrillo 2014, 34–35).
6. The tax deductibility issue raises some intriguing possibilities, such as verifying how much was actually paid in bribes. Would companies have an incentive to overstate such payments on their tax returns? Did the bribed give receipts?
7. Plunkitt may have been at home with nineteenth-century Chinese bureaucrats. Bureaucrats were expected to augment their income by "squeeze (Feuerwerker 1958, 23; see also Hsin-pao Chan 1964, 9–10)."
8. Arthur Mann, in the introduction to Riordon's book, pointed out that Tammany Hall and other big-city machines "acted as a social welfare agency when the poor and the immigrants had nowhere else to turn. What is more, the machine familiarized millions of newcomers to this country with representative government (Riordon 1963, xix)."
9. There was an old boast attributed to Simon Cameron: "An honest politician is one who, when he is bought, will stay bought (https://en.wikiquote.org/wiki/simon_cameron, viewed February 27, 2017, 9:56 pm)."
10. Given the banks' greater knowledge of acquaintances, such lending practices did not necessarily imply poor loans.

11. Carnegie usually was an unruly competitor (McConnell [1930] 1973, 105). He often refused to join price-setting schemes and was almost gleeful in undercutting his rivals' price. J.R.T. Hughes described Carnegie's bravura performance in dealing with a collusive agreement that dissatisfied him: "Carnegie leaped up, announced that he wanted an amount equal to the largest quota, moved his finger around the table from magnate to magnate telling each one his own business and costs and threatening to undercut them all. It was a typical Carnegie display, and it worked (Hughes [1965] 1986, 239)." Alfred Chandler Jr. suggests that Carnegie joined the Bessemer pool to see the cost figures of his rivals (Chandler 1977, 268).
12. The National Biscuit Company (Nabisco) stated in its annual report for 1901 that it had learned its lesson regarding trying to control or to limit competition (Chandler 1977, 335).

Bibliography

Andrews, Edmund. "29 Nations Agree to Outlaw Bribing Foreign Officials." New York Times. November 21, 1997. http://www.nytimes.com/1997/11/21/business/29-nations-agree-to-outlaw-bribing-foreign-officials.html, viewed January 25, 2017.

Carlton, Dennis and Jeffrey Perloff. *Modern Industrial Organization* (Boston, MA: Pearson-Addison Wesley, 2005).

Chandler, Alfred Jr. *The Visible Hand: The Managerial Revolution in American Business* (Cambridge, MA: Harvard University Press, 1977).

Chester, Norman. *The English Administrative System, 1780–1870* (Oxford, UK: Clarendon Press, 1981).

Clay, Karen and Werner Troeksen. "Strategic Behavior inn Whiskey Distilling, 1887–1895." *Journal of Economic History* 62(4), December 2002, 999–1023.

Feuerwerker, Albert. *China's Early Industrialization: Sheng Hsuan-Huai and Mandarin Enterprise* (Cambridge, MA: Harvard University Press, 1958).

Fisman, Raymond and Edward Miguel. *Economic Gangsters: Corruption, Violence and the Poverty of Nations* (Princeton, NJ: Princeton University Press, 2008).

Friedman, Daniel and Daniel McNeill. *Morals and Markets: The Dangerous Balance* (New York, NY: Palgrave Macmillan, 2013). 2nd edition.

Galambos, Louis. "The Trade Association Movement in Cotton Textiles, 1900–1935." *Explorations in Entrepreneurial History* 2(1), Fall 1964, 31–55.

Gerschenkron, Alexander. "Russia: Agrarian Policies and Industrialization, 1861–1914." *Continuity in History and Other Essays* (Cambridge, MA: Belknap Press, 1968).

Gordon, Sanford. "Attitudes towards Trusts Prior to the Sherman Act." *Southern Economic Journal* 30(2), October 1963, 156–167.

Grandy, Christopher. "Original Intent and the Sherman Antitrust Act: A Re-examination of the Consumer-Welfare Hypothesis." *Journal of Economic History* 53(2), 1993, 359–376.

Gunton, George. "The Economic and Social Aspects of Trusts." *Political Science Quarterly* 3(3), September 1888. 385–408.

Hadley, Arthur. "Private Monopolies and Public Rights." *Quarterly Journal of Economics* 1(1), October 1886. 28–44.

Hatfield, Henry. "The Chicago Trust Conference." *Journal of Political Economy* 8(1), December 1899. 1–18.

Hofstadter, Richard. "The Paranoid Style in American Politics." *The Paranoid Style in American Politics and Other Essays* (New York, NY: Alfred A. Knopf, 1965), 3–40.

Chan, Hsin-pao. *Commissioner Lin and the Opium War* (Cambridge, MA: Harvard University Press, 1964).

Hughes, Jonathan. *The Vital Few: The Entrepreneur & American Economic Progress* (New York, NY: Oxford University Press, [1965] 1986). Expanded edition.

Huntington, Samuel. *Political Order in Changing Societies* (New Haven, CT: Yale University Press, 1969).

Kristof, Kathy. "David Versus Goliath: Lawsuit against Wal-Mart Could Change the Face of Retailing." Chicago *Tribune*, June 14, 1994, Sec. 4, 1–2.

Landes, David. "Structure of Enterprises." *The Rise of Capitalism* (New York, NY: Macmillan, 1966). 99–111.

Marburg, Theodore. "Government Business in Germany: Public Policy toward Cartels." *Business History Review* 38(1), Spring 1964, 78–101.

McConnell, Donald. *Economic Virtues in the United States: A History and an Interpretation* (New York, NY: Arno Press, [1930] 1973).

McCraw, Thomas and Forest Reinhardt. "Losing to Win: U.S. Steel's Pricing, Investment Decisions, and market Share, 1901–1938." *Journal of Economic History* 49(3), September 1989, 593–619.

Menes, Rebecca. "Limiting the Reach of the Grabbing Hand: Graft and Growth in American Cities, 1880 to 1930." *Corruption and Reform: Lessons from America's Economic History*, edited by Edward Glaeser and Claudia Goldin (Chicago, IL: University of Chicago Press, 2006), 63–94.

Nichols, Philip. "Outlawing Transnational Bribery through the World Trade Organization." *Law and Policy in International Business* 28(2), Winter 1997, 305–381.

Okazaki, Tetsuji, Michiru Sawada, and Kazuki Yokoyama. "Measure the Extent and Implications of Director interlocking in the Prewar Japanese Banking Industry." *Journal of Economic History* 65(4), December 2005. 1082–1115.

Parrillo, Nicholas. *Against the Profit Motive: The Salary Revolution in American Government, 1780–1940* (New Haven, CT: Yale University Press, 2014).

Public Opinion. "Mr. Blaine on Trusts." Vol. V, No. 20, August 25, 1888, 425.

Riordon, William. *Plunkitt of Tammany Hall: A Series of Very Plain Talks on Very Practical Politics, Delivered by Ex-Senator George Washington Plunkitt, the Tammany Philosopher, From His Rostrum—The New York County Court House Bootblack Stand* (New York, NY: E.P. Dutton, 1963).

Ritchie, Michael. *Please Stand By: A Prehistory of Television* (Woodstock, NY: Overlook Press, 1995).

Rose-Ackerman, Susan. *Corruption: A Study in Political Economy* (New York, NY: Academic Press, 1978).

Rose-Ackerman, Susan. *Corruption and Government: Causes, Consequences, and Reform* (Cambridge, UK: Cambridge University Press, 1999).

Sears, Marian. "The American Businessman at the Turn of the Century." *Business History Review* XXX(4), December 1956, 382–443.

Shulman, David. *From Hire to Liar: The Role of Deception in the Workplace* (Ithaca, NY: Cornell University Press, 2007).

Smith, Adam. *An Inquiry into the Nature and Causes of the Wealth of Nations*, edited by R.H. Campbell and A.S. Skinner (Indianapolis, IN: Liberty*Classics*, 1981).

Standiford, Les. *Meet You in Hell: Andrew Carnegie, Henry Clay Frick, and the Bitter Partnership that Transformed America* (New York, NY: Crown Publishers, 2005).

Stashower, Daniel. *The Boy Genius and the Mogul: The Untold Story of Television* (New York, NY: Broadway Books, 2002).

Stevens, William "Unfair Competition." *Political Science Quarterly* 29(2), June 1914, 282–306 and (3), September 1914, 460–490.

Strouse, Jean. "Capitalism Depends on Character." *New York Times*. July 7, 2002, Sec. 4, 9.

Sullivan, Mark. *Our Times: The United States, 1900–1925. Vol. II. America Finding Herself* (New York, NY: Charles Scribner's Sons, 1927). 6 vols.

Tarbell, Ida. *The Life of Elbert H. Gary: The Story of Steel* (New York, NY: D. Appleton, 1925).

Telser, Lester. "Cutthroat Competition and the Long Purse." *Journal of Law & Economics* 9(1), October 1966, 259–277.

Troesken, Werner. "Exclusive Dealing and the Whiskey Trust, 1890–1895." *Journal of Economic History* 58(3), September 1998, 755–778.

U.S. Industrial Commission. *Preliminary Report on Trusts and Industrial Combinations, Together with Testimony, Review of Evidence, Charts Showing Effects of Prices, and Topical Digest.* Volume 1 of the Commissions Reports (Washington, D.C.: Government Printing Office, 1900).

Watkins, Myron. *Industrial Combinations and Public Policy: A Study of Combination, Competition and the Common Welfare* (Boston, MA: Houghton Mifflin, 1927).

Weiner, Myron. *The Politics of Scarcity: Public Pressure and Political Response in India* (Chicago, IL: University of Chicago Press, 1962).

Whitehorne, Earl. "Some Experiences in Price Cutting." *American Machinist* 68(12), March 22, 1928, 294–296.

CHAPTER 6

John D. Rockefeller and Standard Oil

Many people considered John D. Rockefeller and Standard Oil the epitome of ruthless business practices. In terms of business strategy, Rockefeller and his associates were adept at adapting to the times. Rockefeller was a stickler for cost control; by keeping his costs lower than his rivals, shouldn't Rockefeller have triumphed in the end? Why wasn't he a hero: He helped rationalize the oil industry from its swings of boom and bust? Why does the Standard Oil Company continue to incite opprobrium?

Certainly Standard Oil was a convenient target; John D. Rockefeller and his associates were secretive; they were ruthless, but they were also pragmatic. In many cases, they did not crush a rival until after they had given the rival a chance to join Standard Oil under reasonable terms. Business historians and economists began clearing away the myths associated with Standard Oil's rise. The conventional wisdom that political pressure inspired judicial decisions to curb Standard Oil's and other large economic entities' power proved overdrawn (Pratt 1980, 817).

To be sure, Rockefeller and the Standard Oil Company exploited rebates from railroads that were perceived as unfair, immoral, and probably illegal. Throughout the late 1800s, though, Rockefeller focused on providing high-quality kerosene and other petroleum-based products at low prices, surely goals in the public interest and fulfilling ethical considerations.

D. G. Surdam, *Business Ethics from the 19th Century to Today*,
https://doi.org/10.1007/978-3-030-37169-2_6

The Animus Toward Rockefeller and Standard Oil

Allan Nevins, a Rockefeller biographer, noted in the 1940s that ethics during American industrialization were misunderstood. Nevins wrote, "Rockefeller's economic vision, and the courage shown in his fidelity to it, deserve commendation. He knew that he was carrying through a great experiment, and he believed the experiment sound and fruitful." He also recognized that his associates and he were operating in a time of flux. For instance, in the field of banking, Henry Lee Higginson related to a class of Harvard students that what was considered ethical had changed considerably. In particular, in the 1870s, bankers often mimicked orders placed by rich customers for particular stocks, in order to piggy-back on the customer's supposed information regarding the stock. By 1900, bankers frowned on such actions, and by 1940 the action was punishable. Rockefeller, too, acknowledged that some of the Standard Oil Trust's tactics in the 1870s and 1880s were no longer considered acceptable. Nevins conjectured that a study of business history would reveal that there was an inverse relationship between economic booms and "business laxity" as well as a correlation between business honesty and "social maturity." "All this must be remembered in appraising Rockefeller's weapons and the use he made of them." Nevins disputed the idea that Rockefeller and other titans of industry were motivated by sheer greed but by the challenge of creating a well-functioning industry. He acknowledged that some businessmen were greedy, but truly greedy men rarely accumulated "colossal fortunes" as greed eventually impeded business success. He thought that greedy men, instead, ended up with modest fortunes: "The men who built the really towering economic structures were not thinking primarily of dollars, or they would have halted at the first story (Nevins 1940, 2:710–712)." Although Nevins' observation may have been correct, one would be hard pressed to know how to test this thesis. Rockefeller and his associates had to withstand enormous risks in the face of uncertainty. In contrast, a modern-day lottery player hoping to win a mega-jackpot is unwilling to put forth the enduring effort required to attain both the achievements and wealth of industry leaders.

Historian Thomas Navin suggested that a better way to evaluate a business pioneer was to consider their decisions to act ethically or unethically in the context of their times. Critics often use their advantage of hindsight combined with a naïve belief that business ethics exist in a world that is "comparatively frictionless." He rather snidely wrote, critics "are hampered in arriving at this ideal only by the friction of their own ignorance. That is to say, they are concerned only with what is right and not with what is expedient or possible." Navin details how businesspeople facing real-life frictions may be compelled to "decisions which he realizes are not fair or beneficial." Rockefeller needed the savings in shipping costs associated with the rebates. Navin observes that "Had [Rockefeller] been essentially an unethical business man, he could never have obtained the favorable rebates he did get. Cornelius Vanderbilt knew that he could trust Rockefeller to keep his agreements even when it meant shipping at a loss to Standard."[1]

Navin cautioned that critics of businesspeople were not always accurate: "There are many cases in which the public has been misled, sometimes deliberately, sometimes merely because of improper emphasis." The critics have often been more vociferous than the defenders; many of the targets remained quiet, often unable to respond without divulging strategic information. The critics, too, have often been "men of letters," in contrast to the businesspeople, who are "men of action." The businessperson's motives, though, triggered suspicion that eroded the public's perception of the astute businessperson; many historians and much of the public impugn the profit-seeking motivation, even if such motivation created a company such as Standard Oil, "one of the best-managed corporations in the world, even if it produces goods of incomparable quality and with an efficiency which makes competition nearly impossible." Rockefeller and his associates' triumph over more favorably situated rivals were undercut in the public's mind by their seeking of profits; they, presumably, would have received plaudits, had they run their enterprise as a non-profit endeavor. Businesspeople, too, were sometimes their own worst enemies, as losers in the game castigated the winners. Although Rockefeller and Standard Oil attempted to buy out (and often at generous terms) rival firms, the independent oil firms that refused Standard Oil's offer gave bitter testimony about the allegedly unfair and unethical behavior of the winner. Unethical behavior on the part of an impotent company did not incur the same wrath.

Navin made another provocative point. The industrial captain, such as Rockefeller, found that his company's and the public's interest tended to converge, as the firm grew larger. Standard Oil initially produced kerosene, a product demanded by a wide swatch of the consuming public. Standard Oil could not have maintained its market dominance by relying upon unfair practices. Rockefeller and his associates recognized that, to remain dominant, they had to not only offer low prices but also to produce high-quality kerosene. The public understood that cutthroat competition often created only temporarily low prices. In other words, firms had to constantly serve their customers. "It is said that Standard's second grade of kerosene was superior to the best grades of most competitors."

Navin considered why such early titans of industry, such as John D. Rockefeller, engendered such opprobrium. Navin believed that people who exonerated Rockefeller in the decades after 1900 did so because of his legendary charitable donations and not for his genius in organization. Others excused his actions on the basis that in the last decades of the nineteenth century, business mores were considerably different than those that prevailed by the third decade of the twentieth century (when most of the creators of large companies had been displaced by managers). Of the latter explanation, Navin wrote, "The concession [regarding applying anachronistic ethical standards to Rockefeller] is generous, but not particularly to the point. Even in his own day, Rockefeller was criticized for using such competitive devices as railroad rebates. The difference in ethical standards was one not of time but of level. Rockefeller was operating on one ethical plane and was being criticized on another (Navin 1943, 11–14)."

Rockefeller's Early Days

Rockefeller's father was a peddler of nostrums and medical quackery; a whiff of disrepute hung about Rockefeller's father. As with many famous figures, Rockefeller's youth was shrouded in myth. Although Rockefeller recalled that he learned much from his father, there was some evidence that his father and his father's occupation were bittersweet memories. One commentator characterized William Avery Rockefeller as devoid of a moral code, who boasted, "I cheat my boys every chance I get .... I trade with the boys and skin 'em and I just beat 'em every time I can. I want to make 'em sharp (Flynn 1932, 57–58; see also Chernow 1998, 29; Russell 1934, 314; Cohn 1940, 216)."

As amusing or appalling as this story goes, the earliest of the authors using this story did not list a citation for William Rockefeller's quote, and no other biographer seems to have provided a source (except that they quoted Flynn). Rockefeller biographer Allan Nevins depicted Rockefeller senior differently: "But William was essentially a businessman, highly practical, whose main desire for his sons was that they become shrewd alert businessmen." Nevins described how William trained John and his brothers in business, including lessons in negotiating, as well as personal habits reflecting those of Benjamin Franklin—"industry, punctuality and thrift." John D. might have been an apt student, but it was a little disconcerting to hear his sister, Mary Ann, recall that "He used to buy candy by the pound and sell it to us by the piece and make a profit." One might admire John D.'s acumen and initiative but the candy story revealed a precocious, relentless quest for profits (Nevins 1940, 1:39, 43–44, 68).

Rockefeller learned early on of the benefits of thrift; he recalled his amazement at finding the interest on a loan he made to a farmer rivaled his earnings doing hard physical labor. Years later, he told an audience that he realized, "it was a good thing to let the money be my servant and not make myself a slave to the money." Rockefeller lived by this credo.[2]

There was one unusual aspect to the young Rockefeller. Almost as soon as he began earning money, he began to give money to his church and other charities. His mother may have inculcated this habit, but in any event, John D. Rockefeller was serious enough about giving that he kept detailed records: "From the beginning, I was trained to work, to save, and to give." In later years, when Rockefeller became renowned for his philanthropic work, people wondered whether his giving was motivated by public relations or from a sincere desire to give. Rockefeller remarked, "It has seemed as if I was favored and got increase because the Lord knew that I was going to turn around and give it back." On another occasion, Rockefeller reminisced that a minister preached, "'Get money; get it honestly and then give it wise.' I wrote that down in a little book (Nevins 1940, 1:43, 68, *New York Times*, October 20, 1907, SM1)."

The young Rockefeller went to work as a bookkeeper in a produce commission firm and quickly became a partner by age 20. He did not serve in the Civil War, even though he was of prime age. Although he was not an exceptional student, he did have the ability to understand and to work with numbers. He also realized that paying attention to details was critical. The early experience of loaning money to the farmer triggered his astute use of credit; he quickly gained a reputation as a dependable borrower. During the Civil War, he entered the oil refining business (Gras 1941, 52).

Standard Oil's Goals

Rockefeller and Standard Oil quickly grasped the importance of what Alfred Chandler Jr. termed, "economies of speed." They invested in ever-larger refineries capable of producing more and more barrels per day. The high volume led to falling per-barrel costs of output.

Rockefeller and his associates used their lower cost of output to gain a competitive edge during the 1870s.

In order to capture the gains from declining average costs, though, an enterprising individual or group of individuals had to entice or coerce rivals into joining the burgeoning cartel. Cartels often chose to ruthlessly crush recalcitrant producers using a variety of tactics. The careers of Rockefeller and his associates exemplified the process. Those oil producers and refiners who joined Standard Oil profited handsomely, but the hold-outs sometimes faced business extinction.

Within a couple of decades of the initial strikes in western Pennsylvania, oil was the United States' fourth-largest export. The oil was used for illuminants and lubricants. The Pennsylvania oil fields were chaotic, as oil drilling required small amounts of capital. Adding to the chaos and waste was the "rule of capture," whereby the landowner owned what was beneath the land. The analogy of a milkshake with multiple straws is apt; each drinker had an incentive to slurp as much milkshake (or oil) as possible, a point amusingly made in the "Who Shot Mr. Burns" episode in *The Simpsons.* Someone discovered oil under the Springfield elementary school; Burns bought an adjacent lot and drilled diagonally to suck the oil dry. The ease of entry and ambiguous property rights led to a roller-coaster ride for prices. Chandler documented the price swings in 1862, 1864, and 1871. The price gaps quoted were much narrower not only in dollar terms but also proportionally by 1871. For the oil producers, growing demand in the United States and Europe cushioned the price volatility.

Initially, the oil industry was fragmented. There were the drillers, producers, transporters, refiners, and marketers. Refiners specialized in output. Firms began combining vertically and horizontally. Competition dominated. "Under these conditions, the location of refineries with respect to transportation as well as to the market frequently proved to be an important determinant of success." The cost of transporting crude and refined oil loomed large; producers located where there were multiple railroads and quickly learned to play the railroads against each other. The railroads, as America's first inter-regional firms, found themselves competing for business. "A wildly fluctuating market, whose unpredictability was based on perennial imbalance between supply and demand, caused both producers and refiners to seek some way of stabilizing their positions. It was John D. Rockefeller and his associates who successfully analyzed and manipulated this complex situation in order to control the competitive climate of the whole industry."

Henry Flagler, a Rockefeller ally, negotiated a deal with the Lake Shore Railroad, a subsidiary of the New York Central. Flagler promised to ship 60 carloads of oil a day, if the railroad would charge him $1.30 instead of $2.00 for crude between Cleveland and New York. The general manager of the railroad testified that the guaranteed shipment allowed him to regularly schedule a single train made up solely of tank cars. Even with the reduced rate, the railroad made a good profit. The general manager rebutted other refiners, who complained about the favorable rate, by stating, "this arrangement was at all times open to any and all parties who would secure or guarantee the like amount of traffic or an amount to be treated and handled in the same speedy and economical manner." Rockefeller and Flagler got two of their Cleveland competitors to join in this railroad deal. Several oil refiners grasped the benefits of aligning with Standard Oil and, by the end of 1871, the "conquest of Cleveland" was effected. Standard Oil's control of these companies was kept secret; executives of the absorbed companies became Standard Oil executives. Those producers who did not join were driven out of business (Chandler 1985, 256, 345–349).

With regard to favorable railroad rates, Standard Oil executives probably realized that such rates were possibly illegal and quite certainly destined to arouse public ire. On an economic level, however, were uniform rates optimal? What if there were lower marginal and average costs to shipping large batches than small batches? If rates were based on marginal costs, then didn't it make sense to give price discounts to larger customers? Railroads were not the only large organizations attempting to practice price discrimination; utilities often gave volume discounts. Even today, under the state- and municipal-controlled utilities, different rates are charged to industrial and private domestic customers.

Witnesses testified that Standard Oil not only got rebates on freight rates for its own shipments but that railroads frequently paid the company rebates based on the shipments of its competitors (drawbacks). Standard Oil witnesses pointed out that such railroad rebates were not illegal during the 1870s and up until the formation of the Interstate Commerce Commission. Although the drawback and rebates on railroad freight rates gave Standard Oil a big advantage, whether this was unethical is unclear. The railroads preferred the large shipments (that were cheaper on a per-unit basis than small shipments). The railroads, however, may have been violating their charters. The Supreme Court rulings and various state and federal legislation defined railroads as common carriers charged with the public interest. As common carriers, the railroads legally had to charge uniform rates. John Archbold and John D. Rockefeller testified that they believed other large-scale shippers received rebates, and that Standard's competitors would have received rebates had they shipped the same volume of oil with similar regularity as did Standard Oil. Rockefeller argued that the railroad rebates benefited the consumers in the form of lower prices, which may well have been true. Rockefeller denied that railroads frequently paid drawbacks to Standard Oil based on other oil producers' shipments; Rockefeller acknowledged one instance where a "small sum" was received briefly but that the company had refunded the money "before any action was brought in the courts." Although Rockefeller's statement may have been true, one does not have to be very skeptical to question his statements regarding the drawbacks. In any event, the report acknowledged that "It is not claimed by anyone that the railroads in making these rates are doing anything illegal, or that the Standard Oil Company is receiving any illegal advantage. It pays exactly the same rates as its competitors pay when they make shipments in the same way; its only advantage comes from the fact that, considering the way the tariffs are made up, its refineries are more variably situated (U.S. Industrial Commission 1900, I:28)."[3]

The Pennsylvania Railroad incorporated the South Improvement Company. The railroad hoped to control the oil shipments to port cities through a system of quotas, rebates, and drawbacks. The stabilized freight rates would benefit the railroads, and the large oil producers would benefit from the rebates and drawbacks on shipments. The nonmembers would pay the published rates, an action tantamount to their death knell. The Pennsylvania hoped to monopolize the rail traffic through the South Improvement Company. For Rockefeller and other members, another advantage of joining was the railroad's provision of daily reports of oil shipments. Such information was highly valued by Rockefeller, who always had a keen eye for data. The Rockefeller group would get a large proportion of the shares of the South Improvement Company; there was also hope that the oil producers would find a way to limit production in the hopes of maintaining a minimum price. The independent oil producers responded by forming a Petroleum Producers Union "whose initial goal was to control overproduction and periodic price wars." Such goals were not necessarily inimical to Standard Oil's (Chandler 1985, 350–351; Berk 1994, 90; Gras 1941, 5).

The South Improvement Company scheme failed once the public became aware of it. Nonmembers and other companies complained vociferously and threatened to halt shipments of crude oil to the refiners. Other opponents sought to revoke the company's charter. The Pennsylvania Railroad eventually revoked the charter before the South Improvement Company ever shipped a barrel. The conquest of Cleveland and the company's involvement with the South Improvement Company tainted Standard Oil's reputation for decades to come. Rockefeller and his associates, though, recognized the advantages of stability and control of the refining industry. They intended to create stability with voluntary cooperation, if possible, or by ruthless measures if necessary (Chandler 1985, 351).

Despite these despised, heavy-handed activities, even Rockefeller's critics noted his strengths. Journalist Ida Tarbell's series of articles makes it clear that, aside from his rebates and drawbacks from railroads, Rockefeller possessed superior managerial skills that lowered his production costs. The independent producers were often careless and profligate: "If he had been contented to economize and to accept small gains, even the small producer could live on a much lower prices than $3; but nobody in the Oil Regions in 1872 looked with favor on economy, and everybody despised small things." Instead these producers were "notoriously extravagant in the management of their business. Rarely did an oil man write a letter if he could help it. He used the telegraph instead .... Frequently wells were abandoned which might have been pumped on a small but sure profit. In those days there were men who looked on a ten-barrel (net) well as hardly worth taking care of .... The one great thing which the Oil Regions did not understand in 1872 was economy (Tarbell 1904, I:393)."

Eradicating Competition

Although Standard Oil dominated the Cleveland refiners, refiners in Philadelphia, Pittsburgh, and New York remained independent. Standard Oil resorted to its tried method of offering stock exchanges and gained control of several large refiners; perhaps as important, the company gained skilled and experienced executives, including John D. Archbold, who had been an "implacable foe" of Standard Oil but now became one of their key executives. Once again, Rockefeller and Standard Oil pledged their acquisitions to secrecy, with each company operating as though nothing had happened. They masked the takeovers by creating the Central Refiners Association, but unlike previous associations, Standard Oil's control of stock in the various companies made the cartel agreement stick. Each refiner leased their plant to Standard Oil. The Pittsburgh refiners and

Pennsylvania Railroad refused to join, so the Central Refiners Association failed. Rockefeller decided to rely on Standard Oil's dominance in refining and favorable railroad rates to stabilize the market. By the end of 1878, the combination controlled more than 90 percent of the total refining investment of the country (Chandler 1985, 353–354).

Another alleged Standard Oil tactic was to undercut potential rivals. Ida Tarbell documented cases where retailers of refined oil products were shadowed by Standard Oil sales representatives. The Standard Oil men would promptly offer lower prices and better service than the upstarts. In this way, most of the new companies were forced out. While the alleged predatory pricing persisted, buyers gained; presumably, after the rival was eliminated, the fear was that the buyers would be forced to pay monopoly prices. This may not have been predatory pricing if Standard Oil had lower costs. The company may not have had to slash prices below its marginal or average variable costs. Norman Gras rebutted Tarbell's interpretation. He characterized many of the authors on business history to be biased against business operators, especially Ida M. Tarbell's work on Standard Oil. Gras implied that Tarbell had a grudge against John D. Rockefeller. Gras admitted that Rockefeller's silence and hardball tactics made him an easy target for Tarbell. "So bad was the reputation of this concern [Rockefeller and the Standard Oil] that no evidence in its favor could be considered genuine (Gras 1945, 143)."[4] Although Rockefeller's penchant for secrecy made him suspect in the eyes of his rivals and the public, one wonders what purpose would have been served by his divulging all of the company's plans.

Henry Demarest Lloyd's *Wealth against Commonwealth* was also influential in shaping public opinion about John D. Rockefeller. Allan Nevins described Lloyd's sensationalistic work as showing "the same distortions and downright errors of his earlier writing. As a piece of business history (which it purports to be) it is ludicrous; as a contribution to biographical data upon Rockefeller it is at best misleading, at worst maliciously false. Its significance lies in the distorted stereotype of Rockefeller which it helped fasten upon the public mind."[5] Lloyd was astute in his timing; by 1894, the animus toward the big industrialists may have been at high tide. Many readers were more than willing to accept Lloyd's allegations, and a flood of vituperation engulfed Rockefeller and Standard Oil. There were critics of Lloyd, with academic economists giving the work their ultimate sign of contempt by ignoring his book (Lloyd 1963).[6]

Nevins identified three attacks upon Rockefeller that swayed the public by depicting him as malevolent. Rockefeller allegedly forced a poor widow with an oil property to accept an unconsciously low price for it, leaving her in penury. Nevins refuted the story and documented that the Widow Backus became a wealthy woman. Lloyd claimed that Rockefeller was involved in a plot to blow up a rival plant; he even asserted that the plant in Buffalo exploded, but the reality was that there was no explosion and no attempt to do such a thing. Rockefeller was called as a witness for the *prosecution* [italics Nevins]. Lloyd also implied that Rockefeller attempted to bribe the Ohio legislature to elect Henry Payne to the U.S. Senate. No bribery was ever proved, and the story was implausible. Payne was a Democrat and known as a politician with integrity; Rockefeller was a Republican. Lloyd left out some key information that made his insinuation seem preposterous. To be sure, Rockefeller and his associates were slow to grasp the need for a competent publicist to refute such charges: "Rockefeller, believing a dignified silence the best policy, did not comprehend until too late that it was construed as an admission of guilt all along the line (Nevins 1953, 1:330–333)."

Standard Oil's Organization

The discovery of oil at Baku on the Caspian Sea in 1880 threatened Standard Oil's dominance. The Nobel family invested heavily in developing the field. The Russians planned to build a railroad from Baku to the Black Sea, so as to send the refined kerosene to European markets. The Baku oil made high-quality kerosene; between the Russian oil's proximity to Europe and Baku oil's quality, Standard Oil knew that by 1885, competition would be ferocious. Rockefeller and his allies recognized they needed to cut costs even more, but in order to do so, they needed legal consolidation and administrative centralization. The goal was to centralize decision making with the authority to "build, reorganize, and shut down refineries and then to administer the rationalized network of production, transportation, and marketing facilities."[7]

In order to achieve its goal, the Standard Oil alliance needed a legally identifiable enterprise. The executives decided upon creating a trusteeship that complied with common law while affording secrecy. "Trustees, because they were legally agents for stockholders and not for the corporations involved, could testify truthfully about Standard Oil without revealing information that investigators sought to uncover." Therefore, Standard

Oil's involvement in other companies could remain obscure. There were nine original trustees, including John D. Rockefeller and his brother William, along with Henry Flager and John Archbold. These men now had the power to create the desired centralized administrative control.

Standard Oil in 1885 controlled the three largest refineries in the world at Bayonne, New Jersey, Philadelphia, and Cleveland. The ensuing economies of scale cut costs further, which was needed, since independent refiners succeeded in cutting average costs to 1.5 cents a gallon. Standard Oil cut its average cost from 0.543 cents per gallon in 1884 to 0.452 cents in 1885, and its profit margin rose from 0.530 to 1.003 cents during the same period. To put this achievement in perspective, Standard Oil's costs were not only far below their American competitors' but sufficiently low enough to compete with the Nobels for European markets, even though Standard Oil faced higher shipping and distribution expenses than the Nobels (Chandler 1985, 357–362). Even Rockefeller critic Ida Tarbell presented data showing that the average price of crude fell from $2.75 per barrel in 1873 (it had been markedly higher in previous years) to below $1.00 in many of the years after 1878 (Nevins 1940, 2:718).

The Standard Oil Trust differed from the Standard Oil combination because of its committee and staff organization. The centralized decision making proved a major improvement, although Chandler remarked that even in the 1890s, the trust's administrative organization did not forecast demand for its products or for capital needs; budgeting; or coordinating the flow of goods. At times, the subsidiaries and affiliates worked at cross purposes.

John D. Rockefeller may well have experienced anxiety regarding the decades of building Standard Oil. As the nineteenth century waned, another challenge appeared. Thomas Edison and George Westinghouse's harnessing of electricity threatened to destroy consumer demand for kerosene, thereby knocking out Standard Oil's main raison d'être. Another source of anxiety was the discovery of oil in northern Ohio and Indiana near Lima. In one sense, the new oil fields meant that the depletion of the Pennsylvania fields would not ruin the east coast refining business. The Lima oil contained high amounts of sulfur and required investments in pipelines; the sulfur content meant that Standard Oil and other refiners had to devise new refining processes. At the turn of the century, discovery of oil in Texas also threatened Standard Oil's dominance. Alfred Chandler Jr. observed that "over these fundamental shifts in the market, Standard Oil, for all its economic power, had no control whatsoever .... Thus even before the breakup of Standard Oil the industry had developed into an oligopoly characterized by large integrated firms competing for market share (Chandler 1985, 368–369)."

Standard Oil Meets Texans

"Don't mess with Texas!" or "Ride Clear of Texas" might have been good warnings for Standard Oil. When the Spindletop fields in Texas opened up in the first decade of the twentieth century, a new domestic rival arose to challenge Standard Oil's dominance of the American petroleum industry (roughly five-sixths of crude supplies, refining, and marketing of kerosene at times). Although historians of the Progressive Era like to think that the Supreme Court's mandate breaking up Standard Oil in 1911 was a turning point, the court's decision may have simply confirmed a trend in Standard Oil's declining power.

With respect to Texas, Standard Oil ran into a fierce provincialism. Texans did not want Standard Oil to come in and usurp Texan control of the new fields. Texas courts had earlier imposed strict antitrust laws. The legislature passed laws prohibiting combinations in restraint of trade and precluded companies from owning stock in another company. These laws, passed in 1889, were at the behest of farmers and ranchers, who were fighting oligopolists in cotton bagging, beef, and other industries. The law limited each business incorporated within the state to a single corporate purpose, which made vertical integration difficult. Because Texans were jealous of their control of Texas oil fields, the newspapers, politicians, and jurists scrutinized Standard Oil's operations; certainly Standard Oil's use of clandestine allied firms and secrecy redounded against them in the court of public opinion in Texas.[8] Such skullduggery was not mere paranoia on the Texans' part. Historian Joseph Pratt relates how George Burt, "got off a train in Beaumont, bought a large tract of land near Spindletop, constructed a high fence around the land, and built one of the largest and best equipped refineries in the state." Standard Oil bankrolled, staffed, and sold the oil from Burt's plant. Texans were pleased with the *fait accompli*, despite the plant's association with "the Octopus," as Standard Oil was nicknamed; the plant "was a potent force in the prosperity of South East Texas," and Pratt noted, "[Texans] were not eager to cut off the tentacle that was feeding them."

Despite the Texans' suspicions of Standard Oil, the more pragmatic (or cynical) among them welcomed Standard Oil's infusion of capital with which to develop Spindletop. One newspaper opined that Beaumont, Texas, was "the one place on earth where Standard is to be devoutedly [sic] wished." Pratt characterized these shenanigans as being "accepted in the way an older, nonbelieving child greets the arrival of Santa Claus: winking at Standard's disguise, many in the region gladly accepted the economic gifts that it bought." As the years went by, the drumbeat against Standard Oil crescendoed and the company moved many of its operations to Baton Rouge, Louisiana, where it built a massive refinery.

Ironic consequences attended Standard Oil's involvement in the Texas oil industry. "[Standard] filled a symbolic role that was perhaps even more important to the survival and growth of Gulf Oil and Texaco. As the focus of public and political attention, Standard protected the growing Gulf coast companies from political forces that might have blocked their expansion. From their inception, these new oil companies were larger than most corporations previously chartered in Texas, but because they were perceived as smaller, 'Texas' alternatives to the giant 'foreign' Standard Oil Trust, they enjoyed a great deal of political leeway in their operations."

Texas courts had battled the Standard Oil Company in the years prior to the discovery of oil at Spindletop. The courts faced a dilemma in the years after the Spindletop discovery; if the courts strictly enforced the state's antitrust laws, they might have throttled the budding Texas oil companies, especially if the courts prohibited any attempts at vertical integration. In the end, state officials and judges, assuredly reflecting the wishes of most Texans, played the ethically dubious game of keeping the antitrust laws on the books but selectively enforcing them. The Texas courts and legislature blocked any potential Standard Oil domination of Texas oil fields: "allow[ing] Standard Oil to take a limited role in developing the new Texas field, yet blocked the former monopolist from crushing its youthful competitors," thereby contributing to the rise of an oligopoly that displaced Standard Oil's monopoly in the years before the Supreme Court's decision in the Standard Oil case (Pratt 1980, 815–827, 837).

Supreme Court Breaks Up Standard Oil

The Supreme Court responded to the public's clamor to do something and broke up the Standard Oil Trust in 1911. Thomas Navin points out an irony: "the company had developed to a point where the best interests of the public were tantamount to the best interests of the company."

The court ruled that trust had to be dissolved, so as to create a competitive market. Although Standard Oil had long faced foreign competition, the discovery of oil in Texas and, later, Oklahoma and California, eroded the company's dominance even in America. Navin noted that the price of oil, which had dropped during the Standard Oil's dominant days, now began to rise rapidly, despite the increased competition (Navin 1943, 14; Gras 1941, 53).

The Supreme Court's efforts at trust busting may have come too late to really affect the oil industry. At the time the Supreme Court ruled to break up Standard Oil, there were a number of foreign and American competitors, including holdovers such as Pure Oil and Tidewater, as well as the fledgling Texas companies. Indeed, most modern Americans no longer associate oil production with Pennsylvania and Indiana but primarily with Texas, Oklahoma, Louisiana, California, Alaska, and, in recent years, North Dakota. The Court's rulings, however, did affect later industry leaders' decisions on whether to further concentrate industry productive capabilities. The offshoots of Standard Oil, though, played a role in determining prices. "Instead of competing for a share of the market on price, the companies advertised their brands of products with catchy slogans and improved the facilities and services at the growing number of retail gasoline stations which these companies came to own or to franchise (Chandler 1977, 402)."

Conclusion

John D. Rockefeller and his associates were pioneers of creating a business organization featuring horizontal and vertical integration (Hidy and Hidy 1955, xxiii, 4, 8, 715–717; Bridges 1958, 11). Standard Oil succeeded in reducing prices for high-quality petroleum products. They employed novel tactics in their endeavor, some of which skirted legality and others were ruthless. Other industry leaders, such as Carnegie, James Duke, and the meat packers, employed similar tactics in concentrating their industries into the hands of a few.

Rockefeller reflected in 1907 that "Commercial morality improving? Why, I think it always has been very high, the highest, I think, in any department of life .... No one who does not know can imagine the high standard of integrity maintained among business men. The whole system of business may be said to rest on honor. I say to you that the very highest examples of honor and high-mindedness I have ever seen have been among business men. It is false and cruel to malign them. The conduct of the Standard Oil Company has been in the hands of high-minded, honorable gentlemen (*New York Times*, October 20, 1907, SM2)."

Rockefeller and the Standard Oil Company rose to greatness largely because of savvy, but many of their methods antagonized the public. The public deemed secrecy, tactics designed to mislead, knocking out rivals, espionage, and price-cutting to be unfair and unethical, if not strictly illegal. Some of these charges were overblown or were not necessarily unethical, such as price-cutting due to efficiency or some aspects of secrecy. Perhaps the most vexing question was whether lower prices and better quality offered by Standard Oil justified questionable tactics.

Notes

1. This is similar to how many lawyers pursue negligence cases: Some plaintiffs' attorneys seem to believe that we live in a world where nothing bad would happen except through negligence.
2. The author shares Rockefeller's amazement at earning interest on his savings account; as a seven-year-old, the added pennies of interest each quarter pleased the author no end. The author considers it a seminal moment in his life.
3. Other Standard Oil officials gave similar testimony, including the story of refunding the drawback.
4. For the economics and antitrust of alleged price-cutting, see Telser (1966, 263–268) and Gellhorn (1976, 366–370).
5. Turner presents a more favorable view of *Wealth against Commonwealth* in his article (1994, 67–68).
6. Lloyd wanted Americans to return to the ethical code of man should love his neighbor as himself. He criticized orthodox economics, especially laissez-faire economics and its claim to have reconciled self-interest with the harmony of others (Turner 1994, 54–57).
7. Russian oil eventually captured 20 percent of the European market by 1889 (Chandler 1985, 363).
8. One bizarre story, which even the *Oil Investors' Journal* labeled a "jack-assey story," had the Standard Oil building a pipeline under cover of night designed to pump salt water from the Gulf of Mexico into the Spindletop field (Pratt 1980, 821). Even Montgomery Burns of *The Simpsons* would find such an audacious attempt incredible, although he might have wished he had "thought of that," however.

Bibliography

Berk, Gerald. *Alternative Tracks: The Constitution of American Industrial Order, 1865–1917* (Baltimore, MD: Johns Hopkins University Press, 1994).

Bridges, Hal. "The Robber Baron Concept in American History." *Business History Review* XXXI(1), Spring 1958, 1–13.

Chandler, Alfred Jr. *The Visible Hand: The Managerial Revolution in American Business* (Cambridge, MA: Harvard University Press, 1977).

Chandler, Alfred Jr. "The Standard Oil Company—Combination, Consolidation, and Integration." *The Coming of Managerial Capitalism*, edited by Alfred Chandler, Jr. and Richard Tedlow (Homewood, IL: Richard D. Irwin, 1985).

Chernow, Ron. *Titan: The Life of John D. Rockefeller, Sr.* (New York, NY: Random House, 1998).

Cohn, David. *The Good Old Days: A History of American Morals and Manners as Seen through the Sears, Roebuck Catalogs, 1905 to the Present* (New York, NY: Simon and Schuster, 1940).

Flynn, John. *God's Gold: The Story of Rockefeller and His Times* (New York, NY: Harcourt, Brace and Company, 1932).

Gellhorn, Ernest. *Antitrust Law and Economics in a Nutshell* (St. Paul, MN: West Publishing, 1976).

Gras, Norman. "A New Study of Rockefeller." *Bulletin of the Business Historical Society* 15(4), October 1941, 49–58.

Gras, Norman. "Shifts in Public Relations." *Bulletin of the Business Historical Society* 19(4), October 1945, 97–148.

Hidy, Ralph and Muriel Hidy. *Pioneering in Big Business, 1882–1911* (New York, NY: Harper & Brothers, 1955).

Lloyd, Henry. *Wealth against Commonwealth* (Englewood Cliffs, NJ: Prentice-Hall, 1963).

Navin, Thomas. "Evaluating the Methods of the Business Administrator." *Bulletin of the Business Historical Society* 17(1), February 1943, 11–14.

Nevins, Allan. *John D. Rockefeller: The Heroic Age of American Enterprise* (New York, NY: Charles Scribner's Sons, 1940). 2 vols.

Nevins, Allan. *Study in Power: John D. Rockefeller, Industrialist and Philanthropist* (New York, NY: Charles Scribner's Sons, 1953). 2 vols.

New York Times. "Rockefeller Sees No Portent of Disaster." October 20, 1907, SM1.

Pratt, Joseph. "The Petroleum Industry in Transition: Antitrust and the Decline of Monopoly Control in Oil." *Journal of Economic History* XL(4), December 1980, 815–37.

Russell, Bertrand. *Freedom versus Organization, 1814–1914* (New York, NY: W.W. Norton, 1934).

Tarbell, Ida. *The History of the Standard Oil Company* (New York, NY: McClure, Phillips, 1904). 2 vols.
Telser, Lester. "Cutthroat Competition and the Long Purse." *Journal of Law & Economics* 9(1), October 1966, 259–277.
Turner, Michael. "Henry Demarest Lloyd and Business Ethics in late Nineteenth- and Early Twentieth-Century America." *Business History* 36(4), October 1994, 53–78.
U.S. Industrial Commission. *Preliminary Report on Trusts and Industrial Combinations, Together with Testimony, Review of Evidence, Charts Showing Effects of Prices, and Topical Digest.* Volume 1 of the Commissions Reports (Washington, DC: Government Printing Office, 1900).

CHAPTER 7

Rise of the Big Retail Merchants

There have been a variety of retailing methods throughout history. Retailers and customers struggled to find better ways for conducting mutually beneficial transactions. The costs of searching for retailers with the desired commodities and ascertaining whether merchants and customers were trustworthy created obstacles in making trades. Most retailers treated customers fairly in order to avoid punishment; because it was good business; and, frequently, because this was their inherent goal.

A group of entrepreneurs transformed retail shopping during the second half of the nineteenth century. The names Bon Marché, Field, Selfridge, Sears, Ward, Woolworth, and Wanamaker became nationally and, in some cases, world renowned. Their creators believed in giving consumers good-quality products at reasonable prices. They built emporiums, mail-order houses, and five-and-dime stores.

Customers gained, some producers gained (from having regular orders from department stores), and retail workers benefited to some extent, but transforming workers into a disciplined force imposed costs. Then again, once potential workers understood the expectations of the job, they could self-select into retail or into other jobs. Since all of us are consumers, retail ethics loom large in our daily experiences.

D. G. Surdam, *Business Ethics from the 19th Century to Today*,
https://doi.org/10.1007/978-3-030-37169-2_7

Caveat Emptor

What are we to make of the common sense notion that most consumers are not qualified to judge product quality of complex items (and perhaps some not-so-complex items)? Most people don't know how a computer works. When they walk into an electronics store, are they vulnerable for being ripped-off? What protections do consumers have? They can compare warranties or query the salesperson. Read *Consumers' Report*. Ask a friend. Or, wonder of wonders, depend upon the merchant's integrity.

The last possibility is not whimsy. We shop at Target and Nordstrom's because they have a reputation for providing quality products. As George Stigler points out, the successful retailers prospered for years, because they met their consumers' wants and desires. They cultivated reputations for fair and scrupulous dealing. Stigler argues that caveat emptor did not preclude another form of protection for the consumer: the force of competition. Aside from price, many sellers compete on the basis of quality of product and service. Many people believe that merchants compete primarily on the basis of price, so sellers of shoddy products, because of their lower costs, must drive out high-quality products. Of course, a moment's reflection will reveal this to be false. There exists a continuum of quality for most commodities and services.

Product quality tends to improve. Televisions, cars, stereos, computers, microwaves, and cell phones are better than even a few years ago. Foodstuffs are better. A fundamental problem facing statisticians who calculate price indices and real national output is adjusting for quality improvements.

Do consumers need regulatory protection? George Stigler examined the ability of government regulatory agencies in protecting the consumer. He proposed something novel: to empirically test the effectiveness of the government regulations, using the Securities and Exchange Commission's (SEC) regulation of the New York Stock Exchange. He found that the rates of returns before and after the SEC's review of prospectuses of new stocks did not "appreciably improve the experience of investors in the new issues marketed by its expensive review of prospectuses." Stigler dismissed the argument that if the regulators are lax or corrupt or incompetent, then we merely need to replace them with more competent and diligent officials. "If commissioners have often been lazy or timid, or deeply subservient to the industry they purport to regulate, it is inexcusably romantic to assume that all future appointments will be regulatory saints." He lamented public regulation's ability to weaken consumers' defenses against fraud, often imposing new burdens upon consumer, "without conferring corresponding protections. The doctrine of *caveat emptor* has not lost its force: the only change is that now the consumer must beware of different threats, and threats which he is less well equipped to defend himself against." Stigler concluded that consumers must be perpetually vigilant. "[U]nder the earlier regime of *caveat emptor*, the consumer was protected basically by his own care and intelligence and by the most powerful of allies, competition. Public regulation weakens and sometimes destroys these defenses against fraud and negligence, without replacing the protections they used to afford (Stigler 1975, 179, 181–182, 185–186)."

Why are the protections of the consumer reduced under regulation? Suppose the Community Cable Company (CCC) gives lousy service. Under competition, the more abusive the CCC, the more incentive the consumer has in seeking other cable services. Thanks to regulation, suppose CCC is the only cable game in town. In order to get relief from the abusive government-created monopoly, consumers have to petition and lobby for a legislative change. Clearly, the time and effort deter many consumers from doing so. Consumers may have to grit their teeth and accept the rotten service or forego cable. Competition still works to some degree in this scenario; a monopolistic cable company faces competition from rentals and sales of videos, internet streaming of programming, and from the television networks. One could even say that movie theaters and professional sports also provide competition to the cable company.

Consumers may also occasionally benefit from the help of another industry in battling the government-protected monopoly. Network and non-cable television stations may clamor to break up the cable monopoly to get some benefits for themselves. Only by happenstance, though, do these groups and the consumers have common interests.

Drummers and Traveling Salesmen

Retailers have used various means of offering their products to potential buyers, from fixed location to roaming sales representatives. Traveling salesmen had long been the stuff of legend. Fictitious character Willy Loman was one. The perception of itinerant salesmen, including peddlers, evolved over time. Three centuries ago, a pamphlet placed peddlers—watch out for the coming alliteration—with "prostitutes, pimps, and pawnbrokers." The public associated traveling salesmen with immorality and deceit, never mind the jokes relating traveling salesmen and farmers' daughters (French and Popp 2008, 792–793; see also Westerfield [1915] 1968, 316–318).[1]

Historian Timothy Spears studied the traveling salesmen known as drummers. Wholesale merchants (jobbers) in eastern cities hired drummers to go to outlying territories and solicit orders from retailers. The idea was to cultivate relationships with retailers and thereby spare the retailers the long trips back east. The drummers scorned the usual peddler or door-to-door confidence men. Because these drummers, as with other itinerant salesmen, were on the road, living in hotels, eating in restaurants, and entertaining themselves with various commercial leisure activities, plenty of rumors circulated around them. Some of the salesmen, such as Edward Palmer, reveled in their ability to hoodwink customers. Palmer's book, *Forty Years of Hustling*, was perhaps braggadocio but was in a vein with American tall tales.

Aspects of drumming were already established practices. When country retailers visited New York City, wholesalers often plied them with food, drink, and entertainment. Such customs horrified clergy, who worried that the country retailers were being corrupted by the big-city sophisticates. Spears relates how Henry Ward Beecher worried about the city's "high life" and "varied phases of lust." Reverend James Alexander derided the drummer's "smirking, and bowing, and treating" and "playing the spaniel" while "groveling" for a local retailer's business. In other words, commentators worried about the quid pro quo of "licentious pleasures for business favors," with one likening the wholesaler or drummer to a worm: "So the mercantile borer assails, obtrudes himself upon, and insinuates himself into the good graces of a country merchant."

Some drummers recollected that they "never misrepresented an article" and that they adhered to a code of ethics "that reinforced the goal implicitly shared by retailer and wholesaler alike: getting the goods to the consumer." The astute drummer worked to improve his retailers' positions in the market by giving advice on purchases and by organizing his stock. Although such efforts were self-interested, it was a self-interest that also benefited his client. One way to improve a retailer's position and to get a sale was to cut prices. The wholesalers were often displeased by price cuts, but retailers often insisted; drummers were caught in the middle. Such negotiations, of course, were rife with potential misrepresentation; retailers could claim that other drummers had offered lower prices, while drummers could bleat that by offering discounts their profits fell to unacceptable levels (Spears 1995, 17, 35, 60, 63, 72; see also Cohn 1940, 541). Perhaps some drummers used twentieth-century automobile sales tactics: "I'll have to ask my boss whether I can offer such a price."

Wholesalers began instructing their drummers how *not* to act. These companies eschewed use of "pertinacity and impudence" but advocated using "sound, logical arguments ... [instead of] glibness of tongue." The result was that there probably was a difference, on average, between the drummers and the peddlers, based on the former's "desire to nurture long-term commercial relationships."[2] Some drummers, though, proved unscrupulous, and commercial travelers' fraternal organizations tried moral suasion to dissuade such miscreants from their ways. Often the fraternal organizations appealed to the miscreants' self-interest: It was better business to be honest. Editorial writers preached morality in the commercial travelers' publications, such as the *Sample Case* (Spears 1995, 102, 163).

In contrast with drummers, selling vacuum cleaners proved a problematic endeavor. Selling vacuum cleaners door-to-door was a long-standing tradition in the United States and Great Britain. The industry was rife with exploitation of customers by sales representatives and exploitation of sales representatives by management (and sometimes vice versa). A key characteristic was the unlikely event of repeated transactions between an individual sales person and a particular customer (Scott 2008, 762–782; *Bulletin of the Business Historical Society* 1935, 27).

Retail Experience, Circa 1840s

Twenty-first-century shoppers would find wandering into a retail store in a major city in 1850 to be off-putting. Much of the merchandise was out of reach behind counters. Unctuous salesmen handled the merchandise and quoted prices, usually based on their assessment of the customer's willingness to pay. The salesmen were often obnoxious in persuading customers to buy something. One writer satirized clerks by describing how they tried to trick customers into thinking they were getting marked-down goods at "cost," even though the goods—which were "fit for moths only"—were actually marked up "just one hundred and fifty per cent more than the miserable stuff cost at auction." If a male customer balked and pled poverty, the savvy clerk would ask, "Is it for *her*?" The clerk would then intimate that the customer could have it "*at a sacrifice* [Italics in the original] (Hundley [1860] 1979, 108–109)!" Very generous of the clerk, who still priced the merchandise at a 100 percent markup. On other occasions, male clerks became obsequious when dealing with ladies of wealth: the clerk's behavior transformed, "affable, how polite, how cringing, how nimble of feet, how full of smirks and grimaces! With happiness divine beaming in his glowing face, he tumbles down silks, brocades, velvets … after all his toil and flatteries, his bows and smirks, he is in the end most humble thankful to sell madam a simple yard of *rubin de fil* (Atherton [1949] 1968, 46)."[3] What if a customer changed his or her mind and wanted their money back? Too bad. Once the customer was out the door, the sale was considered final.

"A Late Retailer" published *A Peep into Catharine Street, or the Mysteries of Shopping* in 1846. Catharine Street was a prominent retail street in New York City. The author began by describing the temptations facing retailers; the attrition rate among retailers proved ferocious, and the author asserted that many retailers succumbed to unscrupulous tactics to defraud creditors and customers as retailers' own literal shelf-life was likely to be brief. The author devoted most of his book detailing the frustrations of dealing with customers, who were frequently fractious, indecisive, and opportunistic. Haggling over prices proved a verbal tug-of-war. Of course, retailers hoped to get the highest price possible. Customers, too, indulged in hardline bargaining in hopes of paying the lowest price possible (A Late Retailer 1846, 7–10).

Nineteenth-century retailers, though, admitted that—in the past—ethics were not as high as they currently were. Of course, such reminiscences may have been self-serving. William Ablett, author of *Reminiscences of an Old Draper*, recalled the retail antics of his youth, when, "various unprincipled tricks were practiced in selling goods that would not countenanced for a moment in drapers' shops of the very lowest standing now-a-days." He mentioned that the owners never directly ordered salesmen to use these tricks, but that they were aware of such shenanigans and said nothing (indeed, they rewarded such efforts with higher salaries). "Customers were bullied into buying goods they did not want." Ablett claimed that such tactics were not needed anymore, as the buyers were more astute in purchasing merchandise.

The owner of the store who employed Ablett precipitated another shenanigan. Presaging modern stores that are seemingly perpetually "Going Out of Business," this owner decided to claim there had been a fire that had damaged his merchandise. He spread the word through the neighborhood. The staff singed merchandise to give the appearance of fire damage.

They were also pestered by impatient "importunities of the old women … who persisted in clawing hold of these burnt ensigns, which they insisted should be sold to them forthwith, at a nominal rate, which, of course, would not have answered our purpose at all." The sale was a huge success, Some customers were impertinent enough to ask whether the damaged merchandise was covered by insurance, presumably out of curiosity, concern, or, more likely, to be able to jaw-bone the retailer into further price reductions. The clerks "confidentially" informed a few customers that the low sale prices "would be our employer's ruin (Ablett 1876, 8–9, 31–34; see also Cox and Hobley 2014, 74)." The word "sale" appeared to trigger a Pavlovian response among the customers, who made frenzied purchases and overflowed the till.

Some merchants relied upon more than just the misunderstood caveat emptor. If an immigrant came into the store and tried on a hat, a clerk might read a document that stated that a woman who tried on a hat for two minutes was obligated to buy it. Naturally the befuddled immigrant was no match for the officious-sounding clerk. Some retailers went to elaborate lengths to cheat customers. One retail stunt was to buy men's suits from a wholesaler. The retailer then bought some cheap watches that he inserted into the trouser pocket. In the act of trying on the trousers, the customer would feel the watch and "conclude it had been left by another customer, and would be so intent on stealing it that he would readily pay $25 for a $15 suit (Cohn 1940, 541)."[4]

Early American Retailers

American Alexander Turney Stewart was an unsung pioneer of retailing. He introduced or refined several innovations in retailing. He operated a dry goods store in New York City in the 1830s and 1840s (years before Aristide Boucicaut opened his Bon Marché in Paris). His store exemplified many of the characteristics of later department stores, such as a central, downtown location; several departments within the store; free services; one price to all; low mark-ups; cash sales only; sophisticated advertising and promotion; dependence on fast turnover; buying wholesale for cash; and disposing old stocks through bargain sales (Resseguie 1965, 303; Chandler 1977, 227–229).

Stewart believed that housing several departments in one store made shopping convenient for customers, creating, in effect, a one-stop shopping experience. Modern-day Target and Walmart stores are echoes of

Stewart's insight. By paying cash for goods, Stewart received a small discount, often 2 percent, which he could share with customers in the form of lower retail prices. By emphasizing cash purchases by customers, he avoided the entanglements of credit; he could also charge lower prices because of the cash policy. When he extended credit to a few customers, the terms were for 60 days or less. Stewart believed that his ability to satisfy customers with quality and low prices justified his insistence on cash purchases, whenever possible (Resseguie 1965, 303–306, 312).[5]

As early as 1823, Stewart was advertising his goods; in his advertisements, he stated that he had purchased goods wholesale with cash. "His plan was to purchase goods for cash, in large quantities, so as to be able to sell a large amount of goods at a small profit (Resseguie 1965, 306, New York *Herald*, April 12, 1876, 7)." His basic markup was 10 percent, which became his motto: "Ten per cent and no lies!" His competitor, Richard Lathers, relied upon a strategy of selling for the highest price he could get. Lathers later recalled what Stewart had told him, "That is not my [Stewart's] habit. I study to put my goods on the market at the lowest price I can afford and secure a reasonable profit. In that way I limit competition and increase my sales; and although I realize only a small profit on each sale, the enlarged area of business makes possible a large accumulation of capital and assures the future." A hundred years later, though, according to Edward Filene, some retailers still operated with the idea of making "high profits by buying cheap and selling dear, instead of serving the customer better and receiving the highest total profits as a reward for this better service (Resseguie 1965, 306–308, Lathers 1907, 44; Filene et al. 1937, 293)."

To establish his credentials for integrity and truth, Stewart did not rely upon persuasive advertising by touting (or misrepresenting) the qualities of his merchandise. His advertising usually simply stated what was available. Stewart did not emphasize sophisticated window displays. He insisted that his sales people tell the truth and not to embellish the characteristics of the goods; several of his sales people left, because they could not behave in such a manner. Stewart's stores were popular, so customers appear to have appreciated his penchant for simple honesty and low prices.

Stewart was a pioneer in the one-price policy. Rather than use customers and sales people's time in haggling, he set one price for each piece of merchandise. All customers could purchase at this price.[6]

Customers were free to examine merchandise and to decide to leave the premises without purchasing anything. Stewart's sales staff were instructed that customers were not to be cajoled, browbeaten, or intimidated into buying items. The old "closed door" system persisted into the twentieth century in London, where sales staff continually accosted customers. Harry Selfridge believed in Stewart's policy of letting customers browse and leave unmolested; some London magistrates disliked Selfridge's policy, claiming that it encouraged shoplifting (Resseguie 1965, 308–311; Selfridge 1935, 53)!

At this point, it is useful to consider the maligned "middleman." We may wish that we could evade the "middleman," such as a retailer, and pay lower prices, but the retailer actually saves us resources. Rather than having to expend time, energy, and money in investigating product quality and availability, we trust and rely upon the retailer to be the expert. We are paying the retailer for the service of selecting product lines for us that are priced commensurate with the quality. Nordstrom's provides expert advice on upper-end priced clothes, while K-Mart provides expert advice on lower-end priced clothes. Ethical retailers reduce uncertainty relating to both price and quality. The new retailers eradicated most of the wholesale middlemen by the end of the nineteenth century. In alliance with small urban retailers, dry goods jobbers protested the department stores' competition; these losers in the competition demanded protection from the department stores' lower prices (Chandler 1977, 229; Nelson 1976, 281–293, 2001, 213).

Creating a New Shopping Experience

Modern commerce transformed selling into an industry, an industry based on shop windows. The shop windows became pleasurable spectacles, a process comparable with motion pictures. These entrepreneurs made shopping more convenient and pleasant; they also made it, to use the words from *The Maltese Falcon*, "the stuff that dreams are made of (Bowlby 1985, 5–6)."[7] Many people took pleasure walking by retail store windows and contemplating the goods displayed. For most people, it seemed an innocuous way to spend the day. Even Holly Golightly window shopped in *Breakfast at Tiffany's*. Less than two hundred years ago, the idea of the hoi polloi leisurely lolling by retail shops was controversial. Pioneering retailers radically transformed the shopping experience in Britain, France, and the United States.

Aristide and Marguerite Boucicaut built their Bon Marché into one of France's finest department stores. French retailers previously had often been enmeshed within a guild system that proved conservative. Retailers usually specialized in a line of goods, and there were strict divisions of the market. The guilds tried to protect each merchant's trade. The guilds also set minimum selling prices and so on. Retailers were constrained with respect to permissible advertising. French retailers worried that there were only so many customers and sales to go around, and if one retailer gained some customers it was at the direct detriment of another retailer. Instead of devoting time to devising innovations to attract more customers, shopkeepers concentrated on bargaining and haggling. Individual retailers, given protection from encroachment upon "their" customers, were free to extract the highest prices they could from their customers. Given this mindset, "Undoubtedly some shopkeepers were scrupulous ... many others were not, and most likely one entered a shop prepared for deception rather than service (Miller 1981, 21–23)."

The Boucicauts with their Bon Marché encouraged Parisians to walk around; Boucicaut understood that "spectacle and browsing were integral to the success." Their sales staff exerted little overt pressure to buy. In Great Britain, retailers such as Fred Fenwick created a sensation by announcing the "silent sales assistant." Instead of customers being accosted by a salesperson, he urged, "Walk around today, don't buy. There is time for that another day." Historian William Lancaster characterized Fenwick's message as, "extremely subtle and loaded with economic and social implication .... Careful marketing ensured that some items were affordable to the less well-off, but of equal importance was the creation of an ambience which gave full vent to the complexities of the British class system .... Poorer folk could enter a new world of material fantasy, they could see it and even touch it and expect its glamour to rub off on their own small purchases." Lancaster added that "the items purchased by poorer folk were of good value (Lancaster 1995, 30–31)."

Mail-Order Retailing

Farmers lived a long way from the burgeoning department stores and rarely had access to low-priced merchandise. Aaron Montgomery Ward recognized that farmers had to pay high prices for goods at their local general stores. Part of this was because local merchants often had miniature monopolies based on location, as they might be the sole retailer for miles around. If they proved too successful, though, another retailer was likely to set up shop. The local merchants, unable to buy large quantities and facing high transportation costs, often had to charge higher prices than retailers in larger cities, who had more clients and competition. The local merchant was the tail end of a long chain of vendors. Ward hoped to buy wholesale or to manufacture goods himself and then sell directly to farmers (Hoge 1988, 8–9; Montgomery Ward & Co 1972, 3–4).

Ward began business in 1872. One of his advantages was to be named purchasing agent for the Illinois Grange, giving him access and credibility with the organization of farmers. His position gave him access to the Grange's mailing list and meetings; one could argue that using his position to further his own business was a questionable use of his position. Ward went to the Grange meetings and explained what he was trying to do. He knew that selling good-quality products was paramount, regardless of the prices he charged. Ward encouraged Grange members to pool their orders to save on shipping costs; he also offered to pay Grange members to visit his firm in Chicago to see that he was bona fide. He relied upon satisfied customers, who would tell their friends and family members (Hoge 1988, 10, 13; Montgomery Ward & Co 1972, 7).

Ward saw an opportunity to *serve* farmers, thanks in part to cheap, government-sponsored and subsidized, shipping. Ward saw his mission as providing a wide variety of quality goods at reasonable prices to farmers on America's prairies. He saw himself as a servant of farmers. "The job was not to sell so much as to find out what was needed. The objective was not to get the customer to accept what wasn't needed, but to encourage the farmer and his wife to realize what they did need. The idea was to educate the farmers to the latest improvements and to make him aware of better values." Ward figured that by offering well-made articles at low prices, his business would grow; as his business grew, he could generate sufficient volume to get further discounts on purchases and also to widen his offerings. By offering low, fixed prices and a money-back guarantee, he persuaded hundreds of thousands and eventually millions of rural buyers to trust him (Hoge 1988, 15).[8]

For Ward, the issue of selling by mail order revolved around trust. How could he induce farmers, many of whom were too skeptical of city "slickers" to relinquish their scarce currency? He canvassed many of the farmers' granges, introducing himself and obtaining orders. Sometimes a Grange's order would be opened in front of members from other granges; since the merchandise was good quality, these other members would be converted. He then hoped to receive laudatory word of mouth that would create new business. He was an early proponent of offering a money-back guarantee. Some observers believed that the *consumers* would abuse the money-back guarantee and drive Ward out of business; in essence, the trust between Ward and his consumers was bilateral. By establishing trustworthiness and reliability, Ward's sales increased rapidly. Ward was fortunate in his timing, as the Grange movement had reached its apogee (Hoge 1988, 15–16; Montgomery Ward & Co 1972, 7–9, 12–13).

Ward encountered opposition from country store owners and jobbers who supplied such stores. His plan threatened their businesses. The Chicago *Tribune* initially reported that Montgomery Ward was a fly-by-night business and panned his efforts at offering quality goods at relatively low prices: "the profits amount to something worthwhile, for it is known that a certain proportion of the multitudes of circulars issued fall into the hands of credulous fools, who place boundless faith in anything which is set up in type and printed." Ward turned this criticism, unfounded though it was, into an opportunity. He got the editors to examine his business and within a few weeks, the newspaper issued a retraction and provided favorable press: "We have taken pains to investigate this business, and have no question that Montgomery, Ward & Co. are doing a legitimate trade." Because Ward shipped cash-on-delivery (C.O.D.), farmers did not even have to remit money until they had a chance to inspect the goods (Chicago *Tribune* 1873a, 3, b, 5; Hoge 1988, 14; Montgomery Ward & Co, 1972, 9–10). Readers might recall their initial skepticism toward Amazon.com. Was it really that good a deal? It was.

Ward, in contrast to Richard Sears, was careful with the copy in his catalogs. He ensured that the descriptions of the merchandise were accurate. He also rigorously tested the products he offered for sale. By 1875, his catalogs stated, "We Guarantee All of Our Goods … if any of these are not satisfactory after due inspection we will take them back, pay all expenses and refund the money paid for them." Eventually the guarantee became the pithy motto: "Satisfaction Guaranteed or Your Money Back (Hoge 1988, 16–17; Montgomery Ward & Co 1972, 16–17, 42)."

Ward recognized that his organization required careful, quick-acting workers to fill the orders. He paid attention to details in planning his facilities, making sure they were clean and presented no dangerous machinery. He ran training and educational classes. He treated his clerical staff, comprised mostly of women, well. He also established a sick-and-death [sic] benefit association (Montgomery Ward & Co 1972, 48–49).

Over the years, Ward upgraded his clientele and catered less and less to the lowest-income customers. In retrospect, he may have created an opening for Sears, who would meet the wants and needs of such indigent customers.

A few decades later, Richard Sears decided to use a similar business model as Montgomery Ward. He was a master of writing advertisements. The sheer volume of copy that he wrote for his catalogs boggles the mind. As an example of his bombast, Sears outdid the Ward slogan, "The Cheapest Cash Supply House in America," with a Sears Roebuck slogan, "The Cheapest Supply House on Earth (Hoge 1988, 19–20)!"[9] Sears, presaging the National Football League, put the establishment date on the catalog front cover in Roman numerals (he assumed most customers could not decipher MDCCCXCIII for 1893); he hoped that people would think his firm a long-established one. Although his ads were in very small type and jammed together, he offered poor Americans low, low prices: "However small the ad, the prices screamed to all (Hoge 1988, 26–27)."[10]

Montgomery Ward executives probably thought Sears would go bust; they likely disparaged his catering to the lower end of the market. Ward executives were not so naïve to completely dismiss Sears' potential threat, but they obliquely criticized their rival in the Ward catalog: "We sell everything except trash. Your interests are ours. We sell no shoddy, second-hand or fire-sale goods. We do not wish to be classed with the numerous swindlers of our city." Somewhat more self-serving, if accurate, the catalog stated, "DO AS YOU WOULD BE DONE BY [caps in original]—This is a rule which we try to live up to and upon which we have built our business." Ward expected a reciprocity between his company and his customers; he would play fair by them and expect the same from them (Hoge 1988, 28).

Sears may have been an entrepreneurial and marketing visionary, but his attention to detail was lacking. Sears' business partner, watch repairer Alvah Roebuck, despaired about the business and feared bankruptcy and personal liabilities, so he sold out to Sears for $25,000. Had Sears gone bust, he might have been an interesting footnote for a book such as this, as an example of a fly-by-night operator of the late Gilded Age. Fortunately for Sears, new partner Julius Rosenwald created order from the chaos. The two made a formidable team; although Sears was probably reasonably ethical, Rosenwald earned a reputation for high standards of conduct. The company became proficient at quickly and accurately filling thousands of orders each day (Worthy 1984, 21–22, 24–25).

During the business slump of 1907, Sears Roebuck offered to let customers pay for orders using personal checks instead of cash, even though many banks had closed or were teetering. Many customers post-dated their checks, and the company honored them. Rosenwald believed that demonstrating trust and goodwill toward Sears' customers was the right (and profitable) thing to do. The policy was a great success, and most all of the checks cleared. In fact, over the years, bad checks were well under 1 percent of total payments by checks, an astonishing testimony to the honesty of Sears' customers. Within a decade, customers learned to trust Sears, as they had done with Montgomery Ward; Sears learned to trust its customers (Hoge 1988, 56). For modern readers accustomed to internet firms using customer ratings of vendors and vendor ratings of customers, the Sears experience serves as a harbinger of such mutual-trust.

Although Sears was a master of writing advertising copy that caused merchandise to fly off the shelves, Rosenwald insisted on a more restrained and truthful style of advertising. Rosenwald presumably promulgated the following in the Sears Advertising Guide issued in 1908: "Exaggerated claims and unrestrained superlatives undermine customers' confidence. Therefore avoid free use of such expressions as Best, Finest, Biggest, and avoid all statements the truth of which may be questioned." He also urged his copy writers: "Appeals to patriotism as an argument to induce buying are to be avoided." Such policy reflected Rosenwald's belief regarding business morality: "More and more the man who sells has come to realize that he has a very definite responsibility toward the man who buys (Cohn 1940, 541, 546; see also Hoge 1988, 56)."

A ramification of Rosenwald's emphasis upon honesty was the gradual elimination of patented medicines from the catalog. Sears sold a considerable amount of medicines in 1905, but by 1915, it was down to a single page for aspirins and Epsom salts. Not only were there few ads for nostrums remaining by 1915, the ads no longer used bombast and ridiculous claims. Naturally, Sears' loss of business meant increased business for other vendors (Cohn 1940, 223, 230–231).

Rosenwald's business plan was to, "Sell honest merchandise for less money and more people will buy." Rosenwald supplemented this pithy statement with three corollaries. First, buy in volume and get lower wholesale prices. Second, reduce the cost of shipment. Third, use a smaller markup on each item and depend upon selling a sufficient larger volume. In all of these cases, Rosenwald intended to maintain the quality of the goods sold. Rosenwald's philosophy envisioned a reciprocal relationship: "Treat people fairly and honestly and generously and their response will be fair and honest and generous." To lose a customer meant that Sears Roebuck failed the customer in some fashion. Rather than lament such a loss, Rosenwald had his staff contact inactive accounts among their customer base to ascertain why they had stopped buying from Sears and what the company could do to set things right (Worthy 1984, 27; see also Hoge 1988, 64).

Rosenwald also benefited Sears' customers by setting up a laboratory in Chicago to test goods before selling them. He benefited his workers by setting up a profit-sharing and pension fund. The fund comprised Sears' stock that earned dividends and appreciated in value. Sears employees of the mid-century did quite well. From today's perspective, having the employee pension to be based upon just Sears stock would be a cause for concern, even alarm (as witnessed by the unfortunate workforce at Enron, whose pensions were invested in Enron stock). In any event, the Sears pension fund did well for decades during the mid-1900s.

Sears was fortunate in finding a successor to Rosenwald who possessed competence and ethics. Before becoming Sears' leader in the 1920s, Robert E. Wood worked at Montgomery Ward after serving in Europe during World War I (Worthy 1984, 14–15, 32, 151–152).

Wood's approach to business ethics was similar to Rosenwald's, although Wood's breadth of vision was perhaps wider. During the Great Depression, Wood wrote in the Fall 1934 catalog: "I believe we could easily increase our present gross profit, but I do not believe it good policy to do so. We must do our part in holding down the increase in the cost of living to the American people." Wood presaged the stakeholder theory by decades by identifying customers, employees, and stockholders as the "great interests in the business": "The stockholder comes last, not because he is least important, but because, in the larger sense, he cannot obtain his full measure of reward unless he has satisfied customers and satisfied employees." Wood later expanded his philosophy. He argued that retailers should consider the interests of customers, employees, the community, and then the stockholders, with the customers coming first. "The customer comes first, for unless he gets good values, courteous and fair treatment, is satisfied in every respect, he will not continue as a customer, and the business eventually decays and dies."

Retail owners needed to consider themselves as trustees for their employees. In this capacity, they needed to uphold employees' rights, as well as help improve their workers' standard of living (an attitude similar to that held by Josiah Wedgwood). "If employees have confidence in the fairness and sense of justice of their employer, and feel that he is truly interested in their welfare, that his feeling for them springs from his heart as well as his head, the employees will respond, and there is a vast difference in the quality and quantity of the work performed and of the amount of supervision required between such employees and those who feel just the opposite to their employer." Retailers needed to be active members of their communities. They needed to help support charities and social welfare programs. Wood then considered stockholders. "All I can say is that if the other three parties above named are properly taken care of, the stockholder will benefit in the long pull." Sears stockholders generally did pretty well.

Allowing for self-serving or public relations considerations, Wood and Rosenwald genuinely believed in these ideas. Wood's stakeholder theory neglected suppliers (although he worked well with his suppliers), but otherwise could be found in business ethics forums even today. The key to their beliefs resulted from not viewing people, whether customers, employees, suppliers, or fellow residents, as objects to be used to achieve ends (Worthy 1984, 63–65).

Montgomery Ward ended in 2001. Sears is struggling against the onslaught of online vendors, especially Amazon.com. As I wrote this, an article in the *New York Times* chronicled how Sears lost more than $9 billion in the previous five years, despite closing 150 stores (as well as over 350 K-Mart stores it owned). Its stock prices ranged around $9, a far cry from its high of $190 (Solomon, January 18, 2017, B7). The Schumpeterian concept of "perennial gales of creative destruction" has blown through retailing. A hundred years from now, a historian revisiting the history of retail may denote the demise of Amazon.com.

Catering to the Lower-Income Groups

Frank W. Woolworth remembered the callous and humiliating treatment he received at the hands of a supercilious salesman, who disdained the young Woolworth's scruffy appearance. Woolworth harbored ambitions of becoming a clerk in the local store and eventually of owning his own store. He vowed to treat all customers with respect and dignity. Woolworth also wanted to cater to working-class and less-prosperous customers; he searched for bargains on moderate quality goods that he bought in bulk and sold at low prices (a strategy that Walmart would exercise decades later).

Woolworth worked for a local retailer. One of the retailer's friends had bought some merchandise and advertised it for five cents for each item. He was able to lure in customers, who eventually moved toward the more expensive items. Woolworth, though, was fascinated by the nickel price aspect. Why not an entire store of five-cent merchandise? Woolworth believed that such a store, with a low markup and five-cent prices would create enough sales volume to earn the retailer a steady profit. Customers could browse the merchandise that was open for inspection, instead of in counters or on shelves behind counters. Sales would be cash only. Woolworth took the one-price policy another step. All of his merchandise was initially five cents; later he introduced ten-cent items, too (becoming a five and dime). Woolworth was familiar with the alternative pricing strategy, where retailers rarely marked prices on goods. Clerks memorized prices or were prompted by "complicated price codes." Often there were two prices listed; the higher price was quoted first, and, if the customer balked, the clerk retreated to the second, "rock-bottom" price (Plunkett-Powell [1999] 2001, 26, 32, 36–38).[11]

Woolworth was so successful that he achieved an accolade accorded to successful entrepreneurs: the entry of imitators. On the other hand, "unfriendly" competitors co-opted Woolworth's idea and, sometimes, his name in opening their stores. One of Woolworth's cousins, Herbert Woolworth trained with F.W. and went off on his own. Herbert imitated Frank Woolworth's stores and used the "Woolworth" name to get the public to think he was F.W. The original Woolworth felt aggrieved at this blatant betrayal. Despite such shenanigans, Woolworth surmounted such challenges (Plunkett-Powell [1999] 2001, 72–73, 76).

The dime store chains contested the lower end of the market. F.W. Woolworth and other pioneers quickly dominated this market, and later entrants into the dime store market rarely succeeded. At first, regular department stores and other observers viewed the dime stores as the "poor person's department store." But as the dime store chains began siphoning business, rivals of other types of retail stores started whining that the five-and-dime stores were competing unfairly. These stores were accused of driving out small retailers in towns, thereby ending the dream of retail ownership that had encouraged many Americans of limited capital.

The critics argued that once the small retailers were forced out, the five-and-dime stores could become local monopolies and gouge the local customers; the descendants of such critics use similar arguments against Walmart and other large discount retailers. The critics did not appear to appreciate the irony of their remarks, as most of the dime store chain owners were the epitome of small town, Protestant young men with ambitions. Woolworth, Sebastian Kresge, the Kress brothers, John J. Newberry, and William T. Grant grew up in small towns or rural areas. Some worked on farms and others for small retailers. They usually had a little more education than the typical male in their locales, but they rarely enjoyed a college education. They became rich by offering good values for the low prices and by creating the image that all of their customers, even the poorest, could still afford to buy anything in the store (Raucher 1991, 132–137).

Woolworth proved loyal to his former employer and his employees through the years. When he heard that his old employer had become impoverished, Woolworth helped his friend get back into business. He promoted two of his early women workers to managing stores, which was an audacious decision for the era. However, he did not promote additional women to management positions. He considered his employees "part of his extended family." He was happy to promote his employees. As with a majority of his fellow employers of the period, Woolworth took it for granted that his female employees would earn less than his male employees. He felt he was giving the "counter girls" an opportunity. One of his male executives persuaded Woolworth to raise the female clerks' starting salary from $1.50 per week to $3.50 (Plunkett-Powell [1999] 2001, 67).

As the retail workforce became feminized, the industry gradually began promoting women to management and even senior management positions, decades ahead of many other industries. The logic was impeccable. Women shoppers determined the bulk of expenditures for their families, and women sales staff and buyers were better attuned to female customers than their male counterparts. Although the Sister Carries of the world, as memorably drawn by author Theodore Dreiser, may have predominated, women who persevered and gained senior management rungs earned far more than women working in industrial plants; they also had better fringe benefits (Lancaster 1995, 176–177). These women were pioneers in attaining the "middling sort" of living standards in England and America. This is not to say that they did not face barriers to senior management positions, but simply to point out that retail differed from other industries.

Woolworth anticipated modern-day concerns about sexual harassment. The company policy mandated dismissal of any man making sexual advances (wanted or unwanted) to female employees or drinking in public. Most of the dime store owners also avoided hiring men who liked to gamble or engage in risky behavior. Kresge justified its low salaries to men who were prospective managers, in order to inculcate habits of thrift. The company's thinking was that how a man spent his personal money was reflective of how he would spend the company's money. Dime store chain owners wanted pliable managers, who were team players with executives higher on the corporate ladder, but able to be mentors for employees beneath them (Raucher 1991, 140–41).

Resistance to Large Retailers

A century and a half's experience with large retail stores offering a wide panoply of goods makes it difficult to realize how controversial such businesses were at their inception. Social critics found plenty to dislike about French, British, and American department stores.

There were plenty of critics of the new department store retailers. William Stead's provocative *If Christ Came to Chicago!* excoriated the retailers; his description of their activities painted a modern version of Sodom and Gomorrah. He accused Marshall Field for having succeeded "in ascending a pyramid largely composed of human bones (Stead 1894, 63; Lancaster 1995, 59)."[12] Indeed, the frontispiece to Stead's book shows Christ rebuking a facsimile of Marshall Field.

Critics of the big retailers claimed the fancy displays induced customers to buy things they did not "need." Some consumers spent money on "luxuries" they could not afford. Underlying both these arguments was an air of condescension. Did adults know how to handle their money? Of course, nineteenth-century critics were not entirely wrong; there was an element of truth in their criticisms. Twentieth- and twenty-first-century psychologists have documented that some shoppers can't help themselves.

Small- and medium-sized retailers feared the growth of large department stores. The aggrieved retailers fought back, and the Bon Marché's weak points were its employment of female clerks and the enticement of female customers. Emile Zola was an outspoken critic of the large department stores. He employed a demoiselle as the protagonist of one of his novels, similar to Dreiser's *Sister Carrie*. Various social and religious commentators speculated on the morals of the female clerks; because most were single, often living out of their family homes, they evoked prurient interest. They spent their days working with male clerks, and observers imagined and published absurd accounts of the female clerk's nighttime activities. To be sure, some females (and males) were intoxicated by their freedom, but given the long hours of work, one wonders whether the staff members were too exhausted to party. Since the shop staff fell between the working class and middle class, the imputation of debaucheries among working-class women were easily transferred to female shop workers. The Boucicauts were devout Catholics and very concerned about the moral behavior of their workers. In part, their concern was understandable—part of the appeal of their store was the probity and reputation of the sales staff. Department store owners had to rebut charges that their establishments fostered immorality, especially with regard to unchaperoned women "any form of misbehavior was regarded, as a threat to the functioning of the store." To rebut such insinuations was the challenge facing Boucicaut and his peers and partly explains his obsession with protecting his workers' reputations (Miller 1981, 83–87, 193–196).

Working Conditions

Astute retailers, such as Harry Selfridge, recognized that their sales staff were paramount. "When an assistant is serving a customer the whole reputation of the store is in the hands of that single assistant (Cox and Hobley 2014, 138)."

Prior to the rise of the French department stores, small- and medium-sized shops paid employees fixed salaries and worked them 12 hours or more per day; the Bon Marché offered shorter hours to its workers, but even these privileged workers were susceptible to being called to work overtime without pay. Sales workers were not permitted to sit down in French stores, similar to American stores. Boucicaut paid his employees commissions on top of a nominal salary. A diligent salesperson earned above-average amounts; because of the elimination of time-consuming bargaining, commissions made sense for the Bon Marché. A drawback was that commissions created an individualistic ethos and competition between workers; from Boucicaut's perspective, though, the commissions had the additional benefit of deterring unionization efforts.[13]

One of Boucicaut's innovations was creating an organization to handle the large volume of business. To prevent chaos from the high-velocity turnover and myriad of goods and sales staff, everything was routinized. The insistence on properly filling the paper work and following the rules, of course, rankled many employees. Since the Boucicauts and other employers' attempts to control workers were no secret, presumably the Bon Marché would begin to attract a self-selected group of workers who found the strictures less onerous than more free-spirited workers.

To further buttress this idea of becoming an organization person, Boucicaut created a retirement program for his workers; the workers saved some of their paychecks, and the Boucicauts invested the savings into the company. Of course, to eventually garner the promotions and pensions, workers had to make working at the Bon Marché a career. "Career also meant subservience to the regulations of the house. To rise meant to display obedience and loyalty as much as talent." The pensions and provident accounts also impeded the formation of an employee union. The Boucicauts were adamantly opposed to unions (Miller 1981, 79–83, 93, 102–103).

The large Parisian store owners, such as the Bon Marché, tended to treat their salespeople better than their counterparts in England and America did; they offered paid sick leave, health care, and annual vacations. The health care was a particularly welcome benefit, as sales staff were susceptible to respiratory diseases. The Bon Marché and Louvre had a set of fringe benefits that presaged modern benefits, including maternity leave and even gifts for newborn children. One retailer ran a day-care facility (McBride 1978, 676–678; Lancaster 1995, 20).

The obverse side of the Bon Marché's enlightened employee policies was the possibility of dismissal. Employees had to adhere to the procedures and rules; failure to do so often meant instant dismissal, regardless of a worker's prior experience and record. The Bon Marché was not the most ruthless retail employer; other retailers facing recurring off-seasons were merciless in dismissing employees during slack times.[14]

Sales people labored under a myriad of regulations, punishable by fines. William Whiteley had thousands of people working under him. He issued a staff rulebook with 176 separate rules. Some of the rules, such as no bad language, no fighting, no liquor, and no standing on chairs, seemed sensible. The other rules appeared more annoying, such as no noise, no loitering, no gossiping, and others. Two authors wryly noted, "For good measure, rule 176 covered 'any mistake not before mentioned (Cox and Hobley 2014, 37).'"

Unlike most other merchants, Harry Selfridge did not expect his sales staff to accept abuse from customers. Selfridge, a protegee of Marshall Field in Chicago, wrote, "The time has passed when an irritable customer, no matter who he or she may be, can, whether right or wrong, ride roughshod over the young man or woman behind the counter and demand his or her dismissal." He acknowledged that sometimes the sales staff was correct and the customer wrong. He also understood that employees made mistakes, so he advocated a rule of "Don't make the same mistake twice." He urged his managers to use encouragement more than criticism when training and monitoring employees; Selfridge thought it better to "cement the loyalty and determination to do continually better" among his employees, and he also mentioned applying the Golden Rule.[15] He also advised paying employees a decent wage or salary instead of holding "wages down to the breaking point; for there is so much more to the employee than two arms and two legs. There is the spirit of enthusiasm and earnestness and 'I will,' which means more to the employer than ten pairs of arms and legs .... And loyalty is a quality to be earned by the employer from the employee, and only earned by fair, friendly, generous treatment (Selfridge [1918] 2013, 76–77, 83 113–114)."

Forming a Better Class of Retail Workers

Aristide Boucicaut, as with other similar-minded retailers in Great Britain and the United States, sought to elevate the stature of his sales staff. Retail clerks had a rather disreputable image; playwrights often satirized their swings from obsequious to disorderly and untrustworthy. From their physical appearances, including clothing, to their demeanor, retail sales staff working for the Bon Marché and similar stores had to present a gentlemanly or ladylike mien.

Some of the workers were literally part of the household, as they lived in quarters on the upper floors of the new building. The living quarters included a library, lounging rooms with a piano and billiards tables, and dining facilities. The meals were free, although biographer Michael Miller suggested the free meals meant lower salaries, but given his previous information on salaries and commissions, this would seem difficult to disentangle. By housing workers, Boucicaut could exert greater control over their free time. Boucicaut provided educational opportunities and concerts, but he forbade card playing and strictly prohibited mixing of the sexes, aside from the common library. Modern-day readers may find the Boucicauts' prudery off-putting, but given the mores of the time, their edicts were wise. Families worried about their daughters working in Paris; employers, including the Boucicauts, strove to assure parents that their daughters' chastity was being protected as much as possible. Similar to college dormitories well into the twentieth century, the Bon Marché living quarters had a concierge and curfews. Underlying these rules and efforts at control, employers were hoping to transform their working-class staff into bourgeois (Miller 1981, 105–109, 171–172).

One potential reason why department store owners and their labor force had fewer strikes than in other industries might have been that the workers enjoyed stable, albeit lengthy, hours unlike many workers. Sales staff who avoided running afoul of the myriad rules and the persnickety floorwalkers and supervisors could anticipate a steady income. The sales force may have been afforded an element of protection denied to mine workers; the public dealt directly with sales workers, unlike miners. Although customers may have been condescending toward sales workers, they could see such workers as living, breathing people. Miners were often in isolated regions, away from the public's consciousness, and they were begrimed, offending upper-class sensibilities.

Most of the department store owners eventually followed the lead of Boucicaut and American Edward Filene, who saw his workers as assets to be nurtured and treated as individuals and not interchangeable pawns: "whose sole purpose was the maximization of profit could never be part of the department store milieu." Filene and the International Association of Department Stores were at the forefront of using scientific management to promote welfare (and paternalism). They openly disagreed with Henry Ford and other leading industrialists (Lancaster 1995, 131, 144–145).

Store owners, though, resisted legislation that allowed salespeople to sit down. According to testimony given to a Select Committee of 1886, retailers worried that customers entering a store and finding assistants sitting would have the impression that "the shop was not well patronized and did but little business." Female workers found the no-sitting rule to be particularly onerous. Given the styles of the day, wearing a corset and standing for 12 or more hours was undoubtedly vexing (Lancaster 1995, 135; see also Steele 2001, 67–71).

Women and Retailing

Women had been the primary buyer for their families well before the department stores. Historian William Lancaster concluded, "[I]t was freedom afforded to such large numbers of women by the new type of shopping that caused unease in a society dominated by patriarchal values. With hindsight we can see .... that these women, particularly the workers, were pioneers of the new urban sociability." Female retail employees attained a financial independence novel in history (Lancaster 1995, 188; McBride 1978, 675; Vickery 1993, 274–301).

Some commentators of women and shopping took a more favorable view: "women's consumption could be advocated unequivocally as a means towards the easing of their domestic lot and a token of growing emancipation." No less an advocate for women's rights than Elizabeth Cady Stanton told her audiences in the 1850s about a congressman's wife, whose husband complained about her cooking (despite an ill-equipped stove). Stanton advised the woman to, "GO OUT AND BUY!" [Caps in original] The new stove, of course, was bound to cause the congressman to go into conniptions. Stanton urged the wife to, "sit in a corner and weep. That will soften him! Then, when he tastes his food from the new stove, he will know you did the wise thing. When he sees you so much fresher, happier in your new kitchen, he will be delighted and the bills will be paid." An advertisement writer a century later would be hard pressed to come up with better copy. Stanton's advice, which jars modern readers, was a forerunner of "relative emancipation in women's active role as consumers (Bowlby 1985, 20, 22)."[16] Women did most of the shopping for the family, so they had discretion. One wonders, though, whether the husband reserved the final say so on major purchases.

One historian, though, presents a more extreme criticism of women and shopping: "It was above all to women that the new commerce made its appeal, urging and inviting them to procure its luxurious benefits and purchase sexually attractive images for themselves. They were to become in a sense like prostitutes in their active, commodified self-display, and also to take on the one role almost never theirs in actual prostitution: that of consumer (Bowlby 1985, 11)."

Contrary to many Marxist interpretations of women shoppers and workers, women, even prior to 1800, occasionally flexed their collective muscles for various social and political causes. Women abolitionists used boycotts of slave-produced products; women also banded together to protest high meat prices. The shibboleth "the customer is always right" had implications for women, as women were the predominant shoppers. Department store owners often cooperated with suffragists, even allowing them to use display windows for campaign purposes. Some offered special clothing for suffragists. As many window display experts were women, the suffragists could draw upon a talented pool to promote their cause. "Women have long been aware of [their collective power] and have been highly innovative in expressing their power for the common good as well as for themselves and their families (Midgley 1992, 35–40, 49–50, 57–58; see also Lancaster 1995, 190–192, Cox and Hobley 2014, 119; Thompson 1971, 76–136)."[17]

Consumer Malfeasance and Shoplifting

Customers want to pay as low a price as possible, and there is a tussle between consumers and retailers. Some customers believe a price of zero is optimal (even if the retailer does not). The word, "free," sets hearts aflutter.

One of the retailers' new tactics raised concerns. Aristide Boucicaut displayed his merchandise in the open; customers could touch and finger merchandise. Some critics worried that giving customers access to merchandise would trigger shoplifting by consumers. Shoplifting, of course, predated nineteenth-century retailers and their shopping venues. A Shakespearean contemporary, Robert Greene, wrote a manuscript offering advice for potential shoplifters: be "attired in the form of a civil country gentleman (Shteir 2011, 16)." The English eventually made stealing more than five shillings' worth of merchandise a hanging offense.

Opponents of the large department stores attacked the largely female clientele and tied this to shoplifting. Female customers were supposedly susceptible to kleptomania. The allure of so many desirable objects that they could see, touch, and sometimes smell proved overwhelming. A juicy topic for Victorian readers on both sides of the Atlantic was the alleged propensity for middle- and upper-class women to shoplift. Although retailer William Whiteley's claim that "for every male he caught, 300 female shoplifters were detected," seems exaggerated, the problem of female shoplifting became a lively topic of debate (Lambert 1938, 126; see also Lancaster 1995, 185).

Presumably nineteenth-century women had two advantages as shoplifters relative to men. Their voluminous dresses afforded many a hiding place, and their femininity, especially for middle- and upper-class women, made apprehending, accusing, and searching them problematic. In most cases, the stores let them go with what William Lancaster characterized as "a gentle ticking-off (Lancaster 1995, 185; Shteir 2011, 38)."[18] The female kleptomaniac became the material that pseudo-science thrived upon. The public was titillated by the idea that respectable women were shoplifting, although most of the stealing was done by professionals. Shoplifting was enough of a problem that inspectors had to monitor not only the clerks' performance but also keep watch for thefts. To bolster the store's anti-theft defenses, the Bon Marché offered a bonus of money and two evenings off for employees identifying a shoplifter (Miller 1981, 197).

Contemporary experts offered pseudo-scientific explanations for the alleged propensity that bordered on the ridiculous. Kleptomania was a common explanation for female shoplifting; more modern researchers have broadened the explanations to include a sense of entitlement—poor women seeing desirable goods beyond their budgets may have felt that society's injustices made it permissible for them to redress the inequity. The changing nature of shopping and the physical layout of stores potentially contributed to the decision to steal; shopping became more impersonal; and the easy access of goods for inspection made it easier to shoplift. Product placement often dictated putting the most desirable or valuable goods at eye level, certainly within easy access (Phillips et al. 2005, 68, 70).

Some physicians claimed that women apprehended for shoplifting at department stores pleaded they only stole from such venues and not elsewhere. One historian stated, "the psychiatrists vied to produce the most lurid account of department store temptations." Women found department stores destinations filled with "distractions or adventures," where they found tempting items on sale. Then, in a burst of purple prose, a contemporary wrote, "Women of all sorts, drawn to these elegant surroundings by instincts native to their sex, fascinated by so many rash provocations, dazzled by the abundance of trinkets and lace, find themselves overtaken by a sudden, unpremeditated, almost savage impulse." One could argue that, if true, the description confirmed the retailers as savvy in their merchandising. The author continued to the crime itself: "They place a clumsy if furtive hand on a display and voila, with one unthinking stroke, they wipe out the most respectable past, improvise as shoplifters, and render themselves criminal." Then, in a finishing conclusion worthy of a Jack Webb summary in the television police drama *Dragnet*, "Soon they will have to explain themselves before the authorities and justice (Miller 1981, 202)."[19]

From a societal perspective, the fact that many shoplifters were women from bourgeois backgrounds proved troubling. These women could afford the items they stole, which were, in many cases, mere trinkets or baubles. Male observers attributed female shoplifters' actions to women's helplessness in the face of temptation. A critic huffed, "the department stores make great profits .... However the prosperity of these colossal enterprises must not take place at the expense of public morality (Miller 1981, 205)."[20] Other critics claimed that women ignored their family responsibilities as they roamed the Bon Marché.

Another potential for consumer malfeasance lurked. Retailer Alexander Turney Stewart practiced a modified version of a "money-back guarantee." Most retailers of his time considered all sales final. Once the customer left the premises, he or she was stuck with the purchase. Stewart allowed customers to return merchandise for exchange or cash refund. Later retailers would carry the policy to extremes and leave themselves open to consumer fraud. Some customers saw nothing wrong with wearing an article of clothing and then returning it for a refund, even though there was nothing wrong with the garment. Stewart anticipated such unethical behavior by taking back unsatisfactory merchandise but at a modest discount, such as giving credit for nine yards of cloth if ten were returned. His policy "discouraged indiscriminate and unreasonable exchanges and 'safeguarded the interests of subsequent customers who always reaped the benefit.'" He also adjusted the terms of credit or refund, if the price of the returned good had dropped during the interim (Resseguie 1965, 311–312). He appeared to have understood the concept of "moral hazard," and discouraged customers from making frivolous or fraudulent returns.

Modern-Day Shoplifting

Shoplifting continues to be a costly crime. Dramaturgist Rachel Shteir cites figures of $11.69 billion annually, or over one-third of all "shrink" (profit margin); another authority estimates that store theft amounted to $450 per American family annually. A similar figure of £180 in "crime tax" per family was cited for the United Kingdom. Since supermarkets, for instance, operate on margins as low as 1 and 5 percent, a thief walking out with a $5 item can require the store to sell up to another $500 of merchandise to recoup the loss (Shteir 2011, 8).

By the 1960s and 1970s, the counterculture movement became more brazen about stealing from capitalist-owned retail stores. Jerry Rubin and William Powell published *Do It: Scenarios of the Revolution* and *The Anarchist Cookbook* respectively. Rubin was a 32-year-old yippie and one of the Chicago Seven, while Powell was a 19-year-old. Rubin gleefully advised his readers to steal: "all money represents theft … shoplifting gets you high. Don't buy. Steal." Borrowing a page from the Elizabethan shoplifters who wore silk to blend in with the nobility and gentry browsing and shopping, Powell suggested young people dress up as "establishment squares" to steal. Both Rubin and Powell imbued shoplifting with a sort of juvenile call for revolution. Abbie Hoffman, author of *Steal This Book*, was already a little old to be cavorting with college students in the late 1960s. He debated a Harvard sociologist, Seymour Lipset. After Lipset made the obligatory remark, "Stealing is stealing even if you call it revolution," Hoffman claimed that "Saying that shoplifting accounts for high prices is like saying that people using colored toilet paper are responsible for the ecological mess. All our ripoffs together don't equal one price-fixing scheme by General Electric (Rubin 1970, 122; Powell 1971; Hoffman

1971, Shteir 2011, 52, 55)."[21] One can only wonder what Marx, Lenin, Stalin, and Mao would have thought of such puerile acts.

What did young revolutionaries do when they grew up? Rubin was hoisted upon his own petard when someone stole stuff from his apartment: "In advocating stealing …. I guess I didn't make clear the difference between stealing from General Motors and stealing from me." Powell became an Anglican and renounced his own book. No one asked whether Hoffman was miffed when people took advice and stole his book.

Shteir, too, expresses skepticism regarding shoplifting as a revolutionary act: "At first, I found these ideas rhetorically and imaginatively jejune. 'Why I Love Shoplifting from Big Corporations' read more like a summa of adolescent grudges than a sophisticated political treatise." Perhaps because such calls to revolution at the local mall are so jejune, they appeal to young minds. The Freegans, a radical group of anti-consumerists [sometimes spelled Fregans], rely on the old canards that starving people should steal food and that stealing from rich owners is not immoral.[22] There is also the "Robin Hood" aspect of shoplifters sticking it to "The Man" (or increasingly, "The Woman"). Shteir goes on to highlight how shoplifting is just one of an array of stealing. People download music illegally; such activities progress from using reel-to-reel or cassette recorders to reproduce music. P2P file sharing is dubbed "trading," and a few found guilty are dealt with harshly. Some commentators or participants claim such activity is not stealing, that these people would never shoplift. Because music is less tangible than a piece of food, it was not a "stealable object (Shteir 2011, 62, 66–70, 97–98)."

Similar sentiments existed in the United Kingdom. Father Tim Jones, an Anglican vicar, counseled starving congregants in York to shoplift: "I would ask that they do not steal from small, family businesses, but from national businesses." One critic said that Father Jones was "one psalm short of a sermon." Jones, unruffled, shot back, "Walmart is a trade union recognition short of an ethical employment policy." A serious critic concluded that stealing food out of dire straits "just mimics the theft at the top," creating a vicious cycle and contributing to a crumbling society. Left unstated was how many York residents were on the brink of starvation.

Shoplifting transcended cultures and political milieu. In Japan, senior citizens became the biggest perpetrators of shoplifting, as the country's social structure weakened. In Russia, where as Shteir snidely but accurately put it, "only after the fall of communism did enough products appear on store shelves for people to shoplift," one entrepreneur created a game whereby businessmen pay a fee to enter a store to find out who can steal the most expensive item without getting caught. Chinese loss prevention officers, however, played rough with an alleged shoplifter, beating her to death.

Some American retailers fight against shoplifting, sometimes using excessive means. Retailers install magnetic detectors and employ guards. Sometimes they use "mystery or secret shoppers" who spy on shoppers. Retail store guards may or may not have training in apprehending suspects; in many states, such guards are "exempt from laws binding the police and protecting individual rights and due process. In general, no authority requires store security to Mirandize detained alleged shoplifters." Dillard's takes a particularly militant stance toward shoplifters by hiring moonlighting police officers. Such "loss prevention" officers are more likely to resort to handcuffs and guns than other store guards, sometimes with unfortunate consequences. An off-duty police officer who shoots a suspected shoplifter in the store or on the store's parking lot can assert he or she was acting in their capacity as a police officer, relieving the store of responsibility in wrongful death or personal lawsuits.

One need not be a psychic to predict that African-American shoplifters were punished more severely than white shoplifters throughout American history. Loss prevention officers at Dillard's have killed six alleged shoplifters—all but one African-American—between 1994 and 2011. In one wrongful death case, the deceased's family won a verdict of $800,000 plus interest. Dillard's reacted by suppressing unfavorable stories about these incidents, using morally dubious economic coercion, such as threatening to cancel advertising from newspapers and television stations reporting on the killings. Shteir concluded her book by advocating for retailers to make public their methods of dealing with shoplifters; she argues that transparency is needed (Shteir 2011, 174–176, 215–219).

Sources of Scandals

Victorian readers in England and the United States feared (or perhaps were titillated by) the potential for women to lose their chastity in various public spaces. Department stores came in for intense scrutiny by morality watchdogs. When William Whiteley opened a luncheon room in his store in 1872, he anticipated meeting his customers' desire for a place to refresh, but his idea met a storm of criticism. Whiteley, with his notorious reputation as a womanizer, was probably not the best retailer to introduce a luncheon room. According to the critics' worldview, white slavers, cads, and other predatory men (and occasionally women) lurked; seemingly innocent places such as powder rooms and luncheon rooms were potential places of danger. Female workers, too, were susceptible to degradation. William Stead, among other critics, claimed that department store owners paid insufficient wages for a working woman to support herself, forcing her to resort to prostitution. He added a kicker: Department stores with their boundless temptations of fancy clothes and luxurious products tempted female customers to overspend and then be forced to earn money in dishonorable ways. The reality seemed pretty tame; given the large number of women, it was inevitable that some would succumb to a less respectable life. Stead trumpeted the fact that Selfridge admitted that three women in five years had "gone bad," to buttress his argument, but Selfridge employed hundreds, if not thousands, of workers during those five years. Store owners sought respectable girls with education (and physical attractiveness, too); the sales, buyer, and management positions required an increasing ability to handle rapid turnover of merchandise and to monitor a growing workforce (Lancaster 1995, 178–181, 203; Stead 1894, 234, 244).

A more reliable source of moral turpitude regarded the action of some owners and managers and their relations with female staffers. William Whiteley and Harry Selfridge were notorious womanizers. They slept with some of their workers, among other women. Whiteley's escapades resulted in his murder by an enraged illegitimate son of one of his lovers; he was also involved in a well-publicized separation case (the press dubbed it the "Great Whiteley Divorce"). Although people disapproved of such shenanigans, there was no cry for what we now call sexual harassment laws in the late Victorian/early Edwardian years. Not only were Whiteley's and Selfridge's dalliances risky and likely to trigger adverse publicity, their behavior had a negative effect upon the employees. One director related, "The day Gordon [Harry] Selfridge walked up to a till and removed a fiver to pay for his and his girlfriend's lunch was the day he was finished as a trader (Lancaster 1995, 121, 183)."

Conclusion

The big retailers of the nineteenth century advanced ethical business practices. Their innovations helped customers find good-quality merchandise at reasonable prices. By serving their customers better, several of the pioneering department store owners became very wealthy, which seems a just outcome. To be sure, by twenty-first-century mores, some of their practices left something to be desired. They fought unions and held patronizing attitudes toward women (and, sometimes, children); then again, by the mores of their time, they treated their female employees better than their peers in other industries.

Americans of the twenty-first century are voracious shoppers. In the vast majority of purchases, customers feel satisfied. There remain some unscrupulous retailers, but the odds of such retailers becoming fabulously wealthy are slim. Market competition, especially when commodities are purchased repeatedly, tends to winnow out fraudsters.

The internet has given birth to new ways to shop. Amazon.com and eBay have proved formidable competitors to the nineteenth- and twentieth-century retail goliaths. Montgomery Wards, Marshall Fields, Woolworth, K-Mart, and quite possibly Sears have either gone out of business or been subsumed within some conglomerate. Amazon.com and eBay, as well as various travel sites, introduced a bilateral rating system; customers rate vendors, and vendors rate customers. Although one is entitled to think that only the disgruntled will take time to rate their transaction partner, the rating system works well. Vendors with strong reputations can charge a premium, as customers seek them out. Presumably vendors may avoid customers with bad records (Frankel 2006, 51–52; Seabright 2004, 147).

Notes

1. French and Popp provided several unflattering depictions of traveling salesmen.
2. J.P. Johnston's *Twenty Years of Hus'ling*, written in 1888, mocked the commercial travelers. Johnston bragged about his ability to "hustle" instead of wasting time "getting acquainted." Johnston's method involved pushing ahead, fast pitch, quick sale, and, presumably, rapid disappearance (Spears 1995, 103; Johnson 1908).
3. Uriah Heep might have made a cracker-jack sales clerk.
4. Barry Levinson's movie *Tin Men*, depicted a variation of this stunt whereby the aluminum siding salesman would casually drop a $5 bill on the ground, pick it up, and say to the prospective customer, "Did you drop this?" By establishing his reputation for "honesty," the salesman prepped his customer/victim.

5. Takatoshi Mitsui ran a kimono shop in Japan during the 1670s. He presaged Stewart's tactics of cash-only sales. He also set fixed prices and eliminated haggling; this policy proved quite popular (Yamamura 1973, 178).
6. Some historians attributed the one-price policy to John Wanamaker, but a Wanamaker biographer made the distinction that Stewart originated and Wanamaker "established" the policy (Appel 1940, 53–59).
7. The author of this book would argue the department store and its kin can be more aptly described as *extractive* industries. They serve to extract money from wallets and purses; the escalators are eerily reminiscent of the conveyor belts in mines.
8. Ward often emphasized the fact that he bought direct from the producer, saving money for his customers and himself (Montgomery Ward & Co. 1972, 12).
9. Why Sears restrained himself from using, say, "The Cheapest Supply House in the Galaxy," is an interesting question?
10. Sears employed another subterfuge in his watch business. He sent out thousands of postcards in facsimile handwriting. He relied upon his customers' credulity in thinking the handwriting was real. On the other hand, the prose in his ad copy proved effective (Hoge 1988, 21).
11. The author worked for a retail drug store; the price code used the word, "REPUBLICAN," which in addition to representing the owners' political persuasion, also stood for the digits 0–9.
12. For a more flattering description of Field, see Darby (1986, 25, 36).
13. The commission system afforded sales clerks an opportunity to escape a working-class standard of living, but clerks undoubtedly had to bite their tongues or turn the other cheek in dealing with obstreperous customers, and such customers were apparently plentiful in the nineteenth century (Miller 1981, 91–92).
14. In film director Ernst Lubitsch's charming *Shop Around the Corner* with James Stewart and Margaret Sullavan, the two stars are bickering clerks in a small shop in Budapest. At a key point in the film, the owner, Matuschek, summarily dismisses the Stewart character—whom he mistakenly suspects of having an affair with his wife.
15. Selfridge learned from Marshall Field, whose slogan was, "Give the lady what she wants (Wendt 1952)."
16. Bowlby noted, "This apparently foolproof recipe—his fury, your tears, a nice meal, a 'fresher, happier' you, then finally his conversion—is an interesting lesson in that much-vaunted nineteenth-century feminine power of 'influence.'" The advice "comes from woman to woman, not from a man, and involves first bypassing and then mollifying a male authority (Bowlby 1985, 22)."

17. Militant suffragists went on a rampage and broke windows in March 1912; they did not distinguish between anti- and pro-suffrage retailers. Those retailers who supported suffrage and whose windows were smashed, carried on without comment (Cox and Hobley 2014, 122).
18. Cox and Hobley described how difficult it was for store staff and detectives apprehend upper-class females (Cox and Hobley 2014, 75).
19. At least the contemporary had the self-control not to add "where she [the female shoplifter] will suffer the torment of the damned," or some similar dramatic denouement.
20. See Emma Goldman's similar tirade (Shteir 2011, 41).
21. Hoffman and his sidekicks pulled off one amusing stunt, though, when they went through the New York Stock Exchange and tossed money, most of it play money, among the traders, some of whom scrambled for the loot (Rubin, *Do It*, 117).
22. In a sense, the philosophy was reminiscent of playground morality: It's okay to steal, if the other party stole first!

Bibliography

Ablett, William. *Reminiscences of an Old Draper* (London, UK: Sampson Low, Marston, Searle, & Rivington, 1876).

Appel, Joseph. *Growing Up With Advertising* (New York, NY: Business Bourse, 1940).

Atherton, Lewis. *The Southern Country Store, 1800–1860* (New York, NY: Greenwood Press: [1949] 1968).

Bowlby, Rachel. *Just Looking: Consumer Culture in Dreiser, Gissing, and Zola* (New York, NY: Methuen, 1985).

Bulletin of the Business Historical Society. "The Persistent Fringe of House to House Selling in American History." IX(2), March 1935, 24–28. No author.

Chandler, Alfred Jr. *The Visible Hand: The Managerial Revolution in American Business* (Cambridge, MA: Harvard University Press, 1977).

Chicago *Tribune*. "Grangers, Beware!" November 8, 1873a, 3.

Chicago Tribune. "Montgomery, Ward & Co.," December 24, 1873b, 5.

Cohn, David. *The Good Old Days: A History of American Morals and Manners as Seen through the Sears, Roebuck Catalogs, 1905 to the Present* (New York, NY: Simon and Schuster, 1940).

Cox, Pamela and Annabel Hobley. *Shopgirls: The True Story of Life behind the Counter* (London, UK: Hutchinson, 2014).

Darby, Edwin. *The Fortune Builders* (Garden City, NY: Doubleday, 1986).

Filene, Edward, Werner Gabler, and Percy Brown. *Next Steps Forward in Retailing* (Boston, MA: E.A. Filene, 1937).

Frankel, Tamar. *Trust and Honesty: America's Business Culture at a Crossroad* (Oxford, UK: Oxford University Press, 2006).

French, Michael and Andrew Popp. "'Ambassadors of Commerce': The Commercial Traveler in British Culture, 1800–1939." *Business History Review* 82(4), Winter 2008, 789–814.

Hoffman, Abbie. *Steal This Book* (New York, NY: Pirate Editions, 1971).

Hoge, Cecil Sr. *The First Hundred Years Are the Toughest: What We Can Learn from the Century of Competition between Sears and Wards* (Berkeley, CA: Ten Speed Press, 1988).

Hundley, Daniel. *Social Relations in Our Southern States* (Baton Rouge, LA: Louisiana State University Press, [1860] 1979).

Johnston, J.P. *Twenty Years of Hus'ling* (Chicago, IL: Thompson & Thomas, 1908).

Lambert, Richard. *The Universal Provider: A Study of William Whiteley and the Rise of the London Department Store* (London, UK: George Harrap, 1938).

Lancaster, William. *The Department Store: A Social History* (London, UK: Leicester University Press, 1995).

A Late Retailer. *A Peep into Catharine Street, or, The Mysteries of Shopping* (New York, NY: J. Slater, 1846).

Lathers, Richard. *Reminiscences of Richard Lathers: Sixty Years of a Busy Life in South Carolina, Massachusetts and New York* (New York, NY: Grafton Press, 1907).

McBride, Theresa. "'A Woman's World': Department Stores and the Evolution of Women's Employment." *French Historical Studies,* 10(4), Autumn 1978, 644–683.

Midgley, Clare. *Women Against Slavery: The British Campaigns, 1780–1870* (London, UK: Routledge, 1992).

Miller, Michael. *The Bon Marche: Bourgeois Culture and the Department Store, 1869–1920* (Princeton, NJ: Princeton University Press, 1981).

Montgomery Ward & Co. *1872–1972 A Century of Serving Consumers: The Story of Montgomery Ward* (Chicago, IL: Montgomery Ward & Co., 1972).

Nelson, Robert. *Economics as Religion: From Samuelson to Chicago and Beyond* (University Park, MD: Pennsylvania State University Press, 2001).

Nelson, Robert. "The Economics of Honest Trade Practices." *Journal of Industrial Economics* 24(4), June 1976, 281–293.

New York Herald. April 12, 1876 (obituary for Alexander Stewart).

Phillips, Simon, Andrew Alexander, and Gareth Shaw. "Consumer Misbehavior: The Rise of Self-Service Grocery Retailing and Shoplifting in the United Kingdom c. 1950–1970." *Journal of Macromarketing* 25(1), June 2005, 66–75.

Plunkett-Powell, Karen. *Remembering Woolworth's: A Nostalgic History of the World's Most Famous Five-and-Dime* (New York: St. Martin's Griffin, [1999] 2001).

Powell, William. *The Anarchist Cookbook* (Fort Lee, NJ, Lyle Stuart, 1971).

Raucher, Alan. "Dime Store Chains: The Making of Organization Men, 1880–1940." *Business History Review* 65(1), Spring 1991, 130–163.

Resseguie, Harry. "Alexander Turney Stewart and the Development of the Department Store, 1823–1876." *Business History Review* XXXIX(3), Autumn 1965, 301–322.

Rubin, Jerry. *Do It: Scenarios of the Revolution* (New York, NY: Simon and Schuster, 1970).

Scott, Peter. "Managing Door-to-Door Sales of Vacuum Cleaners in Interwar Britain." *Business History Review* 82(4), Winter 2008, 761–788.

Seabright, Paul. *The Company of Strangers: A Natural History of Economic Life* (Princeton, NJ: Princeton University Press, 2004).

Selfridge, Harry. "Selling Selfridge." *Saturday Evening Post* 208(4), July 27, 1935, 16–53.

Selfridge, Harry. *Romance of Commerce: An Abridged Version of the Classic Text on Business and Life* (Avon, MA: Adams Media [1918] 2013).

Shteir, Rachel. *The Steal: A Cultural History of Shoplifting* (New York, NY: Penguin Press, 2011).

Solomon, Steven. "Sears Sells Something for Everyone. And That's the Problem." *New York Times*, January 18, 2017, B7.

Spears, Timothy. *100 Years on the Road: The Traveling Salesman in American Culture* (New Haven, CT: Yale University Press, 1995).

Stead, William. *If Christ Came to Chicago! A Plea to the Union of All Who Love in the Service of All Who Suffer* (London, UK: Review of Reviews, 1894).

Steele, Valerie. *The Corset: A Cultural History* (New Haven, CT: Yale University Press, 2001).

Stigler, George. "Can Regulatory Agencies Protect the Consumer?" *The Citizen and the State: Essays on Regulation* (Chicago, IL: University of Chicago Press, 1975), 178–188.

Thompson, Edward P. "The Moral Economy of the English Crowd in the Eighteenth Century." *Past and Present* 50, February 1971, 76–136. No issue number.

Vickery, Amanda. "Women and the world of goods: a Lancashire consumer and her possession, 1751–81." *Consumption and the World of Goods*, edited by John Brewer and Roy Porter (London, UK: Routledge, 1993), 274–301.

Wendt, Lloyd. *Give the Lady What She Wants!: The Story of Marshall Field & Company* (Chicago, IL: Rand McNally 1952).

Westerfield, Ray. *Middlemen in English Business, Particularly between 1660 and 1760* (New York, NY: Augustus M. Kelley, [1915] 1968).

Worthy, James. *Shaping an American Institution: Robert E. Wood and Sears, Roebuck* (Urbana, IL: University of Illinois Press, 1984).

Yamamura, Kozo. "Economic Responsiveness in Japanese Industrialization." *Business Enterprise and Economic Change: Essays in Honor of Harold F. Williamson*, edited by Louis Cain and Paul Uselding (Kent, OH: Kent State University Press, 1973), 173–197.

CHAPTER 8

Early Twentieth-Century Aspects

By the twentieth century, Americans, Europeans, and other former British colonies enjoyed an unimaginable prosperity and higher standards of living. Greater educational attainment accompanied the growing prosperity. By the first decades of the twentieth century, new industries such as automobile manufacturing and, later, radio began assuming larger proportions of America's (and European countries') gross domestic product.

Although economists debate how education affects productivity, one suggests that another unheralded aspect is what "people decide to make of the potentialities of capitalism. The values that determine these decisions are essentially ethical and aesthetic. Capitalism is an economic system that vastly widens the practical field of ethical and aesthetic choice but often in misunderstood ways (Ways 1964, 214)."

Americans began to accept big business as a permanent fixture. Since many of the leading industrialists were retired and replaced by executives and managers, most of whom had no family ties to the firms they oversaw, the animus toward big business softened. The public recognized big business' contributions to rising living standards. Prosperity blessed a wider swath of the population. The introduction of electricity in homes created a demand for a myriad of household appliances. Americans became impatient with saving to buy such items and increasingly opted to buy now, pay later. They also began dabbling in the stock market during the 1920s, lured by the reports of fabulous "killings" and instant wealth. Naturally there was a learning experience for both novice consumer credit users and

D. G. Surdam, *Business Ethics from the 19th Century to Today*,
https://doi.org/10.1007/978-3-030-37169-2_8

investors. The good times and feelings evaporated during the Great Depression, and businesspeople's prestige plummeted.

During the early decades of the twentieth century, religious and academic thinkers created new approaches to thinking about business ethics. Many popular speakers and writers emphasized the idea that "ethics pays," while academics often promoted corporate social responsibility or stewardship as ethical guides. Businesspeople formed associations that pushed for self-regulation in an attempt to forestall government regulation.

Softening Attitudes to Big Business

The American public grew accustomed to big business. A 1950s survey showed "a substantial majority reacted favorably to big business," with 76 percent of the respondents agreeing with the statement, "good things outweigh the bad things" with regard to big business. Another survey revealed in 1951, "Stronger feeling was shown against labor unions than against big business (Fisher and Withey 1951, passim; Hofstadter 1965, 212–214)." Elmo Roper found that "the public has mixed feelings about big business. There is pride over the achievements of big business but some apprehension over the possible abuses of power inherent in big business (Roper 1949, 165–174; Hofstadter 1965, 21)."

By the mid-twentieth century, America was at the apogee of its relative economic power. Germany's and Japan's economies were just beginning to revitalize. Great Britain was no longer so great, and the USSR was capable of mass producing impressive quantities of military goods and some desirable, but more often undesirable, consumer goods. Americans certainly recognized their economic prowess, but as John Kenneth Galbraith wryly noted, "the foreign visitor, brought to the United States by the Economic Cooperation Administration, visits the same [large] firms as do attorneys of the Department of Justice in their search for monopoly (Galbraith 1956, 96; Hofstadter 1965, 215–217)."

Because of America's somewhat fortuitous economic strength, large corporations began offering lifetime employment while also boosting wages for union workers. Indeed, during the 2016 Presidential election, some American liberals posted material on Facebook and the internet hearkening back to the good, old days of the 1950s, when unions were strong and blue-collar workers enjoyed prosperity. Such nostalgia had a basis in fact. The GI Bill allowed many white veterans with limited means to attend college and to compete for good jobs in corporate America.

There was a marked improvement in the chances of middle- and lower-class men to gain upward mobility: "the modern corporation has proved to be a better medium for social mobility and opportunity than the old system of individual and family entrepreneurship." Many Americans wanted jobs in corporate America (Hofstadter 1965, 218, 223; see also Whyte 1956, 79; Riesman 1964, 309–323).

Americans of the 1950s displayed a very different attitude toward big business executives than those of 2019, with many agreeing with the portrayal of such executives as having "a strong and practical sense of responsibility to the public, and an awareness of the ethics of present-day business competition." Other beliefs included the idea that big business "nourishes diversity," and that "we are living in what is probably the most highly competitive society men have ever known." The public displayed some animosity toward antitrust prosecutions due to "grave implications for national security." Even Adolph Berle, who had worried about corporations in the 1930s, "urged liberals to reconsider their former, and historically justified, antipathy to big business and to judge it in the light of its achievements in increasing income and distributing property (Berle 1959, 11–16)."

Perceived State of Business Ethics in the Early 1900s

The field of business ethics changed in the early twentieth century. New participants got involved, such as business associations, business schools, and journalists; these new participants joined clergy in bemoaning the rapidly changing economies of the United States and Great Britain. The rise of large corporations coincided with or created social problems, as did the growing separation of ownership and management (Abend 2014, 96). Business associations often espoused a form of self-policing, although there were complaints about such efforts. Business schools brought together academics, who specialized in studying business. The business ethicists often had backgrounds in philosophy but lacked direct experience in business; many, indeed, seemed inherently anti-business.

Many of the ethicists a century ago stressed the same factors as those of today—morality, fairness, honesty, and service—which is not surprising. What was novel was that there were now popular business magazines to convey the message. Ernest DuBrul, an executive at National Machine Tool Builders Association, asserted, "The cynic about business ethics pretends to believe that as a cold business proposition it does not pay to be ethical, and that the whole movement to establish better ethics in business is merely a futile gesture. But if the truth were known, it would be seen that ethical conduct in business is absolutely reflected in the balance sheet." DuBrul's argument was not very convincing, as he compared the fate of two competitors. One competitor used the "unethical" practice of "sharpshooting" or giving discounts, while the other competitor adhered to its list price. The latter firm, although enjoying lower sales volume, made greater profits. The sharpshooting manager eventually lost his job, as his company's profits faltered (DuBrul 1926, 78).

Not all business executives were so sanguine. John Flynn opened his article, "Dishonest Business," by blunting stating: "I lay down this proposition—that the ethics of business is on a very low plane." Flynn dismissed anecdotal evidence about exceptional business executives or to executives' exemplary behavior outside of business. His condemnation was nuanced: "I do not say that business men are scoundrels. Indeed I know they are not. These gentlemen, before they are business men, are men, and as such have a collection of frailties to which all save a few heroic souls are heir." He then highlighted a key point: "Business is a pursuit. It is the pursuit of money." He admitted that pursuing profits did not lead to the level of immorality associated with war (due to the lack of physical violence), but he insisted that definitions of business morality were so elastic that laypeople viewed many acceptable business practices as unethical.

Flynn attributed any improvement in business practices of the 1920s to governmental scrutiny and regulation: "There is no doubt our modern business man does not resort to these petty-larcenous practices [that he had previously enumerated] to the same degree as his praying and hymn-singing predecessor." Instead he identified "new diseases of big business" that emanated from a diffusion of ownership among thousands of stockholders, who were largely powerless to control managers: "the current brand of ethics looks with tolerance upon a reasonable latitude within which directors may exploit their corporations for their own enrichment."

Flynn commented on the recent Teapot Dome scandal, whereby "the conduct of these men [associates of the Henry Sinclair and Edward L. Doheny interests] was approved throughout, not merely by a few familiars, but by their directors, numbering half a hundred men who might be considered among the leaders in the oil industry. They could see nothing in all of these transactions to warrant any lack of confidence in the conspirators." He then inveighed against the newly devised "investment trust," which appears to have been a forerunner of today's mutual fund.

He admitted that the pooling of small investors' investments managed by professionals could be beneficial by creating diversified portfolios and expert advice, but he felt that all too often, "many of them are just catch-alls for stocks and bonds of investment houses. Yet upon their directorates will be found hundreds of leaders in business all over the country. Upon what principles of ethics can this situation be defended?"[1]

Was there any way to improve business ethics heading into the 1930s (Flynn's article appeared in *Forum* in December 1929, so he might have known about the stock market crash)? He thought that business leaders needed to establish and enforce "ethical ideals" instead of making self-serving paeans regarding business ethics; otherwise the level of ethics in business would not rise (Flynn 1929, 351–355).

Journalist and business executive Julius Klein, writing just a few months after Flynn, was much more optimistic about the state of business ethics as the Great Depression loomed. He made the valid point that the misbehavior of the few should not necessarily tar the reputation of an industry. As another example, Klein pointed out that there were 13,000 business organizations; the Federal Trade Commission apparently had "pounced upon some lumber group and half a dozen others for distorting the policies of such trade associations to the attainment of sinister objective." He considered the journalists' coverage of this as distorting public perception, given that the media was trying to "condemn thousands of others whose purposes are manifestly not only honest but thoroughly in the public interest. Almost every one of them has as one of its major objectives the setting up of rigorous codes of ethics, and any straying individuals is promptly and usually effectively checked."

Klein backed up his statements by citing changes in the market for credit; advertising; and heightened competition that pushed businesspeople to become more ethical. The improved communications and transportation capabilities of the 1930s America with, say, the 1880s America, was a big change. New industrial leaders had emerged; Klein acknowledged that some of these leaders engaged in "unprincipled policies in regard to wage earners and consumers." But the changes in technology made it more difficult for unethical businesspeople to escape unscathed compared with "the old days when smug secure isolation made possible countless breaches of commercial and industrial ethics without serious danger of detection." He emphasized that dishonesty did not pay, before quoting John Wanamaker: "money is not made by aiming at money, but by doing things well." Klein concluded that a businessperson's "code of behavior has, if anything, to be a little above that of the rest of the community."

The growing use of credit by ordinary consumers and businesspeople reflected the growing confidence in the honesty of most businesspeople. Klein argued, "These elements simply cannot exist in an atmosphere of chicanery." For Klein, the burgeoning credit trade was a "symbol of the fundamental integrity of our business world." He took a swipe at the "good old mid-Victorian era," by saying that goodwill was not an element in that business world, but he provided no evidence for such a claim.

Along with the growth of credit, the increased spending on advertising demonstrated growing concern to create goodwill and develop a reputation for honesty, as consumers could quickly discern and repudiate products using deceptive advertising. Industries, too, used advertising to proclaim and to ensure the sound, ethical policies of its members. Finally, Klein believed that there were more firms competing for consumer dollars. He characterized the situation as "imperator emptor," that is, "the buyer is boss."

For these reasons, Klein thought that "shortcomings in business behavior today seldom arise from intentional malevolence; they are the result of misinformation and unintentional blundering rather than deliberate misbehavior." He did not attribute this elevation of ethical behavior to some inherent virtue of contemporary business participants but due to a fear of detection and punishment. Competitors were quick to highlight unethical behavior on the part of rivals. Things had changed considerably during the previous decades: "No industry, however, maliciously inclined, can afford to follow Boss Tweed's [a manipulator of politicians] arrogant example and demand, 'What are you going to do about it?'—because the answering chorus from a hundred directions is: 'Plenty!' And there is abundant power to back up that threat. Business ethics these days simply must be—and are—sound; otherwise modern business could not continue to function as it does (Klein 1930, 129–133)."

Judge Elbert Gary asserted that business ethics had improved in the two decades since 1900. Gary attributed this trend to the force of public opinion and the profitability of being known as an ethical firm. He admitted that circa 1900, "the managers of some of the large private business corporations apparently believed that if their conduct was within the strict and technical rules of law it was immune from public or private attack; that if the provision of no public law was violated the corporation should be permitted to secure unlimited profit and might treat indifferently its customers, its employees, its competitors and even the general public." When he delivered a speech at Northwestern University in June 1922, he claimed, "I think it properly may be claimed multitudes of leading business men during the last two decades have voluntarily devoted more and more time and energy in a conscientious desire to conduct their business in accordance with the rules of propriety and honesty (*Nation's Business* 1922, 53; Abend 2014, 103)."

Early Proponents of Prosperity Gospel

During the early decades of the twentieth century, the hope of attaining a material "good life" spread beyond the Anglo-Saxon Protestants to various ethnic groups. Although radio and television evangelists (and presumably internet evangelists) later elicited widely varying responses, they seemed to emphasize getting a return on charitable giving or appealing to God for prosperity.

Russell Conwell (an ironic surname, to be sure), a Baptist preacher, spent decades touring America preaching the virtue of amassing wealth. His "acres of diamonds" lecture was very popular and worth quoting at length. Unfortunately, the printed word alone undoubtedly does his presentation injustice.[2] One is advised to look up his recorded speeches on YouTube.

"I have come to tell you what in God's sight I believe to be the truth … that the men and women sitting here … have within their reach 'acres of diamonds,' opportunities to get largely wealthy." He lauded America as a place where opportunities abounded for acquiring wealth. He admitted that many people found it off-putting for a minister to exhort parishioners to seek wealth. His rejoinder was "to make money honestly is to preach the gospel …. The men who get rich may be the most honest men you find in the community." He chided people who clung to the belief that only the dishonest and dishonorable became rich, "that is the reason why you have none, because you have that idea of people." Here he pulled a number out of the air, claiming that 98 percent of the wealthy businessmen were honest; dishonest men of wealth were rare but appeared frequently in the press, creating a distorted view of businessmen in general. Economists Thomas Stanley and William Danko might agree with Conwell that the vast majority of American millionaires earned their money honestly and without fanfare; most of them are what we might call "the anonymous rich (Conwell 2010, 6–7; Stanley and Danko 1996, 1–11)."

Conwell understood that people would find his message inconsistent with his profession. "We preach against covetousness …. Christians get the idea that when we stand in the pulpit we believe it is wicked for any man to have money—until the collection-basket goes round, and then we almost swear at the people because they don't give more money." This was a provocative point for a preacher to make. "Money is power … you can do more good with [money] than you could without it." His candor was admirable, perhaps foolhardy: "I am always willing that my church should raise my salary, because the church that pays the largest salary always raises it the easiest …. The man who gets the largest salary can do the most good with the power that is furnished to him."

What about the poor? Conwell had an answer for them, too. His answer was in line with that espoused by Eliza Doolittle's father, Alfred, in the musical version—*My Fair Lady*—of George Bernard Shaw's *Pygmalion*. Conwell stated that he sympathized with the poor, but he made a distinction between the "worthy" and the "unworthy poor;" the latter were undeserving of pity or of help. He then made a stunning remark: "It is all wrong to be poor, anyhow." Conwell then provided an equivalent of a moral whiplash by piously decrying the worship of money, or in his colorful phrase, "[the] man who hugs the dollar until the eagle squeals has in him the root of all evil."

Conwell demonstrated the credibility of his main thesis that a businessperson does well by serving others in the middle of his "acres of diamonds" talk. He related how he used to mind his father's store. He admitted that he ignored customers' wants and requests. Business owners needed to "carry [their] religion into business" in the sense of ascertaining and meeting their customers' wants. He related how he ignored a customer who sought a jackknife. By going out and obtaining a jackknife, "I would have actually done him a kindness, and I would have received a reward myself, which it would have been my duty to take."

According to Conwell, profit taking was not just permissible but righteous; he provided a provocative version of the "just price." He argued that a seller had "no more right to sell goods without making a profit on them" than someone who dishonestly overcharged. Conwell added, without knowing that he was alluding to economists' concepts of consumer and producer surplus, "I should so sell each bill of goods that the person to whom I sell shall make as much as I make."

Conwell used retailer Alexander Turney Stewart to illustrate a point. Stewart, when a lad of modest means, scraped together \$1.50, he gambled

87.5 cents of it by buying needles, threads, and buttons for re-sale. Unfortunately, people did not want these items. Conwell believed this initial loss was of inestimable value for Stewart, since Stewart learned not to gamble in business and, instead, learned to fulfill buyers' wants and needs. Stewart was astute enough to make rounds of his neighborhood asking people what they wanted. He then spent his remaining 62.5 cents in purchasing things people wanted (Conwell 2010, 7–12).

A few decades later, Bruce Barton, author of *The Man Nobody Knew*, saw similarities between Jesus of Nazareth and successful business executives in that both preached service to others (in the latter case, service to customers); that good service sometimes resulted in great rewards was simply an inadvertent outcome of the focus upon providing service. Barton preached that God wanted people to enjoy prosperity and presaged many modern-day evangelists with their prosperity gospel (Barton 1992; Frey 2009, 133).

Christian Moralists During the Progressive Era

The "business ethics pays" argument met resistance. Many Christian business ethicists argued that the "business ethics pays" theory was "morally hideous." Other Christian thinkers incorporated business piety within the broader piety and attempted to show that the concepts were complementary. Minister Henry Boardman cited I Timothy 4:8 (King's James version): "Godliness is profitable unto all things, having promise of the life that now is, and of that which is to come." Boardman stated, "religion imparts to every young man who embraces it, much KNOWLEDGE which is indispensable to his highest temporal interests and happiness." If this wasn't clear enough, he continued, "Personal piety is especially valuable to Young Men, inasmuch as it both qualifies and disposes them TO FORM THOSE HABITS WHICH ORDINARILY INSURE SUCCESS IN BUSINESS [all caps in original] …. The most valuable qualities for the management of business, are the appropriate fruit of religious principles. Such qualities are prudence, frugality, diligence, industry, and stern, unyielding rectitude (Abend 2014, 119, 131)."

Immanuel Kant had weighed in on the subject of "whether the action which accords with duty has been done from duty or from some purpose of self-interests." He noted that a shopkeeper should not overcharge an inexperienced customer, but that a prudent merchant should set a fixed general price for all buyers; the shopkeeper would then be acting honestly.

For Kant, though, the key was whether the shopkeeper did this "from duty and principles of honesty" or whether "his advantage required it." Apparently the shopkeeper's action was not morally satisfactory, as the action was based upon a "self-interested purpose (Kant quoted in Abend 2014, 147; see also Kant [1998] 2016, 13)."

Yet, Christian morality, however, is not without its self-interested aspects. Even those Christian ethicists who hope to direct businesspeople toward a loftier plane of ethics ultimately confront the incentive of eternal life (or the disincentive of eternal damnation). A Christian businessperson may either fear damnation or hope for eternal life; these motives may affect behavior and could justifiably be called "profit-seeking," if we expand the definition of "profit." Throughout history, people have used an all-seeing deity to help keep business participants to hew the straight and narrow. Sociologist Gabriel Abend observes that "omniscience lent itself to consequentialist fear-of-punishment and hope-of-reward uses, e.g., 'God is watching, he knows what you are thinking, so even in your thoughts you should not sin,'" and similar admonitions (in a sense, one's own conscience is an inner "God is watching"). Not to be flippant, but adults endow Santa Claus with an "eye in the sky" power, as he knows whether children have been naughty or nice. Such ideas complemented business ethicists, who "have a practical, not theoretical, job, so they no doubt profited from these uses. Yet, the moral problem is that they smack too much of surveillance," by an eye in the sky authority, who will eventually assign punishments. "Are these practical uses theologically and morally kosher (Abend 2014, 153)?" Appeals to conscience, too, could become tainted by self-interest; the quest to maintain a pure soul is presumably affected, if not dominated, by a desire for goodness, eternal life, and other rewards.

Another debate revolved around moral relativism. Retailer Edward Filene told an audience interested in the Morals of Trade: "Morals are temporal and local. They are local because people live in different places, where conditions are different; and they are temporal because people live in different times and times change." Abend asked whether Filene and others, who held similar views, were arguing solely on an empirical basis that what is considered ethical in business has varied throughout history, or is there some normative content? Abend suggested that the type of economic organization may determine what is right and wrong, but he admitted that Filene did not make this clear (Filene 1935, 13; Abend 2014, 292–293).

Corporate Social Responsibility and Stewardship

An influential approach to business ethics during the Progressive Era was corporate social responsibility (CSR), whereby businesspeople were advised to be perceived as good community members, who never mentioned profit-seeking but emphasized their company's civic services. The rationale underlying CSR was seemingly that a reputation for adhering to CSR boosted profits. Two business ethicists recently argued: "We are convinced that the companies playing a leadership role in addressing these challenges (low levels of trust, high levels of inequality, and rising levels of environmental damage) will reap sound business benefits in terms of long-term competitive advantage, better risk management, and new market opportunities." In case the reader remained unclear as to the authors' intent, they ended their Preface with: "we lay out the case for how companies can benefit from creating value for both shareholders and society alike and how society can benefit from a greater alignment between private initiative and public interest. We write with the strong conviction that principled business leaders, at all levels of a company, can build great companies while also contributing to more prosperous countries and communities." Are the business leaders who follow these authors' prescriptions really principled, or are they mimicking principled business leaders (Jackson and Nelson 2004, x–xi; see also Abend 2014, 85–86)?

There was nothing wrong with boosting profits, but such a situation did not seem very ethically satisfying. If doing good no longer paid off, would business executives revert to some sort of Hobbesian state? Since antiquity parents and educators inculcated basic moral precepts in children. The stories touting the virtue of honesty were examples; from Aesop to Jataka tales of Teravada Buddhist tradition, children learned that honesty was expected, but there was a "relevant causal claim: ethics pays."

The current CSR school had predecessors among American business executives. Julius Rosenwald and several of the British Quaker entrepreneurs of the Victorian Era espoused being good citizens and treating all parties with fairness, although they sometimes fell short by twenty-first-century standards. Even hardcore market economists recognize the drawbacks of firms creating negative third-party (externality) effects and suggest decision makers should account for such effects (as well as, presumably, positive third-party effects), although they rarely couch such in moral terms.

Stewardship also became a popular approach to business ethics. Unlike ancient dead Egyptians and some other groups, most western thought denied that a person could take their earthly wealth with them. For Christian businesspeople, stewardship was the recognition that all things were God's, and the businessperson had, at best, temporary use of resources under their command. For some commentators, God's ownership extended to the individual person and their time. Christian business ethicists co-opted the stewardship concept in warning against predatory business practices with regard to competitors and customers (Abend 2014, 88, 342).

Francis Peabody took these concepts further than most: "[Jesus] does not ask of a man a fair proportion of his personal profits; he asks the whole of one's gains—and the life which lies behind the gains—for the service of the kingdom." On another occasion, Peabody stated, "[t]his is the paradox of property. To own is to owe. Possession means obligation .... Ownership is stewardship (Peabody 1916, 118, 215; Abend 2014, 343)."[3]

One contemporary writer believed there was no distinction between a businessperson's secular and sacred duties; his belief was supported by other Christian business ethicists of the early twentieth century. The idea that "business is business" as separate from everything else was a convenient canard for business participants. Many business owners might have fought hard during the week and then reflected on their otherwise pious lives on Sunday. Another writer urged businesspeople to consider every day as though it were Sunday (Abend 2014, 349).

Secular Approaches

During the early decades of the twentieth century, businesspeople created national organizations, such as the Chamber of Commerce and the Rotary. Arthur Frederick Sheldon was a Rotarian, who created the slogan, "He Profits Most Who Serves Best." The national organization adopted the somewhat ambiguous slogan. Some Rotarians found the slogan off-putting, due to the prominence of the word, "profits." Sheldon attempted to explain, "Service to others is enlightened self-interest. Selfishness is the road to self-destruction." Some observers worried that the public misconstrued the slogan and associated the Rotary with "a body of men gathered together for financial gain," sort of a modern-day guild. Of course, Sheldon and his critics might have relied upon another use of "profit" from Mark 8:6 (King James Version): "For what shall it profit a man, if he shall gain the whole world, and lose his whole soul."

American businesspeople in the early twentieth century relied upon codes of business ethics, including one promulgated by the Chamber of Commerce. One scholar argued that the codes often became vacuous and were more useful for "their rhetorical uses, and the background elements they are underlain by."

The Chamber of Commerce was an attempt to give small business owners—the Main Street proprietors—a lobbying voice. The corporations, of course, had sufficient cash to influence legislators. Small business owners hoped to protect themselves from onerous regulation and perhaps to get some favorable pieces of legislation. The conduit of information would also flow in the opposite direction, as government bureaucrats would now have a handy means of informing small businesspeople (Abend 2014, 109–110, 163, 166–169).

During the 1920s, businesspeople sought to head off unfavorable government legislation and hoped to create self-enforcement and punishment of misbehaving business operators. Herbert Hoover put the alternatives starkly: either businesses must clean up their industries or the government would (try to) do so. The formation of business associations served two purposes: The organizations established standards of practice and enforced such; commentators touted the democratic nature of these rules, often hashed out by committees in meetings. The reader might cast a skeptical eye upon "ethics by committee." Associations then published their codes of business ethics in the press, both to ensure all members had an opportunity to view the rules and for public consumption (Hoover 1924, 7; Abend 2014, 178, 181–183).

Another development was formal training of aspiring business professionals. The rise of business schools, often endowed by prominent business entrepreneurs and executives, created tensions within the academy. For as long as scholars and business practitioners have co-existed, scholars have held an animus toward business and the people that conducted business. The twentieth-century introduction of well-funded, highly publicized schools of business was sure to raise hackles within and outside academia. Dean John Madden (New York University), who when taunted that he was presiding "over a school that prostituted higher education," responded that "there was one thing worse than being a prostitute, and that was to be the pimp living off her earnings (Abend 2014, 224)."

Even within the business world, there were opponents of professionalizing business. Many of the titans of industry had relatively meager higher education experiences. They learned by doing or had an innate sense of how to conduct business. The growing complexity of business and the information flow feeding successful businesses, though, required greater analytical skills. The business schools claimed to train young minds to master interpreting financial reports, basic financial concepts, and economics. As early as 1903, though, the *Wall Street Journal* worried that concentration only upon technical aspects of business (and journalism) was insufficient. The writer urged some training "of the consciences of their students in habits of spontaneous morality." In order to inculcate business ethics, the writer advocated, "a thorough groundwork of university training on the philosophy of right action would be of inestimable value. The young men thus instructed ***might not always follow his instructor***, but at least he would not have the excuse of ignorance [italics mine] (*Wall Street Journal*, October 10, 1903, 1)."[4]

Progressive Era Regulation

Although Russell Conwell and Bruce Barton urged people to seek riches by serving others, many Americans remained wary of untrammeled profit-seeking. Throughout history, people sought regulation to limit undesirable behavior. In the case of restricting businesspeople, such regulation may have had perverse effects. A rule of "Beware businesspeople seeking regulation" would serve well. For instance, representatives of a particular trade implored the governor of a Midwestern state to support legislation to license their trade. "'Governor,' the men said, 'passage of this licensing act will ensure that only qualified people will practice this occupation; it will eliminate charlatans, incompetents or frauds; and it will thereby protect the safety and welfare of the people of this state.'" The governor knew from experience to be skeptical. "'Gentlemen,' he asked, 'are you concerned with advancing the health, safety and welfare of the people under the police powers of the state, or are you primarily interested in creating a monopoly situation to eliminate competition and raise prices?' The spokesman for the occupational group smiled and said, 'Governor, we're interested in a little of each (Law and Kim 2005, 723).'"

Milton and Rose Friedman note that barriers to entry, such as requirements of degrees from approved medical or law schools, are not necessarily created just to raise the incomes of incumbent practitioners. The incumbents use a rather convoluted argument that if too many people enter a profession, "[incumbents and new entrants] will be driven to resort to unethical practices in order to earn a 'proper' income. The only way ... in which ethical practices can be maintained is by keeping people at a standard of income which is adequate to the merits and needs of the medical [or law] profession." The Friedmans responded that such reasoning was "objectionable on ethical and factual grounds. It is extraordinary that leaders of medicine should proclaim publicly that they and their colleagues must be paid to be ethical (Friedman and Friedman 1962, 152)."[5]

New Forms of Policing Unethical Behavior

By the 1920s, unethical business practices, including "falsely characterized consumer goods, fraudulent employment scams, and real estate swindles," amounted to an estimated 1 percent of American gross domestic product. Swindlers diverted capital from honest, productive business; reduced profits that might have gone to reputable companies; and undermined the public's trust in America's retailers and markets. All too often, though, even relatively reputable companies cut corners in their sales tactics and advertising. Such tactics as the bait-and-switch irritated customers. From retailers to advertisers to financial leaders, maintaining the public's faith in American business was paramount.

Organized crime rings formed to defraud manufacturers and wholesalers. "Credit trimmers" set up phony identities as independent retailers—trading on stolen or fictitious references; establishing businesses that they purchased; or piggy-backing on an existing store's good name. These pioneers of identity theft and unauthorized use of credit to obtain goods and services were a nuisance that threatened to bankrupt honest businesses. Another popular fraud was publishing phony financial newsletters touting dubious stock choices. The perpetrators were often scornful of their victims and created and sold/distributed lists of "suckers" among stock promoters and other list brokers. In some cases, the swindlers were brazen enough to humiliate their victims by informing them that they had been mulcted; the swindlers sometimes added the gratuitous advice that the swindled had gotten something for their money—a lesson in the "ways" of the market (Balleisen 2009, 118–120, 125).[6]

Fraudsters then and now relied upon their victims' embarrassment of having been defrauded. Pursuing justice against fraudsters was a lengthy, often frustrating process. Often victims were willing to proceed only far enough to get some reimbursement, but few pressed their case through criminal proceedings, allowing fraudsters to cheat and cheat again. Although historian Edward Balleisen wrote, "Silent suckers furnished authorities with no basis to launch an investigation"; he could have just as well reiterated the old pirate saying (revised to fit the current situation) that "silent suckers tell no tales." America of the 1920s and 1930s was too big geographically and still lacked a sophisticated enough communication system to track fraud rings across state lines. Although the Inspector Service of the Post Office dealt with fraud using the mail system, the federal government was not an efficient arm of the law with regard to fraudsters. The National Association of Credit Management (NACM) and National Vigilance Committee attempted to create national registries of swindlers, including compiling "rogues' galleries," but such efforts were insufficient (Balleisen 2009, 134–135).[7]

The NACM decided to set up volunteer groups of industry executives as early as 1900 to investigate claims of dubious behavior by debtors and creditors. As a sign of the times, the NACM dubbed these groups as "vigilance committees." Advertising clubs began in 1910 to ferret out misleading advertising. The creation of the Better Business Bureau (BBB) was a national effort across industries to create an antifraud publicity campaign to educate and alert American consumers. The BBB was able to draw upon top public relations talent in crafting its message. The BBB cracked down on newspapers and magazines, advocating tightened standards of advertisements in those publications; of course, the publications were wary of losing customers, including the lucrative patent medicine market.

The BBB sent in "shoppers" to take notes about various retailers. Retailers occasionally designed incentives that inadvertently or purposefully encouraged sales staff to violate store policies in order to move slow-moving goods. Many retailers had store detectives to monitor employee behavior, which, of course, created a separate set of problems.

Attempts to regulate advertising ran afoul of freedom of speech. The BBB often represented larger, well-established businesses. Their targets were frequently new, start-up businesses, many run by immigrants. Efforts to impose more rigorous safeguards against commercial speech raised judicial concerns, and the BBB had difficulty prevailing in court cases. On the other hand, when the BBB accused business owners of unacceptable practices, the accused often filed libel suits; courts often rejected these suits. As government regulators increased their scrutiny, the BBB, New York Stock

Exchange, and other established self-regulatory groups often supplied information or instigated investigations.

As the BBB's funding came disproportionately from large vendors, smaller vendors and others accused the organization of functioning as advocates for their well-heeled sponsors. The BBB responded by claiming to have admonished Macy's department store and forcing the Firestone Tire company to revise their advertising campaigns; the BBB also attacked the credibility of its critics. The BBB characterized their critics as unscrupulous business practitioners, professional cranks, and loud-mouthed politicians bent on gaining publicity for taking on the BBB (presumably in the name of "the little guy"). Some of the criticism was valid, and the New York City BBB was embarrassed when it placed Richard Whitney, president of the New York Stock Exchange, on its advisory board. A few years later, Whitney was imprisoned for financial improprieties (Balleisen 2009, 121–131, 133, 146–147, 153–157).

Other critics of the Better Business Bureau likened its tactics to those running "protection rackets," especially as local BBBs dunned small businesses for annual dues. Critics claimed that BBBs were more likely to investigate small business owners, who refused to join and to pay dues. The heavy-handed treatment also served to protect incumbent business owners, who were often members, from upstart entrants. There was credence in the critics' complaints, as the BBBs failed to identify any of the stock market shenanigans taking place during the 1920s.

To be sure, the demographics of BBB members probably reflected mainstream, large corporate American executives of the 1920s—almost uniformly northern European males, who attended Protestant churches. These business executives' mindset pertaining to Catholics, Asian-Americans, African-Americans, and immigrants from southern and eastern European, many of them Jewish, was probably not too different from that of typical Main Street Anglo-Saxon Protestant (or, for that matter, the then-popular Ku Klux Klan). The BBB and NACM undoubtedly viewed such groups with suspicion and/or condescension. Balleisen compared the executives' ethnocentrism with regard to fraud with public health initiatives dealing with the allegedly "great unwashed."

The BBBs used different tactics in dealing with, say, misleading advertising. If the identified business was well established, the BBB would start with discreet moral suasion. If such persuasion failed, the BBB resorted to public disclosure and, in cases of willful refusal to mend his or her way, filing legal actions with state or federal authorities. Only a small proportion of accused businesses ended up in court. Although the BBBs had some well-publicized successes getting favorable state or federal legislation enacted or gaining convictions of con artists, they admitted that their efforts were, at best, unable to stymie more than a small proportion of fraudulent activities. Legislation simply forced, albeit at perhaps greater inconvenience and greater costs, fraudsters to resort to new tactics. But the BBBs, too, just as any crusade, had to find new bogeymen to keep its momentum; fortunately for the BBBs, the infinite ingenuity of fraudsters created new topics (Balleisen 2009, 137, 149, 152–157).[8]

During the 1920s, prosperity created new waves of potential "suckers." Many Americans purchased Liberty Bonds during World War I, so they had gotten their financial feet wet. Whether purchasing new electrical appliances or investing in financial securities, however, many Americans were swimming in unfamiliar financial waters. That these neophytes made errors of judgment seemed inevitable; there was a learning-by-doing process involved. New investors may have read of big-time investors accumulating fabulous wealth by "making a killing" on the market. Securities advisors may have faced new investors' unrealistic expectations, and cautious, conservative advisors may have been swamped by more aggressive and perhaps less-scrupulous peers. In retrospect, the idea of placing money with door-to-door securities salesmen seems risible, but some twenty-first-century investors, with the benefit of historical lessons, fell for swindles, too. As Balleisen put it, "These commercial neophytes struggled to navigate the information asymmetries of a complex modern economy, and they often chased after fantasies of easy riches without even the most cursory of investigations." Chinese consumers are currently learning similar lessons (Balleisen 2009, 124; Stevenson 2018, B1 and B2).

An observer might grant grudging respect, without condoning, to the fraudulent securities operators. To evade federal statutes and also to promote sales, such nefarious operators created their own "independent financial newsletters and dailies" that purported to be neutral but "puffed" securities in which the publishers had an interest. The promoters, in a precursor of tele-marketing, internet pornographic sites, and other marketing efforts in our times, shared or, more likely, sold address or phone lists of gullible customers. Reputable securities vendors—and there were undoubtedly some of these around during the 1920s; they just failed to attract the publicity that their less-scrupulous peers did—fought these thieves. These reputable dealers were concerned about individual investors, but they also resented the siphoning of investment funds by the fraudsters. Thoughtful, forward-thinking business executives, too, worried about an erosion in both actions and perceptions of young Americans with regard to business behavior (Balleisen 2009, 119–120).

Advertising

As the American economy evolved into a national marketplace, large firms began using national advertising to sell their output. Cheaper paper and printing techniques, aided by railroads to distribute and telegraphs to collect information, contributed to the diffusion of advertising. Advertising was becoming more sophisticated and advanced from merely brokering advertising space in newspapers and periodicals to actually writing copy and creating advertising campaigns. Advertising professionals began to curb out-and-out lying and focused on creating and maintaining credibility among publishers and consumers.

Early twentieth-century legislators were not particularly interested in advertising, aside from "unfair" competitors using misleading advertising to get more of their share of an industry's business. If the Federal Trade Commission had been charged with addressing "petty squabbles and dishonesties," then it would have paid more attention to advertising. Most legislators and business participants probably viewed puffery and moderate exaggeration as inherent in advertising (Tedlow 1981, 40–45).

The federal efforts to stymie fraudsters using advertising proved frustrating. Senator Francis Newlands (D-NV) astutely recognized the fiendish imagination of such operators: "it would be folly for us to attempt by a definition of each practice to cover the field, because we have the testimony of experts in business that unfair competition is so multiform that if we condemn 20 practices that exist today, 20 more will be invented tomorrow." Another Senator quipped, "Unfair competition, like fraud, is a creature of protean shapes. It assumes one attitude today and another tomorrow. As with fraud, so it will be with unfair competition. In fraud there is a constant race between the rogue and the chancellor. In unfair competition there is going to be a constant race between the corporation and the Commission, and of course, opinions will have to be ground out accordingly." Legislators and witnesses testifying before Congressional committees agreed that false advertising contributed to unfair competition. Unscrupulous vendors used dubious advertisements to steal sales from reputable vendors; denigrate rival products; and sometimes to steal trademarks of honest vendors (U.S. Congress 1914, 51:11188–11189, 11,598; Tedlow 1981, 40, 47).

An example of alleged unfair advertising revolved around department stores. Department stores sometimes claimed that they could charge lower prices than smaller competitors because they bought in bulk; large stores proclaimed such in their advertisements. Some critics of department stores claimed that the stores did not actually buy the goods more cheaply from wholesalers or producers but that such low-priced items were loss leaders intended to lure customers into the store. Other witnesses dismissed such arguments by pointing out that consumers gained from the low price, regardless of whether the department store saved by buying in bulk or simply priced below its cost. These witnesses suggested that the Federal Trade Commission should not deny customers a chance to pay bargain prices, even in the face of untruthful advertising.

In 1931, the Raladam case threatened to undermine what progress had been made in fighting misleading and fraudulent advertising. Edward Hayes had owned Raladam since the turn of the century. His "Man Medicine" promised to make "'Old Men' boys again." As with many fraudsters, Hayes figured that the conned buyers would be so embarrassed that they would not report the fraud. Although Hayes was astute in his understanding of the male psyche, he ran afoul of the United State Post Office, whose officials took a dim view of using the mails to perpetrate a fraud. Exit "Man Medicine." Enter "Marmola." Hayes was a persistent fraudster. Marmola contained thyroid extract and a changing concoction of ingredients that "depend[ed] on what was available cheaply at any given time." Hayes billed Marmola as a weight-reducing pill and claimed its thyroid extract would help combat the thyroid problems that supposedly caused obesity. He marketed his pills to wholesale and retail druggists and shipped by express, thereby avoiding the postal service. Federal authorities deemed Marmola to be potentially dangerous and wanted Hayes to include a statement stating the dangers involved. Hayes won a court decision. He found physicians willing to testify to Marmola's efficacy. The court, however, based its decision upon its interpretation of the Federal Trade Commission's charge: "no matter what the public interest, the Commission was bound by the language of the statute to act only when competition was adversely affected by unfair practices. 'This cannot exist unless there is competition, and there cannot be competition unless there is something to compete with.' The FTC failed to make this showing. From now on, the court seemed to be saying the Commission would have to hold in check its tendency toward becoming a consumer-protection agency and keep in mind that it was conceived in an anti-trust context." The Supreme Court affirmed the circuit court's decision, stating, "The paramount aim of the act is the protection of the public from the evils likely to result from the destruction of competition or the restriction of it in a substantial degree .... Unfair trade methods are not per se unfair methods of *competition* (Tedlow 1981, 47–50)."[9]

The role of the wholesale and retail druggists should give pause. Presumably these "experts" should have been a frontline defense against fraudulent medicines such as Marmola. Of course, if the pills were popular, a wholesaler or a retailer might hesitate to refuse to sell such an item.

What products could be advertised ethically? Patent medicines certainly raised controversy. More recently, tobacco companies have been chased of off American television screens and radio broadcasts. Such government intervention was associated with an uptick in tobacco companies' profits, possibly because the companies' advertising had become a Prisoners' Dilemma situation: Each firm had an incentive to advertise and hope to increase market share, but all firms doing so may have left market shares unchanged. Unless the combined advertising increased the aggregate quantity consumed, the companies may have been collectively worse off by incurring the expense of advertising on television and radio while not greatly altering market shares. The government's prohibition, therefore, may have been a boon (Mitchell and Mulherin 1988, 855–856; Warner 1979, 439–441).

Cigarette manufacturers, however, remained free to advertise on billboards and in magazines. During the early 1990s, R.J. Reynolds introduced "Uptown" menthol cigarettes. The new product was aimed at African-Americans, which was not a novelty in itself. Naturally such targeting raised hackles. The American Cancer Society wrung their hands and said that the advertising exploited blacks, particularly those living in disadvantaged urban areas. An advertising director for *Essence* magazine admitted the company was ambivalent about accepting advertising dollars for "Uptown." One marketing professor remarked, "The irony is that if R.J. Reynolds made shoes or shirts and specifically marketed to blacks, they would probably be regarded as progressive and socially positive (Ramirez 1990, D1)." Underlying the critics' laments was a thinly veiled condescension toward blacks that, in essence, they were particularly susceptible to being duped by a tobacco company. Naturally, few, if any, people explicitly raised or investigated such a possibility.

Executives Begin Using Public Relations Campaigns

Businesspeople's favorable public relations may have attained an apogee in Great Britain during the nineteenth century. The British public recognized the nation's dominance in world trade; the people enjoyed higher standards of living than almost anywhere else. A belief gained currency that British entrepreneurs and industrialists needed only a clear playing field, and they would prevail; Americans, too, began to embrace such beliefs.

During the early 1900s, business leaders began to understand the ill effects of poor public relations. John D. Rockefeller's Standard Oil had long been in the cross-hairs of crusaders and muckrakers. The company's penchant for secrecy and stealth redounded again it, when the Supreme Court ordered a breaking up of the company. Norman Gras coined the phrase, "The public be pleased (but fooled)," to describe the situation; he did not mean that the business leaders purposefully misled the public. Such firms as U.S. Steel, under Judge Elbert Gary, started disclosing financial information, which was disseminated in such a way to preclude insiders' advantage in possessing information. But the company was careful in what it divulged (Gras 1945, 111–112, 120). Gary's actions may have been designed for public consumption, but he succeeded in preventing the Supreme Court from forcing U.S. Steel to break up.

Gras attributed J.P. Morgan's predilection for secrecy as incurring public suspicion; the desire for secrecy arose from the delicate, confidential nature of banking. Regardless of whether such secrecy was prudent and honorable, the public seemed to interpret the secrecy as "grasping at power which only a government should exercise. Accordingly, it was easy for the Democratic Party to make the firm a political football."

Gras expressed many interesting opinions regarding business ethics. He observed that the "relatively low ethical standards of American business men through the generations" haunted business men of the mid-twentieth century. He advocated the need for the public to understand what successful, honest businesspeople did for society and that business was not inherently predatory. He advised businesses to be more, to use a twenty-first-century buzzword, "transparent." He saw little reason for businesses to maintain so much secrecy. One of his more provocative observations was larger companies tended to be more ethical, because the executives feared to act unfairly or to countenance their subordinates to act unethically and risk public censure. After noting that "many" owners of small businesses were honest, he remarked, "the highest degree of cheating and misrepresentation is probably found in their midst." He concluded, "business is becoming ethically sounder as well as technically more efficient as it grows in size." How one could test his hypotheses is an interesting question.

Firms initiated public relations campaigns. John Wanamaker, the Philadelphia retailer, pioneered institutional advertising. Firms began publishing favorable information about themselves or getting newspapers and magazines to run laudatory stories. Rather than have company founders issue positive (self-serving) information regarding the firm, Gras stated that lawyers were usually involved, because their expertise enabled them to advise companies on remaining just within the letter of the law and also to disarming attacks from legislators and the public (Gras 1945, 121–126, 141). Pioneering publicist Ivy L. Lee published a "declaration of principles" for the new business publicity and information practitioners. Corporations hired newspaper men to act as "apologists." Opponents of such manufactured "news" called such writing "whitewashing" and that the practitioners were "space grabbers." *Printers' Ink and Editor & Publisher* bemoaned the blurring of legitimate news and ersatz news, to little avail (Bernays 1971, 300–301).

The early days of advertising professionals featured plenty of flamboyant characters. George Washington Hill sought an advertising campaign to catapult his Lucky Strikes to the top of the cigarette market. Modern-day readers may marvel at the idea of opera stars endorsing Lucky Strikes cigarettes as "kind to your throat." Hill wanted to get women to smoke Lucky Strikes, but he was stymied by the fact that the green cigarette pack repelled women, because the color "clashed with their costumes." Edward Bernays, then a young advertising executive, advised changing the dominant color of women's fashions to green. Hill demanded to know what such a campaign would cost, and Bernays made a wild guess of $25,000. Hill immediately ordered, "Spend it."

In his reminiscences, Bernays claimed that his firm was "able to pursue socially laudable goals and aid our business clients simultaneously. We helped to kill the communal drinking cup when we were retained by the Dixie cup makers. This ushered in the era of paper cups and improved health conditions." Bernays described how newspapers and publicity people held a reciprocal relationship: editors would write recurring "puffs" in return for free passes on railroads or, in the case of professional team sports, passes to ballgames. Owners of professional sports teams often hosted lavish buffets for reporters after games. Some people in the newspaper industry urged editors and reporters to stop engaging in such dubious activities (Bernays 1971, 300, 304–305, 311). In terms of public relations, Gras identified industries such as the department stores, corner stores, auto makers, and producers of art goods and cosmetics generally with having the best public relations, while the stock speculation, investment banking, coal, railroad, public utilities, liquor, petroleum, steel, and textiles industries had the worst public relations. Perceived and actual monopoly power generally invited criticism, as monopolies were not always known for good service. Part of the poor public relations characterizing some industries emanated from sore losers—the smaller owners, who lost in the economic struggle—who groused about dominant firms. Other factors tending to diminish a firm's or industry's standing with the public included those who fought labor unions or paid low wages. Industries that provided services without charge or acceding to customer complaints earned good public relations. Then again, people had frequent interactions with their local department stores. Department store owners, with their credo, "The customer is always right!," naturally fared well. Industries providing commodities that "people are eager for or identify with themselves" often had favorable public relations, as satisfied customers boasted about where they purchased the desirable items.

By 1945, small business owners ranked second in public favor, with only war veterans faring better. Gras noted the irony of petty capitalists having more esteem than the investment bankers: "The bankers had some good policies but could command few votes; the petty capitalists have few good policies but muster the votes." He highlighted a conundrum facing business owners and managers: they could cater to public opinion and face adverse effects upon profits or ignore public opinion, gain unfavorable publicity, and protect profits (at least in the short run). After all, businesspeople presumably knew their business better than the public, and "the business executive may be far-sighted and the public near-sighted." He bemoaned a false dichotomy used by Franklin Roosevelt, who suggested there was a choice between human and property rights, with the public unthinkingly agitating for the former. Gras disputed the dichotomy, "in truth, there are no rights except human rights." He used a Venn diagram showing property rights as a subset of human rights (Gras 1945, 140, 142, 145).

Early Twentieth-Century Buccaneers

There remained a sufficient number of unethical business operators to keep news reporters busy and the public piqued. The City of Chicago was a colorful and sometimes toxic brew of corruption, innovation, and vision. Charles Yerkes monopolized the traction system, and Samuel Insull dominated the electrical system. They were, however, vastly different operators. Yerkes enriched himself at the expense of his consumers. Insull was once Thomas Edison's secretary; he quickly realized that the unique aspects of the electrical power industry meant that some sort of government regulation was inevitable and quite likely desirable.

Yerkes was blatantly contemptuous of customers, voters, and probably the city politicians he allegedly bribed. Insull accepted that he had to work with the politicians. Rather than bribe them, he insulated his utility from the deleterious effects of the political system. He made sure that his utility was efficient and innovative; in addition, he bought out other lighting companies and obtained the exclusive right to use some key equipment. By doing so, no potential entrant could build a modern central station without his approval. He was able to offer electrical services at cheaper (and falling) rates than any potential rivals, although his ability to deny potential entrants the key technologies ensured his monopoly power (McDonald 1958, 244–245). Yerkes was opportunistic. He once declared, "The secret of success in my business, is to buy old junk, fix it up a little, and unload it upon other fellows." Early in his career, Yerkes had overleveraged his holdings and faced ruin. The Chicago Fire of 1871 caused the Philadelphia city officials to demand immediate settlement of his debts; Yerkes refused to repay the debts and was convicted of embezzlement and served seven months (roughly one-third of his sentence) in jail. The interesting aspect was that Yerkes' peers believed that he had been convicted on a technicality and agreed to continue doing business with him. The City Council even canceled his debt, giving rise to Yerkes' somewhat disingenuous claim, "I don't owe a dollar in Philadelphia."

Yerkes moved on to Chicago and gained control of Chicago's streetcar lines. He did, in fact, modernize the system, going from horse-drawn to cable cars to electric-powered railcars. He controlled 48 separate lines and built the famed "Loop" around the downtown area south of the Chicago River. What the good citizens of Chicago did not understand was Yerkes' financial machinations. A contemporary labeled Yerkes, "a buccaneer from a Pennsylvania penitentiary," but just how penitent Yerkes was after his time in jail was an open question. Yerkes' financial tactics were "to borrow money, obtain leases, offer dividend guarantees, juggle accounts, create subsidiary corporations, and then issue watered securities. His bookkeeping methods and business tactics were so complicated that a clear account of how he captured control of Chicago's street railways can scarcely be made (Roberts 1961, 344, 346, 348)."

Although Yerkes could manipulate finances almost magically, his other strength was getting municipal grants of monopoly rights. He was astute in knowing how to bribe members of the City Council; presumably the City Council members were not aggrieved at being bribed, as they received race horses, homes, and money in the bank (Peterson 1952, 69; Roberts 1961, 351; *Chicago Tribune* 1895b, 2, c, 6, d, 1, e, 1, 8, 1896b, 1, c, 1, 4).

Yerkes was not too interested in the day-to-day running of his railroads. His street railway cars were dilapidated and filthy. He ran open cars during the winter and closed cars during the summer in the days before air conditioning. His stockholders suggested that the crowded, inadequate cars be improved, but Yerkes responded contemptuously, "It is the people who hang to the straps who pay you your big dividends (Chicago *Tribune* 1895a, 6, 1896a, 1, 4, 1899b, 6, c, 1; Roberts 1961, 352)." More than William Vanderbilt, whose "the public be damned" was quoted out of context, Yerkes could have adopted the quote as his motto. Yerkes cared little about public safety or the safety of his riders. When his cars hit pedestrians, the unfortunate injured were sent to railway offices, "where they were refused medical aid until they had signed liability waivers (Roberts 1961, 352; *Engineering News* 1898, 246)."

Chicago notables discovered that Yerkes was not a man to be trusted. Marshall Field and other wealthy Chicagoans invested in the Chicago North Shore Railway Company, hoping to connect with Yerkes' North Chicago Street Railway. Just as they were completing their line, Yerkes refused to let the lines connect until the North Shore Railway gave him half of an increased stock issue. What was surprising was the willingness of some of Chicago's wealthy to trust Yerkes as late as 1896.

Yerkes wanted a 50-year franchise extension for his railroad monopoly. He displayed an amazing gall by saying the state of Illinois should intervene, because he could not get "honest treatment from the mercenary and corrupt City Council of Chicago." The Illinois Senate approved the bill giving Yerkes what he wanted; in the aftermath, Chicago reformers proclaimed that Yerkes had bought the Senators and House members at the tune of $500,000 (Roberts 1961, 352, 355–357; Chicago *Tribune* 1897a, 1–2, b, 1–2).

Chicago's Mayor Carter Harrison and the reformers were skilled in the rough-and-tumble world of Chicago politics. They put the squeeze upon aldermen whose power rested on saloons, gambling establishments, and houses of prostitution, threatening to disrupt those business unless they agreed to oppose the Allen bill and Yerkes. Somehow the reformers stymied Yerkes. One need shed no tears for Yerkes, as he sold his holdings to two of his friends for $10,000,000. These friends, who were either remarkably naïve or wildly optimistic, soon complained that Yerkes sold them watered stock. Yerkes immigrated to London and built that city's Underground, amid much corruption (Roberts 1961, 367, 371; Chicago *Tribune* 1898, 2, 1899a, 5, d, 8).

Samuel Insull benefited from Yerkes' ham-fisted attempt to get a 100-year franchise for his transportation company. One Democratic Party faction pushed through a 50-year franchise for a potential lighting company, Commonwealth Electric Company. When the politicians discovered there was no way their nascent company could co-exist with Insull's Chicago Edison Company, they sold the franchise to Insull for $50,000. Insull was astute enough to forestall any political interference or raiding by periodically cutting his rates, which he was able to do by increasing his utility's efficiency. Only once did the city legislators mandate a rate cut, which the current mayor vetoed. Insull made the cut anyway.

Chicago, of course, was and remains notorious for political corruption. Insull refused to bribe any politician, believing it to be impractical. His belief was if he bribed one, he would end up having to bribe all. Unlike his contemporary, Yerkes, Insull understood that as politicians needed to earn a living (presumably beyond their pay as city alder-people), it was better to "win the respect and the friendship of politicians." He made regular campaign contributions to all candidates and did small favors, such as offering real (not "ghost") jobs for politicians to distribute. He also accepted the reality that political friends sometime had to make public denunciations out of political expediency.[10]

Insull opted to curry favorable publicity. His rate cuts made him popular in Chicago, and he earned a reputation as "a man who was able to remain honest and yet play the political game with the most able professionals." He encouraged private citizens to buy stocks in his utility companies, making them "public utilities." The goal was to forestall further public regulation or ownership of the utility companies (McDonald 1958, 245–247; see also Insull 1924, 328–329; McConnell [1930] 1973, 127).[11]

Alleged Stock Market Manipulations

A Congregationalist Reverend C.H. (Charles Hunter) Hamlin made a distinction between speculation and gambling: "The risks inseparable from real work, from moving the crops and the manufacture of raw material, are right, but a risk which is all risk and no work is gambling …. Necessary hazard is as right as needless hazard is wicked." Another commentator waxed nostalgic for the 1890s gambler, who was "content to bet on things out of sight merely for the joy of gambling." On the other hand, he asserted, "ninety per cent of market trading was gambling; options and futures trading was pure gambling. The sportsman-editor could see no skill in the market or the lotteries that were sweeping the nation." The commentator probably conjured the 90 percent figure from his imagination; he was more accurate with regard to the lack of skill needed to play the lottery. The futures market, however, more likely entailed skill (or inside knowledge) (Hamlin 1895, 413; Curtis 1891, 281–292; Cowing 1957, 404–405).

The gambling simile was not too inapt, though, as fraudulent "bucket shops" fleeced naïve investors, who were, more or less, true gamblers. The "bucket shop" had elements of modern-day mutual funds, in the sense that they enabled small investors to trade in fractional lots and more easily diversify their portfolios. Unlike legitimate mutual funds, the bucket shops piggy-backed upon stock quotations and never purchased any shares. The "business plan" of a bucket shop relied upon a constant stream of dupes, or the truth of an axiom: "the public is always wrong." In a way, these bucket shops were precursors of today's popular "fantasy sports leagues," whereby participants construct rosters of players and vicariously live through their chosen players' productivity (or lack thereof). In any event, the bucket shop operators were nimble of feet and glib of tongue, so they were able to string along the unwary. If there was a protracted bull market, many investors gave money to the bucket shop operators, but sometimes the operators would be over-extended by the run-up in stock prices, so their nimbleness of feet proved handy. Disappointed investors might find themselves standing in front of a locked office door with scant hope of retrieving their money.

The established New York Stock Exchange and Chicago Board of Trade disliked the bucket shops' competition, both because the bucket shops siphoned off money that might have been invested in the Exchange or the

Board of Trade and because the bucket shops gave investing a bad reputation. The established exchanges made an agreement with Western Union to monitor their stock quotation services, so as to squeeze out the bucket shops (analogous to a sports fantasy league being denied access to the daily box scores). The bucket shops cried foul and insisted that they were offering a valuable service, which, perhaps, some were. Some of the bucket shop operators' claims were odd: customers "could limit [their] losses better, do business with much less money, and be charged smaller commissions." The bucket shop operators' better argument, from a public relations perspective, was to bleat that they were victims of monopolists, and many Americans lent a sympathetic ear to such claims.

William Givens warned novices about the dangers of sending their money to Wall Street. His 1905 article, "Does Wall Street Pay?" listed amateur speculators' self-defeating tactics: "buying high and panicky, taking small profits and big losses." He claimed that 80 percent of the market investors lost. Certainly some of his charges have some element of truth even today, as investors storm into markets that have been bullish for a period of time. His conclusion, "Wall Street is a paying proposition only for the broker and the 'insider,' not for the average customer," may have been overwrought, even for 1905. A broker detailed his experiences and mentioned that many brokers did not give advice, since "relations were more amicable if the client could not blame the broker for his losses." He condemned his own industry by reporting that "Brokers … were not scrupulous enough in encouraging business, and financial writers were often well rewarded for the seemingly disinterested market advice they offered the public. Tips were calculated to mis-lead, and half a dozen giants really controlled the stock market (Givens quoted in Cowing 1957, 405–410; *The Independent* 1907, 669–672)."[12]

Stock market speculators and the investment industry encouraged small investors to jump into the market. The public seemed mesmerized by the flamboyant actions of Will Durant, Jesse Livermore, and Michael Meehan, among others. Earl Sparling wrote a popular book, *Mystery Men of Wall Street*, in 1930. After the stock market crash of 1929, weaknesses in the market became apparent. But before the crash, many industrial leaders urged novices to invest in the market. The New York *World* quoted John J. Raskob, a General Motors executive: "We help our laboring men to save and to invest in General Motors and we have no labor troubles (McConnell [1930] 1973, 129)."

In the aftermath of the stock market collapse of 1929 and ensuing Great Depression, America searched for scapegoats. Some financiers' malfeasance was exaggerated by unscrupulous politicians. Arthur Taylor examined the collapse of the Insull empire in 1932. He noted that the financial framework "was always suspected of containing a good deal of 'water.' This means that there existed the suspicion that a number of Insull companies were worth far less than the securities which the companies had issued. If the suspicion is well founded, book value might have represented the claim of a stockholder to a portion of assets so overvalued by the accountants that their value bore no relationship to reality."[13] The public investors discovered when the Insull Utility Investments Company went into bankruptcy in 1932 and was reorganized in 1937, "less than $5,000,000 had been paid out on an investment of $185,000,000." Insull's operating electric and gas companies, however, incurred losses that were minimal, "less than one tenth of one per cent of the publicly owned securities of Insull companies." Many of the other operating companies fared the depression without reorganization or loss. Taylor concluded that "The significance of [his] study, rather, lies in the fact that the 24.1 per cent loss to the public investors in the Insull securities is far less than a partially informed public opinion believes it to be. The percentage of loss, furthermore, is lower than that sustained by investors in some other significant areas of the economy." He concluded that the opprobrium attached to Insull might someday be revised more favorably (Taylor 1962, 192–200).

Charles Edwin Mitchell proved another useful scapegoat. Mitchell was born in a middle-class family, although he had the opportunity to graduate from Amherst College. He started an investment banking house in 1911 and then joined National City Bank, as well as City Bank Farmers' Trust Company. President Franklin Roosevelt insisted on Mitchell's forced resignation in disgrace in February 1933. The government then indicted Mitchell for income tax evasion. Mitchell defeated the trumped-up income tax charges and by 1935 became chairman of another investment house. Once again, the government prosecuted him during an antitrust case against seventeen investment banking houses; Judge Harold Medina dismissed the case in May 1953, while chastising the government for bringing the case.

National City Bank took advantage of the Federal Reserve Act of 1913's provision that banks could now operate branches abroad to expand their operations to 14 countries. The bank also looked to expand their customer base to individual investors. Mitchell was in charge of creating a nationwide retail distribution system and succeeded within a few years. Economic historians Thomas Huertas and Joan Silverman explained that "The new distribution channels these provided added to the National City Company's ability to place securities, enhancing its role as a leading underwriter."

Mitchell, similar to many of the big retailers, succeeded in providing new services to the average American. National City and other large banks had catered primarily to wealthy customers and large corporations. Presumably bankers had to overcome public suspicion of them. National City Bank and other banks began offering banking services that people in the twenty-first century take for granted: passbook savings accounts and unsecured personal loans. National City Bank thrived and had hundreds of thousands of individual accounts. The bank followed a conservative policy of maintaining a high degree of liquidity and little leverage; these conservative policies enabled the bank to survive the early years of the Great Depression. "To Mitchell himself the bank's financial strength was his 'deepest source of pride (Huertas and Silverman 1986, 82–86).'"

Mitchell ran afoul of an unscrupulous federal official, Ferdinand Pecora, chief counsel of the Senate Banking Committee. Pecora and others adhered to the now-discredited belief that the banks and bankers had been responsible for the economic disaster through their underwriting and distribution of securities. The banks, therefore, not only engaged in, gasp, speculation but also encouraged others to do so. Mitchell and Silverman excoriated Pecora for his shoddy portrayal of Mitchell that was devoid of facts; Pecora's persecution of Mitchell rested upon political calculation. "Pecora felt it necessary only to show that leading bankers had fostered speculation and had personally engaged in it." Mitchell was an obvious target for political reasons. The Roosevelt administration did not want to charge A.P. Giannini, head of Transamerica Corporation, because he was a Democrat. Pecora stated that he chose Mitchell because Mitchell's National City was a huge bank with a solid reputation with scrupulous management. If Pecora could destroy Mitchell, then he could tar all banks with complicity for the economic woes.

Pecora leveled three charges at Mitchell: Mitchell was personally corrupt; National City and he peddled 'unsound' securities; and he promoted speculation by others. These charges incited public outrage, which probably wasn't difficult in the early 1930s and led to the Glass-Steagall Banking Act of 1933. Pecora thought he had a smoking gun in the fact that Mitchell made over $1 million in 1929 but had not paid any income tax (due to a capital loss in the sale of National City stock to his wife). Naturally posturing politicians—are there any other kind—got involved. Senator Burton K. Wheeler (D-MT) gave a sensational quote to reporters: "The best way to restore confidence is to take these crooked presidents out of banks and treat them the same way they treated Al Capone when Capone avoided payment of his tax." The Roosevelt administration was only too glad to add to the lynch-mob attitude by indicting Mitchell and forcing him to resign. Roosevelt was rooting for Pecora and the courts to convict Mitchell.

The tax angle was a stroke of genius. Few Americans could have then (and now) understood the details of the financial deals, but they could (mis)understand tax evasion. The press quickly turned on Mitchell, calling him a variety of unsavory adjectives. One commentator said, "The only difference between a bank burglar and a bank president is that one works at night (Huertas and Silverman 1986, 88–92)." All this outrage and condemnation was misdirected, and a jury acquitted him. The tax deductions were legal. Attorney General Homer Cummings was peeved and declared, probably through clenched teeth, "nevertheless I still believe in the jury system (*Literary Digest* 1933, 6)."

During the trial, Mitchell's testimony indicated that he bought some shares on October 29, 1929; he did so to rectify "imprudent" purchases made by subordinates without his knowledge. Mitchell pledged his own fortune in doing so. "It was testimony to his belief that the U.S. system of corporate organization concentrated responsibility 'in the hands of one accountable individual.'" Huertas and Silverman added that selling stock to his wife, although legal, proved suspicious in the eyes of the public; Mitchell did this, of course, without foreknowledge of the looming economic catastrophe, but the authors reflected, "What might have been prudent tax planning in 1929 was perceived by 1933 as callous greed (Huertas and Silverman 1986, 93, 95–96; see also *Time*, November 18, 1929, 45)."

The charges that National City Company and other investment bankers peddled worthless foreign securities have taken hold among historians. Another charge was that National City Company and Mitchell underwrote unsound securities, but Huertas and Silverman demonstrated that the vast majority of the bond issues underwritten by the company were "rated as investment grade securities (Baa or better) when they were offered to investors." Under the Glass-Steagall Act, such quality bonds were approved.

National City Company's advertising was culpable in the sense that it portrayed the company not as sellers of securities but as financial advisers to prospective, often novice, investors. It purported to educate first-time investors and encouraged the investor to query National City Company representatives regarding investment decisions, as an investor would "in discussing legal problems with his lawyers or his health with a doctor." Such a message was ill-advised, as the financial representative might not be as interested in the well-being of the client as an attorney or physician would be. The underwriting process itself sent a "seal of approval" to investors, as the company assured buyers that the bonds were "priced fairly" and reflected the current risk; of course, current risk was no sure indicator of future risk. Mitchell and the company "warned investors that bonds carried risk and that every added measure of security in a bond 'has its own special price tag attached (Huertas and Silverman 1986, 96–98).'"

Even when Mitchell tried to do the right thing, such as offering to lend up to $25 million to shore up the call loan market during a panicky day in March 1929, people later accused him of sustaining the boom and exacerbating the stock market crash. The National Portrait Gallery perpetuated this idea during a 1980 exhibit: "Having thus demonstrated the ineffectiveness of the traditional instruments of financial control, the head of the nation's largest commercial bank made it perfectly clear that speculators would not be shaken from their stock market fantasy by anything unless than major disaster." Part of the controversy emanated from the Federal Reserve Board's simultaneous attempts to reduce speculative loans, and Senator Carter Glass (D-VA) accused Mitchell of "slapping the Federal Reserve Board squarely in the face … [treating its policies] with contempt and contumely." But another contemporary believed that Mitchell's actions were those of a "courageous man" who recognized the dangers of "shutting off of new money" to sustain investors. Huertas and Silverman disputed Senator Glass' accusation, observing that Mitchell had received approval from the Federal Reserve Bank of New York's governor, as well as the Federal Reserve Bank's support of the discount rate. "Even the Federal Reserve Board agreed that Mitchell had done the right thing (Huertas and Silverman 1986, 99–100; *New York Times*, March 29, 1929a, 1, *New York Times*, March 29, b, 2, *New York Times*, March 30, c, 1)."[14]

Mitchell and the central bankers thought the economy was self-correcting, so they thought that raising interest rates was the correct policy; as Milton Friedman and Anna Schwartz pointed out, such a policy was probably the reverse of what should have been done (Huertas and Silverman 1986, 100–101). In that sense, Mitchell bore some responsibility for the debacle, although his mistakes were not made from corrupt motives. Mitchell's tale was a cautionary one. Public hysteria whipped up by unscrupulous politicians or government officials is difficult to defuse.

Conclusion

By the 1920s, some noted business leaders waxed complacent. Judge Elbert Gary improved some aspects of corporate behavior. He instigated publicly available quarterly financial reports. These reports reduced the opportunity for company officials and board members to use insider information for profits. He also allowed stockholders to speak at stockholder meetings, and he even suggested that the general public's interests be considered when making company policy. He claimed that "Sunday school principles" might be appropriate for a large corporation. All of these suggestions, he admitted, could improve U.S. Steel's reputation in the eyes of the public (Green 2010, 113).

Judge Gary wrote in 1922 that business executives previously believed that "if their conduct was within the strict and technical rules of law it was immune from public or private attack .... By such as these moral principles were ignored." He asserted that in the first decades of the twentieth century, leading business executives "have voluntarily devoted more and more time and energy in a conscientious desire to conduct their business in accordance with the rules of propriety and honesty (*Nation's Business* 1922, 53)."

Gary's "Sunday school principles" did not extend to letting his workers attend Sunday services, as he wanted his workers to work on Sundays. He refused to accede to his workers and the public's clamor for a day of rest on Sundays. He apparently misled the public by claiming that U.S. Steel had ended the 12-hour workday. On the other hand, the company avoided industrial strife by a variety of unsavory means. Workers had to sign "yellow-dog contracts," whereby they promised not to join a union. Suspect union participants quickly found themselves without a job at U.S. Steel or any rival firm in the industry. Somehow the company got its workers to accept such draconian working conditions (Green 2010, 113, 126).

The Great Depression exposed limitations to self-regulation and also eroded consumers' and investors' trust in big business, especially banks. In the future, however, Americans would return to the buy now, pay later approach with enthusiasm. By the 1950s, big business was back in good graces with the American people.

Notes

1. For a revisionist view of the Teapot Dome scandal, see (Libecap 1984, 381–382, 383–390; Stratton 1957, 387–393; *Newsweek*, December 11, 1944, 38, 40; *New York Times*, April 22, 1928, 1, 21; Waller 1962, 343, 351–352).
2. Conwell is almost too delicious a pun to pass up in a book on business ethics, but there is no evidence that he was insincere.
3. One wonders how palatable such observations were to early twentieth-century business executives; it seems doubtful that many twenty-first-century businesspeople would entertain such a rigorous precept.
4. The idea that ethics instructors are not necessarily arbiters of right and wrong is useful.
5. For a more recent opinion, see Kleiner (2014, no page numbers).
6. Although the technology changes, almost a century later, many of the same practices still persist.
7. American law enforcement struggled to track serial killers until the 1980s, so the ineffective tracking of fraudsters is not a surprise.
8. These publicized efforts and recurrent stoking of fears were tactics used again and again by do-gooders, such as the Public Broadcasting Stations. Pledge drives rely upon touted successes, *Downton Abbey*, for instance, and fears of no more *Downton Abbey*'s, if viewers failed to send in enough money.
9. For the futility of some regulatory acts, see Tedlow (1981, 53–54); Handler (1939, 91, 97).
10. Illinois probably leads the nation in the number of its ex-governors serving time in prison, four of the last seven.
11. Had the muckrakers been around in 1928, they might have characterized Insull's efforts as "Robber baron with a smile."
12. Presumably small investors would have faced a learning curve. Today's small investor, having access to mutual funds and index funds, might fare better.
13. This resembles the Enron collapse 80 years later.
14. Supreme Court Justice Louis Brandeis was among those bemoaning an alleged bank trust (centered in New York). After much political posturing and a lengthy court case led by Roosevelt lackey Arsene Pujo, Presiding Judge Harold Medina dismissed the case with prejudice and scolded the

government attorneys. Historian Vincent Carosso detailed the ill-founded allegations, politically motivated of course (Carosso 1973, 431–432, but also 423–437; *U.S. v. Henry S. Morgan*, et al., Corrected Opinion of Harold R. Medina, 3:63; Hofstadter 1965, 215; U.S. Congress 1912, L:4931). It is probably redundant to mention that 2016 Presidential candidate Bernard Sanders voiced concerns about Wall Street bankers' undue influence; again, such concerns are easy to understand and may be true this time around. Espouse a conspiracy theory enough times and one time it will stick.

Bibliography

Abend, Gabriel. *The Moral Background: An Inquiry into the History of Business Ethics* (Princeton, NJ: Princeton University Press, 2014).

Balleisen, Edward. "Private Cops on the Fraud Beat: The Limits of American Business Self-Regulation, 1895–1932." *Business History Review* 83(1), Spring 2009, 113–160.

Barton, Bruce. *The Man Nobody Knows: A Discovery of the Real Jesus* (Cutchogue, NY: Buccaneer Books, [1924] 1992).

Berle, Adolf. *Power without Property: A New Development in American Political Economy* (New York, NY: Harcourt, Brace, 1959).

Bernays, Edward. "Emergence of the Public Relations Counsel: Principles and Recollections." *Business History Review* XLV(3), Autumn 1971, 296–316.

Carosso, Vincent. "The Wall Street Money Trust from Pujo through Medina." *Business History Review* XLVII(4), Winter 1973, 421–437.

Chicago Tribune. "More Street Car Accommodations Needed." January 15, 1895a, 6.

Chicago Tribune. "Kind to Mr. Yerkes." January 29, 1895b, 2.

Chicago Tribune. "The Latest Street Railway Ordinance." January 29, 1895c, 6.

Chicago Tribune. "Fraud in the Loop." September 3, 1895d, 1.

Chicago *Tribune*. "Grabs All in Sight." December 10, 1895e, 1 and 8.

Chicago *Tribune*. "Seats or No Fares." February 21, 1896a, 1 and 4.

Chicago Tribune. "Gives Mr. Yerkes a New Franchise." April 29, 1896b, 1.

Chicago *Tribune*. "Yerkes' Exodus Is Near." December 27, 1896c, 1 and 4.

Chicago *Tribune*. "Yerkes as a Target." March 11, 1897a, 1 and 4.

Chicago *Tribune*. "New Bill Worse Yet." March 12, 1897b, 1 and 2.

Chicago Tribune. "Board Opposes the Franchise." December 8, 1898, 2.

Chicago Tribune. "Traction Men to Meet." May 7, 1899a, 5.

Chicago Tribune. "Overhead Trolley Not the Issue." May 11, 1899b, 6.

Chicago Tribune. "Nine Hurt in Trolley Crash." July 2, 1899c, 1.

Chicago Tribune. "First and Last Days of State Street Cable Line." July 2, 1899d, 8.

Conwell, Russell. "Acres of Diamonds." AmericanRhetoric.com. 2010.

Cowing, Cedric. "Market Speculation in the Muckraker Era: The Popular Reaction." *Business History Review* XXXI(4), Winter 1957, 403–413.
Curtis, William. "The Increase of Gambling and Its Forms." Forum XII(2), October 1891, 281–292.
DuBrul, Ernest. "Business Ethics and Balance Sheets." *Nation's Business* 14(2), February 1926, 76.
Engineering News and American Railway Journal. "Council Report on the Street Railways of Chicago." Vol. XL, No. 16, October 20, 1898, 246–247.
Filene, Edward. *Morals in Business* (Berkeley, CA: University of California, 1935).
Fisher, Burton and Stephen Withey. *Big Business as the People See It* (Ann Arbor, MI: Survey Research Center Institute for Social Research, University of Michigan, 1951).
Flynn, John. "Dishonest Business." *Forum* 82(6), December 1929, 351–355.
Frey, Donald. *America's Economic Moralists: A History of Rival Ethics and Economics* (Albany, NY: State University of New York Press, 2009).
Friedman, Milton and Rose Friedman. *Capitalism and Freedom* (Chicago, IL: University of Chicago Press, 1962).
Galbraith, John. *American Capitalism: The Concept of Countervailing Power* (Boston, MA: Houghton Mifflin, 1956).
Gras, Norman. "Shifts in Public Relations." *Bulletin of the Business Historical Society* 19(4), October 1945, 97–148.
Green, Hardy. *The Company Town: The Industrial Edens and Satanic Mills That Shaped the American Economy* (New York, NY: Basic Books, 2010).
Hamlin, Rev. Charles Hunter. "Gambling and Speculation: A Symposium." *Arena* XI(2), February 1895, 413–416.
Handler, Milton. "The Control of False Advertising under the Wheeler-Lea Act." *Law and Contemporary Problems* 6(1), Winter 1939. 91–110.
Hofstadter, Richard. "The Paranoid Style in American Politics." *The Paranoid Style in American Politics and Other Essays* (New York, NY: Alfred A. Knopf, 1965), 3–40.
Hoover, Herbert. "If Business Doesn't, Government Will." *Nation's Business* 12(7), June 5, 1924, 7–9.
Huertas, Thomas and Joan Silverman. "Charles E. Mitchell: Scapegoat of the Crash?" *Business History Review* 60 (Spring 1986), 81–103.
Independent. "Confessions of a Stock Speculator." Vol. 52, March 21, 1907, 669–672.
Insull, Samuel. *Public Utilities in Modern Life: Selected Speeches, 1914–1923*, edited by William Keily (Chicago, IL: Privately Printed, 1924).
Jackson, Ira and Jane Nelson. *Profits with Principles: Seven Strategies for Delivering Value with Values* (New York, NY: Currency Doubleday, 2004).

Kant, Immanuel. *Groundwork of the Metaphysics of Morals*, edited by Mary Gregor and Jens Timmermann (Cambridge, UK: Cambridge University Press, [1998] 2016). Revised edition.

Klein, Julius. "The Dividends of Honesty in Business." *Forum* 83(3), March 1930, 129–133.

Kleiner, Morris. "Why License a Florist?" *New York Times*, May 28, 2014, no pages. https://www.nytimes.com/2014/05/29/opinion/why-license-a-florist.html. Viewed March 4, 2018, 3:05pm.

Law, Marc and Sukkoo Kim. "Specialization and Regulation: The Rise of Professionals and the Emergence of Occupational Licensing Regulation." *Journal of Economic History* 65(3), September 2005, 723–756.

Libecap, Gary. "The Political Allocation of Mineral Rights: A Re-Evaluation of Teapot Dome." *Journal of Economic History* 44(2), June 1984, 381–391.

Literary Digest. "Mitchell's Acquittal and the Banking Administration." July 1, 1933, 6.

McConnell, Donald. *Economic Virtues in the United States: A History and an Interpretation* (New York, NY: Arno Press, [1930] 1973).

McDonald, Forrest. "Samuel Insull and the Movement for State Utility Regulatory Commissions." *Business History Review* XXXXI(3), Autumn 1958, 241–254.

Mitchell, Mark and J. Harold Mulherin. "Finessing the Political System: The Cigarette Advertising Ban." *Southern Economic Journal* 54(4), April 1988, 855–862.

Nation's Business. "Judge Gary Believes That Our Business Ethics Are Improving." August 1922, 52–54.

New York Times. "Sinclair Acquitted of Oil Lease Fraud; Jury Out 2 Hours." April 22, 1928, 1 and 21.

New York Times. "Glass Assails Mitchell for Bank's Aid to Market; Stocks Up in Buying Rush." March 29, 1929a, 1.

New York Times. "Money Crisis Past, Mitchell Asserts." March 29, 1929b, 2.

New York Times. "Congress Inquiry Likely into Stock Speculation; Mitchell Explains Stand." March 30, 1929c, 1.

Newsweek. "The Record Stands." December 11, 1944, 38 and 40.

Peabody, Francis. *The Christian Life in the Modern World* (New York, NY: Macmillan, 1916).

Peterson, Virgil. *Barbarians in Our Midst: A History of Chicago Crime and Politics* (Boston, MA: Little, Brown, 1952).

Ramirez, Anthony. "A Cigarette Campaign under Fire," *New York Times*, January 12, 1990, D1.

Riesman, David. "The Found Generation." *Abundance for What?: And Other Essays* (Garden City, NY: Doubleday, 1964), 309–323..

Roberts, Sidney. "Portrait of a Robber Baron: Charles T. Yerkes." *Business History Review* XXXV(3), Autumn 1961, 344–371.

Roper, Elmo. "The Public Looks at Business," *Harvard Business Review*, XXVII, March 1949, 165–74.
Stanley, Thomas and William Danko. *The Millionaire Next Door: The Surprising Secrets of America's Wealthy* (Atlanta, GA: Longstreet Press, 1996).
Stevenson, Alexandra. "Online Investors In China Lose Billions." *New York Times*, January 29, 2018, B1 and B2.
Stratton, David. "Behind Teapot Dome: Some Personal Insights." *Business History Review* XXXI(4), Winter 1957, 385–402.
Taylor, Arthur. "Losses to the Public in the Insull Collapse, 1932–1946." *Business History Review* XXXVI(2), Summer 1962, 188–204.
Tedlow, Richard. "From Competitor to Consumer: The Changing Focus of Federal Regulation of Advertising, 1914–1938." *Business History Review* 55(1), Spring 1981. 35–58.
Time. "Business and Finance: Troubles of Mitchell." November 18, 1929, 45.
United States of America, plaintiff, against Henry S. Morgan, Harold Stanley, et al., doing business as Morgan Stanley & Co., et al., defendants (New York, NY: Record Press, 1950–1954), 3 vols.
U.S. v. Henry S. Morgan, et al., "Corrected Opinion of Harold R. Medina." (New York, NY: 1954?).
U.S. Congress. *Congressional Record: Containing the Proceedings and Debates of the Sixty-Third Congress, First Session*. Vol. L (Washington, D.C.: GPO, 1912).
U.S. Congress. *Congressional Record: Containing the Proceedings and Debates of the Sixty-Third Congress, Second Session*. 63rd Cong., 2nd Sess. Vol. LI (Washington, D.C.: GPO, 1914).
Wall Street Journal. "Schools of Business and Journalism." October 10, 1903, 1.
Waller, Robert. "Business and the Initiation of the Teapot Dome Investigation." *Business History Review* XXXVI(3), Autumn 1962, 334–353.
Warner, Kenneth. "Clearing the Airwaves: The Cigarette Ad Ban Revisited." *Policy Analysis* 5(4), Fall 1979, 435–450.
Ways, Max. "Postwar Advance of the Five Hundred Million." *Fortune*, LXX(2), August 1964, 104–109 and 212–214.
Whyte, William. *The Organization Man* (New York, NY: Simon and Schuster, 1956).

CHAPTER 9

Anxiety Over Product Safety

Although many people think that businesses compete primarily on the basis of price, the evidence suggests that producers compete upon many facets: price, quality, safety, convenience, location, reputation, among other facets, what economist Sherwin Rosen denoted as *hedonic pricing* (Rosen 1974, 34–55).

Product safety provides a clash between deontological and teleological approaches to business ethics. Does a producer have an ethical duty to produce the highest-quality product possible? Should a producer cut back on quality in some instances? What responsibilities do producers have for warning consumers regarding potential defects in their products?

The Ford Pinto was a prominent example of alleged violations of ethical behavior. The case has become a staple for discussion in business ethics classes. Unlike the public's perception, the Ford Pinto case revealed some ambiguities regarding the ethical aspects.

Consumer Activism

The consumer movement was regaining momentum in the 1960s, as it had during the early 1900s. Ralph Nader was one of the most publicized crusaders. George Stigler was skeptical of Nader and his ilk; after documenting industry abuses, Nader called for better regulations and better regulators. Stigler believed that such posturing was likely to have minimal effect. He pointed out that Nader and other prominent consumer

D. G. Surdam, *Business Ethics from the 19th Century to Today*,
https://doi.org/10.1007/978-3-030-37169-2_9

advocates seeking publicity sought new situations from which to stoke the fires of consumer outrage. Even if the consumer advocates got new legislation passed, they usually didn't have the time or the inclination to sit through the interminable hearings on appropriations, the selection of new regulatory appointees, and to write the minutiae of the law. The industry, of course, had an incentive to mold any legislation in ways that either minimized harm to its interests or maximized benefits. Stigler believed that consumers were better off using the traditional defenses available to them, including eternal vigilance and competition in the marketplace, as "Each of the traditional defenses is available to individuals and small groups—changes in policy and adaptation to new circumstances do not require new changes in the ponderous, expensive, insensitive machinery of a great state. It is of regulation that the consumer must beware (Stigler 1975, 188)."

We could revise our basic question to: What protections does industry have against unscrupulous or inept reporters? The media seized upon a rather flimsy charge against Motorola and its cellular phone. The evidence against Motorola was largely circumstantial, yet the media went into a frenzy. Motorola was forced to settle with the plaintiff, simply to stanch the negative publicity. Negative publicity, even if false, was damaging to a company. The *Economist* reported that Motorola stock fell by 15.4 percent. The evidence suggested that overhead power cables were riskier than cellular phones (*Economist*, February 6, 1993, 88–89). National Broadcasting Company's (NBC's) disreputable reporting tactics regarding the General Motors (GM) gas tanks were scandalous. The exploding gas tank on GM's pickup was reminiscent of Ford's Pinto in the 1970s.

Consumers, too, have responsibilities. Should the producer be forced to "dumb down" her products, to foresee every foolish use a consumer might put a product to? Should the legal responsibility of the producer be simply to produce a product that the ordinary prudent reasonable American could use with safety?

Value of Life

How much is a human life worth? Many of you may be discomfited by that question. After all, isn't a human life priceless? Doesn't a human life have infinite value? Have the economists gone too far by setting a price on life itself? The question is germane with respect to product safety.

People implicitly placed less than an infinite value upon their lives. If the goal was to maximize one's life expectancy, a person would be wise not to use the stairs, cross busy streets, go canoeing, or work in a coal mine.[1]

Well, economists are not the only group willing to affix a monetary value upon human life. Lawyers have also done so. The courts have accepted that a monetary value may be placed upon a human life in a wrongful death suit. Factors that affect the value of a person's life include their age, occupation and (actual and potential) earnings, marital and family statuses, lifestyle (risk-taking versus cautious), state of health, subjective personal factors (pleasant versus unpleasant personality or appearance), and sometimes a horror factor (dying in bed versus dying in some horrendous manner).

Previous attempts to assess damages of bodily injury or death date to the Jewish *Mishna*, which contains a considerable amount of debate on redressing reparations for injuries. The discussion resembles modern-day human capital analysis, including estimating the value of an injured slave. The Jewish community preferred to rely more upon reparations than the Old Testament eye-for-an-eye justice. In considering the reparations, jurists considered injury items consisting of damage, pain, healing, inactivity, and indignity to the injured party.

The social status of the injured party mattered when calculating a value upon indignity or insult. In Talmudic society, though, status was not simply a function of wealth but also a matter of learning and perhaps ancestry. Social scientist Ephraim Kleiman explained, "Compensations based on status cannot, therefore, be regarded as being systematically associated with income."

The *Mishna*'s approach to estimating compensation for pain was similar to modern-day "willingness-to-pay" approaches. The question, "How to estimate pain where there was also damage?…Estimate how much a man would demand to have his arm cut off," raised scorn among some rabbis: "To have his arm cut off? This is not [a case of] pain only; all five [injury] items are there! Moreover, are we dealing here with idiots!" Kleiman observed that "people generally don't go about, offering their arms for amputation in exchange for pecuniary compensation." The rabbis struck upon a clever comparison. Suppose a man was due to be punished by the state; his punishment is to have his arm cut off either by a theoretical potion (which acts painlessly) or by a sword. The man was going to lose his arm regardless of his choice, so the difference was between a painful and painless way. This proved an astute way to think about the "willingness-to-pay" approach. Kleiman observed that there is "no market for pain creation, [but] there may exist a market for pain avoidance (Kleiman 1987, 266–273, 279–282)."

There are two basic approaches in estimating the value of life. A common method is the human capital approach that equates the value of a life to the market value of the output produced by an individual during his or her expected lifetime.[2] One of the drawbacks of the human capital approach is that if there is gender or racial discrimination in earnings, the approach attaches an artificially low value on the lives of women and some ethnic or racial groups. Another drawback is that this approach essentially places a "$0" value on nonmarket activities. It does not consider the pleasure of life itself. A chronically unemployed worker (or a retired person) has almost a "zero" value of life.

The willingness-to-pay approach avoids the problems associated with the human capital approach. Economists and lawyers apply the willingness-to-pay approach to product safety. A person's decisions with respect to how much money the person is willing to pay for small reductions in the probability of dying provides an estimate of the value the person places on his or her life. By viewing a person's choices, a statistician can deduce the value the person places on *their* life. This presupposes, however, that people can find information pertaining to the probabilities and severity of the risks involved and that they are able to *understand such information* (which, apparently, they are not apt at doing).

Suppose an airbag costs $600 and reduces the probability of a person dying by 1 in 10,000. We could then deduce that the person places a value of at least: (Cost/Reduced Probability of dying) = ($600/0.0001) = $6,000,000 = (Value).[3]

This approach has a big advantage in that it implicitly incorporates the total value of life, not just the job-market value. Thus, our calculation includes the value of foregone earnings plus the nonmarket value received from good health. This accounts for the generally higher value of life estimates generated by the willingness-to-pay approach than obtained with the human capital approach. Unfortunately, this approach has some indeterminacy. The implied value of human life varies considerably for even a particular individual. Given that people may not know how much a device will affect their probability of dying, one should not be surprised by the variance.

It is important also that a person *voluntarily* accepted a risk. Forcing you onto a rocket ship with a one-way ticket while handing you $3,850,000 (the average value of life estimated some years ago) would not be adequate compensation. People who accept a particular risk may be the most competent to accept the risk (perhaps they view the probability of death as being lower for themselves than for the average person). Some people may gain some satisfaction from accepting a risk. Daredevil Evel Knieval certainly comes to mind (Viscusi 1978, 359–386; Phelps 1997, 537–538).

There is another facet to the public's unwillingness to place an explicit value on a human life. One author shows that the public is more willing to accept such analysis when applied to a large, anonymous group, such as five owners of Pintos will die over the next year without an altered gas tank (that could cost $15,000,000 collectively). However, when the victim is no longer anonymous, the public exhibits less willingness to apply the analysis. One commentator refers to this as the trapped miner syndrome: The public is willing to expend vast sums to rescue a solitary (identifiable) trapped miner, whereas the public may be hesitant to invest vast sums for general mining safety improvements. Even if an accident is a freak occurrence, the mere presence of a badly injured, perhaps crippled and disfigured, victim can easily sway a jury (Schelling 1984, 113–119).

Finally, the public appears particularly unwilling to allow a business to cut its costs in order to improve profits. Thus, if Ford chose to save $100,000,000 and not install a safer gas tank, the public is outraged. However, if the public knows that Ford's Pintos are less safe, then the public would *bid down* the price of the Pinto, and much of the savings would accrue to the public. If car producers compete solely on the basis of cost, then any "cutting corners" will essentially go to the consumers in the long run. Of course, producers compete on the basis of quality and safety, too, so it is not clear that cutting costs is the sole consideration.[4]

Auto Safety

Auto safety presented an excellent example of ethical considerations with regard to product safety. Automobile death rates since World War II have generally fallen. The death rate per 100 million miles driven plummeted in the United States, from 11.22 deaths per 100 million miles in 1945 to 5.2 in 1961; the rate fell below 2.0 by the early 1990s and hovered around 1.1 during the past decade. The largest decrease in the per 100 million miles driven rate, moreover, occurred *prior to* the 1960s burst of automobile safety legislation. Essentially, Ralph Nader and his ilk got the Congress to pass the legislation that merely codified an accomplished fact: Driving was becoming safer even in the absence of legislation. Nader's crusade coincided with a temporary surge in the death rate during the mid-1960s. Much of the surge, however, was likely due to a demographic shift: the entrance of Baby-Boom drivers. The rate continued its long-term decline after the mid-1960s, although a minor increase occurred in the late 1970s, before drifting to the 2.73 range by 1983 (U.S. Department of Commerce 1975, II:719–720; U.S. Department of Commerce 2011, Table 1, 103).

What reduced the death rate per 100 million miles? Were the automobiles outrageously unsafe before 1946? Indeed, if consumers knew that automobiles were dangerous, were they not assuming the risk?

Consumers clearly do not place an infinite value upon their lives when they purchase a car, as they trade off safety for other attributes (sportiness, price, fuel efficiency, ease of handling). How consumers view different bundles can be deduced by their decisions on which bundle of attributes they buy. Buyers' voluntary choices reveal their objective and subjective valuations of the different bundles. Forcing them away from their voluntary choice creates a large presumption that their perceived well-being or satisfaction is reduced because of the coerced transaction.

The airbag, for instance, took years to be embraced by most consumers; in fact, the government had to make it mandatory. Initially offered as an extra, Detroit had difficulty in persuading the majority of consumers to purchase airbags. Were people cheap? Stupid? Daredevils? Or did people simply think the airbags were not a cost-effective way to improve safety? At several hundred dollars a pop (pardon the pun), the airbags were an expensive extra. The passive restraints (lap and shoulder belts) were a fraction of the cost of airbags and only marginally less effective (Levitt and Dubner 2009, 149–150).[5] Could it be that people were voting with their pocketbooks? For the hundreds of dollars of cost, some people did not think the incremental improvement in safety worthwhile.

The government can provide information by conducting and publicizing tests. A private company such as *Consumer Report* might be feasible, but often information, once produced, is easily disseminated; the producer has difficulty capturing the full benefits from producing the information. Is there, moreover, an incentive for the government to produce good information, or is competition the best way to ensure quality information?

Do crusaders disseminate accurate information about the safety of various automobiles? Sometimes the safety zealots make assessing safety attributes of various models of cars more difficult. The media concentrates on certain unsafe aspects of an individual model of car. Unfortunately, the fixation on exploding gas tanks or a propensity to rollover can convince people to avoid buying vehicles that have solid *overall* safety records. Ralph Nader's crucifixion of the Chevrolet Corvair was misplaced. In 1972, the National Highway Traffic Safety Administration reported that the Corvair had no "abnormal potential for loss of control or rollover." Reporters damned Ford for the placement and design of its gas tank in the Pinto. Also, *60 Minutes* bashed the Audi 500 as being prone to suddenly accelerating out of control. Government safety experts discovered that the Audi "would indeed accelerate suddenly—whenever the driver made the mistake of stomping on the gas pedal instead of the brake." Overall, the Audi had one of the lowest fatality records. The brouhaha about the General Motors (GM) full-size pickup with its exploding side gas tanks again showed the journalistic myopia. Besides NBC's journalistic ethical lapse (by rigging an igniting device that was detonated just prior to impact), the trucks had a lower rate of fatal side crashes than Ford pickups (Chapman 1993, 4:3).

General Motors executives reacted stupidly and unethically to Nader's crusade. They hired detectives to find incriminating evidence against him, but these investigations failed to find anything and the spying boomeranged against GM. When the public discovered GM executives' unethical conduct, the company was forced to issue a public apology to Nader and settled a lawsuit with him for $425,000 in 1970 (worth about $2.5 million in 2016 dollars) (Cullen et al. 1994, 265; *Wall Street Journal*, August 14, 1970, 4).[6] The ensuing publicity and Senate hearings resulted in regulations.

Nader, of course, railed against business leaders' fixation on profits at the expense of consumer safety: "under existing business values potential safety advances are subordinated to other investments, priorities, preferences, and theme designed to maximize profit." Three business ethicists asserted that "Nader was not so naïve or dogmatic as to accuse executives of consciously setting out to make dangerous vehicles. Rather, he was asserting that the blind pursuit of profits creates conditions within corporations that are conducive to the production of defective cars. Specifically, he understood that companies place a high priority on two factors that they see as essential to high sales and profit: style and cost (Nader 1965, 236; Cullen et al. 1994, 264–265)."

Safety Sells?

From the auto producer's viewpoint, enhanced safety features can be a marketing coup. Auto advertisements on television today often stress safety features (as well as durability, handling, sportiness, practicality, price). Consumers vote with their dollars (the Edsel being a car equivalent of George McGovern or Barry Goldwater). If consumers vote for safety features (such as air bags), auto makers will respond.

Automobile manufacturers of the past were loath to highlight safety aspects of their vehicles. During the 1930s, much of the call for auto safety concentrated on driver error. A *Reader's Digest* article bemoaned the carnage on the nation's roadways (30,000 per year, based on a much smaller population and much less driving) (Furnas 1935, 21–26). The manufacturers found it easier to blame driver error, and certainly such an explanation seemed plausible.

Paul Kearney's 1957 article in *Harper's Magazine* presented an interesting precursor of the automobile safety debate. Kearney remarked caustically, "Having long ago classified the consumer as a moron, the manufacturers are certain that if anybody breathes the forbidden word ['accident'] the prospect will dash across the street and buy another make of car, one which doesn't have accidents (Kearney 1957, 41)."[7]

About the same time Kearney was writing his article, a Ford executive, Charles Sorenson, asked, "What are the prospects today for a light, cheap car, one in the tradition-shattering role of the Model T?" He noted that such a car was possible under 1956 technology, but he saw little demand for such: "Today's cars are more wasteful of power and fuel than any that have gone before (Sorensen 1956, 110)." The Ford Pinto would answer Sorensen's question.

Some 13 or so years before Lee Iacocca, president of Ford Motor Company, launched the idea of the Ford Pinto, Kearney was lauding Ford as *the leader* in automobile safety. He described Ford's "revolutionary disregard of the trade taboo [against mentioning safety]." Ford pioneered crash research in 1951, even working with safety experts from universities and other research organizations. Kearney attended an automobile show in New York in December 1956. Some of the manufacturers were touting some safety devices, but these features were overshadowed by Detroit's obsession with power. Kearney noted that one manufacturer was offering optional seat belts, but who "proceeded to *unsell* me on the safety device;" in fact, he wrote, "the safety theme got pretty short shrift." The prevailing theme was, instead, "if you have sufficient power you can get away from where the accident happens before it happens. Such, in a nutshell, seems to be Detroit's alibi for its frantic horsepower race." Kearney admitted the performance features were "splendid things," but he pointed out the absurdity of the exaggerated emphasis on performance: "they are essentially what the race driver wants at speeds far beyond our street and highway limits." He cited studies showing that the vast majority of accidents occurred at relatively low speeds. He also advised that automobile manufacturers should imitate the aircraft industry, whose experts discovered that many deaths and injuries resulted from pilots striking some projection within the cockpit (Kearney 1957, 38–41).

Ford temporarily basked in the warmth of public applause for their emphasis on safety. Major periodicals such as *Time* and *Newsweek* lauded the move, as did safety experts and physicians. General Motors, however, chided Ford for emphasizing safety. GM allegedly made "snide insinuations about safety" and promoted anti-seat belt (mis)information. GM executives also exerted pressure on Ford executives to "lay off" safety. GM may have read the public's attitudes more accurately, however, as its Chevrolet Division blew past Ford by "emphasizing styling and performance based on a new V-8 engine." Ford reacted by retrenching their safety advertising and imitating GM by highlighting styling and horsepower. Ford sales dropped off, and its executives concluded that "safety doesn't sell (Fielder 1994, 289; see also Eastman 1984, 231)."[8]

Kearney addressed the salient question: "Do customers want this protection?" According to a contemporary survey conducted by the *New York Times*, "safety equipment was the first consideration of 60 per cent of the buyers, especially of women." Of course, survey instruments are notoriously unreliable. Better evidence was the success of Ford's padded dash, an optional feature; Ford also sold enough seat belts "to protect 350,000 riders." About a third of the people who preferred Ford vehicles listed safety as one of their reasons for their preference. Kearney extolled the safety features of Ford's new vehicle; these included impact-resisting door-latches that kept passengers from being hurled out of vehicles, plastic dash pad, seat belts attached to the car frame not the floor plate or the seats, deep-dish steering wheels, and locking seat tracks. Other manufacturers were just beginning to offer similar features. On the other hand, manufacturers were removing center-posts that protected occupants during vehicle roll-overs.[9]

Kearney urged the industry to create an impartial testing laboratory, similar to the Underwriters' Laboratories or Consumer Reports to test their products. He wondered why the insurance companies did not get involved; the insurance and auto industries certainly had the resources to launch such a project (Kearney 1957, 42–43).

Ford Pinto Case

The Ford Pinto case is a staple for business ethics courses. The facts are pretty straightforward, although the analysis and the conclusions often leave much to be desired. The vehicle's infamy rests, to a large degree, upon journalist Mark Dowie's scathing expose in *Mother Jones*. Business ethics textbooks frequently take Ford executives to task for proceeding with the vehicle, even though the placement of the fuel tank was a known design flaw. The flaw could have been remedied by installing a plastic bladder that cost $11. The authors of these textbooks frequently disagreed with Ford's main defense: a detailed cost/benefit analysis that concluded the bladder was not cost effective. The $11 bladder, however, appeared to have been one of the more expensive potential solutions to the gas tank problem (Birsch 1994a, 3–14; 1994b, 147–163).

The Ford Pinto case demonstrated the complexity of ethics among different groups: businesspeople, journalists, consumers, and government officials. Journalist Mark Dowie's job was to write an attention-grabbing article.

In the late 1960s, Ford executive Lee Iacocca mandated a small, economical vehicle (under 2000 pounds for under $2000) to contest Volkswagen and the Japanese producers in the market for smaller vehicles. Drivers of small vehicles typically faced greater risks than drivers of larger vehicles, so the Pinto was already likely to earn a mediocre safety record (Cullen et al. 1994, 270).

The key aspect of the Ford Pinto was company's decision to place the fuel tank behind the axle instead astride the axle. A gas tank was an inherently dangerous part of an automobile; few designs had only benefits without accompanying flaws. Ethicist Douglas Birsch observed that placing the tank behind the axle was not unique to the Pinto, as such "was standard for the industry in regular sized cars and was also the standard for the Japanese subcompacts." Ford manufactured the Capri, a vehicle with an over-the-axle tank. This design fared well in crash tests, but the design had some drawbacks, "since it required a circuitous filler pipe, which was more likely to be dislodged in an accident. The tank also was closer to the passenger compartment and therefore might increase the threat of fire to the passengers. In addition, the higher placement of the tank raised the center of gravity of the car and might have adversely affected handling." The behind-the-axle model had some safety benefits, although not with regard to rear-end crashes (Birsch 1994a, 7–9; Strobel 1994, 44–45).

Mother Jones and *60 Minutes* spearheaded the campaign against Ford and the Pinto. Like Nader, the journalists were shocked and outraged at the automobile producers' perceived callous indifference toward increased safety at the ostensibly minor cost of $1 to $11 per car. *Mother Jones* used lurid graphics on its cover to heighten the horror and outrage of it all. Of course, Ford was excoriated for its greedy search for profits. Detroit, in general, was blamed for promoting style over safety.

Dowie and *60 Minutes* made Ford officials' explanation for the placement of the gas tank appear flippant. Asked about the Pinto gas tank, a Ford engineer admitted: "You have no idea how stiff the competition is over trunk space. Do you realize that if we put a Capri-type tank in the Pinto you could only get one set of golf clubs in the trunk (Dowie 1977, 23)?" Dowie and *60 Minutes* apparently considered trunk space to be trivial, even frivolous.

The Pinto became a national joke, even making Johnny Carson's *Tonight* show. The movie comedy *Top Secret* used the Pinto's alleged lethality for a sight gag. However, was Dowie's searing indictment of the Ford Motor Company justified? Was Mike Wallace's outrage that "top management of the Ford Motor Company is going to sit there and say, 'Oh, we'll buy 2000 deaths, 10,000 injuries, because we want to make some money or we want to bring in a cheaper car,'" justified (Schwartz 1991, 1029)?

Journalist Mark Dowie found scandalous Ford's use of cost-benefit analysis that "places a dollar value on human life." Dowie used an internal Ford memo as the "smoking gun" to indict Ford: "Ford's cost-benefit table is buried in a seven-page company memorandum entitled 'Fatalities Associated with Crash-Induced Fuel Leakage and Fires.'" The memo argued that there was no financial benefit in complying with proposed safety standards that would admittedly result in fewer auto fires, fewer burn deaths, and fewer burn injuries (Dowie 1977, 20, 24).[10]

Dowie won a Pulitzer Prize for his indictment of Ford and their flamboyant vehicle in *Mother Jones*. He over-estimated the number of potential fatalities and injuries due to the Pinto's gas tanks' vulnerabilities. Dowie claimed that between 500 and 900 fire-related deaths occurred with Ford Pintos, a claim that was baseless. Birsch related that "Mark Dowie said [in a phone conversation] that he derived his estimate of the fire related deaths from his interpretation of information received from 'The President's Fire Commission.' Based on the greater amount of information available today, he admitted that his number might be high, but insisted that Ford's number was too low. He agreed with our claim that no one will ever know exactly how many people died in Pinto fires caused by low-speed, rear-end collisions." Given that Dowie did not couch his statement with any disclaimers, his journalistic ethics could be questioned; an astute reader could have asked: "Where did he get these numbers?" Birsch examined fatality data from different sources and none of the sources attributed even 100 deaths (over a number of years) to low-speed, rear-end collisions involving Ford Pintos. The National Highway Traffic Safety Administration (NHTSA) released a report in 1994 studying the Ford Pinto and Mercury Bobcat. Between 1975 and 1977, they found 33 "Fatalities in Accidents with Fire" and 41 "Total Number Pinto Occupant, Fatalities in Accidents with Fire." The NHTSA admitted that the accident report coding may have missed some fatalities from fire, if such fatalities occurred after the accident (Dowie 1977, 18; Birsch 1994a, 9–10; National Highway Traffic Safety Administration 1994, 81–87).[11]

Ford officials used dubious figures and assumptions in their cost-benefit analysis (they estimated 11 million Pinto-esque vehicles being sold, but the actual number of Pintos sold ended up at 2 million). The government figure of roughly $200,000 per life included just $10,000 for pain and suffering. Dying or being injured by fire is a particularly unpleasant way to die, so one could hardly justify this as an accurate value of pain and suffering (Dowie 1977, 26–27).[12]

Ford's Culpability

Ford executives knew that the behind-the-axle design was a fire hazard as early as 1970. They also knew that a rubber bladder was effective in reducing the potential hazard. The executives decided to perform a cost-benefit analysis. Two years later, the federal government instituted strict regulations pertaining to vehicles' ability to withstand a 20-mile-per-hour, fixed-barrier crash without gasoline leakage. Apparently, several automakers, not just Ford, feared such requirements, so they lobbied to prevent these regulations. Journalist Lee Strobel denounced Ford for doing so, since the company knew its Capri car could pass such a test; the company, therefore, knew how to build such vehicles. Strobel, though, missed the point from Ford's perspective; true, they knew how to build a vehicle with an astride-the-axle tank, but such a vehicle would forfeit the trunk space feature (as well as other aspects) (Birsch 1994a, 10–11; Strobel 1994, 46–47).[13]

Mark Dowie detailed how the Ford safety experts convinced the federal safety bureaucrats that a cost-benefit analysis was an acceptable approach to creating informed automobile safety regulations. "This cost-benefit analysis argued that Ford should not make an $11-per-car improvement that would prevent 180 fiery deaths a year." On the other hand, Ford was aware of cheaper alternatives to the $11 bladder option, although one of the alternatives involved placing the gas tank atop the rear axle. Years later, Ford designer Harley Copp testified that Ford was aware of a shield costing $2.35 or a redesigned axle for $2.10 per car (Dowie 1977, 25–27; Strobel 1994, 47–48). In other words, Ford may have intentionally or unwittingly over-estimated the cost of resolving the Pinto's design flaw.

The Ford cost-benefit analysis gave the result that the "total cost" was roughly three times the benefits. If such a ratio was computed correctly, even increasing the $200,000 per life saved figure by another $200,000 per life would not have changed the basic conclusion. Then again, as mentioned, Ford may have over-estimated the cost. The 180 lives per year that Ford used may have been too high, as it appears Ford was estimating deaths not only from Pintos but also from all similar cars. Ford defended its figures by saying it used the National Highway's figures, but an agency official repudiated Ford's use, stating that the estimate was not supposed to be used in a cost-benefit analysis similar to what Ford was calculating. The estimate was intended to be used with respect to the *loss to society of lost productivity from a person's death*. Strobel also documented a second Ford report analyzing a trade-off between installing an $8 safety device that would save 370 lives and 370 serious injuries a year; in this case, the analysis showed roughly equal benefits and costs, although the study used twice as many deaths and serious injuries as the more notorious study (Strobel 1994, 51–53).[14] Douglas Birsch recalculated a cost-benefit analysis for the Ford Pinto using more recent information than Mark Dowie and Ford had at the time. His estimation largely confirmed Ford's calculation. He addressed one issue that Dowie neglected: Who got the cost savings? Birsch stated, "Ford could have simply charged the customer an additional $8 for the car and realized an initial net benefit of $1,373,500 by saving the money spent to settle the civil suits." He does acknowledge that, on the margin, some people would be deterred from buying a Pinto due to the $8 increase in price. In reality, Ford would probably have had to share the $8 per car cost (or savings) with customers.

Birsch states the safety issue starkly (and accurately): "Is it wrong for manufacturers to market any product that could be made safer using current technology? An affirmation answer to this question would produce an unreasonable standard. Many products can be made safer than they are, but consumers would not necessarily want them to be safer if the safety improvement forced other desirable qualities to be sacrificed (Birsch 1994b, 150, 158)." Ford executives recognized that potential buyers of Pinto would weigh the trade-off between greater trunk space and the hazards associated with the gas tank's position. Of course, implicit in the previous statement was that consumers knew of and understood the risk of the gas tank's position, which they probably did not. However, consumers could seek out information regarding safety, and there were dependable providers of such information.

What if Ford had presented potential buyers an option to pay "an extra $6.65" to enable the vehicle to withstand a 30 mph rear-end impact instead of a 20 mph impact. The consumer would be told that the odds of being rear-ended at a speed between 20 and 30 mph were 1 in 250,000. "Would we call [the potential buyer] reckless if he or she declined to pay the extra $6.65?" This would be a variation on the Coase Theorem in the sense that we could assign the responsibility for safety to the consumer or to the producer. The drawback would be that people appear inept at processing rare probabilities (witness the millions playing state lotteries with their terrible expected winnings).

In the wake of the negative publicity surrounding the Pinto, sales of the vehicle sank. The State of Oregon sold all of the Pintos in its motor fleet, raising the question: "Was it ethical for the State of Oregon to re-sell cars because of fears of the cars' dangerous aspects?" Of course, lost in the controversy was that consumers may have over-reacted, a point made by Stephen Chapman years later. The irony was that there were plenty of buyers for the used Pintos, perhaps because the prices were suppressed. An ethicist stated, "The conclusion we correctly draw is that there was a market for a car with a dubious safety record even though the price was much lower than for safer cars and lower than Ford's manufacturing price (De George 1994, 183–187; see also Chapman 1993, 4:3)."[15]

All of this is to say that the facts are not always subject to the same interpretation. Columnist Stephen Chapman used government statistics in hammering consumer advocates and their hysteria. Consumer advocates may have believed that the National Safety Council was in the hip-pocket of Detroit, so they might have discounted statistics gathered by alleged capitalist stooges. A person should generally be skeptical about any statistics. However, what is important and what Chapman discussed was that: "Almost any vehicle can be found to be less than optimal in some feature that affects safety: It is impossible for every one of them to be above average in every category. Investigative reporters and plaintiffs' attorneys often pretend that the only thing standing between Americans and safe cars is dastardly auto executives. But if minimizing risk were the universal priority, everyone would drive Volvo 240 station wagons, which have the lowest fatality around." Chapman lamented that "Not all of us do that, but many of us have avoided one model or another because it's been painted as a peril to life and limb. Chances are that anyone who spurned the vehicles mentioned above actually raised his chances of dying on the road. That's a scandal in itself, but don't expect to see it on *Dateline* (Chapman 1993, 4:3)."

The Pinto Goes to Court

Two court cases revealed the complexities surrounding the Pinto. An Indiana case in 1978 involved three females who died while driving a Pinto, when their vehicle was rear-ended. The Indiana prosecutor pressed charges of reckless homicide against Ford based on the fact that the company knew the Pinto was deficient in rear-end crashes. During the trial, Ford lawyers introduced evidence that the driver had just filled the Pinto's gas tank; she realized that she had not replaced the gas tank cap and had turned around. A van *going 50 mph* rear-ended the stationary car. Attorneys for Ford also emphasized the fact that there were no federal safety standards in 1973 (when the car was manufactured). In any event, these attorneys asserted that the Pinto's gas tank was similar to other manufacturers' gas tanks. Then again, Ford was forced to recall its vehicles, and the evidence indicated Ford was aware of the problem for some time prior to the crash. Although the grand jury indicted Ford on charges of reckless homicide, a jury found in favor of Ford. The negative publicity and charges of unethical behavior, though, resulted in Ford ceasing production of the Pinto (De George 1994, 180–183; Gioia 1994, 105).[16]

In another lawsuit, Richard Grimshaw was riding in a Pinto driven by a neighbor; the vehicle stalled on the freeway and was rear-ended by another vehicle, resulting in a ruptured gas tank and fire. Grimshaw was badly burned. The Ford memo was not introduced as evidence of liability in the rear-end crash, but to demonstrate Ford's corporate mentality. The trial judge ruled against admitting the memo. A second facet of the memo was that it was to be submitted to the National Highway Transportation Safety Administration (NHTSA) (a bureau where cost-benefit analysis is commonplace, albeit discreet). Third, the memo pertained not only to Pintos but also to all cars sold by American manufacturers (12.5 million vehicles, 180 deaths). Contrary to Mark Dowie's complaint, even the NHSTA used the $200,000 value of life figure.

Law professor Gary Schwartz also disputes whether the memo itself would have implied liability on Ford's part. Although the public apparently believes that it is wrong for a producer to make decisions that endanger or sacrifice the lives of customers in order to reduce production costs and increase profits, the theory of liability permits such decisions. He points out that in an earlier case, *Barker v. Lull Engineering*, the California Supreme Court clarified standards of liability: "the manufacturer is liable if the safety risks in the product's design exceed all the benefits of that design—benefits that explicitly include the monetary costs of alternative designs…a philosophy which actually *encourages* manufacturers to consider such trade-offs, a philosophy that specifies that the welfare of society is generally enhanced when the manufacturer chooses a design that strikes the right balance between advantages and disadvantages." Schwartz points out that the California decision reflected interpretations made nationwide; negligence law recognizes that producers should balance risks versus the cost of risk reduction, a legal opinion dating back to *United States v. Carroll Towing Company* (Schwartz 1991, 1021, 1037).[17]

Given the public's antipathy to such reasoning, however, many defense lawyers opt to forego explicitly using the cost-benefit analysis as a defense against liability. Part of the public's antipathy, according to Schwartz, is the disagreement with placing a monetary value on human life. Schwartz points out that the public generally implicitly places a value on their lives: if the public genuinely believed that their life was priceless, what accounts for the limited response of auto owners to recalls? Schwartz cites a study where only 53 percent of owners of Pintos that were recalled bothered responding (Schwartz 1991, 1042).[18]

Conclusion

What was the safety record of the Pinto? According to the journalists, hundreds of people had been killed as a result of the Pinto's supposedly defective gas tanks. The *Mother Jones* article cited 500–900 deaths by 1977. Columnist Jack Anderson claimed that thousands of people had been killed or "horribly disfigured." Amazingly, the NHTSA documented only 38 instances in which the rear-end impact and ruptured gas tank occurred in the Pintos. Of course, some of these deaths might have occurred regardless of the gas tank. Other data, however, show that the Pinto's overall safety record was mediocre—not too good and not so bad. Some evidences indicate that the Pinto did have a higher death rate from fire. Gary Schwartz concludes that the Pinto's firetrap reputation was exaggerated or misconceived, and that the fatalities and injuries associated with the fuel tank placement were modest: "[Yet] a limited core of the firetrap myth seems fair enough: the Pinto's record in rear-end fire fatalities was not only much worse than the all-car average but was apparently somewhat worse than the record of most (though not all) of its subcompact competitors (Schwartz 1991, 1029–1030, 1033)."

The Pinto case demonstrates that ascertaining ethical culpability is difficult, given the conflicting self-interests at stake. Would Ford's theoretical duty to rectify design flaws be rescinded, if the costs greatly exceeded the benefits? Perhaps this indeterminacy is what makes the case suitable for discussion among business ethics faculty and students.

Notes

1. In Alfred Hitchcock's movie, *Psycho*, the private detective, Arbogast, actually engaged in a statistically likelier deadly activity: ascending stairs. Deaths on stairs greatly outnumber deaths from a knife-wielding, mother-fixated, homicidal maniac.
2. The human capital approach requires calculating the present value (PV) of a person's lifetime earnings. This has some drawbacks, such as choosing the interest rate to be used for discounting future income? The rate of interest chosen has a large impact on the values calculated. The PV of lifetime earnings usually peaks in the 20s and then falls. By the time people reach 65, the PV (lifetime earnings) is relatively small.
3. If we knew the person's reservation price—the maximum they're willing to pay for the airbag—we could tighten our estimate of the value that the person places on their life.

4. Donald Hay disputed the morality of using cost-benefit analysis (Hay [1989] 2004, 141–142).
5. See Peltzman (1975, 677–726) regarding effects of seat belt usage in the 1960s.
6. Then again, GM was simply mimicking the Kennedy administration's snooping about Martin Luther King's lifestyle.
7. In fairness, Paul Kearney described his experiences researching electrical hazards in the home; magazines that questioned the safety of electrical appliances found themselves threatened with advertising cancellations—an economic form of censorship. Over time, however, these manufacturers began to find that "safety sells (Kearney 1957, 41)."
8. Steven Levitt and Stephen Dubner described Robert McNamara's efforts to get drivers to buy and to use seat belts; they quoted Henry Ford II as whining, "McNamara is selling safety but Chevrolet is selling cars (Levitt and Dubner 2009, 148–149, 158)."
9. Child seats in automobiles? The author suspects that most Baby Boomers can recall bouncing up and down on backseats of family vehicles or in the back of station wagons.
10. The infamous memo showing Ford's cost-benefit calculation actually pertained to the problem of fuel leakage in the case of a vehicle *rollover*, not to rear-end damage (Schwartz 1991, 1020).
11. The Ford estimates may have underestimated the number of deaths, but the available evidence suggests the true fatality count was much closer to Ford's estimate than Dowie's interpretation.
12. Note that the disappointing sales helped suppress the number of rear-end fatalities associated with the Pinto; however, even if the estimated 33 or 41 deaths incurred were multiplied by 5.5 (11 million divided by 2 million), the total would still fall far short of Dowie's estimate.
13. Lee Vinsel's *Moving Violations* (2019, 71–101 deals with crashworthiness but does not discuss the Ford Pinto; 129–148 covers the limitations of regulation) describes federal regulation of the automobile industry.
14. Steven Kelman disputed the cost-benefit approach. He believed the approach is too utilitarian and contains technical flaws. He argued that there was a difference in what people are willing to accept "for *giving up* something to which he has a preexisting right and the price he would pay to *gain* something to which he enjoys no rights." Available evidence suggests that most people would insist on being paid far more to assent to a worsening of their situation than they would be willing to pay to improve their situation. James DeLong rebutted Kelman's arguments (Kelman 1994, 125–131; DeLong 1994, 138–141). This author agrees in the main with DeLong, but DeLong takes a rather snide stance toward Kelman.

15. Was it possible that some buyers were drawn to the allure of driving the "Deadliest Car in America," as characterized in Dowie's article in *Mother Jones* (Dowie 1977, front cover)?
16. The Pinto was a cultural icon in the sense that *Charlie's Angels* drove one; the show debuted in September 1976, months before Dowie's article in *Mother Jones*.
17. Some readers may object to the courts and argue that something legal may not be ethical.
18. Safety analysts now use dollars per life-year saved.

Bibliography

Birsch, Douglas. "Introduction: The Pinto Controversy" in *The Ford Case: A Study in Applied Ethics, Business, and Technology*, edited by Douglas Birsch and John Fielder (Albany, NY: State University of New York Press, 1994a), 3–14.

Birsch, Douglas. "Product Safety, Cost-Benefit Analysis, and the Ford Pinto Case." in *The Ford Pinto Case: A Study in Applied Ethics, Business, and Technology*, edited by Douglas Birsch and John Fielder (Albany, NY: State University of New York, 1994b), 147–163.

Chapman, Stephen. "Avoiding 'Unsafe' Vehicles Can be a Fatal Mistake." Chicago *Tribune*. March 14, 1993, Sec. 4, 3.

Cullen, Francis, William Maakestad, and Gray Cavender. "Profits vs. Safety." in *The Ford Pinto Case: A Study in Applied Ethics, Business, and Technology*, edited by Douglas Birsch and John Fielder (Albany, NY: State University of New York, 1994), 263–272.

De George, Richard. "Ethical Responsibilities of Engineers in large Organizations: The Pinto Case." in *The Ford Pinto Case: A Study in Applied Ethics, Business, and Technology*, edited by Douglas Birsch and John Fielder (Albany, NY: State University of New York, 1994), 179–194.

DeLong, James. "Defending Cost-Benefit Analysis: Replies to Steven Kelman." in *The Ford Case: A Study in Applied Ethics, Business, and Technology*, edited by Douglas Birsch and John Fielder (Albany, NY: State University of New York Press, 1994), 137–143.

Dowie, Mark. "Pinto Madness." *Mother Jones* 2(8). September/October 1977, 18–32.

Eastman, Joel. *Styling vs. Safety: The American Automobile Industry and the Development of Automotive Safety, 1900–1966* (Lanham, MD: University Press of America, 1984).

Economist. "Cellular damage: Mobile telephones and cancer." February 6, 1993, 88–89.

Fielder, John. "The Ethics and Politics of Automobile Regulation." in *The Ford Pinto Case: A Study in Applied Ethics, Business, and Technology*, edited by Douglas Birsch and John Fielder (Albany, NY: State University of New York, 1994), 285–301.

Furnas, Joseph. "—And Sudden Death." *Reader's Digest.* August 1935, 21–26.

Gioia, Dennis. "Pinto Fires and Personal Ethics: A Script Analysis of Missed Opportunities." in *The Ford Case: A Study in Applied Ethics, Business, and Technology*, edited by Douglas Birsch and John Fielder (Albany, NY: State University of New York Press, 1994), 97–116.

Hay, Donald. *Economics Today: A Christian Critique* (Vancouver, BC: Regent College Publishing, [1989] 2004).

Kearney, Paul. "How Safe Are the New Cars?" *Harper's Magazine.*214(1281), February 1957, 38–43.

Kelman, Steven. "Cost-Benefit Analysis: an Ethical Critique." in *The Ford Case: A Study in Applied Ethics, Business, and Technology*, edited by Douglas Birsch and John Fielder (Albany, NY: State University of New York Press, 1994), 123–135.

Kleiman, Ephraim. "Opportunity cost, human capital, and some related economic concepts in Talmudic literature." *History of Political Economy* 19(2), 1987, 261–287.

Levitt, Steven and Stephen Dubner. *Super Freakonomics: Global Cooling, Patriotic Prostitutes, and Why Suicide Bombers Should Buy Life Insurance* (New York, NY: William Morrow, 2009).

Nader, Ralph. *Unsafe at Any Speed: The designed-in dangers of the American automobile* (New York, NY: Grossman Publishers, 1965).

National Highway Traffic Safety Administration. "Investigation Report, Phase I: Alleged Fuel Tank and Filler Neck Damage in Rear-End Collision of Subcompact Passenger Cars—1971–1976 Ford Pinto; 1975–1976 Mercury Bobcat." in *The Ford Case: A Study in Applied Ethics, Business, and Technology*, edited by Douglas Birsch and John Fielder (Albany, NY: State University of New York Press, 1994), 77–95.

Peltzman, Sam. "The Effects of Automobile Safety Regulation." *Journal of Political Economy* 83(4), August 1975, 677–726.

Phelps, Charles. *Health Economics* (Reading, MA: Addison-Wesley, 1997). 2nd edition.

Rosen, Sherwin. "Hedonic Prices and Implicit Markets: Product Differentiation in Pure Competition." *Journal of Political Economy* 82(1), January–February 1974, 34–55.

Schelling, Thomas. "The Life You Save May Be Your Own." *Choice and Consequence: Perspectives of an Errant Economist* (Cambridge, MA: Harvard University Press, 1984), 113–146.

Schwartz, Gary. "The Myth of the Ford Pinto." *Rutgers Law Review* 43(4), 1991, 1013–1068.

Sorensen, Charles. *My Forty Years with Ford* (New York, NY: Norton, 1956).

Stigler, George. "Can Regulatory Agencies Protect the Consumer?" *The Citizen and the State: Essays on Regulation* (Chicago, IL: University of Chicago Press, 1975). 178–188.

Strobel, Lee. "The Pinto Documents" in *The Ford Case: A Study in Applied Ethics, Business, and Technology*, edited by Douglas Birsch and John Fielder. (Albany, NY: State University of New York Press, 1994), 41–60.

U.S. Department of Commerce. Bureau of the Census. *Historical Statistics of the United States: Colonial Times to* 1970 (Washington, DC: Government Printing Office, 1975). 2 vols.

U.S. Department of Commerce. Census Bureau. *Statistical Abstract of the United States: 2012* (Washington, DC, 2011).

Vinsel, Lee. *Moving Violations: Automobiles, Experts, and Regulations in the United States* (Baltimore, MD: Johns Hopkins University Press Books, 2019).

Viscusi, W. Kip. Labor Market Valuations of Life and Limb: Empirical Evidence and Policy Implications." *Public Policy* 26(3), Summer 1978, 359–386.

Wall Street Journal. "GM and Nader Settle His Suit Over Snooping." August 14, 1970, 4.

CHAPTER 10

Get-Rich-Quick and Ponzi Schemes

People are mesmerized by the prospect of skipping the drudgery and toil of working for decades and carefully living within their means in order to accumulate wealth. Recurring "gold rushes" provide ample demonstration of the get-rich-quick dream. The chimera of instant, toil-free wealth beckons. Private individuals and governments exploit this desire by various unethical means.

Charles Ponzi, Bernard Madoff, and Franklin Roosevelt engaged in establishing schemes requiring later participants to subsidize earlier participants. State governments have tried to raise tax revenue by appealing to residents' get-rich-quick mentality. Although some of these endeavors could be run in an ethical fashion (ignoring the initial appeal to the get-rich mentality), in many cases, these were not.

The U.S. federal government currently runs a legal form of a Ponzi scheme with its Social Security program. What are the differences between a government-run and a privately operated Ponzi scheme, and do they matter from an ethical perspective?

History of Scammers

Catholic and Protestant thinkers grappled with gambling. Protestants had once thought that "God determines randomized outcomes." The corollary of such a belief was that gambling was blasphemous, since it "undermined the 'singular and extraordinary providence of God which controls

D. G. Surdam, *Business Ethics from the 19th Century to Today*,
https://doi.org/10.1007/978-3-030-37169-2_10

a purely contingent event (Bellhouse 1988, 68, 71).'" How to reconcile God's pervasiveness with a chance event (which presumably underlay gambling) was a difficult problem. Thomas Aquinas suggested that "the ultimate reason why some things happen contingently is not because their proximate causes are contingent, but because God has willed them to happen contingently, and therefore has prepared contingent causes from them." Aquinas said little more regarding gambling aside from forbidding winning from minors or people who were out of their minds (who had no ability to alienate their property), out of greed, or by cheating (Poitras 2000, 93–94).[1]

Many Americans sought quick wealth through the stock market. Wall Street financiers and stock manipulators have deservedly and sometimes undeservedly earned opprobrium for their antics. Politicians and the public issue recurrent calls for stricter regulations, with the Dodd-Frank regulations passed in the wake of the 2007–2008 banking meltdown being the latest. A *New York Times* reporter reflected that "the idea that regulators or auditors can protect us from our own excesses is absurd." A historian commented after the Enron debacle, "I can't think of a previous boom period…where it hasn't ended up a bloody mess, with declining asset values and cases of fraud." Another historian stated, "once there are pressures put on profits [due to a boom], the obvious incentive for management to maintain their lifestyle or their stock prices is to fiddle with the books (Akst July 7, 2002, 3:4; Eichenwald December 16, 2002, C3)."

Business executives and promoters were stingy, when it came to doling out financial information. In addition, accounting practices during the nineteenth century were still evolving to meet the new realities. Promoters allegedly manipulated their stock, often supporting its price subsequent to the initial offering. If they had not done so, potential investors would have suspected chicanery. Even current stockholders found it difficult to get information regarding their company's performance. Attorney James B. Dill helped write New Jersey's favorable corporation laws that attracted many corporations. He believed that stockholders might be permitted to have access to the firm's general records but he feared bogus investors who purchased a few shares only to get a peek at the books. Whether such financial spies were prevalent remained unanswered (Sears 1956, 415–418; U.S. Industrial Commission 1900a, I:243; 1900b, I:136).

Similar to drivers who ignored "Bridge Out Ahead" signs, investors became enthralled by the lure of high promised rates of return. The genius of Bernard Madoff was that he promised a relatively modest rate of return (low double-digit annual returns), albeit with implausible consistency. A journalist recalled Anthony "Tino" DeAngelis, the "great salad oil swindler." DeAngelis presided over the Allied Crude Vegetable Oil Refining; the company purchased surplus vegetable oil from the government and sold it for export. Not satisfied with such routine transactions, DeAngelis attempted to speculate in the futures market for vegetable oil; he became over-extended. He induced a large number of *banks* to lend him more funds. "The American Bureau of Statistics reported that the amount of oil handled by Allied was larger than the country's entire production of the commodity; still, no one blinked." In 1963, DeAngelis' tanks of salad oil were revealed to contain water, and he went to prison (Eichenwald December 16 2002, C3). The bankers were left to sort through the financial debris; presumably there were some embarrassing board meetings.

State-Run Lotteries

State lottery and gambling interests purportedly existed for the good of the public. Citizen reluctance to approve and to pay higher taxes spurred legislators to seek new sources of revenues to pay for escalating government expenditures. "Government, which has insatiable needs for revenue, is trying to satisfy those needs by encouraging its citizens to lose money at commercial games. It is a vicious mechanism because it marries insatiable government needs to the appetite of its citizens to step up to the state lottery and lose 50 cents of every dollar they place down (Zuckoff and Bailey September 26, 1993, 18)."

As early as 1612, the Virginia Company of London, which was already losing money, gained the right to run a lottery. Lotteries were often an inefficient form of taxation, as one estimate suggests that half of the proceeds went to the managers, one-third to the players, and the balance to the beneficiary (government). Lotteries were found in Puritan New England, even though many decried lotteries as a "common and public nuisance." Eventually, Massachusetts legislators outlawed the sale of lottery tickets in 1833. The fact that the Puritans allowed lotteries but their descendants did not is an interesting historical anomaly. By 1890, the Congress enacted legislation prohibiting using the mails for purposes of a lottery. Louisiana had gone against the grain and granted a charter for the Louisiana State Lottery to conduct a lottery (that was a monopoly) in return for a fixed sum per year. The company did so well that it offered to increase its yearly sum to one million dollars in 1890 but to no avail.

Commentators often criticized lotteries. Sir William Petty wrote, "A Lottery…is properly a tax upon unfortunate self-conceited fools." A pamphlet entitled, "The Lottery Exterminator," minced no words in stating, perhaps hysterically, "Wives have been induced to rob their husbands—children their parents—servants their masters, and foremen their employers; mothers have neglected their children—disappointed in their ill-founded hopes has driven thousands to suicide;—in short, almost every crime that can be imagined, has been occasioned, either directly or indirectly, by Lotteries (*Bulletin of the Business Historical Society* 1933, 1–4; *Bulletin of the Business Historical Society* 1928, 12–13)."[2]

A bookmaker who had changed his occupation from servicing slot machines to making book reflected: "It's a good deal like collecting money from slot machines except that, instead of getting it out of the machines, I get it out of the boobs. It's a lot better too because there are more boobs than slot machines, they are closer together, they have more money in them, and they open easier (Chase 1928, 340)."

Do state-run gambling endeavors meet the ethical standards expected of private businesses? Many state governments have won large settlements from tobacco companies for those companies' errant behavior. Many state governments' actions in running lotteries, in fact, mimic those of the tobacco companies' disapproved tactics. State lotteries pursue anti-competitive tactics, provide misleading information, and use predatory advertising practices.

Most state lotteries violate the spirit if not the letter of antitrust legislation. These lotteries are protected against competition from privately run lotteries. Although some states allow privately run gambling, state lotteries are usually exclusive and woe to anyone who offers a competing lottery, even a better lottery. According to the Chicago *Tribune*, an Illinois resident piggy-backed on the Illinois lottery. He used the same winning numbers but paid higher prizes than did the state lottery. Naturally, our enterprising entrepreneur went to prison (Wood July 22, 1987, 2:6).

Even more blatantly, some state governments simultaneously proscribed all private gambling under the guise of protecting the public, while being covetous of the revenue from illegal gambling: "The idea was to get gambling revenues away from organized crime, but now states are the beneficiaries, so they want to keep people gambling (Zuckoff and Bailey September 26, 1993, 18)." In an ironic twist, the states' pursuit of gambling revenue has helped make illegal gambling less illicit in the eyes of the public. A former organized crime gambling operator testified that state-run gambling became organized crime's "unwitting front men and silent partner (Better Government Association Staff White Paper 1992, no page numbers)." Most of the arguments made against privately run gambling applied to state-run gambling, too. State lotteries are, in a sense, descendants of the old "numbers racket."

State lottery officials and legislators resorted to disseminating misleading information. To promote the state-run lotteries, most state governments designated the proceeds for education, economic development, or environmental concerns. For most states, money from the lottery that went to, say, education was typically offset by a reduction of funding from the general revenue pool. Bill Honig, former superintendent of California public schools observed, "For every $5 the lottery gives to the schools, the state takes away $4. The public is more reluctant to pass education bond issues because they think we're floating in lottery money (Passell May 21, 1989, E6)." At least Honig's state did not completely offset the revenues from the lottery funds with reductions in funding from the general revenues. The claim that the lottery proceeds were earmarked for some popular purpose was disingenuous at best.

The very idea of devoting lottery proceeds to funding education is abhorrent. Gambling is the very antithesis of education. Whereas education is a slow, patient, difficult process with fairly reliable returns—a trade-off of current pleasure for future gains—gambling, as exemplified by the mega-buck lotteries, is instant gratification of a destructive kind. A character in a Connecticut lottery commercial explained, "I suppose I could have done more to plan my future, but I didn't. I guess I could have put some money aside…or I could have made some smart investments. But I didn't….Heck I could have bought a one-dollar Connecticut lottery ticket, won a jackpot worth millions, and gotten a nice big check in the mail every year for twenty years…[smile breaks over his face] and I did! I won millions—Me (Karl 1991, 13–14)!" Another advertisement mocked prudence and dedication to the work ethic: "No matter what you do for a living, there's an easier way to make money (Goodman 1995, 136–137)." Although many poor people believed that playing the lottery was their only hope of attaining financial independence, the reality proved a cruel chimera. A 25-year-old person foregoing a two-pack per day cigarette habit costing, say, $12 per day would have over $300,000 in retirement funds in today's purchasing power by age 65, assuming a 3 percent rate of return after inflation. Granted this would not be enough to retire on, but, then again, so far they have only sacrificed cigarettes (a couple consuming two grande specialty lattes and two cookies per day would face the same effect). One could, of course, extend this argument against putting $12 a day playing a state-run lottery into savings.

State lottery officials frequently provided other misleading information about the games. The mega-jackpots trumpeted on the television news are strictly accurate in the sense that the $100 million winner will get $100 million over 20 or 30 years. The relevant amount is not the nominal payout, but the *present value* of the payout. Given a choice of $100 million today or $100 million 20 years from now, to take an extreme but simple example (and ignoring tax implications), only the most perverse person would opt for the latter payment option. Having the $100 million today gives you the opportunity to invest the money today, and even the safest bond (yielding, perhaps, a 1 percent rate of return after inflation) would leave you with $122 million in 20 years (assuming you didn't touch the principal or interest and ignoring taxes). The state buys an annuity paying out the nominal amount over the 20 years; such annuities often cost roughly half of the nominal payout. That's why lotteries can sometimes have a larger nominal prize than money actually bet. The Illinois State Lottery revealed the misleading nature of its prizes by allowing winners to accept lump-sum payments generally worth 45–55 percent of the publicized prize. Given the hysteria over interest rates and other financial fine points with regard to consumer loans, the state consumer agencies' silence about this misleading facet undermines their credibility.

An Illinois court case exemplified the dichotomy between the advertised value and the present value of the winnings. Two Illinois Lotto winners sued the state when their winnings were unexpectedly low. The 2 were among the 78 winners of an advertised $1.75 million jackpot. Normally, a single or small number of winners would receive shares of the $1.75 million in 20 installments. Given the large number of winners, the state paid out a lump-sum of $9544.50 to each recipient instead of the advertised $22,435.90 (the jackpot divided by 78 winners). Of course, the state was simply paying the annuity value of the $1.75 million payout. The Illinois Supreme Court eventually ruled that the state could not be sued for breach of contract. The plaintiffs did not allege fraud, but two dissenting judges believed that the plaintiffs had enough evidence for a fraud charge. A chief justice stated in the *Chicago Tribune*, "What is really at issue in this case is the trust and faith of the people of this state who purchase lottery tickets believing that since the lottery is run by the state, it will be run properly. Many people who may not otherwise spend their hard-earned money, trust that a state-run lottery will be fair (Egler June 7, 1986, 1:1)."

Supplying misleading information is not limited to the large lottery jackpots. The state of Oregon has Keno, a video gambling game. There are 80 numbers, and a computer randomly selects 20 numbers. You can play ten different games, ranging from "1 Spot Game" to "10 Spot Game." The names are descriptive—in the "1 Spot Game," you are merely hoping that your selected number is one of the 20 numbers selected (worth $2.50), while in the "10 Spot Game," you are hoping that all ten of your numbers will be among the 20 numbers selected (worth $1,000,000). In most of the multi-spot games, you get smaller prizes if fewer of your numbers are selected. The game plays every five minutes from 6 a.m. to 1 a.m. The official brochure lists the odds of winning. The quoted odds are accurate, but the information is irrelevant. The key information a player should have is the expected value of the bet—the amount you will lose, on average, per dollar bet. "Lose" is apt, as you will surely lose all of your money if you play the game long enough (think of a balloon representing wealth that is gradually deflating). Given the complexity of Keno, ascertaining the expected value requires a sophisticated knowledge of probability. Many people like to play the game with the best odds of winning. Unfortunately, for them, this particular game had the *lowest expected value*. Coincidence? Probably not. Even caveat emptor requires that defects are readily ascertainable. Requiring players to have college-level knowledge of calculating probabilities does not constitute "readily ascertainable." The states should provide the relevant information rather than the irrelevant odds.

State lottery officials hire top advertising agencies to persuade people to play. The advertising typically targets basic feelings such as greed and fear. Many habitual players fear having their favorite number come up on a day that they did not bet. The Massachusetts state lottery uses this particular fear in an advertisement depicting a news reporter interviewing distraught players whose (lottery) number came up on a day they forgot to buy a ticket.

Just as private businesses must maintain existing clientele while simultaneously expanding their client base, state lottery officials confront the challenges of keeping regular customers not only from becoming bored with existing games (seeking new "highs") but also to get them to *intensify* their playing (Zuckoff September 27, 1993, 9). The lotteries must also continually seek new players, especially among younger people. Similar to tobacco and alcohol companies, state lottery officials create easier access to games, encourage frequent participation, and, in a divergence from private businesses, exhort people to play the lottery in order to help education or economic development. So far, lottery officials have not resorted to using cartoon characters to entice children to become lottery players.

Other advertisements targeted specific groups of people, including an infamous billboard in a Chicago ghetto: "This could be your ticket out (Goodman 1995, 135)." A contemporary set of advertisements for Uptown cigarettes ignited a firestorm of protest for similar targeting of African-Americans; eventually, the lottery billboard also triggered a backlash (Ramirez January 12, 1990, D1). Lotteries disproportionately affected the poor: "Not only is the state Lottery notable for offering worse odds than the toughest casino in Las Vegas or Atlantic City, it operates under a system that plays Robin Hood in reverse, taking from poor communities and giving to rich (Bailey and Zuckoff September 27, 1993, no page number)."[3]

State lotteries have two major advantages with regard to advertising compared with privately run companies. State lotteries are often exempt from federal advertising regulations. The Federal Trade Commission either has no jurisdiction or chooses not to exercise any jurisdiction over these lotteries (Zuckoff September 27, 1993, 9). Why should state lotteries be exempt? In addition, state lotteries get free publicity from the news media when there's a huge jackpot. Few of us have avoided watching the breathless young television reporter at some convenience store; the anchors in the studio usually ask whether the reporter has purchased tickets. Business owners, aside from sports teams and motion pictures owners, can only envy such advantages.

As with alcohol and tobacco consumption, there are the inevitable "problem" users. Most state lotteries respond by running commercials espousing "responsible" gambling. A *Boston Globe* investigative report stated that in Nova Scotia, fears of problem gambling induced lottery officials to remove electronic gambling machines from all places except those with liquor licenses (Zuckoff and Bailey September 26, 1993, 18). Assuming that patrons are allowed to smoke there, but heaven forbid they used any kind of recreational drug other than alcohol, the legislation created your "One-Stop Addiction Center."

In a comparison of ethics practiced by state-run versus privately run enterprises, the state lottery agencies do not emerge as paragons. These agencies are often guilty of violating that most elementary of ethical principles—reciprocity—"our laws apply to you but not to us." Many state government officials and legislators actually hold private businesses to *higher* standards of ethical behavior than they are willing to practice.

Ponzi Schemes and Investor Gullibility

Unlike lotteries, Ponzi schemes promise that *every* investor will be a winner, albeit not necessarily of millions but of a handsome return on their investment. Charles Ponzi set up a pyramid scheme right after World War I. He then noticed an arbitrage opportunity with international postal reply coupons. He based his "investments" upon this arbitrage opportunity and promised $15 within three months for every $10 sent in. The initial investors did get the 50 percent rate of return on their money, and, of course, the pyramid grew exponentially (Bulgatz 1993, 13). Naturally, Ponzi's bubble eventually burst. However, each generation seems to have its Ponzi scheme bubble. What is astounding is how many sophisticated people buy into these plans.

Ponzi scheme operators tread a fine line with regard to informing the public. One-shot con artists must avoid publicity, as publicity leads to brushes with the law. Ponzi operators rely upon publicity and reputation in order to attract new investors. The operators, of course, cannot divulge exactly how they can pay such magnificent rates of return. Investors are often satisfied with the explanation that divulging the secret might dissipate the profits. After all, if someone discovers an arbitrage opportunity, such as Charles Ponzi did with regard to the differences in value of the postage reply coupons, then broadcasting it will, in fact, attract other investors who will bid away the opportunity. Some Ponzi scheme operators may claim a form of intellectual property rights or create a moral justification that they discovered the secret to wealth. They thereby enlist potential and actual investors in a conspiracy of silence (Frankel 2012, 36–37, 57).

Tamar Frankel, author of *The Ponzi Scheme Puzzle*, maintained that people taken in by Ponzi schemes exhibited gullibility and failure to "do their homework." She pointed out that Bernard Madoff and other con artists used the lure of limited access to investments to enhance their desirability. She also suggested that although Madoff's experiences offered some valuable insights for future Ponzi scammers, "con artists do not adjust their stories to the current culture and public feeling but rather focus on their potential targeted audiences. For example, a con artist who operated a charitable organization appealed to similar organizations with a story that an anonymous donor would match their investments. This story was convincing because the managers of charitable institutions have donors who do seek to remain anonymous (Frankel 2012, 18, 146; see also Henriques August 20, 2012, B4)."[4]

Ponzi schemers, though, needed to disseminate information regarding the popularity of the venture. Schemers hoped to create herds of investors. A Romanian Ponzi scheme bilked thousands during the 1990s. Romania's Caritas involved a large proportion of the Romanian population and, according to some estimates, up to a third of the country's liquid reserves. One unique aspect of the Caritas was the involvement of a government official and political party in promoting the scheme. Ioan Stoica devised the Caritas; at its peak in the early 1990s after the fall of dictator Nicolae Ceausescu, many Romanians deemed Stoica as heaven-sent or a saint. People who were initially skeptical about the promise of an eightfold increase in their investment in just three months, jumped aboard, when they saw friends and family members receiving checks. With an inflation rate of 250–300 percent, people had seen their savings dwindle to nothingness, adding an impetus to grasp at any investment straw. One woman described the allure: "You put in 100,000, get 800,000 back, take 500,000 of it to buy things you need, and keep playing the game with 300,000—*their* money. Am I playing with *my* money then? No. If it gets lost, have I lost *my* money? No. YOU CAN'T LOSE in this game [italics and all caps Verdery's]." How was it possible to get an eightfold return after only three months? "Many did not find this a meaningful question: they had seen people on TV taking out huge piles of bills, or they knew of someone what had done so, and this was all the explanation they needed….When I asked how they could entrust such large sums to something they didn't understand, they shrugged." People viewed "my" money as something they earned, whereas "their money" was unearned. People professed, "We aren't used to living off unearned money. It seems somehow dishonest to us" and "I'm not used to having money gotten for nothing; it seems *unnatural*." Some Romanians saw the unearned Caritas money as justified, because under the Communist Party regime, "people worked unpaid, now we get a kind of compensation, don't you think?" Other people linked Caritas to the western-imposed globalization. There was an interesting psychological aspect, as people seemed to enjoy getting frequent, small checks more than receiving occasional large checks. The frequent affirmation that they had made the right decision seemed to bolster enthusiasm (Verdery 1995, 3–4; see also Frankel 2012, 40–41).

Madoff's long-running Ponzi scheme was a recent and spectacular scandal. That Madoff was able to bamboozle investors and federal regulators for so many years raises many intriguing questions. Madoff's clients/victims were a sophisticated group. As a well-respected figure in financial circles, his investment prospectus exuded credibility. Madoff's ability to maintain the scheme for decades marked him as a particularly astute practitioner of this form of fraud. His guarantees of relatively modest rates of return boosted the scheme's credibility.

Madoff had worked with the Securities and Exchange Commission. Many people thought it natural that he would start his own investment firm. What was both attractive and off-putting about Madoff's stated strategy was its *consistency* in beating the market. Madoff maintained secrecy about his operations, an attitude that "violated the policies of certain endowments and institutional investors," requiring managers of these funds to investigate potential investments. Madoff did not charge the normal managers' performance fees and chose to remain a broker instead of an adviser-fund manager (which would have invited stricter regulatory scrutiny) (Frankel 2012, 18–19).[5]

One of the saddest aspects of Madoff's scam was his targeting of coreligionists. Elie Wiesel, concentration camp survivor and Nobel Prize winner, was a victim. Wiesel described how respected Madoff was within the Jewish community. Wiesel told a panel that he considered Madoff a "thief, scoundrel, criminal." Wiesel invested with Madoff at the advice of an old friend; the friend lost $50 million. Wiesel and his wife lost their lives' savings, as well as $15.2 million from their charity. Before investing, Wiesel asked other people who had done business with Madoff and received reassurance. Wiesel noted Madoff's secrecy and a myth created around him "that mesmerized investors." Wiesel thought Madoff's punishment should consist of a solitary cell "with only a screen, and on that screen for at least five years of his life, every day and every night, there should be pictures of his victims…[and] a voice saying, 'Look what you have done to this old lady, look what you have done to that child, look what you have done,' nothing else (Strom February 26, 2009, B1)."[6]

Madoff and other fraudsters can rely upon their victims' reticence to go to the authorities and admit that they had been swindled. Sophisticated victims, money managers, and others have plenty to lose by admitting to being duped. No one wants to appear to the public as incompetent, gullible, or foolish. Other defrauded investors remain silent in hopes of bolstering the market price of their shares as they divest. In the wake of a scam's collapse, even those investors who cashed out ahead of the crash—whether or not they suspected fraud—may face legal scrutiny. In addition, alleging fraud may incur the risk of libel. The public does not seem to direct as much animus toward fraudsters, even on a scale of Madoff, as they do criminals who use physical force and violence. Part of the public's indulgence may emanate from Madoff having defrauded wealthy and sophisticated investors instead of poor and unsophisticated investors. But, of course, there is not much money in bilking the latter group of investors. Another aspect is the American belief in self-protection or exercising some caution; in other countries, "the duty of people to deal fairly with others is heavier." Some commentators blamed the victims for having been greedy (Frankel 2012, 146–147, 161–162, 169, 179–180).

Some people were astute enough to recognize a Ponzi scheme but invested anyway, if they believed they were among the earliest participants. They then hoped that other people would sign up. One money manager, Stanley Chais, steered billions of dollars to Madoff's funds; Chais and other money managers earned hundreds of millions of dollars in fees and profits. Chais insisted that Madoff ensure that "none of the Chais accounts should ever report a single losing trade," a record of expertise that was implausible and suggested this money manager likely suspected that Madoff's operation was not legitimate. The Securities and Exchange Commission alleged that some executives of a brokerage firm "knowingly helped finance the Ponzi scheme and conceal it from regulators for years. These defendants asserted they knew nothing about Madoff's deceptions and that they, too, had lost money."[7] Early investors in Madoff's swindle who recognized the nature of the scheme may have urged other people, including friends and family, to enlist. If these early investors did so knowingly, their "lack of empathy is even more pronounced (Henriques June 23, 2009, B1, B4; see also Frankel 2012, 133–134)."[8]

Frankel argued that the suspicious investors, who cashed out in time, demonstrated a lack of empathy for the buyers of their shares. In an episode of *Veronica Mars*, the title character discovered that her high school investment club's shares were worthless due to fraud. Veronica and her chums urged the high school teacher who was advising the club to divest immediately. He replied that he could not do so in good conscience, as he would be injuring the buyer. For a television show, this was a pretty decent depiction of real-life ethical quandaries.[9]

There is another adverse ramification of Ponzi schemers, albeit an indirect one. Frankel worries that relying upon small public investors to protect themselves from fraud may backfire. Overly cautious investors may reduce the incidence of fraud, but their caution imposes higher costs on issuers of securities. These issuers have to expend more resources providing evidence of their honesty and guarantees. In some cases, high-quality securities might have to accept lower prices, and, in other cases, investors may simply stop buying securities. She concludes, "shifting the burden of verifying and caution to investors is not the optimal way to reduce fraud (Frankel 2006, 134–135, 171)."

Social Security as Ponzi Scheme

Businesspeople are often placed on the ethical defensive by government policymakers and bureaucrats. However, the Social Security program is a good example where businesspeople might insist that the government raise its ethical standards to that of business ethics.

Comparing Ponzi's scheme with Social Security is an instructive exercise comparing government officials' ethics versus business ethics (if we consider Charles Ponzi a businessman). Government officials often excoriate businesspeople for employing anti-competitive tactics, endangering the public welfare, using really duplicitous accounting tricks to mislead consumers, employing willfully misleading terminology, exploiting consumers' feelings of greed and fear, and displaying rampant disregard of regulations.

The Social Security program has been dubbed a "Ponzi Scheme," even by some of its supporters. The allegation was unfair to Mr. Ponzi. Ponzi, as would Bernard Madoff and other modern scammers, had to *persuade* people to trust him with their money; taxpayers are forced to pay into the program (Hayek 1960, 293).

Social Security and Medicare are not voluntary for large segments of the labor force; "contributions" are really taxes. On the other hand, politicians extended coverage over time to include many who never "contributed." Both plans currently depend on the ability and willingness of future workers to fund them.

The plan never was actuarially sound; what you "contributed" (Social Security's term) only loosely correlated with what you will receive. Adherents of Social Security built in redistributive aspects to the system. They controlled the flow of information regarding the program. Social Security officials co-opted terms from insurance, including the term "insurance." They also pushed to monopolize retirement funding by denying an amendment allowing companies to opt out of the system by providing a comparable or better plan. Social Security Commissioner Robert Ball admitted in an interview in 1964 that people do not have *legal* rights to their contributions; they have *statutory rights*; in other words, you will receive Social Security payments only at the continued behest of the U.S. Congress (Ellis 1971, 55; *U.S. News & World Report* December 7, 1964, 58; Weaver 1982, 96). The Congress can, in fact, change the rules pertaining to tax-deferred accounts, but you retain your property rights to the money invested. In all likelihood, the Congress will maintain your statutory rights to social security, but your rights are less assured than your 401(k) or 403(b) investments.

There is no "trust fund." In essence, the government conducts an accounting transaction between government accounts; as Milton Friedman wrote, "the accounting sleight-of-hand of a bogus trust fund is counted on to conceal this fact from a gullible public." The situation is analogous to officials of a private company putting company "IOUs" in an account labeled "reserves." Economist Martin Feldstein echoed Friedman's depiction: "Extending Social Security solvency to 2055 [now approximately 2037] is based on a complex accounting sham so duplicitous that it is hard to believe (Friedman January 26, 1999, A18; Feldstein February 1, 1999, A20)." Officials of a private pension company could have faced criminal charges for using some of these tactics.

From the very beginning, advocates for Social Security cloaked the program and its goals with ambiguous, misleading phrases. One unnamed Social Security official told a *Barron's* reporter: "The continued general support for the Social Security system hinges on continued public ignorance of how the system works. I believe that we have nothing to worry about because it is so enormously complex that nobody is going to figure it out (Scheibla April 26, 1965, 9)."

The employer's matching contribution through the payroll tax was intended to make workers think they were getting something for nothing from their employers; if the employers did not have to pay the matching tax, they could have paid their workers higher wages and salaries. President Franklin Roosevelt admitted as much: "I guess you are right on the economics, but those [payroll] taxes were never a problem of economics. They were political all the way through.... With those taxes there, no damn politician can ever scrap my program (Weaver 1982, 82; see also *U.S. News & World Report* December 7, 1964, 63)." Many economists believe that, in essence, workers bear the burden of the entire 15.3 percent of the combined payroll and FICA—Federal Insurance Contributions Act—taxes.

Economist Paul Samuelson recognized the pyramid aspect of Social Security. In 1967, he wrote: "The beauty of social insurance is that *it is actuarially unsound* [italics his]. Everyone who reaches retirement age is given benefit privileges that far exceed anything he has paid in." This is possible because the national gross domestic product grows at compound interest and the national population, especially the number of young people, increases. Samuelson concluded, "More important, with real incomes growing at some 3 per cent per year, the taxable base upon which benefits rest in any period are much greater than the taxes paid historically by the generation now retired....Social security is squarely based on what has been called the eighth wonder of the world—compound interest. A growing nation is the greatest Ponzi game ever contrived. And that is a fact, not a paradox (Samuelson February 13, 1967, 88)." Samuelson developed an economic model demonstrating the feasibility of a perpetual pyramid scheme. Unfortunately, for his prediction, Samuelson was not as keen a demographer as he was an economist (but in failing to see the declining birth rates, he was not alone; prominent biologist Paul Ehrlich also missed some of the trends). Temporary lulls in productivity increases also made the program less sustainable.

Lest you think I exaggerate the misleading nature of both Social Security and Medicare, consider the following remarks of a former U.S. Director of the Budget, Maurice Stans, when asked, "Would you do away with the Social Security trust fund, and simply handle Social Security as a direct obligation of the Treasury?"

> I don't think it really makes any significant difference. There's now less money in the trust fund than is necessary to pay one year's benefits. We have long since abandoned the idea that President Roosevelt originally had when the Social Security fund was set up—the idea of keeping it on an actuarial basis so that the accumulated reserves would be equal at any date to the accrued retirement liabilities. We are now on a basis in which one year's collections from existing taxpayers are paid out in benefits to beneficiaries to the following year. So the trust fund has no particular significance as of now, except as an earmarking of taxes.

A reporter queried, "In what you said about the Social Security fund being adequate for less than one year's benefits, did you mean to imply that benefits are in danger in any way?" "Oh, no—of course not. I merely imply that Social Security payments rest upon the general credit of the Government of the United States, upon its current taxing power, and not upon any accumulations in a trust fund to take care of you and me when we become eligible for benefits (*U.S. News & World Report* January 16, 1967, 68)."

The tragedy of Social Security is that its strength—the stability, if not the certainty of the program—could have been a tremendous blessing for people planning for retirement. Social Security might have at least guaranteed a bare minimum income. There is, instead, uncertainty and fear surrounding the future of the program. The fear of running out of savings or overpaying for an annuity is pervasive. Workers nearing retirement have rather large question marks confronting them: How much will they receive under Social Security; will there be a means test to establish eligibility; and how will any such payments be taxed?

Mr. Stans gave his testimony decades ago. Mr. Ponzi was eventually convicted as a "common and notorious thief," and sentenced to seven to nine years (he served seven). To date, no government official has been imprisoned for the largest Ponzi scheme ever enacted.

Suppose we end Social Security today and made no more payments for beneficiaries (obviously begging the question of whether such an event would be fair or ethical). Some retirees would become destitute. Other retirees would draw down their estates more than they might have. If society decided to assist the destitute retirees, the costs of their benefits would simply be shifted (albeit without the "liability" to future retirees) from Social Security to another federal program. Wealthier retirees would leave smaller bequests to their heirs. Clearly, each dollar reduction in Social Security would not benefit current workers dollar for dollar.

Government Versus Business Ethics

In the cases of Social Security and state-run lotteries, the ethical standards of government officials have been lacking. Owners of privately run gambling establishments can only envy the advantages accruing to government-run lotteries. Charles Ponzi lacked the coercive capability of the federal government to force citizens to participate in his scheme; he also lacked the taxing capability of the federal government. Granted these two significant advantages, however, government officials displayed a cavalier attitude toward their fellow citizens.

The savings and loan catastrophe of the 1980s presaged the housing market disaster of 2007–2008. Part of the problem arose when legislators—Democrats and Republicans alike—saw studies claiming that home ownership was associated with "better citizenship." They jumped to the conclusion that by getting Americans into homes, then—presto!—these people would become better citizens. Politicians mistook statistical association (correlation) with causality; one could easily make the argument that being better citizens made them more likely to be homeowners.

Although it is too early to write a definitive account of the 2007–2008 debacle, economists Charles Calomiris and Peter Wallison made salient points. Fannie Mae and Freddie Mac executives received signals from Democratic congressional leaders that providing financing for "affordable housing" was imperative. The two entities increased their exposure to subprime and Alt-A mortgages in the years leading up to the crash. They justified their GSE—government-sponsored enterprises—activities as making mortgages cheaper, but, in fact, they were "creating risks for the taxpayers and the economy." The two economists asked, "what value were they providing?" Representative Barney Frank (D-MA) lauded the two entities: "Fannie Mae and Freddie Mac have played a very useful role in helping to make housing more affordable…a mission that this Congress has given them in return for some of the arrangements which are of some benefit to them to focus on affordable housing." So even though Fannie Mae and Freddie Mac were in trouble, some congressional leaders were just fine with the situation. On the other side of the aisle, some key Republicans, admittedly less interested in affordable housing, worried that the situation warranted oversight and proposed a solution. "All the Republicans on the Committee supported the bill, and all the Democrats voted against it. Senator John McCain endorsed the legislation in a speech on the Senate floor. Then-Senator Barack Obama, like all other Democrats, remained silent." Calomiris and Wallison concluded, "If the Democrats had let the 2005 legislation come to a vote, the huge growth in the subprime and Alt-A loan portfolios of Fannie and Freddie could not have occurred, and the scale of the financial meltdown would have been substantially less." As usual, the political leaders who missed the opportunity to rein in the troubled entities later disavowed their culpability: "The same politicians who today decry the lack of intervention to stop excess risk taking in 2005–2006 were the ones who blocked the only legislative effort that could have stopped it (Calomiris and Wallison September 23, 2008, A29)."[10]

Federal legislators "got some benefits in the form of political support from the GSE's ability to hold down mortgage rates, but it garnered even more political benefits from GSE's support for affordable housing. The taxpayers got highly attenuated benefits from both affordable housing and lower mortgage rates but ultimately faced enormous liabilities associated with GSE risk-taking.…As if that were not enough, in the process, the GSEs' operations promoted a risky subprime mortgage binge in the United States that has caused a worldwide financial crisis." The GSEs were astute enough to make "available for spending on projects in the congressional districts and states of their supporters. Many of these projects involved affordable housing." GSEs donated millions to the campaign funds of dozens of senators and representatives (Wallison and Calomiris 2008, 1, 3).

Even some well-known economists got bamboozled by the GSE shenanigans. The GSEs paid for academic research by such worthies as Nobel laureate Joseph Stiglitz; Stiglitz coauthored an article in 2002 claiming that "the risk of GSE default producing taxpayer loss was 'effectively zero.'" The article was published in *Fannie Mae Papers*. Stiglitz later recanted (sort of) and stated in an opinion editorial, "We should not be worried about [GSE] shareholders losing their investments. In earlier years, they were amply rewarded. The management remuneration packages that they approved were designed to encourage excessive risk-taking. They got what they asked for. Nor should we be worried about creditors losing their money. Their lack of supervision fueled the housing bubble and we are now all paying the price (Stiglitz July 24, 2008, no page numbers; Wallison and Calomiris 2008, 3)."[11]

A sad and ironic legacy of the "affordable housing" crash was that African-Americans, long the losers in the housing and mortgage markets, suffered mightily from the efforts of their putative friends. Median black household net worth shriveled from $12,124 in 2005 to $5677 in 2009. "Overall, from 2007 to 2010, wealth for blacks declined by an average of 31 percent, home equity by an average of 28 percent, and retirement savings by an average of 35 percent. Although whites lost greater amounts of wealth, their proportional losses were much smaller." The reporter concluded, "The 2007–2008 episode, though, was perhaps just the culmination of disappointment in the wake of the 1968 Fair Housing Act. Despite federal attempts, black households with sufficient savings to make a reasonable down payment were often shunted by bankers and real estate agents to less-desirable neighborhoods and were more likely to lose their homes relative to whites with comparable income and wealth levels. These black households were more likely to be relegated to subprime mortgages (Bouie July 24, 2014, no page numbers)."[12]

Reporter Tanzina Vega bluntly stated, "Blacks who purchased their first homes between 2000 and 2010 would have been wise to hold on to their money instead." Even before the Great Recession and its skidding housing values, "blacks who purchased their first home between 2003 and 2005 suffered a 23% loss in net worth. In the same period, the net worth of white first-time homebuyers jumped as much as 50%. The disparity persisted after the housing market crashed." The crash generated larger proportional losses for blacks than for whites. "Part of the reason why blacks lost wealth is because their homes did not appreciate in value as much as those owned by whites, particularly if those homes are in majority black communities that experienced high rates of foreclosure and declining rates of homeownership (Vega October 8, 2015, no page numbers)."

Conclusion

Would Bernard Madoff, Charles Ponzi, and other get-rich-quick scam artists have behaved differently had they exercised some imagination and pondered the effects of their frauds upon their victims? Would envisioning the misery their scams caused have drawn the scammers back from the precipice? Madoff was defrauding acquaintances and coreligionists, some of whom had survived persecutions and concentration camps and had rebuilt lives with some normalcy. Now they were being exploited by someone they trusted. The scammers did not use weapons nor force, and their victims were gullible, but a strong argument can be made that the scammers deserved more severe sentencing than petty thieves, drug users, or other minor criminals. A defendant in an Armani suit is no more deserving of the court's leniency than the scruffiest, low-income defendant. Unfortunately, jurists seem willing to cut the well-dressed, white-collar criminal a break.

What should society do with duplicitous legislators and government officials, whose capacity to inflict harm often exceeds that of business executives? Legislators and officials can force all of us to participate in ill-conceived programs. From a deontological perspective, did these worthies fulfill their duties? All good intentions provide scant solace for citizens and taxpayers left to deal with the debacles.

Notes

1. John Ashton and Thomas Cary also characterized gambling as a social ill (Ashton 1899, 2; Cary 1845, 13).
2. John Law also criticized state-run lotteries (Murphy 1997, 40).
3. Nor do state lotteries provide free drinks and chits for meals.
4. For another example of a long-running Ponzi scheme, see the case of John G. Bennett Jr. The pedigrees of his victims are impressive (Stecklow 1995, A1 and A8).

5. Tamar Frankel discussed similarities between Ponzi schemes and stock market traders (Frankel 2012, 98–99, 152).
6. For Madoff's response at his sentencing, see Friedman and McNeill (2013, 92–93).
7. An investment record with nary a losing transaction is akin to Disney's labeling of all their movies as "classics," no one, not even the Bard himself, has such a track record. Perfection is for suckers.
8. One could dub this the "Bigger Fool" investment strategy; you are safe as long as there is a bigger fool following you, willing to buy or participate in a game of musical chairs, assuming one has possession of a chair when the music stops.
9. Hillary Clinton's alleged cattle futures deal presumably had a doppelganger, who did the reverse of turning $1000 into $100,000.
10. Fannie Mae and Freddie Mac were already notorious for their accounting frauds in 2003 and 2004; using the argument that they made housing more affordable proved a useful distraction from the two entities' dubious behavior (Wallison and Calomiris 2008, 5, 8).
11. As late as August 2008, Senator Christopher Dodd (D-CT) was opposing Republican efforts to approve new legislation reforming the GSE (Wallison and Calomiris 2008, 5). Another Nobel laureate, Paul Krugman, either misunderstood or was being disingenuous in stating in July 2008, "Fannie and Freddie had nothing to do with the explosion of high-risk lending." He claimed that regulation of Fannie and Freddie in the wake of their accounting scandal had worked: "You could say that the Fannie-Freddie experience shows that regulation works (Krugman July 14, 2008, A17; Wallison and Calomiris 2008, 6)."
12. The Federal Housing Administration had long discriminated against African-Americans and helped ensure white-only neighborhoods and suburbs. Loewen (2005, 128–129, 209–210, 257–258) details the sorry historical legacy.

Bibliography

Akst, Daniel. "Shock by Scandals? These Are Nothing!" *New York Times*, July 7, 2002, Sec. 3, 4.

Ashton, John. *History of Gambling in England* (Chicago, IL: Herbert S. Stone, 1899).

Bailey, Doug and Mitchell Zuckoff, "Poor Communities Lose Big in Lottery," *Boston Globe*, September 27, 1993, taken from Westlaw, no page number listed.

Bellhouse, David. "Probability in the Sixteenth and Seventeenth Centuries: An Analysis of Puritan Casuistry." *International Statistical Review* 56(1), April 1988, 63–74.

Better Government Association Staff White Paper, "Casino Gambling in Chicago," October 1992.

Bouie, Jamelle. "The Crisis in Black Homeownership," *Slate*, July 24, 2014, www.slate.com/articles/news_and_politics/politics/2014/07/black_homeownership_how_the_recession_turned_owners_into_renters_and_obliterated_black_American_wealth.html, viewed February 12, 2017, 11:05am.

Bulgatz, Joseph. *Ponzi Schemes, Invaders from Mars, and More Extraordinary Popular Delusions*; (Harmony Books, 1993).

Bulletin of the Business Historical Society. "'The Lottery Exterminator.'" II(4), June 1928, 12–13. No author.

Bulletin of the Business Historical Society. "Lotteries." VII(4), June 1933, 1–5. No author.

Calomiris, Charles and Peter Wallison. "Blame Fannie Mae and Congress for the Credit Mess." *Wall Street Journal*, September 23, 2008, A29.

Cary, Thomas. *The Dependence of the Fine Arts for the Encouragement, in a Republic, on the Security of Property, with an Enquiry into the Causes of Frequent Failure among Men of business: an Address, Delivered before the Boston Mercantile Library Association, November 13, 1844* (Boston, MA: Charles C. Little & James Brown, 1845).

Chase, Stuart. "Play." *Whither Mankind: A Panorama of Modern Civilization* (New York, NY: Longmans, Green, 1928).

Egler, Daniel. "Winners lose suit on Lotto shortfall," Chicago *Tribune*, June 7, 1986, Sec. 1, 1.

Eichenwald, Kurt. "After a Boom, There Will Be Scandal. Count on It." *New York Times*, December 16, 2002, C3.

Ellis, Abraham. *The Social Security Fraud* (New Rochelle, NY: Arlington House, 1971).

Feldstein, Martin. "Clinton's Social Security Sham." *Wall Street Journal*. February 1, 1999, A20.

Frankel, Tamar. *The Ponzi Scheme Puzzle: A History and Analysis of Con Artists and Victims* (New York, NY: Oxford University Press, 2012).

Frankel, Tamar. *Trust and Honesty: America's Business Culture at a Crossroad* (Oxford, UK: Oxford University Press, 2006).

Friedman, Milton. "Social Security Socialism." *Wall Street Journal*. January 26, 1999, A18.

Friedman, Daniel and Daniel McNeill. *Morals and Markets: The Dangerous Balance* (New York, NY: Palgrave Macmillan, 2013). 2nd edition.

Goodman, Robert. *The Luck Business: The Devastating Consequences and Broken Promises of America's Gambling Explosion* (New York, NY: Free Press, 1995).

Hayek, Friedrich. *The Constitution of Liberty* (Chicago, IL: University of Chicago Press, 1960).

Henriques, Diana. "Madoff Suits Add Details About Fraud." *New York Times*, June 23, 2009, B1 and B4.

Henriques, Diana. "Examining the Ponzi Scheme Through the Mind of the Con Artist," *New York Times*, August 20, 2012.

Karl, Jonathan. "Lotto Baloney: The great state lottery swindle." *New Republic*. March 4, 1991, 13–15.

Krugman, Paul. "Fannie, Freddie and You." *New York Times*. July 14, 2008, A17.

Loewen, James. *Sundown Towns: A Hidden Dimension of American Racism* (New York, NY: New Press, 2005).

Murphy, Antoin. *John Law: Economic Theorist and Policy-Maker* (Oxford, UK: Clarendon Press, 1997).

Passell, Peter. "Lotto Is Financed by the Poor and Won by the States," *New York Times*, May 21, 1989, E6.

Poitras, Geoffrey. *The Early History of Financial Economics, 1478–1776* (Cheltenham, UK: Edward Elgar, 2000).

Ramirez, Anthony. "A Cigarette Campaign under Fire," *New York Times*, January 12, 1990, D1.

Samuelson, Paul. "Paul A. Samuelson on Social Security." *Newsweek*. February 13, 1967.

Scheibla, Shirley. "Robbing Peter: A Critical Look at the Pending Social Security Bill." *Barron's*. April 26, 1965, 9–10.

Sears, Marian. "The American Businessman at the Turn of the Century." *Business History Review* XXX(4), December 1956, 382–443.

Stecklow, Steve. "Incredible Offer: A Big Charity Faces Tough New Questions about Its Financing." *Wall Street Journal*, May 15, 1995, A1 and A8.

Stiglitz, Joseph. "Fannie's and Freddie's Free Lunch." *Financial Times*. July 24, 2008, https://www.ft.com/content/c6999a06-5994-11dd-90f8-000077b07658, viewed March 25, 2018, 11:45pm.

Strom, Stephanie. "Elie Wiesel Levels Scorn at Madoff." *New York Times*, February 26, 2009, B1.

U.S. News & World Report. "How Honest Is the U.S. Budget? Interview with Maurice Stans, Former Director of the Budget," January 16, 1967, p. 66–70.

U.S. News & World Report. "How Safe Is Your Social Security Pension? An Official Interview," December 7, 1964, 58, 63.

U.S. Industrial Commission. *Preliminary Report on Trusts and Industrial Combinations, Together with Testimony, Review of Evidence, Charts Showing Effects of Prices, and Topical Digest*. Volume 1 of the Commissions Reports (Washington, DC: Government Printing Office, 1900a).

U.S. Industrial Commission. *Reports of the Industrial Combinations* (Washington, DC: GPO, 1900b). 5 parts.

Vega, Tanzina. "American Opportunity: Black wealth not protected by homeownership," *CNNMoney*, October 8, 2015, http://money.cnn.com/2015/10/07/news/economy/black-wealth-net-worth/, viewed February 12, 2017, 11:05am

Verdery, Katherine. "'Caritas': And the Reconceptualization of Money in Romania." *Anthropology Today* 11(1), February 1995, 3–7.

Wallison, Peter and Charles Calomiris. "The Last Trillion-Dollar Commitment: The Destruction of Fannie Mae and Freddie Mac." *American Enterprise Institute for Public Policy Research*. September 2008. 1–9.

Weaver, Carolyn. *The Crisis in Social Security: Economic and Political Origins* (Durham, NC: Duke Press Policy Studies, 1982).

Wood, Hank. "Man charged with using lottery to make life greener for bettors," Chicago *Tribune*, July 22, 1987, Sec. 2, 6.

Zuckoff, Mitchell. "State-Run Games Flout Ad Standards," *Boston Globe*, September 27, 1993, 9.

Zuckoff, Mitchell and Doug Bailey. "US turns to betting as budget fix." *Boston Sunday Globe*. September 26, 1993, 1 and 18.

CHAPTER 11

Distributions of Income and Wealth

A vital question for societies revolves around the distributions of income and wealth. A vital question for businesspeople who have accumulated wealth is what to do with their wealth. How a businessperson handles his or her own wealth may reflect their ethical beliefs.

Wealthy businesspeople earned their wealth in a different fashion than did royalty and other elites entrenched by birth. Businesspeople had to persuade consumers to buy their goods and services, whereas the elites of the past often did little to earn their wealth. With the interaction of government and business, though, some people became wealthy by using the government for their own ends.

Distributions of income and wealth continue to vex policymakers and citizens. There is little unanimity about what constitutes just or fair distributions of income and wealth. Philosophers have struggled to construct coherent approaches to these ageless problems. Attempts to even out, say, well-being or satisfaction founder upon individuals' different preferences.

What are the ethical aspects connected with forcible redistribution of income and wealth? Are there ethical drawbacks associated with charity? Did the recipients owe any duties to the taxpayers?

Ancient Views Concerning the Poor

As more complex societies developed, and specialization increased, the need to care for the orphan, widow, and poor remained. Urukagina, king of Lagash, some 4500 years ago, sought to transform his kingdom from

D. G. Surdam, *Business Ethics from the 19th Century to Today*,
https://doi.org/10.1007/978-3-030-37169-2_11

one based on heavy taxation and rife with corruption and seeking military conquest to one demonstrating concern for the unfortunates within society. A later ruler, Ur-Nammu boasted that under his rule, "the orphan did not fall prey to the wealthy," "the widow did not fall prey to the powerful," and "the man of one shekel did not fall prey to the man of one mina." Hammurabi reiterated the intent to protect the weak and unfortunate (Schmidt 1987, 43). The great monotheistic religions, therefore, were not the first to introduce charity into society.

"Confucius only posed the problem," according to economist Jichuang Hu, but Confucius did not resolve the problem of disparities in wealth distribution. Confucius' sympathies were with the feudal ruling class, and he advised the underlings to be "content with poverty" and "know their fate," but he also advised for the wealthy that they should be "rich but not conceited" or "rich and yet good mannered." Hu believed that Confucius never really pondered why some people were rich and others poor (Hu 1988, 49–50). Socrates observed that the king or rich man is often without happiness. Of course, contemporary people sometimes observe that "the best things in life are free." Jacob Viner quoted Jean la Bruyere: "He who is powerful and rich, and to whom nothing is lacking may well formulate the question; its answer, however, should be left to a poor man."[1] Oddly, no one seemed to remark that if the poor man was carefree and happy, all a rich (unhappy) man had to do was to divest his wealth and join the ranks of the poor. Theodicists argued that evil was usually "only apparent, not real." They applied such thinking to poverty. They denied that happiness was directly correlated with wealth. These thinkers claimed that wealth was often a burden, and that inequality in wealth "worked to the advantage of the poor (Viner 1972, 98–99)."

Medieval scholastics wrestled with the problem of wealth. There were multiple sources of "all sin." Ecclesiasticus advised that "For pride is the beginning of [all] sin, and he that hath it shall pour out abomination (Ecclesiasticus 10:13)." Saint Paul, on the other hand, attributed "the love of money" as the "root of all evils (1 Timothy 6:10)," although other translations read "cupidity" instead of "love of money (Little 1971, 18–20)."

St. Ambrose considered wealth and the pursuit of wealth as a potential snare. "It contaminates those who have it, and does not help those who have it not." Wealth distracts the soul "from loving what is virtuous and laudable." Ambrose did not appear to understand that wealth could contribute to the development of resources and of economic prosperity. "Nor did he appreciate the moral significance of wealth as a means whereby character may be educated and moral qualities developed." Ambrose saw only the rich men of his time, "who were singularly greedy, luxurious, and unscrupulous, and he could see little good in the wealth that was responsible for the production of people of this odious type (Dudden 1935, 547)."

Although people in the past exhibited charity and concern for the poor, there were many people who felt social inequality and attendant inequalities in income and wealth, with its accompanying "hierarchy and subordination" were necessary to preserve "order and civil peace." French physician Philippe Hecquet in 1740 commented that "The poor in a state are like shadows in a picture; they create a necessary contrast, which humanity sometimes bemoans, but which does honor to the intentions of providence. No doubt it was ambition, vanity and the eccentricity of men which created the distressing distinction found among them: but it is wisdom that maintains it." The poor, therefore fulfilled a purpose, but, "It is therefore necessary that there be poor people; but there must not be *miserables*. The latter only exist to the shame of humanity, while the former, on the contrary, are part of the order of political economy. Through them, abundance reigns in the cities, all conveniences are found there, the arts flourish, etc. (Hecquet quoted in Viner 1972, 88; Kaplow 1972, 27)."

English writer Soame Jenyns held the thesis that "the divine plan" allowed people widely different shares of wealth, wisdom, and health, but that they received similar amounts of happiness. He believed that the poor received compensation from, "having more hopes and fewer fears, a greater share of health, and a more exquisite relish of the smallest enjoyments." Samuel Johnson, for one, thought such ideas repugnant: "Sir I was once a great arguer for the advantages of poverty, but I was at the same very discontented....You never knew people laboring to convince you that you might live very happily upon a plentiful fortune." Johnson was unique among the English literati in repudiating the Theodicy and Jenyns' "cavalier treatment" of the plight of the poor [which was far worse in 1770 than today]. He disputed that the poor's suffering was ordained by providence: "as far as human eyes can judge, the degree of evil might have been less without any impediment to good."

Thomas Aquinas urged wealthy people to demonstrate "liberality" and "magnificence" with their wealth. The moderately well-to-do could demonstrate the former; the really well-heeled could demonstrate the latter. He suggested spending on prominent, even gaudy projects, similar to Aristotle. Pope Pius XI in 1931 chose to associate Aquinas' concept of "magnificence" to productive investments that would create jobs. The

Pope and Aquinas ignored the opportunity cost—wealth spent on "magnificence" could have created benefits and jobs even if spent on "pedestrian" projects. For Jacob Viner, though, the importance of Pope Pius' pronouncement was its characterizing the wealthy investor in capitalistic projects as possessing virtue (all quotes from Viner 1978, 63, 103–105).[2]

A large proportion of people throughout human history have been poor, often in an absolute sense, whereby the struggle to find enough to eat and adequate shelter was an endless grind. Aquinas recognized the inability to fully succor the destitute. He counseled that under certain dire situations, "then a person may legitimately supply his own needs out of another's property, whether he does so secretly or flagrantly. And in such a case there is strictly speaking no theft or robbery (Aquinas 1964, 38:83)."[3]

Even as late as the eighteenth and nineteenth centuries, vestiges of the idea that the poor were necessary persisted. Hecquet claimed that poverty ensured that there would be sufficient labor for the arduous work, as hunger was a powerful motivation that drove people to undertake even arduous jobs. Bernard Mandeville argued in his *Fable of the Bees*, "No man would suffer to be poor or work hard for his living if it were open to him to do otherwise. It is his need for food and drink, and, in a cold climate, for clothing and a roof over his head, that resigns man to suffer all that he can bear. Without these needs no one would work." A large number of working poor, where slavery was outlawed, was deemed beneficial (Kaplow 1972, 27; Geremek 1994, 232–233).

One nineteenth-century writer used biology, if erroneously, to justify huge disparities in income and wealth; William Sumner Graham argued that if people disliked the idea of the survival of the fittest, they must be prepared for the alternative, the survival of the unfittest. He disputed whether socialism, "a plan for nourishing the unfittest and yet advancing in civilization," was possible (Sumner quoted in Hofstadter [1944] 1959, 57–58). If one was looking for an apologist to justify large disparities in wealth, Sumner could satisfy: "The millionaires are a product of natural selection, acting on the whole body of men to pick out those who can meet the requirement of certain work to be done....It is because they are thus selected that wealth—both their own and that entrusted to them—aggregates under their hands." There was no point whining about the outcome, since it was beneficial: "They get high wages and live in luxury, but the bargain is a good one for society. There is the intensest competition for their place and occupation. This assures us that all who are competent for this function will be employed in it, so that the cost of it will be reduced to the lowest terms (Sumner [1914] 1971b, 90)."

There was room for middle-class citizens, such as Sumner's "Forgotten Man." This character was a responsible individual, who made his way through life and provided for his family without recourse to government largesse. "The 'Forgotten Man' is the simple, honest laborer, ready to earn his living by productive work. We pass him by because he is independent, self-supporting, and asks no favors. He does not appeal to the emotions or excite the sentiments....Every particle of capital which is wasted on the vicious, the idle, and the shiftless is so much taken from the capital available to reward the independent and productive laborer (Sumner 1969, I:477)."

One ramification of Sumner's ideas was that "Every law or institution which protects persons at the expense of capital makes it easier for persons to live and to increase the number of consumers of capital while lowering all the motives to prudence and frugality by which capital is created. Hence every such law or institution tends to produce a large population, sunk in misery. All poor laws and eleemosynary institutions and expenditures have this tendency." Such misguided laws, therefore, harmed the general standard of living by, to use a twenty-first-century concept, "enabling" the poor to live and procreate. In a sense, Sumner saw a relatively fixed economic pie and wanted to reduce the denominator in order to maintain or increase the per-capita slices (Sumner [1914] 1971a, 27–28).

Sumner viewed the accumulation of wealth as a reflection of and reward for personal merit, so millionaires demonstrated a natural outcome of natural selection. Thorstein Veblen, on the other hand, mocked the wealthy business class, painting them as predators and moral delinquents in his *Theory of the Leisure Class.* Veblen's barbed wit was certainly provocative: "The tendency of the pecuniary life is, in a general way, to conserve the barbarian temperament, but with the substitution of fraud and prudence, or administrative ability, in place of the predilection for physical damage that characterizes the early barbarian." Richard Hofstadter explained that for Veblen, "the process of selection, under the conditions of modern society, has caused the aristocratic and bourgeois virtues—'that is to say the destructive and pecuniary traits'—to be found among the upper classes, and the industrial virtues, the peaceable traits, largely among 'the classes given to mechanical industry (Hofstadter [1944] 1959, 153–154; Veblen [1899] 1945, 237–240).'"

The Church's Example

In western Europe, the Catholic Church was the paramount institution for centuries. Although medieval people may not have asked the modern-day question, "What would Jesus do," the church's power and wealth posed vexing questions. Given that the church was an avenue for advancement for ambitious, not always scrupulous, young men and its significant role in the economy, were church leaders more ethical with regard to its wealth-holding than the maturing merchant and trading class?

The church bureaucracy's growing complexity and power often resulted in officials succumbing to the temptation of unearned acquisition of wealth. In addition to potential corruption, there was a likelihood of growing inefficiency that inhered in most complex organizations. The Byzantine process, replete with outstretched palms needing to be greased, resembled trips to nineteenth-century Chicago city hall or immersion in 1930s Soviet bureaucracy. If a corporation knew it faced repeated interaction with the papal government, it could engage a professional resident proctor to deal with the big bureaucracy. In an interesting facet of ethical interpretation, selling church offices (simony), for example, could be seen as a pro quid pro and, "in the eyes of the eleventh century as a sale and hence identified as the heresy of simony. Similarly the established tradition of making a gift to a monastery upon the entry of a new member…had henceforth to be called into question and its legitimacy examined (Little 1978, 31; see also Lynch 1976, 61–75)."

The combination of coins and church desire to accumulate such led to some pretty harsh depictions. Artists portrayed the greedy priest or church official as an ape defecating coins. Sigmund Freud noted the connection between money and excrement: "Dreams with an intestinal stimulus throw light in an analogous fashion on the symbolism involved in them, and at the same time confirm the connection between gold and faeces which is also supported by copious evidence from social anthropology (Freud 1955, 403)."[4]

Well before Martin Luther, critics excoriated Catholic leaders for their preoccupation with wringing money from their property and from their parishioners. The Catholic Church embraced forerunners of commodification. The concept of purgatory inspired sixteen-century priest Johann Tetzel, a contemporary and bête noire of Martin Luther, to allegedly coin the jingle, "Sobald der Pfenning im Kasten klingt, die Selle aus dem Fegfeuer springt (As soon as the coin in the coffer rings, the soul from purgatory springs)," to inspire sinners to avoid purgatory. A Benedictine monk frequently warned church officials of the dangers of avarice among the clergy; he urged the officials to "get rid of money," because "Christ and money" were incompatible. In the rankings of vices, avarice was gaining parity with pride. With all of the upheaval, the tensions arising from the profit economy within medieval society triggered a "spiritual crisis" needing to be dealt with. Christians often "found occasional release" by "pillaging" Jews (Cox 1999, no page numbers; *Beggars All: Reformation & Apologetics* n.d., no page numbers; Little 1978, 36, 41).

The church was wealthy. People wishing to join the order were often knights with wealth; they "abandoned" their wealth to, say, a Benedictine monastery. Although a man relinquished control of his wealth, he still consumed off of it (along with his fellow monks); in a sense, the Benedictines had their salvation and ate it, too. What such entrants gave up was, "not his wealth but his power." Religious reformers considered the Benedictines hypocritical in not renouncing comfortable lifestyles based upon wealth, but the Benedictines "saw no contradiction between their own wealth and their own poverty. What they meant by poverty was poverty of spirit, or humility."

The monks, to be sure, helped the poor, but they were not reticent about spending wealth upon the liturgy and buildings. They often maintained a superior standard of living relative to the peasants. Stephen of Muret explained to a prospective monk that there was a choice to be made between the rude standard of living at Muret or a life at a Benedictine monastery: "Look you can go into any monastery whatever, where you'll find huge buildings and first-rate cuisine all properly prepared and served on time. There you will find animals and great expanses of arable land, but here you will find only the cross and poverty."

There were occasional lay people, though, who put the monks to shame. In the late twelfth century, Waldes, a merchant in Lyons, decided to give away most of his wealth to the poor. He ensured that his daughters were provided for, presumably in modest circumstances. He made restitution to those to whom he lent money at interest. He not only gave his money to the poor, he helped distribute food to needy people.

To contemporary observers, the friars and monks were, in a sense, merchants interested in gaining a surplus (the friars may have seen themselves as do modern-day people, who commend themselves for working for nonprofits). People commented on the Dominicans, spending so much money at Dunstable and collecting revenue through indulgences. A priest even had the temerity to criticize St. Francis, by calling him "an avaricious merchant (Little 1978, 45–46, 81, 121, 201)."

John Wesley and the Problem of Wealth

John Wesley not only founded a denomination but also gave shrewd advice regarding personal finance. Wesley believed wealthy people could attain heaven, but that their path was strewn with a different set of temptations. The wealthy had responsibilities tied to their wealth. "And [Wesley] lived it too. In the year Wesley earned today's equivalent of $1.4 million, he lived on 2% of this income and gave 98% of it away. He did. He 'tithed' 98%. In fact, during Wesley's lifetime he earned the equivalent of $30 million. When he died, [he] left behind only a few miscellaneous coins and a couple of silver spoons. He had given away the rest. He practiced what he preached (Drury n.d., no page numbers)."[5]

Wesley, Benjamin Franklin, P.T. Barnum, Andrew Carnegie, and John D. Rockefeller all left behind advice on both how to attain and how to use wealth. The main rule was simple and eternal: live beneath your means. Wesley gave a sermon entitled, "The Use of Money." His ideas are worth examining in detail. The condensed version goes as follows: "Gain all you can. Save all you can. Give all you can." Naturally he went into greater detail than those three short phrases, but the phrases have the virtue of being easily remembered.

With regard to gaining all you can, Wesley was not granting carte blanche. Gainers should not be engaged in sinful trade, nor should they sully legitimate trade with cheating, lying, or "conformity to some custom which [is] not consistent with a good conscience." In the pursuit of gain, the gainer must not hurt their neighbors, including selling harmful substances nor obtaining the neighbor's property by dubious mean. Sellers could not price their goods below the market price or attempt to "ruin our neighbour's trade." Thus you should, "Gain all you can by honest industry."

At this point, the reader might have thought that Wesley was simply discussing business ethics, but business ethics was intertwined with how one spent the gains. You could "save all you can" by a frugal and modest, not to say ascetic, lifestyle. In today's world, businesses pay attention to prospective and current employees' spending patterns, including checking credit ratings. An indebted employee, especially if the debt was incurred by consumption expenditures, might be tempted to embezzle or act in an unethical manner. Wesley exhorted his listeners to, "Lay out nothing to gratify the pride of life, to gain the admiration or praise of men.... While you are purchasing anything which men use to applaud, you are purchasing more vanity." Such expenditures Wesley likened to, "literally throwing your money into the sea."

Wesley's phrase, "give all you can," simplifies his nuanced advice. He does not advocate spontaneous, unthinking giving. He establishes a hierarchy: "First, provide things needful for yourself, food to eat, raiment to put on, whatever nature moderately requires for preserving the body in health and strength." Then you provide the same for your dependents. If a surplus remains, "do good to them that are of the household of faith." Finally, if there still remains a surplus, "as you have opportunity, do good unto all men." A secular view of the last two priorities might restate them as, "give locally, then globally." By giving all you can, you are not being virtuous as you are simply, "'render[ing] unto God the things that are God's' not only by what you give to the poor, but also by that which you expend in providing things needful for yourself and your household." Near the conclusion of "The Use of Money," Wesley reiterates this point: "'Render unto God,' not a tenth, not a third, not half, but all that is God's, be it more or less…in such a manner, that you may give a good account of your stewardship when ye can be no longer stewards….So 'laying up in store for yourselves a good foundation against the time to come, that ye may attain eternal life (Wesley n.d., Sermon 50, no page numbers).'"[6]

Theories of Just Income and Wealth Distributions

Income and wealth disparities are controversial topics, and people hold strong opinions on the sources of such disparities. Economists attribute disparities to various factors, especially differences in endowed attributes. Some people have more intellectual or physical abilities than other people. Other people have determination or the ability to delay gratification. Each of us has a mix of advantages and disadvantages; to be sure, some people have such severe disadvantages that they are incapable of competing in a market economy. There is an element of chance involved with abilities; A 7′2″ male who can dunk a basketball can make millions of dollars, but he would have found such a skill virtually worthless in 1900. Changes in technology boosted the marketability and incomes of athletes, actors, and musicians.

Business ethicist Richard Chewning identifies an "old ethic" that views inequality as "a positive reality." "From the perspective of the 'old values,' one person's advantage, gained from being superior in ability or position, was *not* to be equated or associated with the lesser condition of another person….The advantage of one person, according to this view, does not create the disadvantage or come at the expense of someone else, per se." The old ethic also understood that every person faces an inner struggle to reconcile good and bad traits. "It was concerned with accentuating the good (recognizing, encouraging, and rewarding individual creativity) and with limiting the bad (capacity for inappropriate self-centeredness, self-will, and greed which are problems of both the advantaged and disadvantaged) through a market mechanism in which competition penalizes inappropriate behavior" and emphasized individual responsibility and accountability, so "the competent climb the economic ladder." In contrast, "the new ethic… sees humanity as only good and inequality as dehumanizing. Here, advantages realized through inequality are viewed as undeserved. Inequality is a negative aspect of reality (Chewning 1984, 7–8)."

In the hands of Benjamin Franklin, virtue assumed a pragmatic self-interest; Franklin believed that incentives mattered, so society should take care to establish incentives that encouraged hard work and thrift and not indolence. He therefore argued that the English poor laws created incentives for people to be lazy, although given the poor laws' stinginess, it was unclear whether such incentives truly motivated people to be lazy. Eighteenth-century French beggars may have lacked the requisite calorie intake to do anything more than sit and beg. In a similar vein, Franklin worried that government provision of aid to the aged and ill would erode people's incentive to save when young (Frey 2009, 27–28).[7]

What are just distributions of income and wealth? Modern theories of just income and wealth distributions emphasize end-state or process approaches. A theory of distributive justice is a set of principles with which we can judge the fairness of a particular *distribution* of economic well-being. An end-state theory of distributive justice looks at the fairness of the outcome; that is, the actual distribution of income. There are two main end-state theories: utilitarian and Rawlsian. End-state theories do *not* necessarily imply that everyone receives the same income.

The utilitarian theory asserts that the fairest outcome is one that makes the sum of the utilities of all individuals in the society as large as possible. Redistribution from one person to another should take place until the added satisfaction from the last dollar spent by each individual is the same. This does not imply equal incomes (if people's utility functions differ). A difficulty with the utilitarian approach is that no one knows their own or another person's utility function; each individual has their own unique utility function. Economist Kenneth Arrow used an example of two persons, one "satisfied with water and soy flour, while another was desperate without pre-phylloxera clarets and plover's eggs." Should society indulge the latter's preferences possibly at the former's expense, or "an individual who is incapable of deriving much pleasure from anything, whether because of psychological or physical limitations. He may well be the worst-off individual and, therefore, be the touchstone of distribution policy, even though he derives little satisfaction from the additional income (Arrow 1973, 254; Mill 1950, 1–80)." More generally, does an educated person require more or less income to have the same utility than a less educated person or does a depressed person need more or less income to have the same utility as an optimistic person?

The Rawlsian theory of fairness holds that the fairest distribution is one that gives the least well-off person the largest possible income, subject to certain conditions. Philosopher John Rawls suggests a realm where people are under a "veil of ignorance" with regard to their eventual social and economic positions. Suppose a group of fetuses in their various wombs are able to convene in one womb—a womb with a view—to discuss their life chances. They may know the expected wealth and the statistical variance for their group, but no individual fetus knows its particular outcome. According to Rawls, they might agree to a simple insurance scheme, whereby the fetuses who later realized good life opportunities would compensate those not so fortunate (Rawls 1970, 136–142; Frey 2009, 180–182). End-state theories now recognize that increasing redistribution reduces the incentive to produce output. Thus, there is likely a trade-off between redistribution and economic efficiency and the extent of the redistribution should take account of the loss in efficiency.

With respect to taxation, utilitarianism and Rawlsian justice allow for redistribution of income. "This result is characteristic of theories that emphasize justice as impartiality. Notice again, that the argument is not that redistributive taxation is in the interest of those who must pay the taxes, but rather that taxpayers should acknowledge that, looked at impartially, it is fair that they should pay. What motivates people to support such taxation is not, on this kind of account, rational self-interest, but some form of moral concern (Hausman and McPherson 1993, 710)."

A process theory of distributive justice looks at the fairness of the method used to generate the income distribution. Philosopher Robert Nozick argues that no end-state theory can be valid and that the fairest income distribution is based on private property rights and voluntary exchange. Nozick's argument starts with a hypothetical income distribution deemed best and then supposes that everyone decides to go to, say, a new rock performer's concert. As a result, the rock artist's income rises. Because the decision to attend the concerts was voluntary, Nozick asserts that the new distribution of income is also fair. Nozick might view the high incomes earned by people protected by licensing laws or other barriers to labor mobility as unjust, as well as overprotection from patent laws. Recent research suggests that many people in the top 1 percent of the income distribution get artificially high incomes because of such protective and discriminatory laws (Nozick 1974, 149–231).[8]

As Economists See It

George Stigler recognized economists' sparse discussion of income distribution: "For the century from Smith to Jevons, economists were correspondingly discreet in their discussions of income distribution. It may be supposed that Smith thought income distribution was a matter for markets to determine when he said, 'To hurt in any degree the interest of any one order of citizens, for no other purpose but to promote that of some other, is evidently contrary to that justice and equality of treatment which the sovereign owes to all the different orders of his subjects (Stigler 1982, 11).'"

Where income equality was discussed, the classical economists usually cited two baneful effects: the disincentive to thrift and work and the deleterious effects upon population (a la Malthus) under an income-redistribution scheme. The classical economists proved wrong; the very success of laissez-faire in raising living standards while increasing the population broke down the second argument (although today's conservatives still cite the effects of welfare payments upon the population of the poor) (Hirsch 1976, 164).[9]

During the 1970s, some economists predicted that the American economy was nearing a "steady state," whereby the stock of wealth would not grow, Economist Paul David wrote that such an event would undermine the argument justifying disparities in wealth holdings because such disparities inspired economic growth. The ethical outcome, then, would be a stronger argument for equal shares of income and wealth. "The steady state would make fewer demands on our environmental resources, but much greater demands on our moral resources (David 1979, 70)."

The attack on large disparities in income distribution received reinforcement in the latter half of the nineteenth century with the rise of marginal utility analysis. Taxation on the basis of minimal sacrifice (the old cliché "a dollar means less to a rich woman than a poor one") became cloaked with economic respectability: the transfer of a dollar from a rich person to a poor person raised the overall level of utility of society under certain—seemingly plausible—assumptions. However, the economists may have been responding to the clamor by the public for defenses of income policies.

Kenneth Arrow pointed out that "If each individual revealed his productivity, it would be possible to achieve a perfect reconciliation of justice and incentives; namely tax each individual according to his ability, not according to his actual output." The difficulty in such a scheme is that individuals would then have an incentive to pretend to be of lower ability than they actually were (Arrow 1973, 260).

For most people, happiness is not predicated on large amounts of wealth. Past a certain subsistence level plus some amenities, additional income and wealth have what economists term "diminishing marginal returns." People gain happiness not only from income and wealth but also from a sense of connectedness, peace of mind, and simple pleasures (Lane 2000, 77–82; Mill 1950, 8–15).[10]

One big ethical problem with government-mandated redistribution is the very act of coercion. A commentator observed, "There is a difference, for example, between giving to the poor because I want to, and giving to the poor because I am required to do so through taxation, even though the consequences are exactly the same (Hay [1989] 2004, 136)." Philosopher Ronald Dworkin coined a slogan, "A more equal society is a better society even if its citizens prefer inequality." An economist labeled this sentiment as, "moralistic aggression." Not all altruists were quite willing participants. "Some 'Robin Hood' altruists, however, seek to escape from paying their full share of the ultimate cost of a reform because it exceeded their benefit. Here we confront the 'limousine liberal,' who supported such causes as busing for racial integration and constructing low-income housing projects in more affluent neighborhoods—but not for his own children and not in his own neighborhood." Morris Silver commented, "Obviously, 'Robin Hood' altruism and 'limousine liberalism' are partial, selective, and hypocritical; but they are also genuine to the extent that reform passage costs (in both time and cash), and tax costs are voluntarily borne by the donor (Silver 1980, 8–9; Hirshleifer 1987, 253)."

Silver provides an explanation of why some wealthy people advocate coercing other wealthy people to provide for the poor: "Assume that the satisfaction of a rich person depends on the satisfaction of the poor, but not on the satisfaction of other rich people." When a rich person donates money to charity, that person gets some personal satisfaction but bears the entire cost. If, instead, the rich person can get the government to collect taxes from other rich people, then the greater amounts given to the poor give satisfaction to the original rich donor but the cost is spread among many. "Thus, he might be unwilling to donate the $1 to charity (the satisfaction being less than the grief), but very willing to vote for the $1 tax (the satisfaction is bigger than in the charity case, and therefore can be greater than the grief) (Silver 1980, 8; Goldfarb 1970, 995)." Is it ethical, however, for the rich man to vote to levy an unwelcome tax upon other rich people, even for a worthwhile cause? Then again, this may be a coordination problem, where all rich people face the same dilemma and therefore may collectively vote for the tax.

In a complex society, there can be advantages from state-provided charity. Religious groups in small communities often have sufficient information to identify needy individuals and worthwhile causes, but in a large community, such information may be difficult to obtain. Charitable organizations may be a halfway solution between individual giving and state-enforced giving. Presumably there can be differing support for state-enforced charitable giving among smaller and larger communities. For donors, "indirect charity also obviates the need for a painful exposure to the needy"; scholar Juan Luis Vives depicted a scene in 1526, whereby donors had to walk between two lines of supplicants, many of whom suffered from disgusting physical afflictions. He advocated a new form of public charity and asked, "Do you think they [the potential donors] can all be so made of iron that they would not be disturbed, fasting as they are, at the sight (Silver 1980, 5–6)?"

To some degree, calls for significant forced income redistribution occurred as the individual slices of the economic pie grew larger; increasing per-capita gross domestic product (GDP) did not quell the sentiment. Herbert Spencer quipped, "the more things improve the louder become the exclamations about their badness." Silver contemplated upon a second aspect of the paradox: the demand for poverty program arose as real incomes soared and, "despite the absence of pressing demands or powerful lobbying groups among the poor themselves!" Silver quoted Lawrence Friedman, who observed that the demand for anti-poverty programs "did *not* boil up out of demands of special-interest groups, such as the poor (Spencer 1891, 1; Silver 1980, 10–11, 37–38)."

Modern-Day Disparities in Income and Wealth

Income and wealth distributions are based on earnings and wealth in a given year. Income and wealth distributions provide snapshots, but politicians and activists focus on such distributions. The so-called 1%ers (with respect to income) of today are unlikely to be there a few years from now. An individual's income and wealth fluctuate along a life cycle, typically peaking in a person's mid-life. As families move along their life cycle, they tend to have higher incomes and to accumulate more wealth. Thus a young family may appear poorer in terms of income and wealth than an older family even though when the younger family reaches the same age as the older family it has the exact same income and wealth as the older family had at that age. A simulation based on a nation with identical families except for their age yields wealth and income Lorenz curves with degrees of inequality that are somewhat similar to those in the United States.

Poverty is defined as having an income less than the government calculated poverty index. In the United States, poverty is essentially relative and not absolute, as incomes at the poverty level afford a level of consumption much greater than that of many people in the world. Such reality, of course, does not deny that it hurts to be impoverished in America. The irony is that as absolute poverty in the United States shrank, interest in redistribution seemed to rise.

Absolute poverty occurs when people struggled just to survive. Parents worried not about credit card debt but how to allay the chronic cries of their hungry children. They faced significantly higher mortality rates for themselves and their children. American producers were so successful that absolute poverty diminished and the American way of life proved irresistible to many people around the world. Writer Isabel Lundberg identified American military personnel as "agent[s] of social change," who were revolutionaries in inciting demand for "the wrist watch, fountain pen, cigarettes, flashlight, chocolate bars, chewing gum, cameras, pocket knives, pills to kill pain, vaccines to save lives, hospital beds with clean sheets, hand soap and shaving soap, gadgets and gewgaws of every description, the jeep, the truck and *white bread* [italics hers]." She wrote that Americans took white bread in supermarkets for granted, but the reality was that both white bread and supermarkets were emblematic for many people outside the United States. "Very few Americans, picking and choosing among the piles of white bread in a supermarket, have ever appreciated the social standing of white bread elsewhere in the world. To be able to afford white bread is a dream that awaits fulfillment for billions of the world's population. To afford it signifies that one enjoys all the comforts of life (Lundberg 1948, 39–40; Deaton 2018, A27)."

An individual's income depends on the factors of production she owns and the prices paid for these factors. Wages are the largest source of most people's income. Wages differ between jobs and this partially accounts for disparities in incomes. Since the 1980s the demand for highly educated workers increased. Meanwhile, the supply of highly educated workers increased relatively slowly—policies implemented during the 1970s to reduce the "oversupply" of highly educated workers had an unintended effect. It is no surprise that wages of highly educated workers rose dramatically in the 1980s. Concurrently, in many OCED (Organisation for Economic Co-operation and Development) countries, a large influx of young workers occurred, depressing wages for younger, less skilled workers (*Economist* July 24, 1993, 71).

With respect to individuals' incomes, people are endowed with different attributes. These disparities are also part of the reason people's incomes differ. People's choices also contribute to the skewedness of the income distribution. The amount of work an individual chooses to supply often increases with the wage paid. We note that most professional people with their high per-hour earnings amplify their incomes by choosing to work significantly more hours per year than the typical manufacturing worker. Wealthier families choose to leave higher bequests. Most people inherit nothing or very small amounts; a very few inherit vast amounts. Such disparities contribute to the skewed distribution of wealth. One other factor looms large. Assortative mating means that people tend to marry within their own socioeconomic class. There are very few Cinderella stories where the Prince marries a drudge. Assortative mating maintains or increases the disparities in income and distribution of inherited wealth (Cowen 2014, no page numbers).[11]

A variation of assortative mating with regard to marriage occurs in the work force. People with higher abilities tend to "mate" with similarly skilled people. Instead of people of varying abilities being randomly thrown together, high ability match with high ability and low ability match with low ability. Because working with low ability may degrade a high-ability person's productivity, such matching redounds doubly against low-ability people: they lack ability and their lack is amplified by having to work with other low-ability people. This matching in the labor force exacerbates income differences, as well as job satisfaction (Seabright 2004, 200).

CEO Pay

Americans have expressed varying levels of concern regarding accelerating Chief Executive Officer (CEO) pay. CEO pay increases outpaced that of most Americans (with the possible exception of entertainers and professional sports athletes); in fact, CEO pay rose proportionally faster than the second-highest-paid executives of Business Roundtable firms. Two researchers reported figures showing that average CEO pay increased from $750,000 to $1.2 million between 1987 and 2001; the increase was 3.4 percent compounded annually. The Democratic Congress of 1993 decided to tax CEO pay in response to labor and other groups' protests over CEO pay. Congress levied higher top tax rates—aimed at CEOs but affecting other high-earning Americans—and limited the executive compensation that could be written off as expenses. Managers and boards of directors quickly shifted executive compensation toward stock options... just in time for the stock market boom of the 1990s (Englander and Kaufman 2004, 432–435).

What were CEOs being paid for? CEO compensation was difficult to distinguish from the rest of the management team and labor's contributions. Daniel Kahneman described how "luck plays a large role, the quality of leadership and management practices cannot be inferred reliably from observations of success." Even if you knew a particular CEO was exceptionally astute, "you still would be unable to predict how the company will perform with much better accuracy than the flip of a coin." Those CEOs and companies lauded in Tom Peters' and Robert Waterman Jr.'s *In Search of Excellence* saw their average profitability plummet after being identified. *Fortune's* "Most Admired Companies" was also a poor predictor, as "firms with the worst ratings went on to earn much higher stock returns than the most admired firms." Kahneman's evidence suggested that investors should run away from CEOs anointed by the business press or with "prestigious press awards." Researchers discovered that "firms with award-winning CEOs subsequently underperform, in terms both of stock and of operating performance. At the same time, these CEOs' compensation increased." Why? One explanation was that such CEOs begin spending more time writing books and sitting on outside boards than tending to their business (Kahneman [2011] 2013, 207, 258; Peters and Waterman 1982).

CEOs were seeking to attain such wealth as would ensure their families' fortunes for generations, just as earlier industry leaders had. There was a big difference, however, in that the Rockefellers and Carnegies had created their wealth; CEOs largely managed the wealth of their shareholders (Englander and Kaufman 2004, 439, 441).

High Price of Being Poor

In the United States, at least, it is expensive to be poor. This statement is not meant flippantly. People should realize that being poor in the United States is an uphill fight. The urban poor in the United States rarely have convenient access to a big discount store, such as K-Mart or Walmart.

Even in the early 1960, some researchers understood that the poor faced disadvantages in the marketplace. David Caplovitz examined various aspects of the economics of low-income Americans during the Kennedy administration. During the postwar period, the poor in America enjoyed material gains with the rest of the population. Rural poor people got electrification and indoor plumbing, especially during the decade after 1945. Almost all American households owned a television by 1960. Caplovitz observed that low-income families purchased major durable goods as a way of demonstrating they were making "some progress toward the American dream of success." For Caplovitz, instead of Thorstein Veblen's "conspicuous consumption" to flaunt wealth and social standing, "it might be said that the lower classes today are apt to engage in *compensatory consumption* [italics his]."[12]

In the early 1960s, low-income people in urban areas did not suffer from a lack of vendors selling consumer durable goods. These retailers, however, often charged higher prices for lower-quality goods compared with Americans in more prosperous neighborhoods. In the 1960s, few, if any, people with low incomes had bank credit or credit cards. The credit terms offered by the retailers in low-income neighborhoods were confusing, even for consumers with substantial education. One professor examined credit terms of leading department stores catering to middle-class customers and found that the "cash price was practically the same in the various stores, but that there were wide variations in the credit terms leading to sizeable differences in the final cost to the consumer."

Low-income customers are greater credit risks than middle-class buyers. The retailers and door-to-door salespeople have to develop skills to determine which buyers have lower risk of default. To stay in business, the retailers have to charge more; how they charge more can be a flexible choice. Generally, the retailers sell poorer-quality goods with a higher markup; such a strategy would not work in more prosperous neighborhoods. "This results in the irony that the people who can least afford the goods they buy are required to pay high prices relative to quality, thus receiving a comparatively low return for their consumer dollar." Although Caplovitz attributes the vendors' ability to get away with such a strategy to their "captive" market, an economist would question his assertion. If such a strategy is profitable enough to make the risk-adjusted profit rate above the market return, other retailers would move in; entry into such a retail market does not require much capital. The merchants indicated that selling goods was not a challenge, but assessing the risk was the key (Caplovitz 1963, 12–14, 18).

Since some of the lower-income customers understood that they were paying more for less, why did they? Caplovitz thought that "some family heads felt that it was easier to buy on credit than to save and pay cash. They made it plain that they were referring to the discipline required for advance saving." Such thinking was not unique to lower-income families; William H. Whyte, who studied young, middle-class families in the 1950s, suggested that "the monthly installment fits neatly into their efforts to budget their income…that [young, middle-class families] too are more apt to think of the monthly payment rather than the cost of the merchandise or the cost of credit (Caplovitz 1963, 97; Whyte 1956, 171)."[13]

Caplovitz did not deny that merchants were providing a service for low-income buyers, but he bemoaned that fact that "the poorest risks are shunted to a special class of merchants who are ready to accept great risk. A close association probably exists between the amount of risk that merchants in this system are willing to accept and their readiness to employ unethical and illegal tactics." The end result was that "the very poor risks [are left] with twin options: of foregoing major purchases or of being exploited (Caplovitz 1963, 180)."

Ethics of Charity

Roman philosopher Seneca defined beneficium: "benevolent action which gives pleasure and finds pleasure in so doing…the reward of all the virtues is inherent in themselves." Voluntary altruistic contributions might not be supplied at a socially optimal level, which could be deemed a "market failure." One solution to such a market failure would be to get the government to coerce taxpayers to fund a greater amount of "altruistic production" in order to reach a socially "optimal level."

Wealthy people often exhibited their wealth by acts of largesse, although such acts were not always ones of pure altruism. The wealthy benefactors sought recognition, salvation, and favor from their bequests. In the ancient world, charity was voluntary, and legislators refused to make contributions compulsory until the late sixteenth century. A modern state might be a "relatively efficient producer of altruistic output. Thus, a portion of its tax receipts are really voluntary charitable contributions." Such an observation might meet with disagreement from taxpayers, who either did not want to contribute to charity in general or the charity targeted for government largesse. Then again, a government-provided charity could coordinate wealthy "benefactors," who were willing to donate, if "all the other rich people do (Silver 1980, xiv, 6–8)."

Medieval Christian thought may surprise modern-day students, especially those familiar with recent Papal announcements on economics and distribution: "Medieval moral theologians were united in holding that an essential part of the merit in charity to the poor was in its being voluntary....For this reason, there was considerable opposition within the Church to tithes....there was [also] strong opposition to provision of poor relief under state supervision and from tax revenues (Viner 1960, 52)."

Thomas Aquinas advised that unless there is dire need for helping the poor, the Church should use its surplus to purchase property and to create future ability to help the poor. If an individual gave beyond the level needed to sustain his or her lifestyle, then this might have been praiseworthy (especially if the individual is entering a religious order). St. Caesarius urged that people give alms to the extent that they did not jeopardize their ability to "sufficient nourishment and a simple wardrobe, avoiding in everything the expenditure and the luxury which corrupt (Viner 1978, 73–74)." Donated alms should not afford the beneficiary an easy life or a living standard above basic needs.

Morris Silver used Abraham Maslow's concept of a hierarchy of needs in discussing the development of a "taste" or preference for altruism. As societies become more affluent, the "demand for altruistic consumption" increases. He identifies classical Athens, Rome, Sung China, and Victorian England, as well as a preponderance of modern-day countries, as reflecting this taste (Silver 1983, 134).

St. Augustine and other fifth-century Christians began emphasizing storing one's treasures in Heaven. Proverbs 13:8 stated that "The ransom of a man's life is his wealth, but a poor man has no means of redemption." An early interpretation stated that a wealthy person could help "save his skin" in a way poor people could not. By the seventh century, though, people began interpreting the verse to mean that souls hung "tremulously between heaven and hell, in sore need of the comfort that only the gifts of the living could provide." A generous donation might succor such a tremulous soul (Brown 2015, 21–22).[14]

Attitudes toward the poor evolved in Europe. Merovingian society disdained the poor, and only after Greek Church fathers' teachings began to influence western Europeans did some forms of poverty gain sympathy and recognition as a spiritual value. In the eleventh and twelfth centuries, poverty increased and forced authorities and the well-to-do to begin considering responses. The Church emphasized charitable institutions and mendicant orders. A researcher remarked that charitable donations were a mixture of "carefully calculated" quid pro quos and compassion. The over-riding desire for salvation and the desire for public acclaim were rarely absent from such decisions. Such calculations were not far removed from those of wealthy Greeks funding liturgies or Roman landowners spreading largesse. Some Catholic and Protestant observers, though, recognized the potential demoralization stemming from indiscriminate spreading of alms. Begging became profitable, relative to working. Reformers bemoaned the sometimes indiscriminate giving that led to embezzlement, misappropriation, and misdirection of badly needed funds. Medieval charity was seen as "fundamentally flawed." The gradual spread of the idea of poverty as a spiritual value provided benefits for wealthy believers: "The poor knew their place and their role in the social order: they were there to enable others to buy salvation through alms-giving."

The realities of the involuntary poor of the Middle Ages, though, clashed with people who voluntarily chose poverty. If poverty were to have spiritual value, it had to be voluntary. Unfortunately, the vast majority of those in poverty did not choose their situation. For these involuntarily poor, the Church exhibited a somewhat different attitude. Fortunately for the wealthy, they could still earn salvation, not by becoming poor, but by practicing charity. Whether the poor recognized or appreciated being trod upon by wealthy people on the road to salvation remains unanswered. In the *Life of St Eligius*: "God could have made all men rich, but He wanted there to be poor people in this world, that the rich might be able to redeem their sins." Bronislaw Geremek observed that St. Eligius' words could be reversed: "God wanted there to be rich people in this world in order that they might help the poor (Geremek 1994, 17–18, 20)."

Christian charity was not a carte blanche; the idea regarding the "deserving poor" expressed so memorably in *My Fair Lady* was just as relevant in the early days of the Church. Able-bodied men might receive temporary aid, but eventually they had to find work. During the Middle Age, attitudes toward the poor changed. "It ceased to be a misfortune, a blessing of Providence, a virtue extolled by Christ in the Sermon on the Mount. It took on a more modern aspect of a crime, 'an assault by the poor upon society itself (Gilchrist 1969, 119).'"[15]

Medieval thinkers categorized poor people as worthy or unworthy, which Geremek argued confirmed the act of charitable giving as a contract, "with alms representing its material, prayer its spiritual, side. If only the fact of giving alms counts, charity was a one-sided affair, concerning no one but the giver." It became a disinterested, altruistic act. There was an alternative perspective that suggested if giving was intended to redeem one's sins or to induce the recipient to, "intercede with God on behalf of his benefactor and pray for him, the disinterested purity of the act of almsgiving was severely weakened." Separating the poor into "deserving" and "undeserving" proved a way to redress this weakness: "St. Thomas Aquinas condemns all those who solicit alms without being forced to do so by dire necessity (Geremek 1994, 47)."

There were, to be sure, some undeserving or opportunistic poor. France and Spain were countries with large numbers of poor people in the early modern era. "Thriftless" men and women made a career of beggary with some "run[ning] scams, communicating among themselves in a thieves' 'canting' language, counterfeiting illness and disease by the application of 'corrosives' and poisons to their own skins 'thereby to raise pitiful and odious sores and move the hearts of the goers by'" in order to get alms (Harrison [1807] 1968, 119–120, 183; Miller [2000] 2012, 38–39).

The Fathers sometimes proposed "almsgiving on a grand scale, and as an obligatory act of justice, not of pity or self-complacent benevolence." Jacob Viner observed that medieval theologians never claimed the poor had a right to largesse from the rich but that the rich had a responsibility to succor the poor. Notably, though, almsgiving was a palliative and not a solution to poverty. God countenanced rich and poor, "so that each could provide the other with the opportunity for the exercise of the virtues appropriate to them, charity for the rich, patience and humility for the poor." What the multitude of poor people thought of such conjectures went unmentioned (Lovejoy 1948, 304; Viner 1978, 20–21).

Industrialists and Philanthropy

Muhammad may have presaged Andrew Carnegie's admonition that "the man who dies rich, dies disgraced." One of the traditional Islamic stories described Muhammad near death and wondering how he could face Allah with all his remaining wealth. Whereupon his wife, A'isha, gave the money to charity. Sayyid Qutb, a modern-day Islamic, recognized that people inherently had a "natural love of wealth for its own sake." He quoted a passage from the *Qur'an*: "Verily the love of wealth is strong." Qutb believed the striving for prosperity and personal possessions was not only natural but also desirable, as it induced people to work hard. He also recognized the importance of property rights, citing the draconian punishments meted to thieves (Qutb 1953, 102–103; Zinbarg 2001, 54–55).

Carnegie and John D. Rockefeller devoted much of their fortunes to philanthropic endeavors. Rockefeller funded colleges for African-Americans and research that led to the eradication of hookworm. Carnegie endowed libraries throughout the United States. He funded a research foundation devoted to promoting world peace. Some of their funding, in retrospect, appears misspent. The Carnegie and Rockefeller institutes contributed to a Station for Experimental Evolution that eventually morphed into the Eugenics Records Office, but many Progressives were adherents of the eugenics movement and supported sterilization programs (Black 2003, 40, 93–94).

Rockefeller was renowned for donating hundreds of millions of dollars to various causes. A few people argued that he did so to curry favor among the public, but he gave consistently, before and after he was rich. Biographer Allan Nevins astutely observed that Rockefeller's donations were notable not so much for their scale but for the thoughtfulness and acumen devoted to choosing among options. Rockefeller and his son hired experts to analyze the requests for donations. They emphasized self-help endeavors and ongoing efforts to ameliorate conditions afflicting the poor. Nevins characterized their efforts, as being "of the highest value." Rockefeller acknowledged that, to some extent, the size of his fortune was a historical accident. Nevins suggested that rather than interpret Rockefeller's remark, "God gave me the money" as a reflection of arrogance, one should realize instead that Rockefeller saw his role as trustee of the money. The statement reflected a, "spirit of utter humility" and a responsibility to disburse the sums prudently; Nevin argued that the Rockefellers succeeded and that "gratitude is really due them (Nevins 1940, 2:712–713)."[16]

Carnegie, in the wake of the Homestead disaster, may have hoped his efforts to bolster world peace and endowed libraries would rehabilitate him in the public's eyes. Jonathan Hughes thought that blanket speculation concerning these men "deprives each man of his individuality, and anyhow, where is the *direct* evident evidence to support such a view," that they gave because of religious beliefs, guilty consciences, or to curry public favor (Hughes [1965] 1986, 432–433)?

Carnegie believed that the wealthy had a responsibility to help those less fortunate, although not by indiscriminate distribution of money. In his *The Gospel of Wealth*, he argued, "It were better for mankind that the millions of the rich were thrown into the sea than so spent as to encourage the slothful, the drunken, the unworthy." He continued by describing a man, who was a disciple of Herbert Spencer, yet gave 25 cents to a beggar on the street; Carnegie commented, "He only gratified his own feelings, saved himself from annoyance—and this was probably one of the most selfish and very worst actions of his life, for in all respects he is most worthy." He preferred to finance self-help projects, such as the famous Carnegie libraries he endowed. Carnegie publicly expressed that he was merely looking after the wealth he controlled; the wealth was a sort of "trust fund (Carnegie 1962, 26–29, 31–32)." Carnegie professed to believe that leaving large bequests to heirs was demoralizing; aside from a sufficiency, he argued that the money left in an estate should be taxed heavily. He fulfilled his belief and left modest inheritances to his wife and daughter (Carnegie 1962, 22–23; Sorvino 2014, no page numbers).

Carnegie believed that the very wealthy were better equipped to disburse money for the common good than if the money were in the hands of many semi-wealthy people making decisions or, heaven forbid, government legislators and bureaucrats. As with many successful people, he assumed the conceit that because he had a genius in one sphere, such genius was easily translated to another sphere: "the man of wealth thus becoming the mere trustee and agent for his poorer brethren, bringing to their service his superior wisdom, experience, and ability to administer, doing for them better than they would or could do for themselves (Carnegie 1962, 25)."

More recent benefactors included the Pritzker family of Chicago. The founding members of the family business immigrated from the Ukraine during the early decades of the twentieth century. They exhibited integrity. On one occasion Abram, patriarch of the family in America, went bust in a Florida land deal. Although he was not legally obligated to do so, Abram paid off his partners. Critics of the family called them wheeler-dealers, but the family rebutted that criticism by responding that they still owned the majority of assets they ever purchased. The family also chose not to invest in tobacco, alcohol, pharmaceuticals, and products that could be injurious to buyers. Unlike the stereotyped aggressive negotiating tactics, the Pritzkers described their approach to negotiation as, "Here's what we'll do—A, B, C. If you like, fine. If not, that's okay, too." Such sang froid makes for dull viewing, had the family's history been depicted in a television "reality show." The family, though, became well known for its ongoing charitable activities, especially in Chicago. They contributed to hospitals, educational institutions, and the like. Often these contributions were made quietly without wish for publicity (Darby 1986, 100–101, 104–107).

Although giving to charity is laudable, the opportunity cost of doing so is often neglected. Norman Gras makes the provocative statement that "There is much to indicate that many of us believe that the goal of business and wealth is charity, but this I would set down as a piece of mediaeval patristic and scholastic social philosophy. The primary goal of business is service to all classes of men here on this earth: it is the production of goods, services, and jobs for the largest number of persons in the most even flow and at the highest rate commensurate with continuity and advance. It involves highly intellectual processes and requires balanced judgments of rare power (Gras 1941, 57)." The question of what Bill Gates or Warren Buffet could have done instead with the money they devoted to charity is a worthwhile one to ponder.

Jacob Viner observed that the medieval scholars failed to consider the opportunity cost of giving alms to the poor, when such alms could have been used to improve the productivity of agriculture and manufacturing. The resulting increase in productivity might have benefited the poor by reducing the price of necessities and creating jobs (Viner 1978, 22–23).

Conclusion

How a person used their wealth was a reflection of their ethical beliefs. Some wealthy people chose to use their wealth to improve their business by providing better quality and lower priced goods and services as well as providing good jobs. Other business leaders used ostentatious donations to curry favor and to gain status, but late nineteenth-century business leaders, such as John D. Rockefeller and Andrew Carnegie, sought to do good and perhaps gain favor and status by helping people less fortunate instead of lavish buildings (although Carnegie, James Duke, Leland Stanford, Cornelius Vanderbilt, and Rockefeller endowed superb universities). Whether these nineteenth-century business leaders expiated any guilt from how they amassed their wealth is in the eye of the beholder. Quite likely, many of these business leaders did not seek expiation, as they may have felt blameless. Rockefeller and Carnegie appear to have acted from a sense of duty.

Notes

1. A clergyman claimed that "The labors of the poor give them health." In addition, this clergyman claimed that the rich with their dissipations often end up in ill-health (Viner 1972, 101).
2. This is similar to John Maynard Keynes somewhat flippant remark about the desirability of government spending on useless projects, such as pyramid building (Keynes 1936, 220).
3. John Locke also shared this view (Sedlacek 2011, 151). Some of the attitudes toward the disparity between rich and poor sound downright bizarre to twenty-first-century sensibilities, although twenty-first-century sensibilities would undoubtedly strike ancient Greeks, Romans, and Christians as equally bizarre.
4. Lester Little describes the ramifications of the growing use of cash (Little 1969, 283–287; 1971, 37).
5. One might compare Wesley's choices regarding wealth with modern-day television evangelists.
6. Pope Leo XIII and Aquinas urged disbursing one's wealth to help the poor, but they added an interesting stipulation: "no one is commanded to distribute to others that which is required for his own needs and those of his household; nor even to give away what is reasonably required to keep up becomingly his condition in life, 'for no one ought to live other than becomingly,'" before concluding, "It is duty, not of justice, but of Christian charity—a duty not enforced by human law (Pecci 1891, paragraph 22)." These attitudes resembled Wesley's.
7. For caloric intake, see Floud et al. (2011, 106–116); Fogel (2000, 76–77).
8. Nozick used the example of people paying to see Wilt Chamberlain play basketball (160–164). For barriers to entry, see Rothwell (2017, no page numbers); Kleiner (2014, no page numbers).
9. Historian Richard Tawney disputed that a trade-off existed between redistribution of income and output: "as though production and distribution were irreconcilable alternatives." He believed that the reduction in social tensions from redistributing income would actually boost output, "since standards of well-being are relative (Tawney [1931] 1964, 120–121)."

10. For a general discussion of happiness, see Fort (2008, 93). Studies lent some support to income's relationship with happiness (Kahneman [2011] 2013, 397). Ian Mitroff conducted a survey asking what gives employees meaning at work. The top response was "to realize one's full potential as a human being." The next two most chosen responses were "to do interesting work" and "to work in an ethical organization." Ranking fifth was how much money they made (Mitroff 2002, 40).
11. Highly educated people could contribute their mite to redressing skewed income and wealth distributions by marrying a high school dropout, but, of course, no one espouses such a policy.
12. David Caplovitz attributed "compensatory consumption" to Robert Merton.
13. Families that always bought on credit owned more appliances than families that paid only in cash (Caplovitz 1963, 97). Poor money management skills also play a role. A recent article in *The Atlantic* detailed how a staggeringly high proportion of even upper-middle-class Americans would have trouble meeting an unexpected $400 expense, such as a car repair (Gabler 2016, 52–63).
14. Note: other translations use, "The ransom of the soul of a man is his wealth."
15. Joannes Andreae rebutted this belief, "Poverty is not a kind of crime (Tierney 1959, 12)."
16. Allan Nevins provided a year-by-year account of Rockefeller's giving (Nevins 1953, 2:479).

Bibliography

Aquinas, Thomas. *Summa Theologiae* (New York, NY: Blackfriars, 1964). 60 vols.

Arrow, Kenneth. "Some Ordinalist-Utilitarian Notes on Rawls's Theory of Justice by John Rawls." *Journal of Philosophy* 70(9), May 1973, 245–263.

Beggars All: Reformation & Apologetics. n.d. "Did Tetzel Really Say 'As soon as the coin in the coffer rings, the soul from purgatory springs?'" http://beggarsallreformation.blogspot.com/2012/01/did-tetzel-really-say-as-soon-as-coin.html, viewed October 16, 2017, 11:27am).

Black, Edwin. *War against the Weak: Eugenics and America's Campaign to Create a Master Race* (New York, NY: Four Walls Eight Windows, 2003).

Brown, Peter. *The Ransom of the Soul: Afterlife and Wealth in Early Western Christianity* (Cambridge, MA: Harvard University Press, 2015).

Caplovitz, David. *The Poor Pay More: Consumer Practices of Low-Income Families* (New York, NY: Free Press of Glencoe, 1963).

Carnegie, Andrew. *The Gospel of Wealth and Other Timely Essays* (Cambridge, MA: Belknap Press of Harvard University Press, 1962).

Chewning, Richard. "Can Free Enterprise Survive Ethical Schizophrenia?" *Business Horizons* 27(2), March–April 1984, 5–11.
Cowen, Tyler. "Assortative mating and income inequality." *Economics*, January 27, 2014. http://marginalrevolution.com/marginalrevolution/2014/01/assortative-mating-and-income-inequality.html, viewed February 17, 2014.
Cox, Harvey. "The Market as God." *Atlantic*. March 1999, 18–23.
Darby, Edwin. *The Fortune Builders* (Garden City, NY: Doubleday, 1986).
David, Paul. "From Growth to the Millennium: Economics and the Transformation of the Idea of Progress." *Economics and Human Welfare: Essays in Honor of Tibor Scitovsky*, edited by Michael Boskin (New York, NY: Academic Press, 1979), 59–73.
Deaton, Angus. "The U.S. Can No Longer Hide from Its Deep Poverty Problem." *New York Times*, January 24, 2018, A27.
Drury, Keith. n.d. *John Wesley's "Trilateral."* http://www.drurywriting.com/keith/wesley.htm. Viewed September 14, 2015. No page numbers.
Dudden, F. Holmes. *The Life and Times of St. Ambrose* (Oxford: Clarendon Press, 1935). Vol. II.
Ecclesiasticus. https://www.kingjamesbibleonline.org/Ecclesiasticus-10-13/, viewed October 3, 10:15am.
Economist. "Rich man, poor man: The gap between high earners and the lowest paid has widened. Why?" July 24, 1993, 71.
Englander, Ernie and Allen Kaufman. "The End of Managerial Ideology: From Corporate Social Responsibility to Corporate Social Indifference." *Enterprise & Society* 5(3) 2004, 404–449.
Floud, Roderick, Robert W. Fogel, Bernard Harris, and Sok Chul Hong. *The Changing Body: Health, Nutrition, and Human Development in the Western World since 1700* (Cambridge: Cambridge University Press, 2011).
Fogel, Robert. *The Fourth Great Awakening & the Future of Egalitarianism* (Chicago, IL: University of Chicago Press, 2000).
Fort, Timothy. *Prophets, Profits, and Peace: The Positive Role of Business in Promoting Religious Tolerance* (New Haven, CT: Yale University Press, 2008).
Freud, Sigmund. *The Interpretation of Dreams*, translated by James Strachey (New York, NY: Basic Books, 1955).
Frey, Donald. *America's Economic Moralists: A History of Rival Ethics and Economics* (Albany, NY: State University of New York Press, 2009).
Gabler, Neal. "The Secret Shame of Middle-Class Americans: Nearly half of Americans would have trouble finding $400 to pay for an emergency. I'm one of them." *Atlantic*, May 2016, 52–63.
Geremek, Bronislaw. *Poverty: A History* (Oxford, UK: Blackwell, 1994).
Gilchrist, John. *The Church and Economic Activity in the Middle Ages* (London, UK: Macmillan, 1969).

Goldfarb, Robert. "Pareto Optimal Redistribution: Comment." *American Economic Review* 60(5), December 1970. 994–996.

Gras, Norman. "A New Study of Rockefeller." *Bulletin of the Business Historical Society* 15(4), October 1941, 49–58.

Harrison, William. *The Description of England*, edited by Georges Edelen (Ithaca, NY: Cornell University Press, [1807] 1968).

Hausman, Daniel and Michael McPherson. "Taking Ethics Seriously: Economics and Contemporary Moral Philosophy." *Journal of Economic Literature* 31(2), June 1993, 671–731.

Hay, Donald. *Economics Today: A Christian Critique* (Vancouver, BC: Regent College Publishing, [1989] 2004).

Hirsch, Fred. *Social Limits to Growth* (Cambridge, MA: Harvard University Press, 1976).

Hirshleifer, Jack. *Economic Behaviour in Adversity* (Chicago, IL: University of Chicago Press, 1987).

Hofstadter, Richard. *Social Darwinism in American Thought* (New York, NY: George Braziller [1944] 1959). Revised edition.

Hu, Jichuang. *A Concise History of Chinese Economic Thought* (Beijing, China: Foreign Languages Press, 1988).

Hughes, Jonathan. *The Vital Few: The Entrepreneur & American Economic Progress* (New York, NY: Oxford University Press, [1965] 1986). Expanded edition.

Kahneman, Daniel. *Thinking, Fast and Slow* (New York, NY: Farrar, Straus and Giroux, [2011] 2013).

Kaplow, Jeffrey. *The Names of Kings: The Parisian Laboring Poor in the Eighteenth Century* (New York, NY: Basic Books, 1972).

Keynes, John. *The General Theory of Employment, Interest and Money* (New York, NY: Harcourt, Brace, 1936).

Kleiner, Morris. "Why License a Florist?" *New York Times*, May 28, 2014, no pages. https://www.nytimes.com/2014/05/29/opinion/why-license-a-florist.html. Viewed March 4, 2018, 3:05pm.

Lane, Robert. *The Loss of Happiness in Market Democracies* (New Haven, CT: Yale University Press, 2000).

Little, Lester. *The Function of the Jews in the Commercial Revolution* (Todi, Italy: Presso l'Academia tudertina, 1969).

Little, Lester. "Pride Goes before Avarice: Social Change and the Vices in Latin Christendom." *American Historical Review* 76(1), February 1971, 16–49.

Little, Lester. *Religious Poverty and the Profit Economy in Medieval Europe* (Ithaca, NY: Cornell University Press, 1978).

Lovejoy, Arthur. "The Communism of St. Ambrose." *Essays in the History of Ideas* (Baltimore, MD: Johns Hopkins Press, 1948). 296–307.

Lundberg, Isabel. "World Revolution, American Plan." *Harper's Magazine*, CXCVII, December 1948, 38–46.

Lynch, Joseph. *Simoniacal Entry into Religious Life from 1000 to 1260* (Columbus, OH: Ohio State University Press, 1976).

Mill, John Stuart. "Utilitarianism." *Utilitarianism, Liberty, and Representative Government* (New York, NY: E.P. Dutton, 1950). 1–80.

Miller, Lee. *Roanoke: Solving the Mystery of the Lost Colony* (New York, NY: MJF Books, [2000] 2012).

Mitroff, Ian. "Spirituality at Work: The Next major Challenge in Management" In *Ethics and Spirituality at Work: Hopes and Pitfalls of the Search for Meaning in Organizations*, edited by Thierry Pauchant (Westport, CT: Quorum Books, 2002), 35–44.

Nevins, Allan. *John D. Rockefeller: The Heroic Age of American Enterprise* (New York, NY: Charles Scribner's Sons, 1940). 2 vols.

Nevins, Allan. *Study in Power: John D. Rockefeller, Industrialist and Philanthropist* (New York, NY: Charles Scribner's Sons, 1953). 2 vols.

Nozick, Robert. *Anarchy, State, and Utopia* (New York, NY: Basic Books, 1974).

Pecci, Pope Leo XIII. 1891. *Rerum Novarum*. vatican.va/content/leo-xiii/en/encyclicals/documents/hf_l-xiii_enc_15051891_rerum-novarum.html.

Peters, Thomas and Robert Waterman. *In Search of Excellence: Lessons from America's Best-Run Companies* (New York, NY: Harper & Row, 1982).

Qutb, Sayyid. *Social Justice in Islam* (Washington, DC: American Council of Learned Societies, 1953). [Name is listed as Sayed Kotb on title page.]

Rawls, John. *Theory of Justice* (Cambridge, MA: Harvard University Press, 1970).

Rothwell, Jonathan. "Myths of the 1 Percent: What Puts People at the Top." *New York Times*. November 17, 2017. https://www.nytimes.com/2017/11/17/upshot/income-inequality-united-states.html. Viewed March 4, 2018.

Schmidt, Thomas. *Hostility to Wealth in the Synoptic Gospels* (Sheffield, UK: JSOT Press, 1987).

Seabright, Paul. *The Company of Strangers: A Natural History of Economic Life* (Princeton, NJ: Princeton University Press, 2004).

Sedlacek, Tomas. *Economics of Good and Evil: The Quest for Economic Meaning from Gilgamesh to Wall Street* (Oxford, UK: Oxford University Press, 2011).

Silver, Morris. *Affluence, Altruism, and Atrophy* (New York, NY: New York University Press, 1980).

Silver, Morris. *Prophets and Markets: The Political Economy of Ancient Israel* (Boston, MA: Kluwer-Nijhoff, 1983).

Sorvino, Chloe. "The Gilded Age Family That Gave It All Away: The Carnegies." *Forbes*. July 8, 2014. https://www.forbes.com/sites/chloesorvino/2014/07/08/whats-become-of-them-the-carnegie-famiy/#640e20867b55, viewed September 30, 2019.

Spencer, Herbert. "From Freedom to Bondage." *A Plea for Liberty: An Argument against Socialism and Socialistic Legislation*, edited by Thomas McKay (London, UK: John Murray, 1891), 1–28. 2nd edition.

Stigler, George. "The Economist as Preacher." *The Economist as Preacher and Other Essays* (Chicago, IL: University of Chicago Press, 1982), 3–13.

Sumner, William. "The Challenge of Facts." *The Challenge of Facts and Other Essays* (New Haven, CT: Yale University Press, [1914] 1971a). 15–52.

Sumner, William. "The Concentration of Wealth: Its Economic Justification." *The Challenge of Facts and Other Essays* (New Haven, CT: Yale University Press, [1914] 1971b). 79–90.

Sumner, William. "The Forgotten Man." *Essays of William Graham Sumner* (Archon Books: 1969), I:466–496. 2 vols. Reprinted from Yale University Press version.

Tawney, Richard. *Equality* (London, UK: George Allen and Unwin, [1931] 1964).

Tierney, Brian. *Medieval Poor Law: A Sketch of Canonical Theory and Its Application in England* (Berkeley, CA: University of California Press, 1959).

Veblen, Thorstein. *The Theory of the Leisure Class: An Economic Study of Institutions* (New York, Viking Press, [1899] 1945).

Viner, Jacob. "The Intellectual History of Laissez Faire." *Journal of Law and Economics* 3(1), October 1960, 45–69.

Viner, Jacob. *The Role of Providence in the Social Order: an Essay in Intellectual History* (Philadelphia, PA: American Philosophical Society, 1972).

Viner, Jacob. *Religious Thought and Economic Society* (Durham, NC: Duke University Press, 1978).

Wesley, John. n.d. "The Use of Money." Sermon 50. *The Sermons of John Wesley. General Board of Global Ministries: The United Methodist Church.* Wesley.nnu.edu/john-wesley/the-sermons-of-john-wesley-1872-edition/sermon-50-the-use-of-money. No page numbers. October 31, 2019.

Whyte, William. "Budgetism: Opiate of the Middle Class." *Fortune* 53(5), May 1956, 133–137, 164, 166, 171–172.

Zinbarg, Edward. *Faith, Morals, and Money: What the World's Religions Tell Us about Money in the Marketplace* (New York, NY: Continuum, 2001).

CHAPTER 12

What About the Children?

Children are a *sui generis*. They have rights, but they are not assumed to have the same responsibilities as adults or to be capable of looking after their self-interest. Adults had duties toward children. Even most libertarians are willing to concede such. However, who should look after the child's interest: the state or the parents?

Adults treated children differently in the past. Children were often an economic liability for many years, and parents in poverty were hard pressed to care for, much less love, their children.[1] Two key issues revolve around children and business. Many businesspeople employed children in the past. As the prevalence of child labor diminished in the western world, many children began having discretionary income to spend. Businesspeople began offering goods and services for children; children became perfect vehicles (targets) for moral activists. What outraged moralists and inspired fear in the past, however, often draws guffaws today.

Children's vulnerability made them good vehicles for moral crusaders and entrepreneurs. Social scientist Karen Sternheimer distinguished between moral crusaders and moral entrepreneurs. Moral crusaders strove to get the public's attention to a perceived threat to society; they perceived themselves as fighting against evil and employed emotional arguments, often centering around the question, "What about the children?" Dangers to children emanated from food, technology, friends, adults, and so on. Sometimes young people were both victims and villains, such as the juvenile delinquents made famous in America (or, the "Teddy Boys" in Great

D. G. Surdam, *Business Ethics from the 19th Century to Today*,
https://doi.org/10.1007/978-3-030-37169-2_12

Britain in the 1950s) during the postwar years. In a public debate, one was hard pressed to argue against protecting children, so the moral crusaders were essentially shooting fish in the political barrel. Moral entrepreneurs often possessed charisma; in addition, Sternheimer thought moral entrepreneurs are "more focused on potential personal gains than moral crusaders (Sternheimer 2015, 8–9)."

The Precarious Lives of Children

Children were not always exalted, nor were they seen as "special." Given the precarious balance between mouths and available calories throughout much of human history, children could even be perceived as economic albatrosses. Unless your child was a prodigy of some sort or ridiculously good-looking and able to perform a soft-shoe routine or some other entertainment activity, it took decades for him or her to become a net economic gain for the family unit. In addition, doting upon a child was to accept a high risk for emotional devastation, given child mortality rates (if you waited a year for the baby to survive, the odds of premature death went down considerably but were still higher than modern-day parents would countenance). Children, though, provided a relatively reliable source of retirement "income." Today, of course, we rely upon government-sponsored retirement income—ironically based upon the productivity of later generations of children turned adults.[2] Ultimately, what our ancestors were confronting were opportunity sets that were much more constrained than what the typical twenty-first-century American parent faces. These severely limited opportunity sets induced behavior on the part of our ancestors that would shock and outrage present-day sensibilities. One should, however, judge the past to a large degree by what was possible in the past, not against the more pristine situation of today.[3] Given our knowledge of childhood development, children of the poor were likely not to be merely physically stunted or wasted but also intellectually diminished. Descriptions of early childhood suggested that many children were malnourished with repercussions upon mental development; parents, too, may not have interacted much with their infants. As advanced a country as France was as the ancien régime waned, a significant proportion of the population received barely enough calories for a career in begging (Floud et al. 2011, 106–116; Fogel 2000, 76–77). One of the triumphs of nineteenth- and twentieth-century free markets was raising living standards sufficiently to greatly reduce these maladies and mortalities; parents today have relatively little likelihood of having to bury a child. Most children in the economically advanced countries are sufficiently healthy that their stature exceeds that of their ancestors; in addition, adequate nutrition helps to increase their intellectual development and ability to fight disease.

Parents treated children very differently in the past. Fidgety children could reduce their mothers' productivity, so women sometimes resorted to giving their narcotics to their children to calm them. Such behavior was common in the field and in the factories. Because women and children who worked in factories were more easily seen by reformers there than those on the farms, the perception grew that working in the *factories* induced mothers to drug their children. The drugging of children combined with other factors to inspire observers to question whether the laboring poor were any better off than the slaves in the Caribbean (Pinchbeck and Hewitt 1973, II:406–407; Duffy 1968, 464).

The dominant European attitude toward children in the seventeenth century was, according to historian John Plumb, "autocratic, indeed ferocious." He quotes a seventeenth-century writer: "The new borne babe is full of the stains and pollutions of sin which it inherits from our first parents through our loins." Parents frequently beat their children. There were plenty of people giving advice regarding raising children throughout history, but only Plutarch, Palmieri, and Jacopo Cardinal Sadoleto "failed to recommend that fathers beat their children (Plumb 1982b, 287; DeMause 1974, 40, 42; Weber 1942, 453)." Undoubtedly there were sadistic parents in the past, but seventeenth- and eighteenth-century parents worried about their children's salvation; because children often died young, there was not much time to spare in inculcating good morals or, at least, preventing bad morals.

John Locke inspired a new approach to child-rearing, one based on more positive responses to children. By the mid-eighteenth century, parents and other adults began viewing children with more benign attitudes. Some adults even advertised that they did not use corporal punishment in their academies of learning, although beating children as a form of discipline (and sometimes gratuitously) continued in the workplace for another century. Parents, to use Plumb's words, "no longer regard[ed] their children as sprigs of old Adam whose wills had to be broken." Children became "consumption" or "status" goods for parents: "[Parents] had come to look upon their children as vehicles of social emulation; hence they began to project their own social attitudes as the moral imperatives of childhood (Plumb 1982b, 291–292)."

Children in the Labor Market

Children had long labored in fields, family crafts workshops, and other workplaces. They were apprenticed in their early teens for years of learning under masters, some of whom were kindly; others were not. English youth in the late medieval period would hire on neighboring farms each year. The flexibility of such labor helped farmers and the youth. By the late nineteenth century, many so-called Progressives began to wring their hands over the fate of child workers. To be sure, many, probably most, children workers earned relatively small amounts of money and often worked long, hard hours, so their formal education languished. Parents with inadequate incomes faced unenviable choices. To see and hear their children (and themselves) suffer from hunger while living in miserable and overcrowded conditions was no doubt disheartening. If a child could go out and earn a few pennies, perhaps sufficient to cover the cost of the child's food, parents were sorely tempted to put the child to work instead of to school. To modern eyes, these parents' decisions were shortsighted, but, again, viewed from the perspective of the struggling poor, the decision made sense. The Progressives were aghast, with one writing, "we have lived not only in neglect but in exploitation of our children (Holleran 1993, 485)."[4]

Demographic changes and industrialization altered the workforce. With high mortality rates, the English population was remarkably young, with not quite half the population being under 20 years old from 1695 into the early 1800s. Such a disproportionate number of youngsters meant that the dependency ratio was quite high during this period (although the youths were offset by the smaller proportion of the elderly and infirm). Child labor in the early modern era did not inspire the moral outrage that was found in later, more prosperous times. Factory work offered alternatives to farm labor, although factory work entailed long hours that were more regular and required punctuality. For those workers who could adjust, wages were higher. In addition, in the textile industries, small, nimble fingers were often an advantage and brute strength less of an advantage, so children could compete with adults with respect to efficiency and productivity. Employing children in factories was an almost seamless transition from working children of the past; if anything, complaints sometimes revolved around how children displaced adult men.

Reformers found child labor an unmitigated harm. Certainly, many children suffered under long hours at onerous, mind-numbing work, sometimes under dangerous or unsanitary conditions. Between a Parliamentary investigation in 1832 and the sometimes overdrawn writings of novelists, nineteenth-century child labor's legacy was dismal. The Parliamentary Commission reported, "of all employments to which children are subjected, those carried on in the factories are amongst the least laborious and of all departments of indoor labour amongst the least unwholesome." Children often labored under worse conditions in small-scale and domestic industries, and domestic service for teenagers and women featured exceptionally long hours under considerable variations in masters and mistresses. The novel feature of factories was the public aspect—onlookers could see a large number of people working under admittedly tough conditions.

Novelists understood that sensationalizing factory conditions sold books and short stories. The novelists sincerely believed that by publicizing what the public wanted, they were also helping to reveal and possibly ameliorate abuses. Their recollection of a "golden age" for British farm workers ratcheted romance to fantasy. William Wordsworth rhapsodized, "Maids at the wheel, Sit blithe and happy." Historian Neill McKendrick cited the low life expectancy, high infant mortality, diseases, and often modest possessions in debunking the nostalgic haze obscuring the reality of life in the past.

McKendrick argued that eighteenth- and nineteenth-century women and children entered the factory labor force to augment family incomes, so the family could purchase decencies and luxuries. Such economic independence for women and, to a lesser degree, children infuriated some observers. Male workers often chafed at the competition for jobs and the alleged suppression of wages associated with the substitution of women and children for men; social critics lamented the idealized version of Victorian-era women as paragons of virtue tending to the domestic hearths and nurturing their children (McKendrick 1974, 156–165; Neff 1929, 13–16).

Poor families in eighteenth-century France might have envied their English counterparts, as the latter usually had a slightly higher standard of living. French families sometimes used their babies as bait to solicit alms. Toddlers were taught to beg, while older children might carry their younger siblings to the streets in order to beg. Poor children were allowed to gather wild fruits and sorrel, which was used to make a "virtually nutritionless soup." Families of sickly boys sought professional castrators to transform the boys into a candidate for the cathedral choir. French families hired out their children to an agent for a fixed sum; the agent then collected a portion of the child's earnings each day. In the Disneyfied version of *Mary Poppins*, Bert the chimney sweep led a whimsical, happy-go-lucky life. The reality for child chimney sweeps proved far nastier and deadlier. Being a sweep was a dreary, dirty job that was injurious to children's development (Hufton 1974, 82, 89, 109).

Economists often used the word "exploitation" to describe workers being paid less than the value of their marginal product. For Progressives, exploitation included not just below-productivity wages, but long working hours, terrible working conditions, and lost schooling. An economist investigated the charges of exploitation of children. He found that "Children's earnings equaled the value of their marginal product; their wages depended on experience and other productivity-enhancing traits. Surprisingly, the evidence for exploitation was stronger in the relatively high-wage North, where mill children may have been paid less than the value of marginal product, perhaps as the result of strict enforcement of child-labor laws. Paying children less than adult males was not necessarily exploitation; what matters was the child's wage relative to his or her productivity (Holleran 1993, 486)."

Labor historians Ivy Pinchbeck and Margaret Hewitt detailed the complexity of the exploitation argument: it was, "the factory owners, anxious to employ the cheapest labour the better to increase their own profits, who were responsible for the presence of large numbers of children among factory populations. This very naïve view over-simplifies a much more complicated situation in which low adult wage rates played a very considerable part and explained a good deal of the anxiety of parents in the mill towns as in rural areas that their children should contribute to their own support." As successive British factory acts and other legislation raised the age at which children could work, many parents found it desirable to deceive employers and authorities as to their children's ages.

Parents in today's poor countries face the same dilemma. They need their children's meager earnings now, but by putting their children to work, they are reducing their children's long-run productivity (and ability to succor the parents in later years). These parents confront a cruel tradeoff. Some parents were callous about sending their children to work, perhaps using the rationale, "I worked, so why shouldn't my children work?" Investigators found that in many cases, children were, "compelled either by the avarice or improvidence of their parents."

Did governments need to mandate compulsory education, imposing immediate costs upon families in order to reach the other side of the productivity gap? A British Factory Act of 1833 required children aged 9–13 to have two hours of schooling each day. The interruption of the workday naturally made such children less desirable to employers. Parents often objected to the law: "To send a child to day-school rarely enters the minds of parents. The child not contributing now to its own support, and parents can less afford to pay school fees than before, and they know that at the age of fourteen the factory will be open and no questions asked whether the child has been to school or not." When children became better substitutes for adult male workers due to changing technologies, then working groups of adults began opposing the employment of children in factories and may have begun supporting the compulsory education laws (Pinchbeck and Hewitt 1973, II:402–405).

Treatment of Child Labor

Children faced abusive treatment at the hands of some employers. Some contemporary observers described scenes of utter horror and depravity: "the infliction of bodily pain by instruments of punishment invented by the sharpened ingenuity of insatiable selfishness." Lord Shaftesbury, a reformer and activist for child welfare, reminisced seeing what, "a set of sad, dejected, cadaverous creatures they were." Historian Lloyd deMause, too, painted a dismal picture: "The history of childhood is a nightmare from which we have only recently begun to awaken. The further back in history one goes, the lower the level of child care, and the more likely children are to be killed, abandoned, beaten, terrorized, and sexually abused (Pinchbeck and Hewitt 1973, II:403; DeMause 1974, 1)."

Economist Clark Nardinelli argued in a controversial paper that using corporal punishment in nineteenth-century British factories was, "an effective method of increasing work discipline and productivity." The Parliamentary Report of the Select Committee, as with most government committee investigations, may have been biased and sought evidence of abuse of children. Nardinelli concluded that beatings were "common but not universal." Regardless of the prevalence of beatings within factories and coal mines, Nardinelli cautioned that these beatings took place in a violent world. Violence was "an accepted method of social control," whether politically or within the home. Ironically enough, Parliament was more concerned about physical violence to children in factories and not so interested in violence toward children within the home (which Parliamentary members probably viewed as a private matter) (Nardinelli 1982, 286, 289, 294; see also Pinchbeck and Hewitt 1973, II:407–410).

Nardinelli developed a theory whereby employers notorious for disciplining child workers would have to pay higher wages than would more benign employers. He used a compensating wage approach: in order to accept a job with a nastier employer, the child or, more likely, his parent would demand a higher wage.

If corporal punishment resulted in increased work discipline that, in turn, led to better productivity, then wages would rise. "It can be shown that if corporal punishment led to increased wages, it must have led to increased discipline and productivity .... If corporal punishment did not raise productivity, its only effect would have been to raise the price of child labor to the firm. The industries employing children were highly competitive, with easy entry and exit. Firms employing corporal punishment would therefore have failed to survive; nonbeaters would have forced child beaters out of the industry. If corporal punishment increased children's wages, then, it must have had an effect on productivity."

Nardinelli found that corporal punishment appeared to boost productivity. Another factor indicating higher productivity was a child's ability to sign their name; researchers often used this ability as a proxy for literacy (admittedly a crude proxy). Because children's jobs did not require education, the positive association between literacy and productivity may have reflected an indirect effect, such as education, that boosted discipline (Nardinelli 1982, 286–289, 292–294; Pinchbeck and Hewitt 1973, II:407–410).[5]

Critics used dramatic statements to condemn child labor: "It pays, my masters, to grind little children into dividends." *Children in Bondage* contained a passage, which portrayed slavery as not so bad but child labor as worse: "This new slavery of the mills is worse than the old slavery of the cotton fields. For the negro of the old days was well fed and sure of shelter; he did his work under the open sky, singing as he toiled, and finding time to weave out of his mystic brain a wild balladry and a poetic folklore. But the slavery of white women and children sucks life dry of all vigor and joy .... It is now the white child who is in bondage (Markham et al. [1914] 1969, 48–49; see also Holleran 1993, 487)."[6]

The child labor legislation may have essentially codified an ongoing shift. Children's participation in the workforce was already beginning to decline, when the laws were passed. Activism against child labor in the

United States coincided with a significant decline in child labor participation between 1880 and 1930, although there was a temporary increase in the years before 1900. Prior to 1880, what child labor legislation was on the books was poorly worded and weakly enforced. Organized labor and women's organizations were prominent in the fight against Child Labor. Organized labor may have held a mix of motivations; prohibiting child labor might have boosted demand for organized labor, but organized labor may have felt genuine concern about children working. Many laborers put their children out to work, as even the small amounts children earned made a difference in the family budget. As adult workers' wages rose, the need for putting their children to work may have waned. Statistical analysis demonstrated that "one of the most common restrictions found in state child labor laws—minimum age limits for manufacturing employment—had relatively little effect on the occupation choices of children at the turn of the century. The occupation rate of 13-year-olds did decline in states that enacted age minima of 14, but so did the occupation rates of children not covered by the restrictions (Moehling 1999, 95)."

Twenty-first-century readers probably consider the abolition of child labor a good thing. Certainly, the Progressives in America and their counterparts in Great Britain did. The actual process of outlawing child labor, though, revealed the issue to be ethically more complicated than a simple relationship between bad employers and innocent children (Brown et al. 1992, 723).

A Childhood Experiment Gone Awry

Americans were not shy about putting children to work selling stuff. Girl Scouts sold their cookies (although the author is waiting for a canny lawyer to file a class action suit against the Girl Scouts for peddling fattening, sugar-laden, irresistible cookies), although rarely door-to-door anymore. On the back of comic books in the postwar period, kids could make money selling packets of seeds. If they sold enough packets, they were eligible for prizes depicted in the advertisement.

A forerunner of such more or less wholesome activities was the Curtis Company's campaign selling its *Saturday Evening Post* magazines to customers. The *Post* was a typical Progressive institution; the magazine disdained wealthy capitalists, who had earned tainted money. Although they countenanced government intervention on occasion, they generally viewed such as a necessary evil.

The *Post* executives sought to encourage business virtues in boys by enlisting them to sell subscriptions to the *Post*. The executives were not looking to encourage all boys, especially the scruffy street urchins shown in Jacob Riis' photos. The magazine's executives sought middle-class, preferably Anglo-Saxon, boys already imbued with middle-class values, who would make a good impression and be honest.

Boys would learn entrepreneurial skills, and the Curtis Company would sell magazines. To encourage the boys, the company occasionally offered cash prizes and a trip to the 1904 World's Fair in St. Louis (immortalized by Vincente Minnelli's *Meet Me in St. Louis*) or the 1904 Presidential inauguration. Come to think about it, a movie based on the boy winning the trip might have been a popular trip down nostalgia lane.

One can envision a 1903 American small town right out of one of the *Post's* Norman Rockwell covers, with boys whizzing by on bicycles and hawking magazines. The *Post* advertised how boys might begin with a handful of subscribers and work up to a subscription list of scores of readers. To inspire the boys, the magazine listed weekly sales leaders who won cash prizes of $5 to $20. The *Post* encouraged boys to set up an "exclusive agency," which smacked of monopolizing a territory: "How to Get the Exclusive Agency for Your Town. In many small towns there is room for only one wide-awake boy. In such towns we are willing to protect good boys against competition from rival boy agents. Send us a deposit and *if your town is not already taken* we will make you an exclusive agent (Cohn 1987, 186–192, 198)." The idea worked well, too well, in fact, as some of the boys began practicing cutthroat tactics.

Boys resorted to anti-competitive tactics. The keen competition resembled that of industry titans, with special pleading, price-cutting, poaching of customers, and so on. One boy, Victor Pelz, feuded with another boy in his town regarding exclusive territories.[7]

Pelz' antics seemed genteel compared with Jay Johns. Johns won a $25 prize based on the number of copies of the *Post* he sold. Johns was nothing if blunt, when he wrote the *Post*: "I want to be the only toad in this puddle. I don't want you to sell to every 'Tom, Dick and Harry.' I can sell more copies than all of them put together anyway. Three of these boys have quit, and to-day I bought out the other two boys by giving them fifty cents apiece. These little fellows only spoil the business. I am now the only boy here who sells *The Post*." Then came his pitch: "If you will agree not to appoint anybody else so long as I sell a lot of copies, you can credit this

$25.00 to my account and send me 100 copies for next week and 125 copies each week thereafter."

Another boy wanted an exclusive territory (the entire town in which he lived), and requested the magazine to reject other boys; to demonstrate his determination, he enclosed a cash deposit for 50 copies a week for months in advance to show he "meant business." Readers may ask what one would call these boys. They weren't juvenile delinquents, but they were certainly juvenile somethings. Author Jan Cohn characterized them as "small-scale buccaneers; the analogy to Captains of Industry."

The *Post*'s success with boys selling magazines induced the magazine to offer prizes based not just on sales but on *increases* in sales. Cohn compared this tactic with "speeding up" a conveyor belt in a factory (such as the Ford Motor Company did in the wake of the fabled $5-a-day wage) (Cohn 1987, 191, 196–211).

Children and Consumerism

As British consumers began to gain a measure of discretionary income above subsistence, they spent more on leisure goods and services. They even indulged their children, buying books and toys. John Newbery pioneered selling books aimed at children. He had a colorful career, starting with marrying his boss's widow; operating a circulating library; and buying a half-share in "Dr. James's fever powders." He inserted blurbs for a fever powder into the children's books that he published. His first book, *A Pretty Little Pocket Book*, was educational in that it informed children about the alphabet. Newbery gave the book away for free (*as long as you read the fine print that required purchasing the book's binding*). Despite this gimmick, *A Pretty Little Pocket Book* sold well, and enabled him to, in the now time-honored fashion, follow up with similar efforts (*Art of Writing* and the *Art of Arithmetic*; it is surprising that he refrained from entitling them *A Pretty Little Book of Writing* or some similar title).

Selling products aimed at children during the eighteenth century was a new phenomenon; in most cases, though, parents made the purchasing decisions. Historians seem to be silent on when children mastered the art of pestering their parents, or whether merchants had devised ways to make their products irresistibly appealing to young minds. Once upper-class consumers started buying toys, books, and clothing, the other classes attempted to emulate them. British workers had a modicum of discretionary income and because their children began having higher odds of surviving infancy and childhood, parents became more willing to "invest" in them (Plumb 1982a, 272–273, 286).[8]

The books frequently had educational or moral content; at first, these books were not designed to "entice the young mind … [as] fairy stories, ballads, riddles and fables were intended as much for adults as for children. Indeed, Aesop was not specifically adapted for children until 1692, when Roger l'Estrange produced an adaptation for children. Toys were often replicas of industrial and scientific tools, although animals and wagons proved popular, too."[9] Plumb observes that children, "had become luxury objects upon which their mothers and fathers were willing to spend larger and larger sums of money, not only for their education, but also for their entertainment and amusement. In a sense they had become superior pets—sometimes spoilt excessively … sometimes treated with indifference or even brutality, but usually, as with pets, betwixt and between." The new indulgence of children did not meet with universal approval. The fears that children could be consigned to hell still nagged at many parents. Other parents, perhaps more conservative than those following Lockean ideas, continued to chastise their children in the earnest belief that doing so was the right and proper thing. Maria Edgeworth scolded parents for wasting money on "useless toys." She was not against all toys, but, presaging modern critics, she disdained the readymade toys that had less potential for childish imagination. She preferred pencil and paper, scissors, hoops, tops, and instructional toys (Plumb 1982b, 300, 310–311, 332).[10]

Advertisers found children irresistible targets. Children began to have discretionary funds, especially by the 1950s in America. Their preferences were malleable. Advertisers were especially drawn to "the boy consumer." Advertisers were usually male college graduates, often from the Ivy League, who wanted their efforts to be recognized as serious and not frivolous. From the advertisers' point of view, "the boy consumer managed to harmonize the consumer ethos with older ideals of industriousness and disciplined entrepreneurship …. In his passionate enthusiasm, loyalty, and salesmanship, the boy consumer displayed all the hallmarks of the successful corporate personality." The advertisers' insecurity was matched by salesmen's concerns over public skepticism of their morality. "The boy even bested the sales professional by virtue of his freedom from professional codes and his trusted position within the family. 'He's got it all over your own men in many ways,' *American Boy* instructed advertisers, 'he's not restricted by sales ethics (Jacobson 2001, 229, 239–240, 249).'"

Girls were not ignored. In a motion picture short series, *March of Time*, an episode titled *Teen-Age Girls* delved into the mysteries of such creatures. The girls were shown at a slumber party in modest pajamas; their activities included painting each other's toe-nails. But some adults expressed befuddlement at this new phenomenon. Although parents had muddled through for millennia without experts to advise them, apparently postwar parents needed the guidance of sociologists and psychologists, even though the girls portrayed in *Teen-Age Girls* ended the film by singing the "Doxology." The narrator optimistically concluded that "the girls would end up as normal American women (Gilbert 1986, 201)."

In the event, marketers catered to children. Sometimes the products they purveyed left something to be desired. Thus, if little Johnny sends off 50 box tops from Corn-Frosted Sugar Cubes for the Amazing X-Ray Eyes ("You can see through anything … except this ad"), should he be protected from rapacious capitalists? Little Johnny is not allowed to sign a contract for this reason.[11] A cynic might argue that the $1.99 plus box tops were a cheap way to learn about caveat emptor. Turning children into skeptics might be pragmatic, but the ethics of doing so seems deficient.

Do You Know What Your Children Are Watching?

Decades before 1950s and the seeming explosion of juvenile delinquents, adults raised similar concerns about the generation of young people in the 1920s. Academics made unsubstantiated statements regarding the deleterious effects of the new culture upon children. A sociologist blamed movies for making young people, "sex-wise, sex-excited and sex-absorbed." In his eyes, movies contributed to "less-concealing fashions, pornographic literature, provocative dances, and briefer bathing suits." Never mind that World War I might have exerted an effect upon young minds, adults blamed the motion pictures, the wild dances, and the greater diffusion of automobiles for eroding America's morals (Butsch 2000, 167; see also Ross 1928, 179; Forman [1935] 1970, 185; Rugg 1931, 499). In fairness to the sociologist, movies in the late 1920s and early 1930s were more explicit than they would be after the industry imposed its own censorship.

What really worried middle- and upper-class Americans of the postwar years was the fear that their "moral authority" was being undermined by unscrupulous pied pipers of consumerism. These characters enticed teenage (and younger) children with desirable products and services that were often associated with lower-class values. James Gilbert emphasized that "peer culture and youth culture had strong economic components since they rested upon the new postwar affluence of teenagers (Gilbert 1986, 215)." Parents and commentators did not expressly link ethics to teenage consumerism, but implicitly they were asking whether it was ethical for companies to pander to childish whims with salacious, low-brow, and morally dubious commodities.

Media historian Bill Osgerby recognized the youth culture's ability to actively shape itself, with the assistance of profit-seeking commercial firms. He quoted Steven Miles' observation that commercial interests and youth have a "mutually exploitative" relationship (although, one might have as accurately labeled it a "mutually beneficial" relationship). "The proposition that young people actively engage with the mass media and to a degree forge it in their own image is a sound one, but is only ever partially realized," as the mass media sets the parameters constraining the youth. Social critic Dwight MacDonald voiced similar thoughts regarding the, "teenage market—and, in fact, the very notion of the teenager—has been created by the businessmen who exploit it (Osgerby 2002, 20–21; Miles 2000, 85; MacDonald 1958, II:58)."

Television producers and executives later created cartoons and children's shows with a large amount of product placement and with only traces of plot and character development thrown in. Children's toys were shown in the most favorable (and artificial) backdrops imaginable. No one's toys were as exciting as those shown on television.

There was a distinction about the concern regarding children, according to media historian Richard Butsch: The reformers were usually concerned about *other* people's children, not their own. The middle- and upper-class reformers bemoaned theater, movies, and music's effects upon working-class and immigrant children. Some reformers hoped to entice children away from the baleful effects of commercialized mass culture with playgrounds and other wholesome endeavors. To be sure, the playground movement addressed a serious issue. An optimistic few thought that motion pictures, at least, could prove beneficial to children, so they pushed for movies with educational and moral content. Whether these reformers would have been gratified by the hygiene movies of postwar America or Big Bird, Bert & Ernie, and other Public Broadcasting Service (PBS) characters is an interesting question (Butsch 2000, 156).

The Horror, the Horror—Crime and Horror Comics

Postwar children often spent their nickels and dimes on morally suspect products. Adult producers purveyed crime and horror comics in order to earn children's nickels and dimes across the United States, Europe, and Oceania.[12] The controversy over comic books continued a long tradition of outrage concerning adolescents' reading material. From the penny-dreadfuls of the late 1800s to the lurid comics (the *Katzenjammer Kids* were a choice target, given the crude and cruel ethnic humor) of the early twentieth century, social critics wrung their hands over the alleged deleterious effects upon impressionable young minds. Punch and Judy—the bickering marital puppet couple—presumably elicited similar laughs from children (and adults) for centuries.

By the 1940s, professors masquerading as pseudo-scientists inveighed against comic books with an unprecedented ferocity. Psychology was popular in the 1940s, and a parade of academics competed to launch the shrillest attacks on comic books by dubious use of psychology theories. Sterling North characterized the comics of 1940 as "lurid publications" that relied upon "mayhem, murder, torture, and abduction—often with a child as the victim. Superman heroics, voluptuous females in scanty attire, blazing machine guns, hooded 'justice' and cheap political propaganda were to be found on almost every page. The old dime novels [which perhaps North might have read as a boy] in which an occasional redskin bit the dust were classic literature compared to the sadistic drivel pouring from the presses today. Badly drawn, badly written and badly printed—a strain on young eyes and young nervous systems—the effect of these pulp-paper nightmares is that of a violent stimulant." Whew! If that wasn't bad enough, he continued by bemoaning, "their hypodermic injection of sex and murder make the child impatient with better, though quieter stories. Unless we want a coming generation even more ferocious than the present one, parents and teachers throughout America must band together to break the 'comic' magazine (North 1940, 21)."

North wrote his screed years *before* the detective, true crime, and horror comic books of the late 1940s and early 1950s hit the newsstands. Marya Mannes, an author and mother, called the postwar comic books, "the greatest intellectual narcotic on the market" and "a waste of time … every hour spent in reading comics is an hour in which all inner growth is stopped." She observed, though, that many low-income American adults read comic books (Mannes 1947, 21, 23).

Proposed regulations of the comic book industry included, "No drawing should show a female indecently or unduly exposed, and in no event more nude than in a bathing suit commonly worn in the United States of America [a marvelously elastic definition, as the bikini had just been introduced in the aftermath of exploding atomic bombs on Bikini atoll]." Almost as an afterthought, another regulation read, "Ridicule of or attack on any religious or racial group is never permissible (*Newsweek*, July 12, 1948, 56)."

Purveying such comic books raised ethical questions, such as whether it was ethical to promulgate salacious material (although it is debatable whether comic book material of the 1940s and 1950s was more disturbing than the goings on in the Old Testament or Shakespearean plays). Certainly, such worthies as Fredric Wertham traipsed across professional ethics with their exaggerated and unsupported condemnation of comics. In fairness to Wertham, crime and horror comic books featured an outlandish amount of mayhem and gore. It would take Hollywood movies decades to catch up. In one issue of *Crime Does Not Pay*, Wertham reported that crime paid in 47 of 48 picture frames. You have to admire the creators, though, for cramming, "ten guillotinings, seven stabbings, six shootings, one fatal shove from a ladder, two shockings, one drowning, and one bludgeoning" into 48 pages. This represented an average of two violent acts per three frames, although it is possible that some frames featured multiple acts of violence; almost as an afterthought, the villain, Paul Chretien, dies in the final frame (possibly from exhaustion). Presumably, character development and subtle plot devices were not staples of the genre. Wertham's claim about comic books was pretentious, "You cannot understand present-day juvenile delinquency if you do not take into account the pathogenic and pathoplastic [infectious] influence of comic books (*Time*, March 29, 1948, 68; Gilbert 1986, 97)."

Wertham was a typical moral entrepreneur. He was parsimonious in spilling ink on citations backing his claims. He claimed that comic books "stimulate unhealthy sexual attitudes; sadism, masochism, frigidity." He then made a suspiciously precise claim without attribution, "seventy-five per cent of parents are against comic books. (The other twenty-five per cent are either indifferent or misled by propaganda and 'research'.)" He also claimed that children felt guilty about reading comic books. With regard to the ethics of the comic book publishers, these executives "seduce the children and mislead the parents. Their mass production is a serious danger to the production of good inexpensive children's books." He did have an ability to weave an effective polemic. He interviewed a 14-year-old boy charged with stealing. Wertham asked the leading question of whether comic books influenced his decision to steal. The boy answered, "Oh, no. In the comic books it is mostly murder." Wertham stated that "Comic books are the greatest book publishing success in history and the greatest mass influence on children (Wertham 1948, 6, 27, 29)."

Legislators worried that comic books and the alleged accompanying delinquent behavior eroded American youth's ability to combat international Communism. Some voices of moderation, including, of all people, Federal Bureau of Investigation (FBI) director J. Edgar Hoover, denied that there would be an "appreciable decrease in juvenile delinquency" if crime comic books were made unavailable to children. Comic strip writer Milt Caniff (creator of rugged he-men, *Terry and the Pirates* and *Steve Canyon*) told a congressional committee that "Practitioners of the inexact science of psychiatry have long served as apologists for the present parental generation by attributing every childhood ill from measles to shyness to the reading of comic book (*New York Times*, November 12, 1950, 1 and 61)."[13] Newspapers and magazine editors and reporters, too, had incentives to publish the most provocative opinions and research pertaining to comic books, as well as comic strips. William C. Gaines' competitors were more than happy to see him become the public's scapegoat. The established publishers knew they could survive a self-censoring board, similar to that employed by the motion picture industry. New entrants, however, often relied upon shocking and innovative approaches to comic books; these potential rivals could be squelched by a censoring board (Gilbert 1986, 162–163).[14]

The postwar boom in comic books spurred Congressional action. Congressional leaders pandered to the electorate during the hearings (legislators apparently could take time from worrying about the hydrogen bomb to delve into the intricacies of children's comics). Senator Estes Kefauver chaired a Senate committee investigating organized crime, but the committee later migrated to juvenile delinquency. Kefauver proved duplicitous in a later hearing on comic books; he invited two pro-comic book experts and then proceeded to publicly discredit them. The Senators, however, avoided stating any opinion on whether comic books were linked to juvenile delinquency (Nyberg 1999, 48; *New York Times*, April 23, 1954a, 29; *New York Times*, November 12, 1950, 1). Producers of such material were viewed with contempt and fear. Certainly, many of the comic book publishers competed by using garish, outlandish, and ghoulish drawings and plotlines. Many children loved these stories. Criminals met violent, gory deaths; ghouls ran amok, sucking blood or worse. Red ink used for bloody scenes led to black ink in the publishers' ledgers. Some of the more established comic book publishers relied on more staid materials, and it was the smaller, independent publishers who were often guilty of pushing the boundaries of bad taste.

EC Comics became notorious. The original owner, Max Gaines, published a series of comics with Biblical storylines. His son, William, opted for imaginative genres. As he stated, "weird," "horror," and "terror" were his key words. The William C. Gaines testimony became legendary. Unfortunately for Gaines, his testimony before a Congressional committee was a fiasco. Gaines later claimed that he was operating on very little sleep. His dispute with a legislator regarding whether a decapitated head was in bad taste was highly amusing, although, obviously, not to the pompous legislators or, in all likelihood, parents across America (Nyberg 1998, 109; Surdam 2015, 98–102).[15] Making Gaines the scapegoat served many interests within the comic book industry and grandstanding legislators, such as Senator Kefauver.

In the end, the industry vowed to clean its nest, although, in reality, such efforts played into the hands of the larger, entrenched publishers. Many of the independent publishers were knocked out of the market, although a concurrent disruption in the distribution network contributed to the demise of many comic book publishers. Gaines survived, but he channeled his efforts into *Mad* magazine. To this day, casualties of the comic book witch hunt lament the dispersion of talent and livelihoods (Surdam 2015, 97–103).

Rock'n'Roll and Payola

The 1950s were a period of paranoia; the Cold War and potential nuclear annihilation had people worldwide on edge. American adults in the 1950s were assaulted by a new menace: loud, simplistic, suggestive rock'n'roll music. The new musical form was a menace that would be condemned by Free World and Communist leaders alike. Rock'n'roll was here to stay, and adults worldwide were appalled. When Elvis Presley, Chuck Berry, Jerry Lee Lewis, and their compatriots exploded onto American consciousness, the response was hysteria. Teenagers waxed hysterical about the new musical form, one that they alone possessed. Adults wailed hysterically about how Elvis and his pelvis portended moral decadence.

The new musical genre seemingly arose out of nowhere, and many adults hoped the fad would soon disappear into the void from which it emanated. The boast, "rock'n'roll is here to stay," however, proved prophetic. Commentators ridiculed the new music. Frank Sinatra, himself a controversial figure from an earlier generation, argued that rock'n'roll was created by, "cretinous goons … [who used] almost imbecilic reiteration and sly, lewd … dirty, lyrics" to marshal every "side-burned delinquents on the face of the earth (Samuels, January 12, 1958, SM16-19)." Psychiatrist Francis Braceland characterized rock'n'roll music as, "a cannibalistic and tribalistic form of music (*New York Times*, March 28, 1956, 33)."[16] The subtext of rock'n'roll being aligned with African-American performers was certainly a factor in the animus.

Legislators quickly seized upon the opportunity to score cheap points against the new music. American adults were already fearful for their children. One senator ranted on the eve of Elvis' debut, "Not even the Communist conspiracy could devise a more effective way to demoralize, confuse, and destroy our future citizens than apathy on the part of adult Americans to the scourge known as juvenile delinquency (*New York Times*, June 29, 1954b, 29)." No one claimed Elvis and his peers were Communist stooges, which was wise, since Russian officials damned the music as vehemently as their American counterparts (rock'n'roll unites the Cold War foes!). According to a Soviet official in the 1980s (just before his death), rock'n'roll was "an arsenal of subversive weapons aimed at undermining the commitment of young Russians to Communist ideology (Martin and Segrave 1993, 247)." If Robert Henrickson and his Communist peer were correct, then rock'n'roll was a truly destructive force.

How did the new music become so popular? Prior to rock'n'roll, such drivel as Patti Page's rendition of "How Much Is that Doggie (In the Window)" succeeded in reaching the top of *Billboard's* popular music chart. How could rock'n'roll have displaced "How Much Is that Doggie?" By 1957, independent labels dominated the popular music charts, using rock'n'roll music. Independent producers such as Sam Phillips took advantage of the ease of pressing small quantities of records by artists, who might appeal to a regional following. The independent producers also benefited from radio's transformation from national network programming to independent, decentralized programming featuring popular music. The multitude of stations meant that music could fill smaller niches and be popular enough to generate profits. The 1950s boosted not just rock'n'roll but also hillbilly, country and western, and rhythm and blues (Chapple and Garofalo 1977, 43–44, 57).

Many American adults believed that the music gained its popularity by foul means; there had to be chicanery lurking. Within a few years, a handy culprit appeared. Alan Freed, a well-known disc jockey and motion picture personality, and other popular disc jockeys admitted to having accepted payments from producers to play their records. The practice, which had existed for decades, was known as payola. Here, though, was a heaven-sent opportunity. Legislators swooped unto the alleged corruption, making ridiculous and lurid accusations. Clearly, American youth had been co-opted by a corrupt process. The despised music could never have made inroads without bribery and deceit on the part of disc jockeys. Legislators appeared to have plenty of time to grill disc jockeys and other small-time operators, even as the Soviet menace loomed. The Congressional hearings, of course, offered a wonderful vehicle for legislators to posture as defenders of truth, decency, and the American way (never mind the fact that cash inducements were certainly a facet of the American way). An example of the derogatory remarks made about the new music, was a question during a hearing: "Well, do you think without payola that a lot of this so-called junk music, rock and roll stuff, which appeals to the teenagers would not be played, or do you think that kind of thing would be played anyway, regardless of payola?" A former Boston disc jockey and recipient of $10,000 in payola replied: "Never get on the air .... Yes, [payola] keeps it on the air, because it fills pockets (Coase 1979, 293)."

There was rank inconsistency in the Federal Communications Commission (FCC) and legislators' cries against payola, when such worthies, "were in the pockets of major broadcasting powers and could be counted on to look the other way when it got to the really big payola of the time, namely the trading in [radio and television station] licenses, price-fixing agreements between the major networks on advertising rates, disguised rate cards, and special kickbacks to advertising agencies buying spot time." FCC Commissioner John Doerfer visited Bimini Island with a media executive. The commissioner traveled to Bimini just once but had his travel expenses reimbursed three times, twice by the executive. The payola scandal was, in essence, part of a larger struggle between ASCAP (American Society of Composers, Authors, and Publishers) and BMI (Broadcast Music, Inc.), the two main publishers of music. "The music industry has moved squarely from publisher domination that favored

ASCAP writers to record and radio domination that uses a looser structure, like BMI's," that revolved around issues, such as advances on royalty payments (Chapple and Garofalo 1977, 62, 66–67).[17]

There was much more to payola than the public appreciated. The episode demonstrated the failure to apply economic understanding to an ethical issue. Ronald Coase wrote an insightful article analyzing payola. His analysis turned much of the conventional wisdom upside down.

Some legislators initially discounted the importance of payola. One senator compared payola with paying a headwaiter to get a better table. Other legislators, though, seized the opportunity to gain publicity and favor with the legions of decency: Commercial corruption and rock'n'roll have got to go. A representative stated that payola, "constitute[s] unfair competition with honest businessmen who refuse to engage in them. They tend to drive out of business small firms who lack the means to survive this unfair competition."

Coase showed that the representative's argument was wrong. Established music publishers and producers gained from banning payola. These established businesses typically had mass marketing and distribution machinery; they had little need to engage in payola. Rhythm and blues, country, hillbilly, and other fringe genres found it difficult to reach a national audience, as established producers of music dominated the airwaves with tried and true musical forms (one could easily add, "tired" to the previous adjectives). It was, the representative's claims notwithstanding, the small, independent producer who benefited most from payola.

Coase pointed out that disc jockeys had to be selective about which songs to accept payola for. A disc jockey considering accepting payment for playing an unknown talent's record needed to weigh the cash benefit versus the potential diminution in his or her popularity. If the disc jockey accepted money to play dreck, his popularity would tank; he might even lose his job. The disc jockey, therefore, would likely only accept payment for songs he thought might have potential. The small producer and payola, therefore, expanded the disc jockey's knowledge of what music was available. The station owner countenanced payola, because the practice made being a disc jockey more attractive, thereby inducing more people into entering the disc jockey market. The owner might have been able to reduce the disc jockey's salary, since the ability to accept payola would more than offset any reduction in salary.

The larger producers, of course, wanted payola squelched. They wanted to prevent entry of innovative producers. Chess, Sun, and, later, Motown became prominent independents (although these companies were often acquired by larger companies); their disseminating the blues, rock, and soul enriched American culture. Payola helped to allow Americans to have a wider selection of musical genres, thereby sparing us, perhaps, from variations on "How Much Is that Doggie (in the Window)?"[18]

Coase concluded that the purpose of the legislative efforts was, "to obtain confessions of guilt from the witnesses and to demonstrate the high moral standards of the congressmen .... In the circumstances it is hardly surprising that widely held misconceptions about payola were perpetuated by the enquiry (Coase 1979, 291, 306–308, 312)."

Children's Television

Newton Minow famously described television as a "vast wasteland." He presumably meant that adults and children alike faced the wasteland, and he made his pithy remark before *My Mother the Car*, *F Troop*, *Gilligan's Island*, and *Hogan's Heroes* debuted (Rothman 2016, no page numbers).[19]

Many adults fondly remember the Saturday morning cartoons of their youth. Such cartoons evolved over the years, from *Bullwinkle & Rocky*, the *Jetsons*, and their compatriots to shows depicting evil businessmen despoiling the environment in the 1970s to other, more progressive cartoons of the twenty-first century. The cartoons of the 1950s and 1960s featured plenty of cartoonish violence, which was perhaps the raison d'être of the genre. *Heckle and Jeckle*, *Tom and Jerry*, *Mr. Jinx, Pixie, and Dixie* (with the deathless phrase, "I hate them meeces to pieces!"), and, of course, the entire Warner Bros. oeuvre that employed anvils, explosions, cliffs, and unblinking realization of impending doom as familiar features (or, to be academic, tropes).

Children's television shows advertised sugar with some cereal thrown in; toys shown under enhanced conditions; and other products. In many cases, children's television producers skipped the middleman and created shows revolving around marketable, licensed character toys (*Transformers*, *Teenage Ninja Turtles*) (Kline 1998, 355–357).

The major networks applauded the creation of the Public Broadcasting Service (PBS). The new network was devoted to televising children's shows and was prohibited from accepting most forms of advertising (aside from acknowledgments of gratitude to corporate sponsors). The networks, therefore, had the pressure to offer educational or uplifting children's programming alleviated while not facing competition for advertising dollars (Bergreen 1980, 254, 258; Gomery 2008, 201).[20]

Ironically, even public television, that alleged bastion of quality programming, was not above sleazy tactics. According to the *TV Guide*, a jeer: "To an unpardonable PBS pledge-drive practice: begging for donations around kids' shows. We've taken public television to task in the past for its frustrating fund-raisers, but our latest blast is aimed at this particularly crass money-mongering maneuver." The writer characterized the pitch or threat: "'Barney's [the orthodontically challenged, purple dinosaur] up next kids—right after you get your mom and dad so they can listen to this important message,' says your average perky PBS type, leaving little Jennifer and Jessica to wonder whether they'll ever see their prehistoric pal alive again if their parents don't pay up. Why not just go all the way like Soupy Sales once did and ask kids to send in 'those little green pieces of paper,' from their parents' wallets? At least you'd skip the middleman (*TV Guide*, March 27, 1993, 6)."

PBS was later chagrined to find that it did not stipulate royalties from the eventually ubiquitous Barney paraphernalia.[21] The *Washington Post* broke the story regarding PBS' lack of royalties from Barney. Peggy Charren, founder of Action for Children's Television, acknowledged the conundrum facing PBS and its parent company, the Corporation for Public Broadcasting. Congress intended that PBS avoid commercialization, lest it be perceived as "choosing programs for their commercial potential." Charren, however, was willing to considering jettisoning this stance, as "it seems idiotic to have all that product and no return to public broadcasting (Edwards, September 13, 1993, no page numbers; see also Everhart, October 4, 1993, no page numbers)."

Economists would predict that television stations would attempt to evade or minimize the effects of the Children's Television Act. Given the yawning loophole provided by the ambiguous definition of educational fare, the stations employed ludicrous definitions of educational. Stations submitted the following as educational fare (along with their rationale):

> "*Super Mario Brothers*—demonstrating the importance of 'self-confidence.'
> *The Jetsons*—teaches children what life might be like in the twenty-first century.
> *Leave It to Beaver*—promoting the values of communication and trust.

> *GI Joe* cartoon—is educational because its heroes 'fight against an evil that has the capabilities of mass destruction of society,' thereby showing 'social consciousness and responsibility (Zoglin 1993, 64).'"

The legislators were shocked by the stations' cavalier actions. The National Association of Broadcasters claimed compliance, "Broadcasters take their children's programming responsibilities very seriously .... We are confident the broadcasters are in full compliance." The legislators remained skeptical. Massachusetts Democrat Ed Markey, in a sound-bite (the adult equivalent of a news Twinkie), retorted: "Children's television on commercial broadcast television today remains the video equivalent of a Twinkie (*Associated Press*, October 1, 1992, no page numbers; Salem, October 12, 1995, no page numbers; Holloway, April 13, 1998, no page numbers)."

Yet, is television an entertainment or an educational medium? Does a child really want to watch television to get a message? And, if so, what message? A writer for *Time*, commented: "The very notion of educational TV often seems to reflect narrow, school-marmish notions. Live-action shows are almost automatically preferred over cartoons, and some sweetly innocent shows, like *Barney and Friends*, seem to win approval largely because they shelter kids from the rude real world—a strange notion of education indeed (Zoglin 1993, 64)."

Conclusion

Dealing with children certainly demands a higher level of ethical standards by employers and sellers. Although a few sellers insinuate that selling the misleading products for "two box tops and one dollar for shipping and handling" is no big deal and, in fact, taught children a valuable lesson ("beware!"), such sellers' actions are unacceptable. Parents, too, share responsibility for putting children to work at early ages (granted many of these parents suffered from severely constricted budgets) or buying junk foods and questionable toys.

On the other hand, moral crusaders and entrepreneurs often exaggerated risks to children. Rock'n'roll has not warped our society, nor did the garish, violent comic books turn children into psychopaths.

Notes

1. Useful histories of children include DeMause (1974); Aries (1962); Pinchbeck and Hewitt (1973).
2. The new form of social security allows a childless bachelor, such as the author, to free ride upon other people's expense in raising a child. Of course, society tries to get childless people to bear part of the expense of education.
3. Aries described the toll high infant and childhood mortality took upon people (Aries 1962, 38–41; Pinchbeck and Hewitt 1973, II:388).
4. On modern-day American farms, small children, as young as six years old, drive large equipment. As the subtitle of a *New York Times* article describes: "Thousands are Injured and Many Are Killed Each Years (Healy, January 29, 2018, A10)."
5. The apparent link between schooling and discipline, or at least discipline amenable to factory work, may have spurred manufacturers to call for more education. Mary MacKinnon and Paul Johnson scathingly rebuked Nardinelli, accusing him of "combining historical ignorance, inappropriate theory, biased sampling, and misspecified econometrics"; academic vitriol rarely attains such levels (MacKinnon and Johnson 1984, 218).
6. Edwin Markham, Benjamin Lindsey, and George Creel may have been Progressives, but their attitudes toward the blacks were condescending: "The young negro, not cunning enough to speed the spindle, is spared … the little darkey is out in the cotton fields under the open heavens (Markham et al. [1914] 1969, 49)." Then again, who knows which of today's commentary will bring a wince to future readers' sensibilities. For a more benign depiction of child labor, see Brown, Christiansen, and Philips' description of rural canneries in early twentieth-century America (1992, 734–738).
7. Victor Pelz parlayed his business aggressiveness into earning a Master's degree at Northwestern University, for which he wrote a thesis dealing with traveling salesmen (Victor H. Pelz papers, 1902–1918, Archives West, http://archiveswest).orbiscascade.org/ark;/80444/xv26428, viewed February 12, 2017, 4:25 p.m.).
8. Modern-day toy and clothing manufacturers openly talk about "branding" children, not with a hot iron of course, but by inculcating brand preferences—McDonald's play areas, Baby Gap, Disney Kids, and so on. With the conglomeration of companies, someday young adults, instead of exchanging astrological signs, may exchange whether they are a "Mattel-Dreamworks" or a "Disney-Sony" person.
9. Pitching children's entertainment that included enjoyable elements for adults continues to modern times; Warner Bros. cartoons and animation

shows such as *The Simpsons*, *Bullwinkle and Rocky*, and *South Park* are aimed at children and adults; the controversy over Bart Simpson's effect as anti-role model seems quaint a quarter of a century on.

10. Jay Nash, too, criticized commercialized toys (Nash 1932, 221–222).
11. Kirk Demarais tracked down many of these products. There were toy soldiers that were basically silhouettes that you could order from the back of comic books, although they are now treasured collector's items (Demarais 2011, 11, 38).
12. Information on Russian comics can be found at https://comicsforum.org/2015/12/09/the-history-of-russian-comics-an-interview-with-misha-zaslavskiy-by-maria-evdokimova/, viewed November 1, 2019.
13. One hopes that Milt Caniff punctuated his blunt remarks with, "Biff!" and "Pow!"
14. During the 1950s, the motion picture industry played juvenile delinquency both ways. James Gilbert pointed out the movie industry, "claimed to be helping in the national fight against delinquency, while it exploited public interest in, and even fear of, juvenile culture (Gilbert 1986, 162–163)." Such films as *Blackboard Jungle*, featuring Bill Haley and the Comets' rock'n'roll anthem, "Rock Around the Clock," proved popular among teenagers, especially as it combined juvenile delinquency with the new musical form. In a pivotal scene of cultural barbarism, the hoodlums destroyed a teacher's beloved collection of vinyl jazz records.
15. William C. Gaines' testimony is preserved at http://www.thecomicbooks.com/1954senatetranscripts.html, viewed November 1, 2019.
16. These remarks were eerily similar to those leveled at ragtime and jazz earlier in the century (McMahon 1921, 116; *Ladies' Home Journal* 1921, 24).
17. See also 64 for earlier controversy between the two groups (Coase 1979, 314–315).
18. Although Chuck Berry's lamentable, "My Ding-a-Ling," was probably a detraction in his corpus of songs.
19. The author wonders about the producers' pitch for the last-named show before the network programming brass: "It's a show about fun and games in a German POW camp."
20. Corporations such as oil companies Mobile, Exxon, Gulf Oil, and Atlantic Richfield found it beneficial to underwrite such prestigious programs as *Masterpiece Theater*. Some humorists nicknamed PBS the "Petroleum Broadcasting System (Bergreen 1980, 258)."
21. This author believes the Barney song, "I love you, you love me; We're a happy family," should be reworded to, "I love you, you buy me; I'm a commercialized property," but perhaps he is too cynical.

Bibliography

Aries, Philippe. *Centuries of Childhood: A Social History of Family Life* (New York, NY: Alfred A. Knopf, 1962).

Associated Press. "TV Broadcasters Making a Joke of Law, Activists Say." October 1, 1992. https://www.deseret.com/1992/10/1/19008064/tv-broadcasters-making-a-joke-of-law-activists-say, viewed November 1, 2019.

Bergreen, Laurence. *Look Now, Pay Later: The Rise of Network Broadcasting* (Garden City, NY: Doubleday & Company, 1980).

Brown, Martin, Jens Christiansen, and Peter Philips. "The Decline of Child Labor in the U.S. Fruit and Vegetable Canning Industry: Law or Economics?" *Business History Review* 66(4), Winter 1992, 723–770.

Butsch, Richard. *The Making of American Audiences: From Stage to Television, 1750–1990* (Cambridge, UK: Cambridge University Press, 2000).

Chapple, Steve and Reebee Garofalo. *Rock 'N' Roll Is Here to Pay* (Chicago: Nelson-Hall, 1977).

Coase, Ronald H. "Payola in Radio and Television Broadcasting." *Journal of Law and Economics* 22(2), October 1979, 269–328.

Cohn, Jan. "The Business Ethic for Boys: *The Saturday Evening Post* and the Post Boys." *Business History Review* 61(Summer 1987), 185–215.

Demarais, Kirk. *Mail-Order Mysteries: Real Stuff from Old Comic Book Ads!* (San Rafael, CA: Insight Editions, 2011).

DeMause, Lloyd. "The Evolution of Childhood." *The History of Childhood*, edited by Lloyd deMause (New York, NY: Psychohistory Press, 1974), 1–73.

Duffy, John. *A History of Public Health in New York City, 1625–1866* (New York, NY: Russell Sage Foundation, 1968).

Edwards, Ellen. "PBS Missing Out on 'Barney' Bucks." *Washington Post.* September 13, 1993.

Everhart, Karen. "Does public TV get a big enough piece of *Barney*? *Current.* October 4, 1993. http://current.org/1993/10/does-public-tv-get-a-big-enough-piece-of-barney/). Viewed January 3, 2017, 7:15pm.

Floud, Roderick, Robert W. Fogel, Bernard Harris, and Sok Chul Hong. *The Changing Body: Health, Nutrition, and Human Development in the Western World since 1700* (Cambridge: Cambridge University Press, 2011).

Fogel, Robert. *The Fourth Great Awakening & the Future of Egalitarianism* (Chicago, IL: University of Chicago Press, 2000).

Forman, Henry James. *Our Movie Made Children* (New York, NY: Arno Press Reprint [1935] 1970).

Gilbert, James. *A Cycle of Outrage: America's Reaction to the Juvenile Delinquent in the 1950s* (New York: Oxford University Press, 1986).

Gomery, Douglas. *A History of Broadcasting in the United States* (Malden, MA: Blackwell Publishing, 2008).

Healy, Jack. "On Family Farms, Little Hands Steer Big Machines." *New York Times*, January 29, 2018, A10.

Holleran, Philip. "Child Labor and Exploitation in Turn-of-the-Century Cotton Mills." *Explorations in Economic History* 30(4), October 1993, 485–500.

Holloway, Diane. "New Kid Shows Comply with Fee, But Nobody's Watching." *Chicago Tribune*. April 13, 1998, no page number. http://www.chicago-tribune.com.

Hufton, Olwen. *The Poor of Eighteenth-Century France, 1750–1789* (Oxford, UK: Clarendon Press, 1974).

Jacobson, Lisa. "Manly Boys and Enterprising Dreamers: Business Ideology and the Construction of the Boy Consumer, 1910–1930." *Enterprise & Society* 2(2), June 2001, 225–258.

Kline, Stephen. "Toys, Socialization, and the Commodification of Play." *Getting and Spending: European and American Consumer Societies in the Twentieth Century*, edited by Susan Strasser, Charles McGovern, and Matthias Judt (Cambridge, UK: Cambridge University Press, 1998), 339–358.

Ladies' Home Journal. "Editorials: Jazz." November 1921, 24.

MacDonald, Dwight. "Profiles: A Caste, A Culture, A Market." *New Yorker*. Part 1. November 22, 1958, 57–94.

MacKinnon, Mary and Paul Johnson. "The Case against Productive Whipping." *Explorations in Economic History* 21(2), April 1984, 218–223.

Mannes, Marya. "Junior Has a Craving." *New Republic*, February 17, 1947, 21–23.

Markham, Edwin, Benjamin Lindsey, and George Creel. *Children in Bondage* (New York, NY: Arno & The New York Times, [1914] 1969).

Martin, Linda and Kerry Segrave. *Anti-Rock: The Opposition to Rock 'n' Roll* (Boston, MA: De Capo Press, 1993)

McKendrick, Neil. "Home Demand and Economic Growth: A New View of the Role of Women and Children in the Industrial Revolution." *Historical Perspectives: Studies in English Thought and Society in Honour of J.H. Plumb*, edited by Neil McKendrick (London, UK: Europa Publications, 1974), 152–210.

McMahon, John. "Unspeakable Jazz Must Go!" *Ladies' Home Journal*, December 1921, 34, 115–16).

Miles, Seven. *Youth Lifestyles in a Changing World* (Buckingham, UK: Open University Press, 2000).

Moehling, Carolyn. "State Child Labor Laws and the Decline of Child Labor." *Explorations in Economic History* 36(1), January 1999, 72–106.

Nardinelli, Clark. "Corporal Punishment and Children's Wages in Nineteenth Century Britain." *Explorations in Economic History* 19(3), July 1982. 283–295.

Nash, Jay B. *Spectatoritis* (New York, NY: Sears Publishing, 1932).

Neff, Wanda. *Victorian Working Women: an Historical and Literary Study of Women in British Industries and Professions, 1832–1850* (New York, NY: Columbia University Press, 1929).

New York Times. "Many Doubt Comics Spur Crime, Senate Survey of Experts Shows." November 12, 1950, 1 and 61.
New York Times, "Senator Charges 'Deceit' on Comics," April 23, 1954a, 29.
New York Times. "Adult Rings Held 'Infecting' Youth." June 29, 1954b, 29.
New York Times. "Rock'n'Roll Called 'Communicable Disease.'" March 28, 1956, 33.
Newsweek. "Purified Comics." July 12, 1948, 56.
North, Sterling. "A National Disgrace." *Chicago Daily News*. Wednesday, May 8, 1940, 21.
Nyberg, Amy. "Comic Book Censorship in the United States." *Pulp Demons: International Dimensions of the Postwar Anti-Comics Campaign*, edited by John A. Lent (Cranbury, NJ: Associated University Presses, 1999), 42–68.
Nyberg, Amy. *Seal of Approval: The History of the Comic Code* (Jackson, MS: University of Mississippi Press, 1998).
Osgerby, Bill. "'A Caste, a Culture, a Market': Youth, Marketing, and Lifestyle in Postwar America." *Growing Up Postmodern: Neoliberalism and the War on the Young*, edited by Ronald Strickland (Lanham: Rowman and Littlefield, 2002), 15–33.
Pinchbeck, Ivy and Margaret Hewitt. *Children in English Society. Vol. II: From the Eighteenth Century to the Children Act 1948* (London, UK: Routledge & Kegan Paul, 1973).
Plumb, John H. "The Commercialization of Leisure." *The Birth of a Consumer Society: The Commercialization of Eighteenth-Century England*, edited by Neil McKendrick (Bloomington, IN: Indiana University Press, 1982a), 265–285.
Plumb, John H. "The New World of Children in Eighteenth-century England." *The Birth of a Consumer Society: The Commercialization of Eighteenth-Century England*, edited by Neil McKendrick, John Brewer, and John Plumb (Bloomington, IN: Indiana University Press, 1982b), 286–315.
Ross, Edward. *World Drift* (New York, NY: Century, 1928).
Rothman, Lily. "The Scathing Speech That Made Television History." *Time*. May 9, 2016. http://time.com/4315217/newton-minow-vast-wasteland-1961-speech/. Viewed November 14, 2017, 7:05am.
Rugg, Harold. *An Introduction to Problems of American Culture* (Boston, MA: Ginn and Company, 1931).
Salem, D'Jamila. "Lawmakers Push New Rules for Children's TV." *Los Angeles Times*. October 12, 1995. No page number.
Samuels, Gertrude. "Why They Rock'n'Roll—And Should They?" *New York Times*. January 12, 1958, SM16–19.
Sternheimer, Karen. *Pop Culture Panics: How Moral Crusaders Construct Meanings of Deviance and Delinquency* (New York, NY: Routledge, 2015).

Surdam, David. *Century of the Leisured Masses: Entertainment and the Transformation of Twentieth-Century America* (New York, NY: Oxford University Press, 2015).

Time. "Puddles of Blood." March 29, 1948, 66 and 68.

TV Guide. "Cheers and Jeers." March 27, 1993, 6.

Weber, Bernerd. "The View of Cardinal Sadoleto on Education." *The Modern Language Journal* 26(6), October 1942, 452–454.

Wertham, Fredric, M.D. "The Comics ... Very Funny!" *The Saturday Review of Literature*. May 29, 1948, 6–7 and 27–29.

Zoglin, Richard. "If Not the Jetsons, What?" *Time*. March 22, 1993, 64.

CHAPTER 13

Twenty-First-Century Situations

The new millennium has not seen a cessation of spectacular lapses in business ethics. Despite a plethora of ethics courses and certification programs, as well as new or revised regulations, some business professionals continue to act in blatantly unethical fashion. There are countervailing trends, however, as Amazon.com, eBay, and other online vendors rely on trust and honesty. Customers rate their experiences with online vendors.

In many ways, the present resembles the past. Accounting tricks, inept regulation, gullible consumers, and callous executives sometimes combine to create a toxic mix. Enron and other early twenty-first-century debacles demonstrate that unethical businesspeople remain.

The Sad Collapses of Enron and Arthur Andersen

With regard to Enron, government regulation failed to protect investors. The documentary, *The Smartest Guys in the Room*, glossed over the role of federal regulators. Enron was not a case of sheer laissez-faire; the documentary mentioned that Enron received approval for a particular accounting interpretation, an exemption of the Investment Company Act of 1940. Enron applied for this exemption and, based upon assumptions described in the application, received the exemption. The company later shifted its business strategy and began engaging in prohibited activities (Frankel 2006, 39).

D. G. Surdam, *Business Ethics from the 19th Century to Today*,
https://doi.org/10.1007/978-3-030-37169-2_13

Enron lobbied Congress to exempt energy and minerals commodities from scrutiny by the Commodity Futures Trading Commission (Schroeder and Ip, December 13, 2001, A1 and A6; Frankel 2006, 150). Congress presumably sought to deregulate the supply of and to create a freer market in energy. Enron operated without sufficient scrutiny, although some commentators argued that it wasn't the lack of government regulation but a failure of Enron's business plan that toppled the company (Frankel 2006, 150–151).

The end of Enron was spectacular and swift; its share price plummeted from $75 to 14 cents per share. People scurried to divest themselves of their Enron shares. Unfortunately for many Enron employees, they could not quickly divest Enron shares that comprised their retirement account. Although many people suffered during a run, Tamar Frankel saw a benefit: "It is self-enforcing…it is likely to shorten the fraudulent scheme in the long term (Frankel 2006, 169)."

In the wake of the Enron scandal, Arthur Andersen, a long-respect accounting firm, disintegrated. Arthur Andersen, the founder, insisted on maintaining high standards of business probity. As a minister eulogized Andersen: "Those principles upon which his business was built, and with which it is synonymous, must be preserved. His name must never be associated with any program or action that is not the highest and the best. I am sure he would rather the doors be closed than that it should continue to exist on principles other than those which he established (Barboza 2002, C6)." Some 55 years after Andersen's death, the company he founded went under.

One of Andersen's loyal lieutenants, Leonard Spacek, had continued Andersen's tradition of moral leadership in the industry. Spacek created the consulting side of the company, but he began to worry that his creation was proving dangerous to the company's ethos. In the 1970s, after he retired from running Andersen, Spacek spoke out publicly for "more standardized reporting practices" and "more integrity in reporting, higher standards and more formalized rules and procedures. He even proposed a kind of accounting court to resolve disputes over issues and procedures." Above all, Spacek and his successor, Harvey Kapnick, urged the company (and other companies) to "keep auditing and consulting work separate." In the wake of the Enron fiasco, Judith Spacek, Leonard's daughter, lamented, "I never thought I'd say that I'm glad my father's dead, but after this started I'm glad he was. I remember him ranting and raving, saying Andersen couldn't consult and audit the same firms because it was a conflict of interest. Well, now I'm sure he's up there twirling in his grave saying, 'I told you so.'" In case readers find these quotes self-serving, accounting professor Daniel Jensen stated: "This is all very sad because it happened to Andersen, which had a reputation of impeccable integrity. And these two men, Andersen and Spacek were tremendously influential in the industry: both had similar characteristics; they were willing to take principled stands (Barboza 2002, C6)." To use an ad hoc argument, an interesting study would have been to see whether companies bearing a person's name tended to experience an increase in unethical behavior after the families are no longer in decision-making positions. By 2000, presumably non-family members ran Andersen, and the company may have simply been a means to an end for these executives.

Reporter Frank Grippo provided a perspective on Leonard Spacek in 2004. Grippo stated that the Arthur Andersen company had changed greatly in the previous two decades and that it was: "no longer the same firm that Leonard Spacek helped form. Few would argue that in the 1950s, '60s, and '70s, Andersen was one of, if not the, most respected of the Big Eight. With tremendously high standards and excellent personnel, it had a wide reputation for being the 'conscience of the profession.'" The company's executives insisted on maintaining "quality and high standards. Unlike the profession today, accountants in those days were 'professionals who happened to be accountants.'" Grippo identified some factors causing the decline, including, "advertising, competitive bidding, and digressing from the core of an accounting and auditing firm. What is certain is that Arthur Andersen became perhaps the most aggressive accounting firm—and strayed from the management philosophy of the genteel and ethical Leonard Spacek. (Grippo 2004, no page numbers)."

Grippo provided examples of Spacek's beliefs. Spacek criticized the Accounting Principles Board's decision "that the dollar effects of a particular accounting practice under consideration should be disclosed in a footnote explanation. Three months later, when pressures had been exerted, the requirement for disclosing the amounts involved was removed and the footnote now need only disclose the practice. Thus, the issuer of financial statements and the auditor in this case are provided a way of ducking their responsibility, leaving the user of our services whom we as a profession are supposed to protect, holding the bag, not knowing whether the amount involved is $1000 or $10 million." With regard to CPA's self-interest, Spacek stressed, "CPAs must be undertaken as a professional responsibility, not as a means of assuring anyone an income.…Once the work is undertaken, we must be able to afford to follow the job through to completion on a proper basis; irrespective of the consequences on our income." Spacek also spelled out the CPA's responsibility: "Why is credence given to such reports [financial statements submitted to the public and to the Securities and Exchange Commission]?...The public assumes that a public accountant's report is free of bias and grounded on facts developed independently of the representations made by the company being reported on. Such reports are accepted as assurances that the company's statements can be relied on (Grippo 2004, no page number)."

A Certified Public Accountant (CPA) audit is supposed to provide a thorough and accurate picture of a firm's financial situation, blemishes and all, so investors and other people can make well-informed judgments. Lest people judge CPAs unduly harshly, remember that employers are hesitant to reveal truthful if damaging aspects when providing letters of references for fear of litigation. Even performance appraisals today are imbued with fears of lawsuits.

As with many of the really dramatic cases of ethical scandals, the Enron/Arthur Andersen episode took place in a world of government oversight and government involvement. Many politicians lauded Enron as innovative company. Enron, as did Bernard Madoff, fooled most regulators. Customers and stockholders discovered, no doubt to the chagrin of many, that government regulation was no guarantor of good behavior.

Conclusion

Enron and the housing market debacle of 2007–2008 clearly demonstrate the growing troublesome relationship between government officials and large businesses in America. The persistence of so-called crony capitalism creates potential for widespread harm from unethical activities. Twenty-first-century consumers and citizens face unprecedented interaction with businesses; businesses compile far more information on customers than did Montgomery Ward back in the 1890s. Such information has become the gold mines of the new millennium. Some companies, such as Equifax, proved lax in protecting sensitive consumer information. Consumers of the twenty-first century must be vigilant regarding their personal and financial information. Rival firms, solo hackers, and foreign government-sponsored hackers are prowling for unprotected information. How firms respond to such attacks may be a primary ethical consideration now and into the future.

Crony capitalism raises serious ethical issues regarding the distribution of income and wealth. American CEO compensation continues to irritate many citizens; the traditional defense of laissez-faire in the market for CEOs appears dubious to many Americans, as CEO pay far outstrips rank-and-file workers and changes in the Consumer Price Index. Certainly the combination of disseminating dubious information and cozy relations between business executives, legislators, and regulators are pathways to corruption that are sure to be trod by future unethical businesspeople.

Despite these differences, the basic transaction of a consumer buying a good or service from a vendor remains the same as it has for millennia. The participants must have a modicum of trust. eBay and other internet marketplaces may prove to be more efficient and more ethical, as both buyers and sellers rate each other. Of course, participants may have an incentive to lie on such evaluations, but presumably reputable providers of such marketplaces have an incentive to maintain the integrity of the rating system.

Contemporary people, no less than primitive people, must remain vigilant. "Trust but verify" and "Who do you trust?" remain as relevant as ever, astonishing changes in our technologies and lifestyles notwithstanding. Business ethics will continue to evolve but also remain similar to the past for the foreseeable future.

Bibliography

Barboza, David. "Where Pain of Arthur Andersen Is Personal." *New York Times*, March 13, 2002, C6.

Frankel, Tamar. *Trust and Honesty: America's Business Culture at a Crossroad* (Oxford, UK: Oxford University Press, 2006).

Grippo, Frank. "Perspective: Leonard Spacek: Ahead of His Time, Relevant Today." *The CPA Journal*, March 2004. http://archives.cpajournal.com/2004/304/perspectives/nv6.htm, viewed Feburary 12, 2017.

Schroeder, Michael and Greg Ip. "Out of Reach: The Enron Debacle Spotlights Huge Void in Financial Regulation." *Wall Street Journal*, December 13, 2001, A1 and A6.

Index[1]

[1] Note: Page numbers followed by 'n' refer to notes.

D. G. Surdam, *Business Ethics from the 19th Century to Today*,
https://doi.org/10.1007/978-3-030-37169-2

O

T

The manufacturer's authorised representative in the EU is Springer Nature Customer Service Centre GmbH, Europaplatz 3, 69115 Heidelberg, Germany. If you have any concerns regarding our products, please contact ProductSafety@springernature.com

Printed and bound by CPI Group (UK) Ltd, Croydon, CR0 4YY
25/09/2026
02222881-0003